SOUL EATER

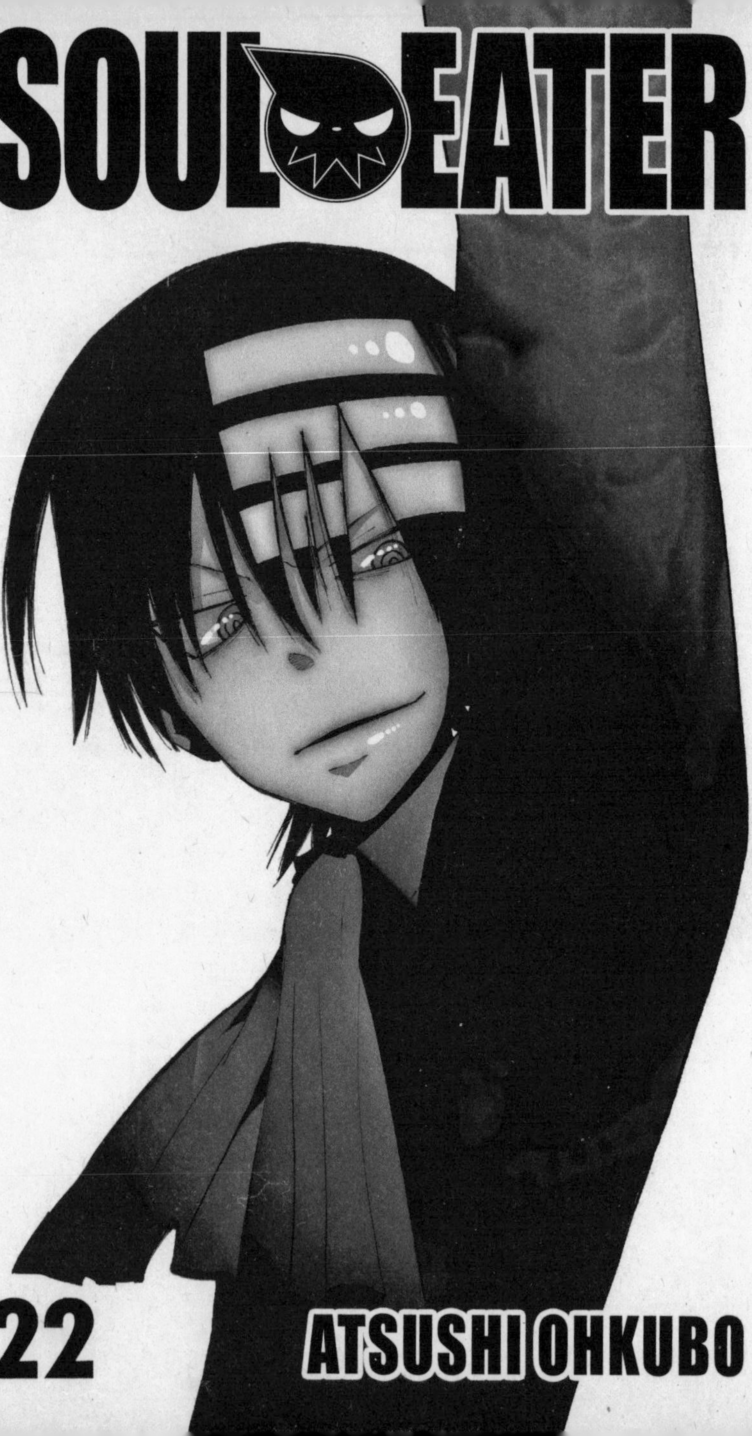

22

ATSUSHI OHKUBO

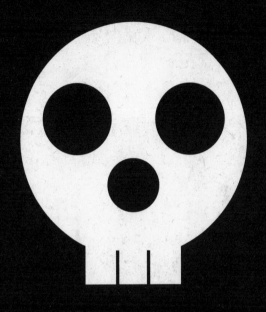

SOUL EATER

vol. 22

by ATSUSHI OHKUBO

The desire and flames named insanity

SOUL EATER 22

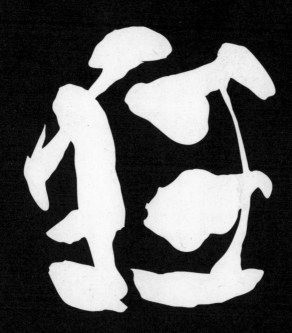

CONTENTS

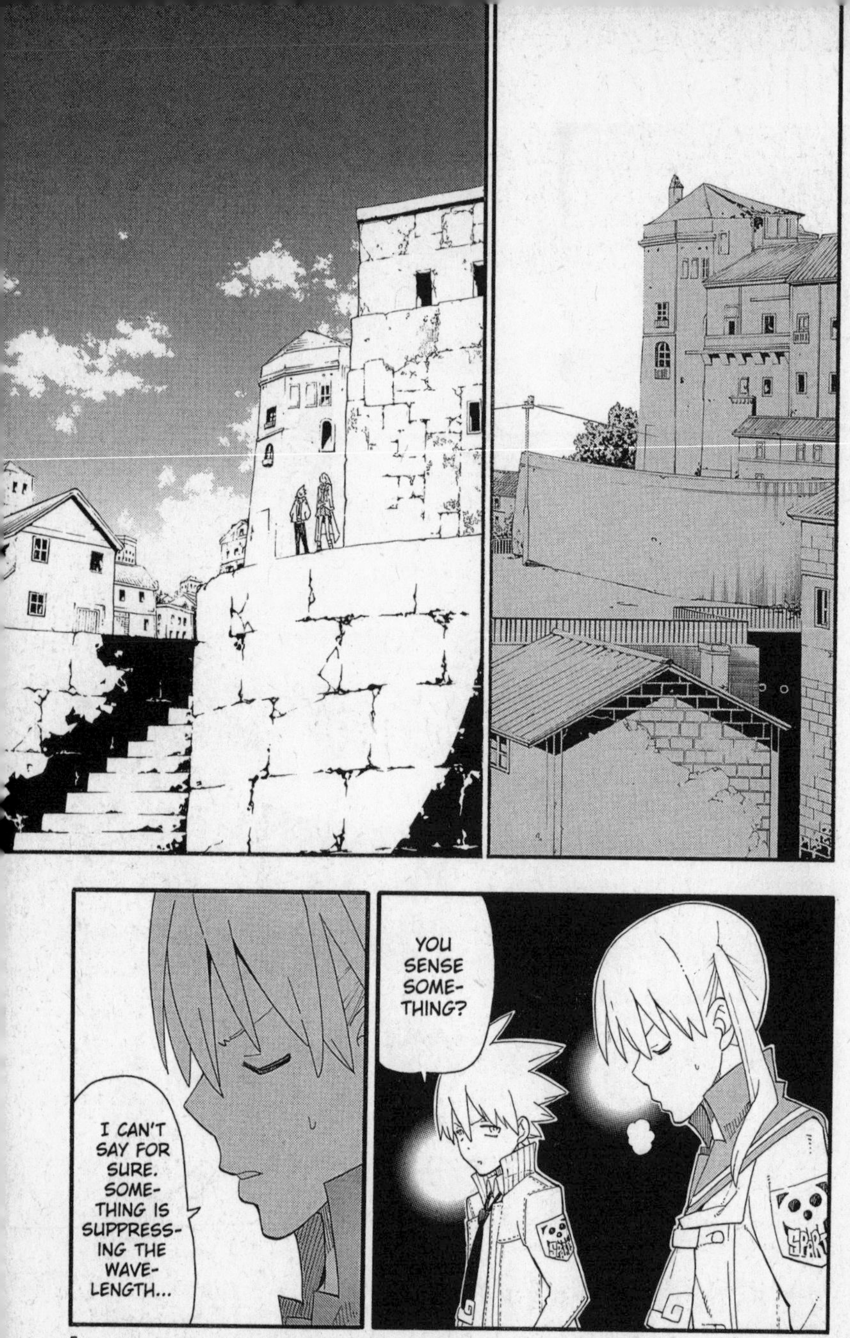
YOU SENSE SOMETHING?
I CAN'T SAY FOR SURE. SOMETHING IS SUPPRESSING THE WAVELENGTH...

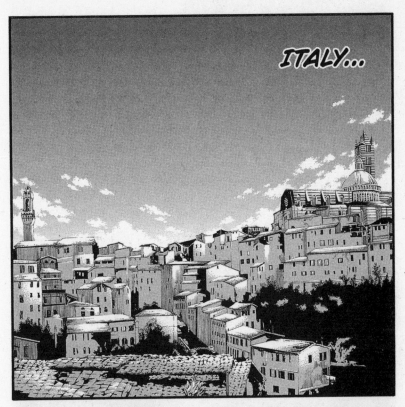

ITALY...

SOUL EATER

CHAPTER 93: WAR ON THE MOON (PART 3)

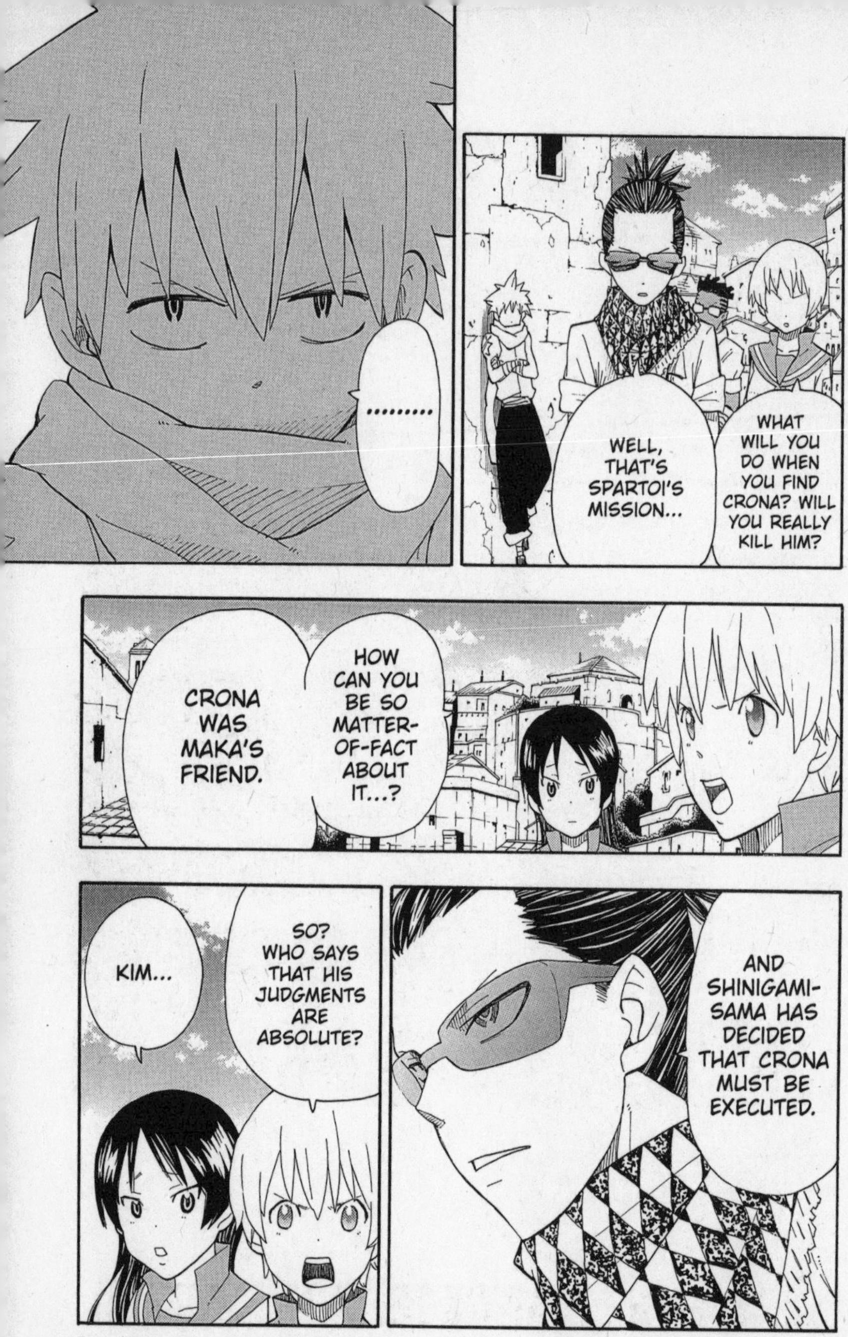
WHAT WILL YOU DO WHEN YOU FIND CRONA? WILL YOU REALLY KILL HIM?
WELL, THAT'S SPARTOI'S MISSION...
....
HOW CAN YOU BE SO MATTER-OF-FACT ABOUT IT...?
CRONA WAS MAKA'S FRIEND.
AND SHINIGAMI-SAMA HAS DECIDED THAT CRONA MUST BE EXECUTED.
SO? WHO SAYS THAT HIS JUDGMENTS ARE ABSOLUTE?
KIM...

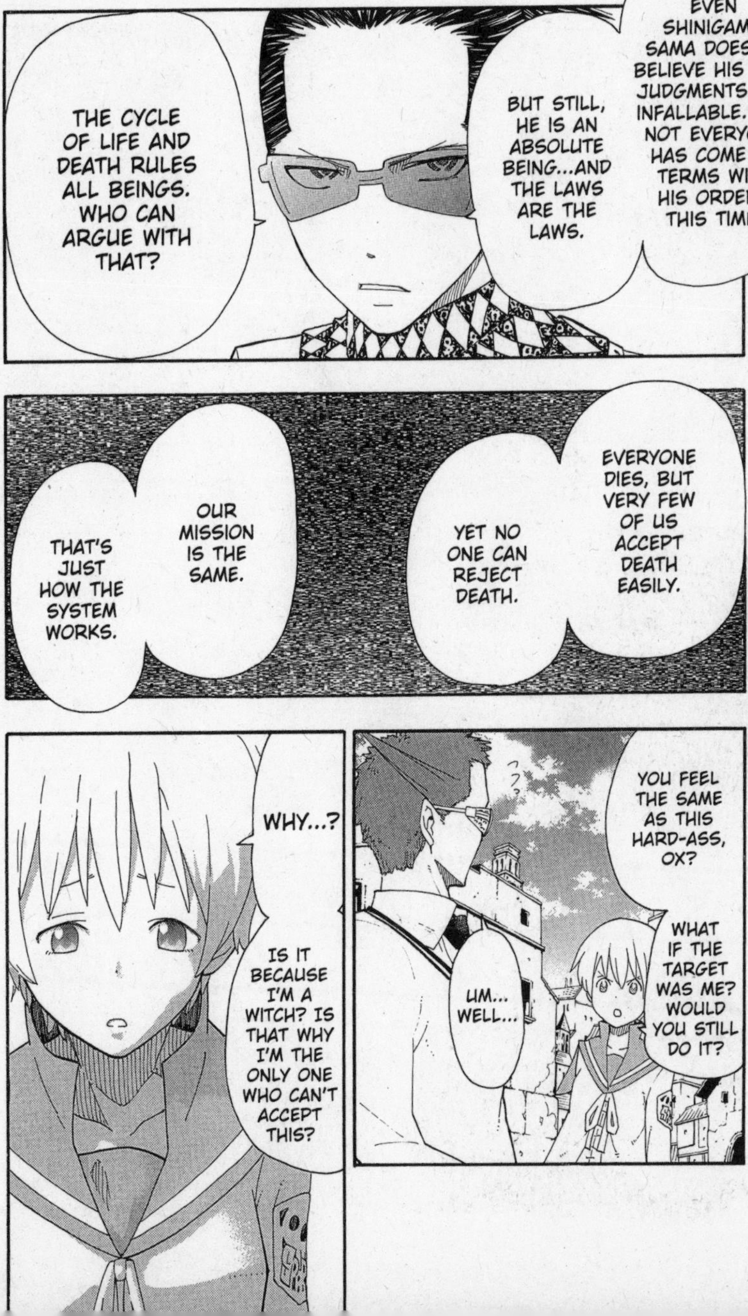
EVEN SHINIGAMI-SAMA DOESN'T BELIEVE HIS OWN JUDGMENTS ARE INFALLABLE. AND NOT EVERYONE HAS COME TO TERMS WITH HIS ORDERS THIS TIME.
BUT STILL, HE IS AN ABSOLUTE BEING...AND THE LAWS ARE THE LAWS.
THE CYCLE OF LIFE AND DEATH RULES ALL BEINGS. WHO CAN ARGUE WITH THAT?
EVERYONE DIES, BUT VERY FEW OF US ACCEPT DEATH EASILY.
YET NO ONE CAN REJECT DEATH.
OUR MISSION IS THE SAME.
THAT'S JUST HOW THE SYSTEM WORKS.
YOU FEEL THE SAME AS THIS HARD-ASS, OX?
WHAT IF THE TARGET WAS ME? WOULD YOU STILL DO IT?
UM... WELL...
WHY...?
IS IT BECAUSE I'M A WITCH? IS THAT WHY I'M THE ONLY ONE WHO CAN'T ACCEPT THIS?

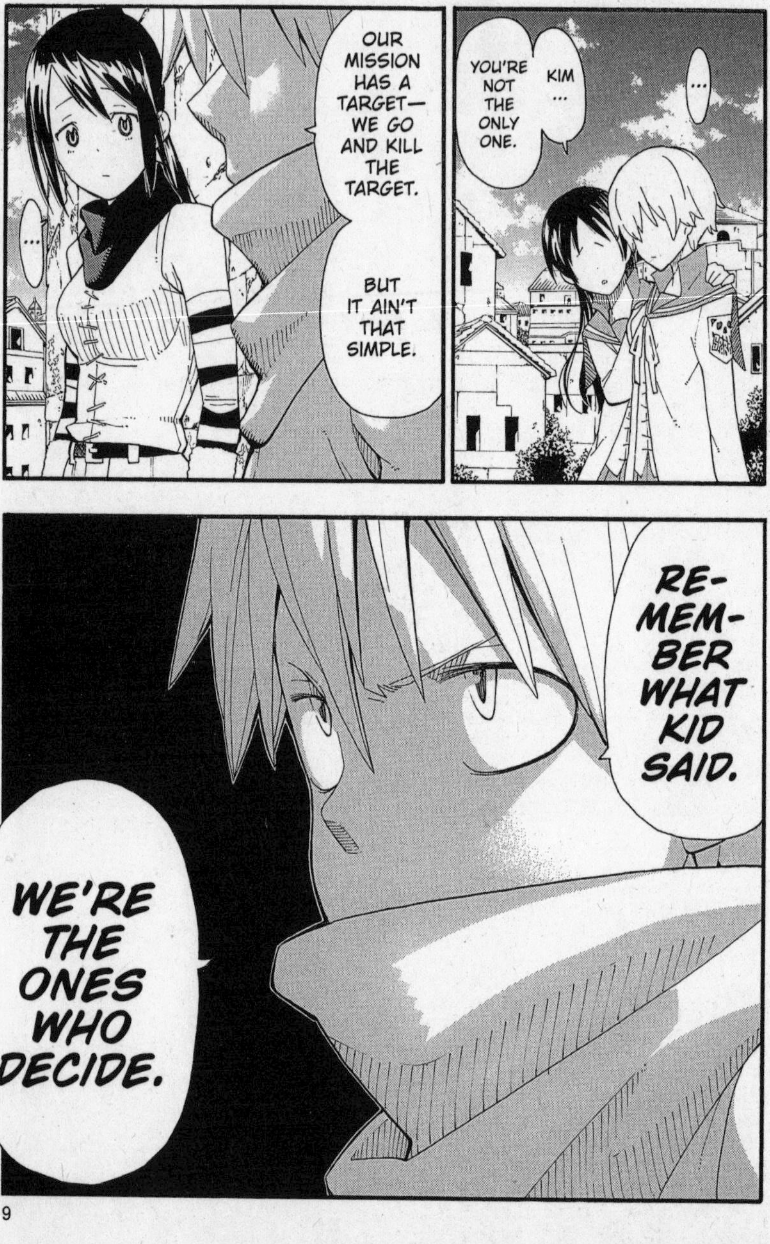
...
KIM ...
YOU'RE NOT THE ONLY ONE.
OUR MISSION HAS A TARGET— WE GO AND KILL THE TARGET.
BUT IT AIN'T THAT SIMPLE.
...
RE-MEM-BER WHAT KID SAID.
WE'RE THE ONES WHO DECIDE.

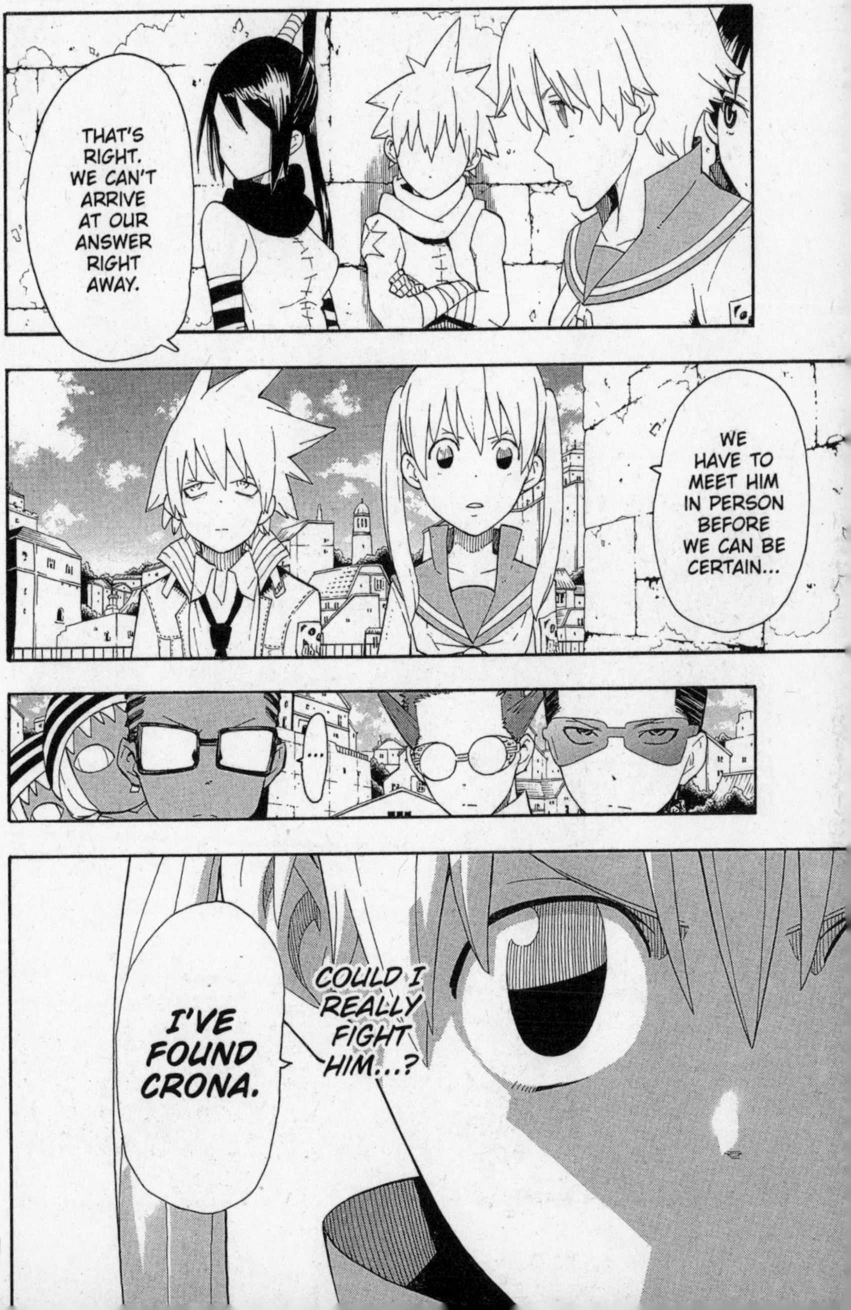
THAT'S RIGHT. WE CAN'T ARRIVE AT OUR ANSWER RIGHT AWAY.
WE HAVE TO MEET HIM IN PERSON BEFORE WE CAN BE CERTAIN...
...
COULD I REALLY FIGHT HIM...?
I'VE FOUND CRONA.

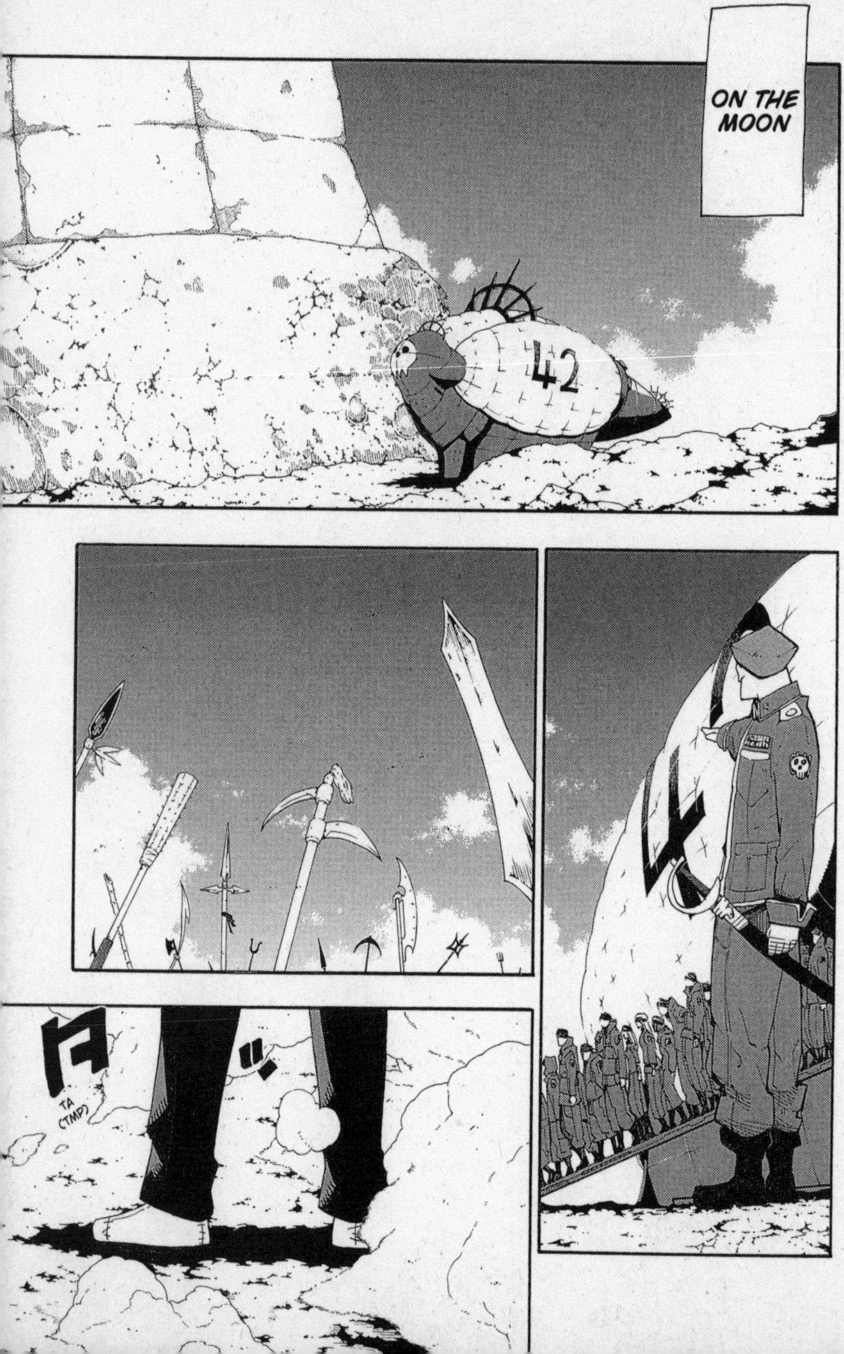
ON THE MOON
TA (TMP)

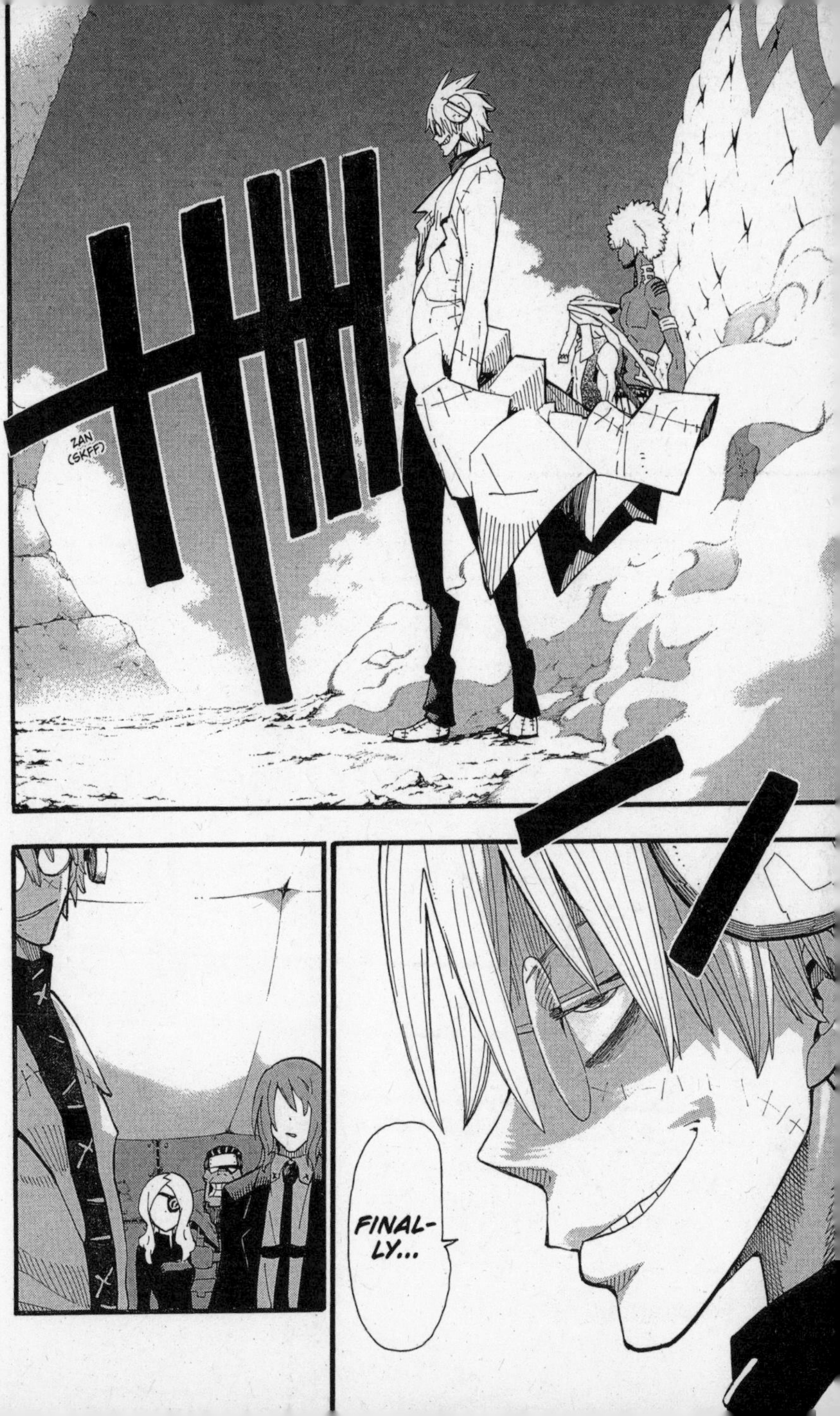
ZAN (SKFF)
FINAL-LY...

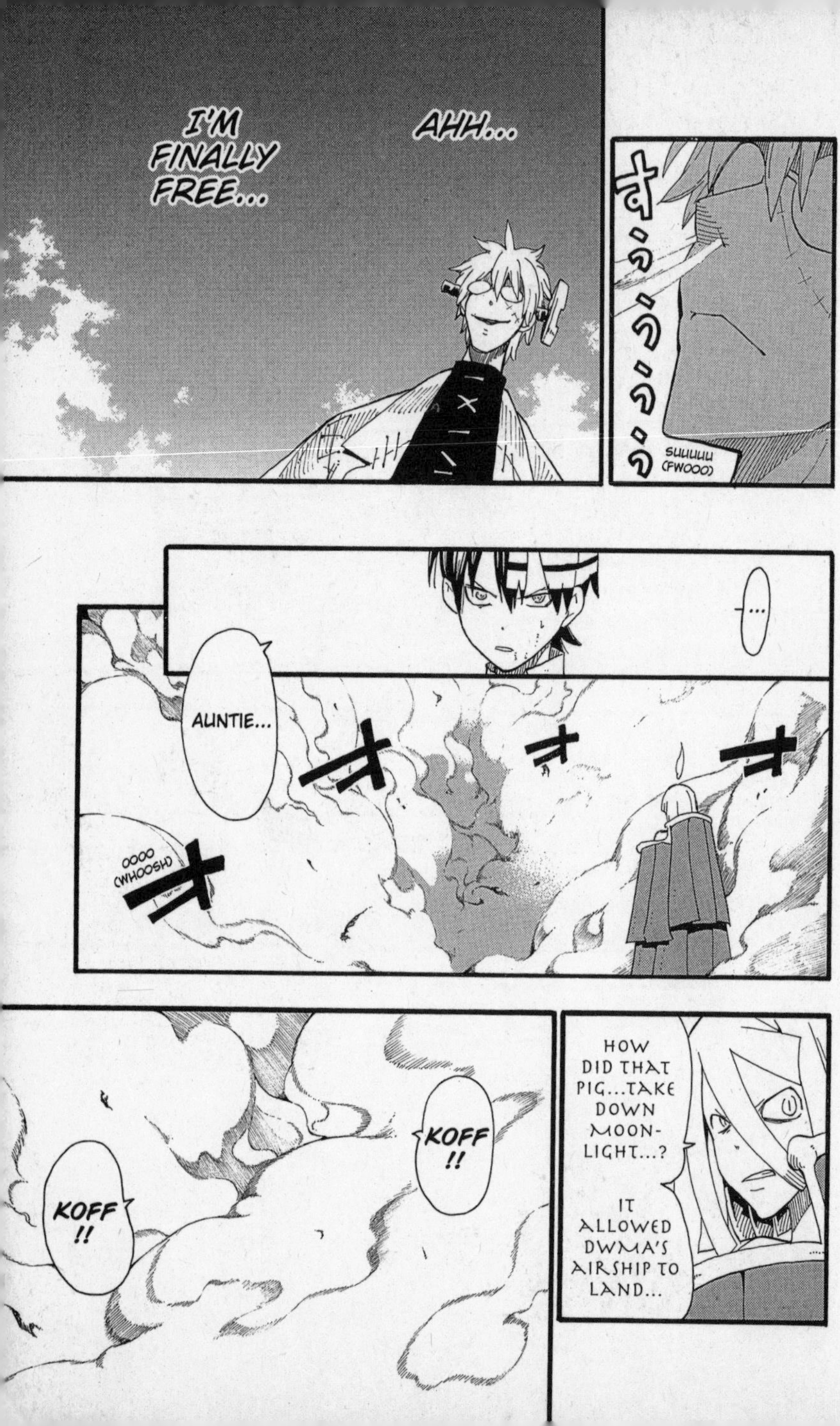
SUUUUU (FWOOO)
AHH...
I'M FINALLY FREE...
...
AUNTIE...
OOOO (WHOOSH)
HOW DID THAT PIG...TAKE DOWN MOON-LIGHT...?
IT ALLOWED DWMA'S AIRSHIP TO LAND...
KOFF!!
KOFF!!

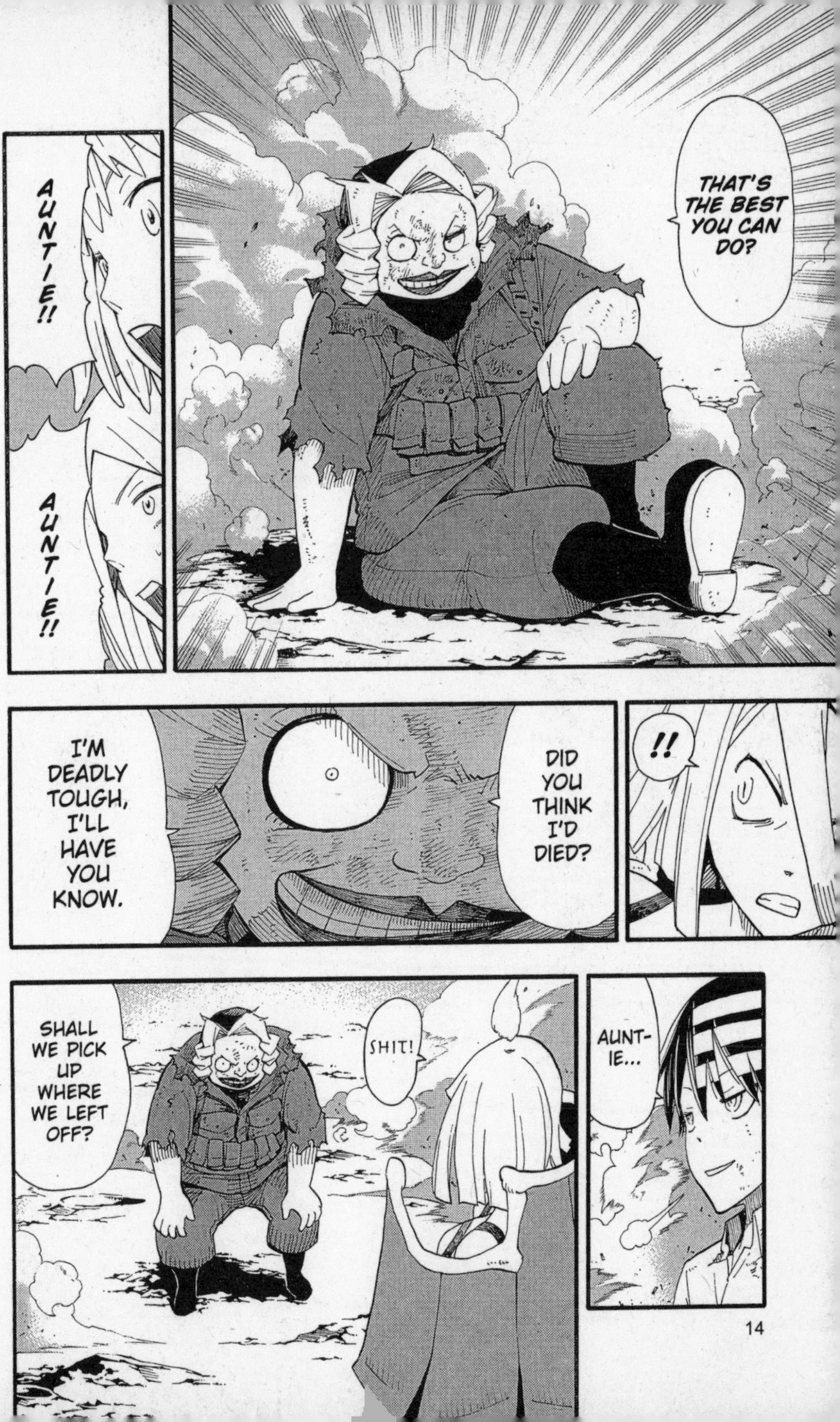
THAT'S THE BEST YOU CAN DO?
AUNTIE!!
AUNTIE!!
!!
DID YOU THINK I'D DIED?
I'M DEADLY TOUGH, I'LL HAVE YOU KNOW.
AUNT-IE...
SHIT!
SHALL WE PICK UP WHERE WE LEFT OFF?

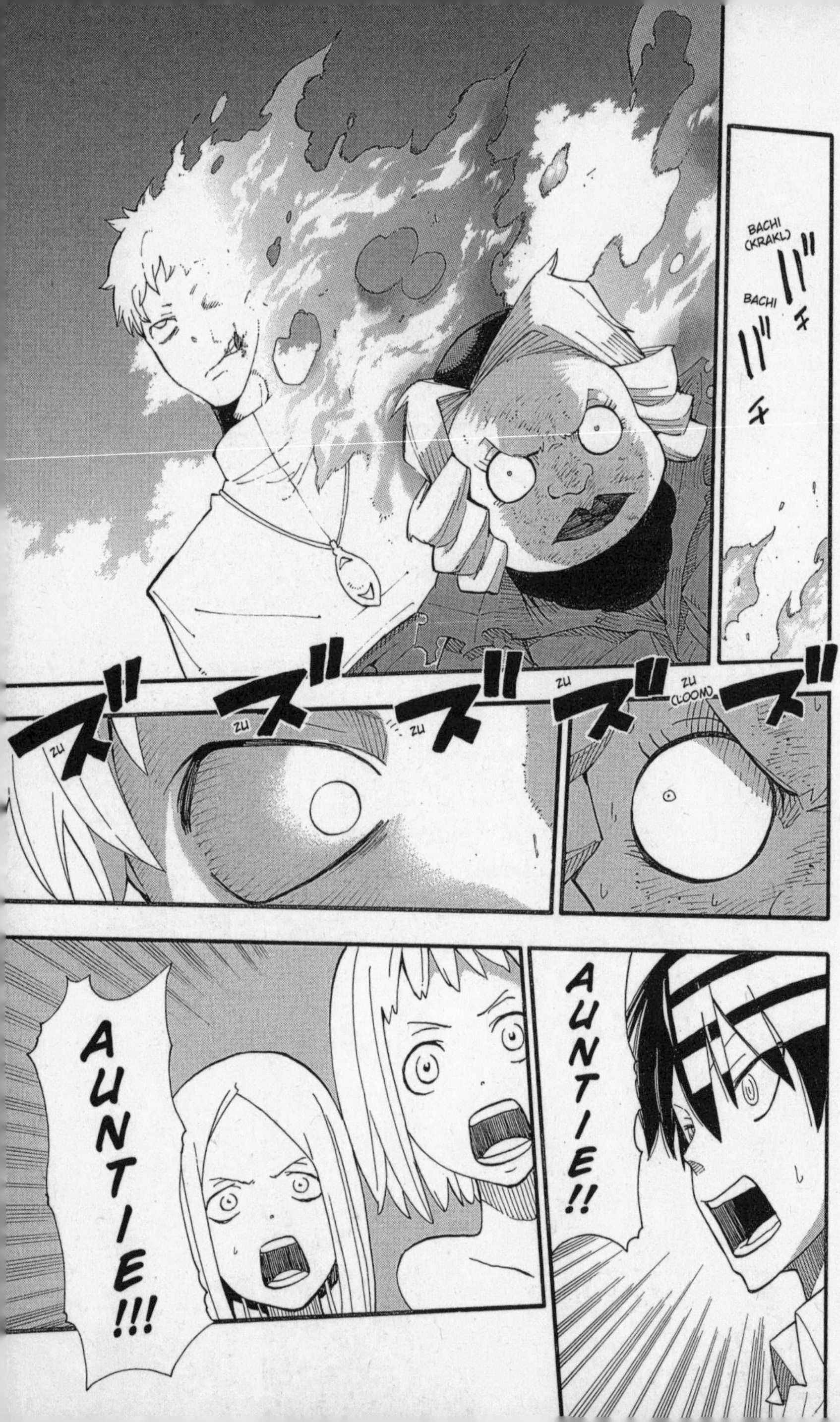
BACHI (KRAKL)
BACHI
ZU (LOOM)
ZU
ZU
ZU
ZU
AUNTIE!!
AUNTIE!!!

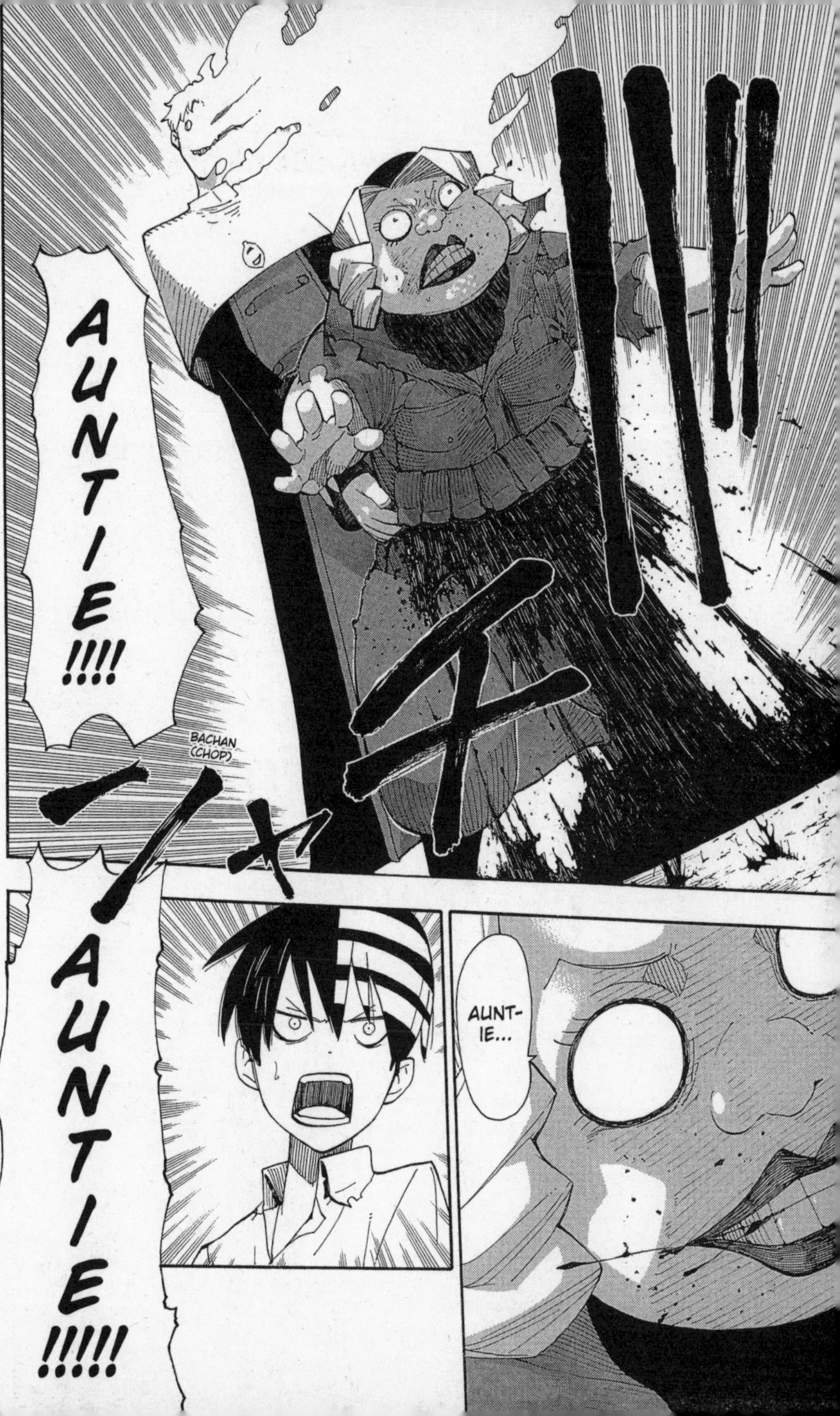
BACHAN (CHOP)
AUNTIE!!!!
AUNT-IE...
AUNTIE!!!!!

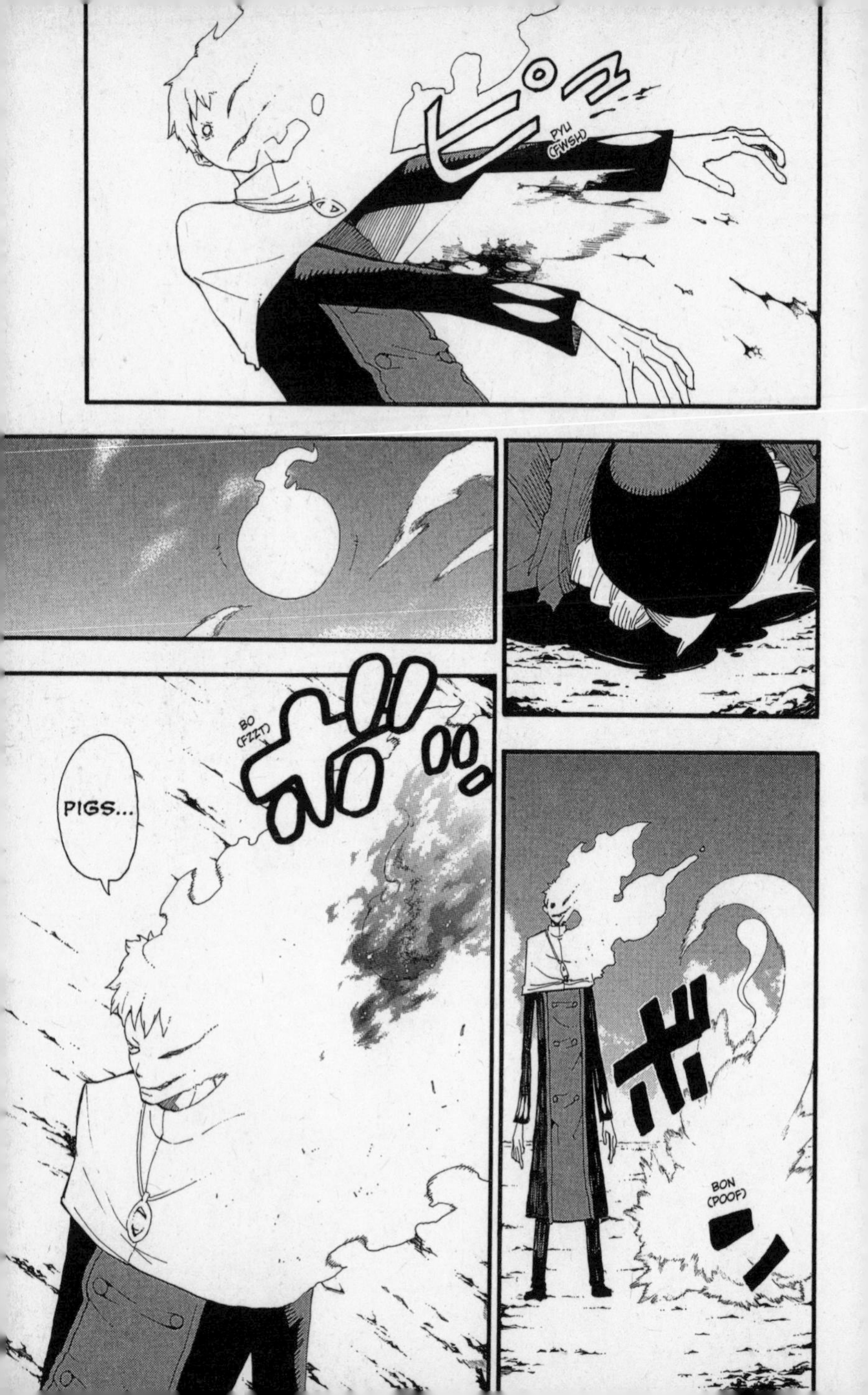
PYU (FWSH)
BON (POOF)
BO (FZZT)
PIGS...

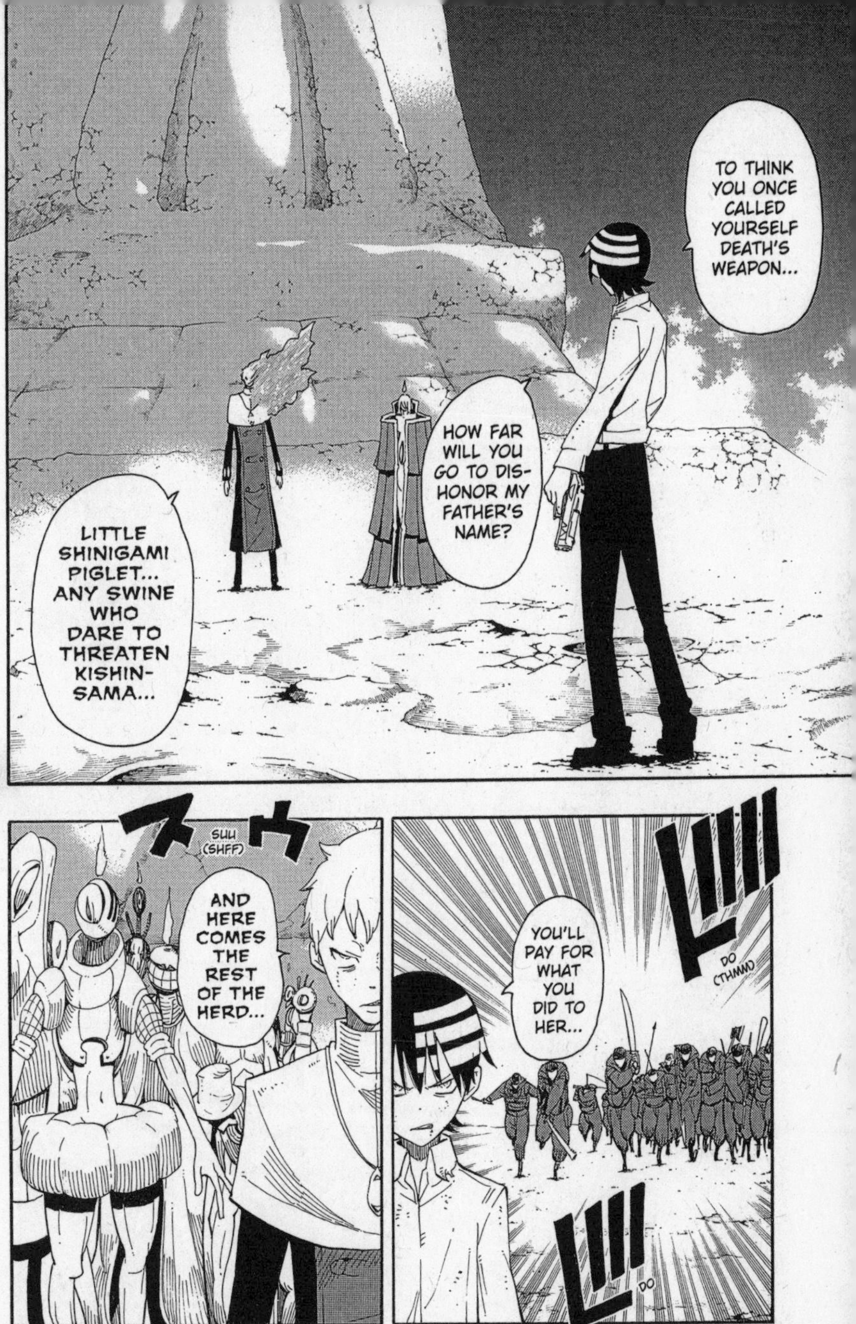
TO THINK YOU ONCE CALLED YOURSELF DEATH'S WEAPON...
HOW FAR WILL YOU GO TO DIS-HONOR MY FATHER'S NAME?
LITTLE SHINIGAMI PIGLET... ANY SWINE WHO DARE TO THREATEN KISHIN-SAMA...
DO (THMM)
YOU'LL PAY FOR WHAT YOU DID TO HER...
DO
SUU (SHFF)
AND HERE COMES THE REST OF THE HERD...

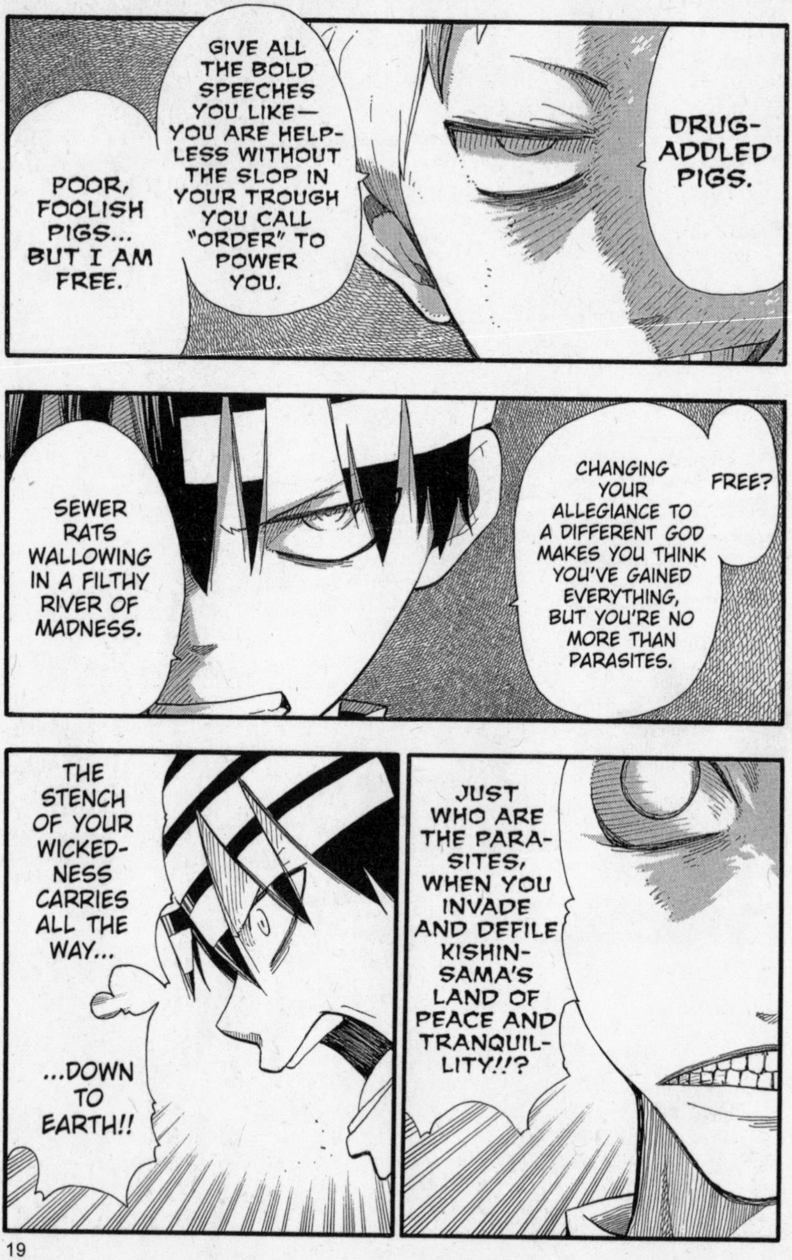
DRUG-ADDLED PIGS.
GIVE ALL THE BOLD SPEECHES YOU LIKE—YOU ARE HELPLESS WITHOUT THE SLOP IN YOUR TROUGH YOU CALL "ORDER" TO POWER YOU.
POOR, FOOLISH PIGS... BUT I AM FREE.
FREE?
CHANGING YOUR ALLEGIANCE TO A DIFFERENT GOD MAKES YOU THINK YOU'VE GAINED EVERYTHING, BUT YOU'RE NO MORE THAN PARASITES.
SEWER RATS WALLOWING IN A FILTHY RIVER OF MADNESS.
JUST WHO ARE THE PARASITES, WHEN YOU INVADE AND DEFILE KISHIN-SAMA'S LAND OF PEACE AND TRANQUILLITY!!?
THE STENCH OF YOUR WICKEDNESS CARRIES ALL THE WAY...
...DOWN TO EARTH!!

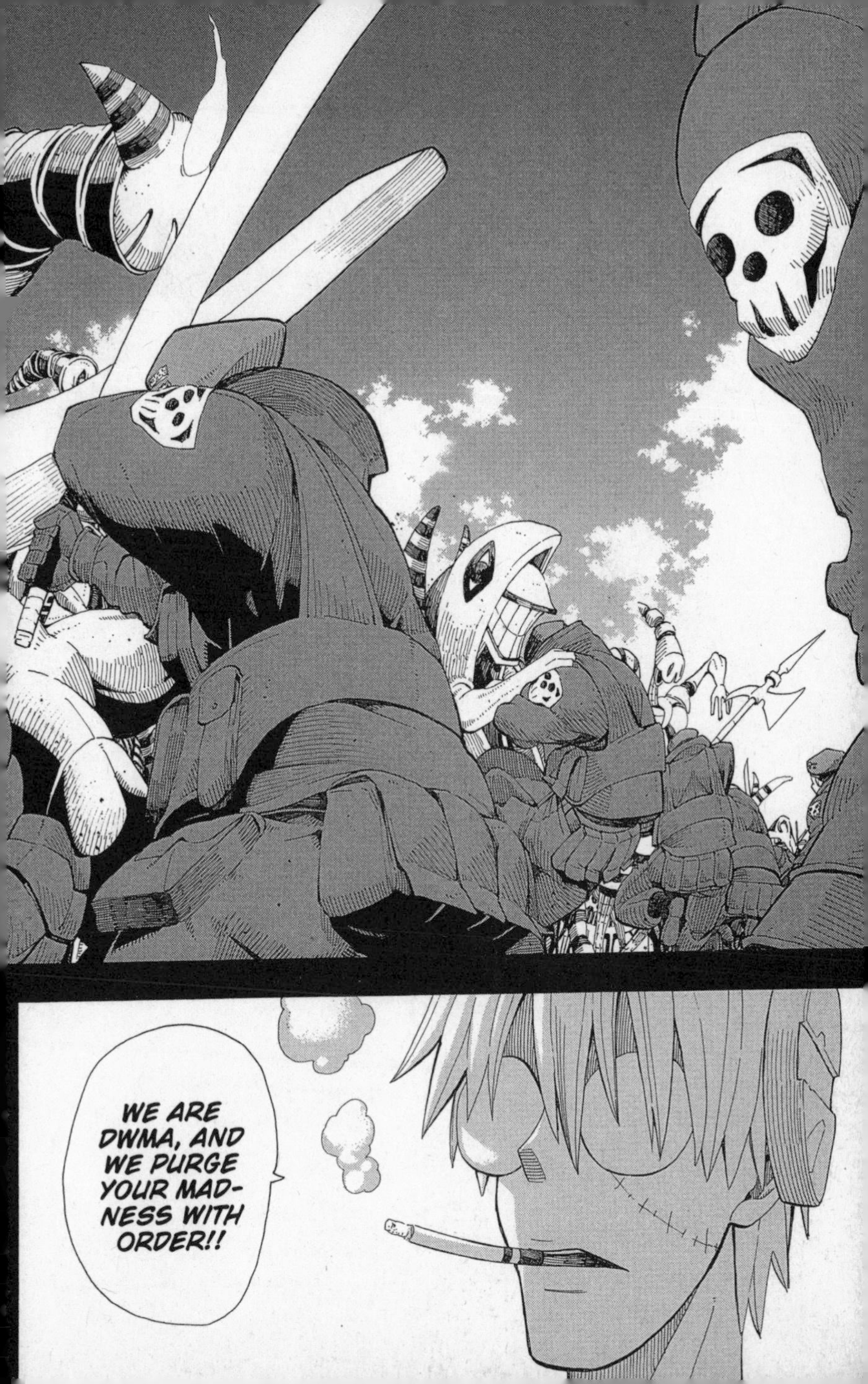
WE ARE DWMA, AND WE PURGE YOUR MAD-NESS WITH ORDER!!

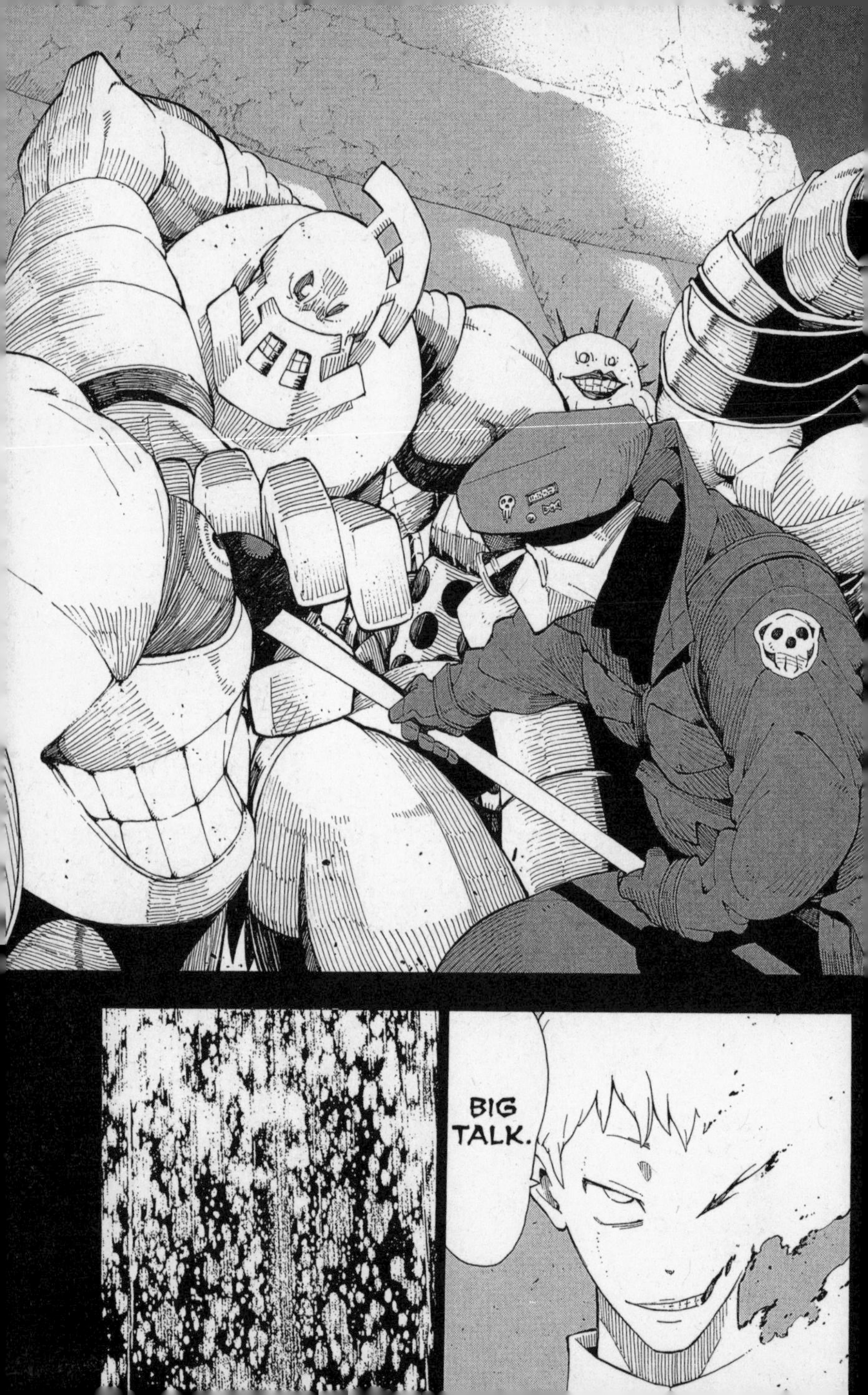
BIG TALK.

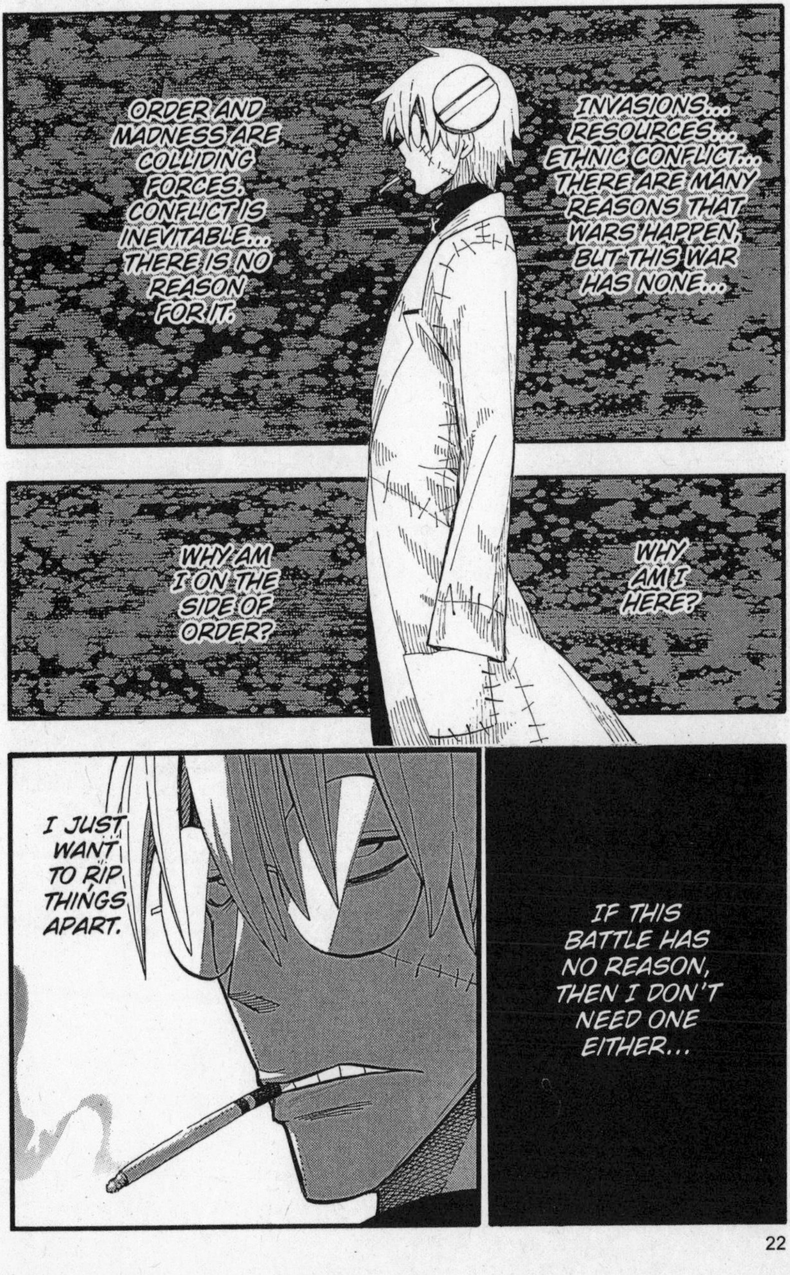
INVASIONS... RESOURCES... ETHNIC CONFLICT... THERE ARE MANY REASONS THAT WARS HAPPEN, BUT THIS WAR HAS NONE...
ORDER AND MADNESS ARE COLLIDING FORCES. CONFLICT IS INEVITABLE... THERE IS NO REASON FOR IT.
WHY AM I HERE?
WHY AM I ON THE SIDE OF ORDER?
IF THIS BATTLE HAS NO REASON, THEN I DON'T NEED ONE EITHER...
I JUST WANT TO RIP THINGS APART.

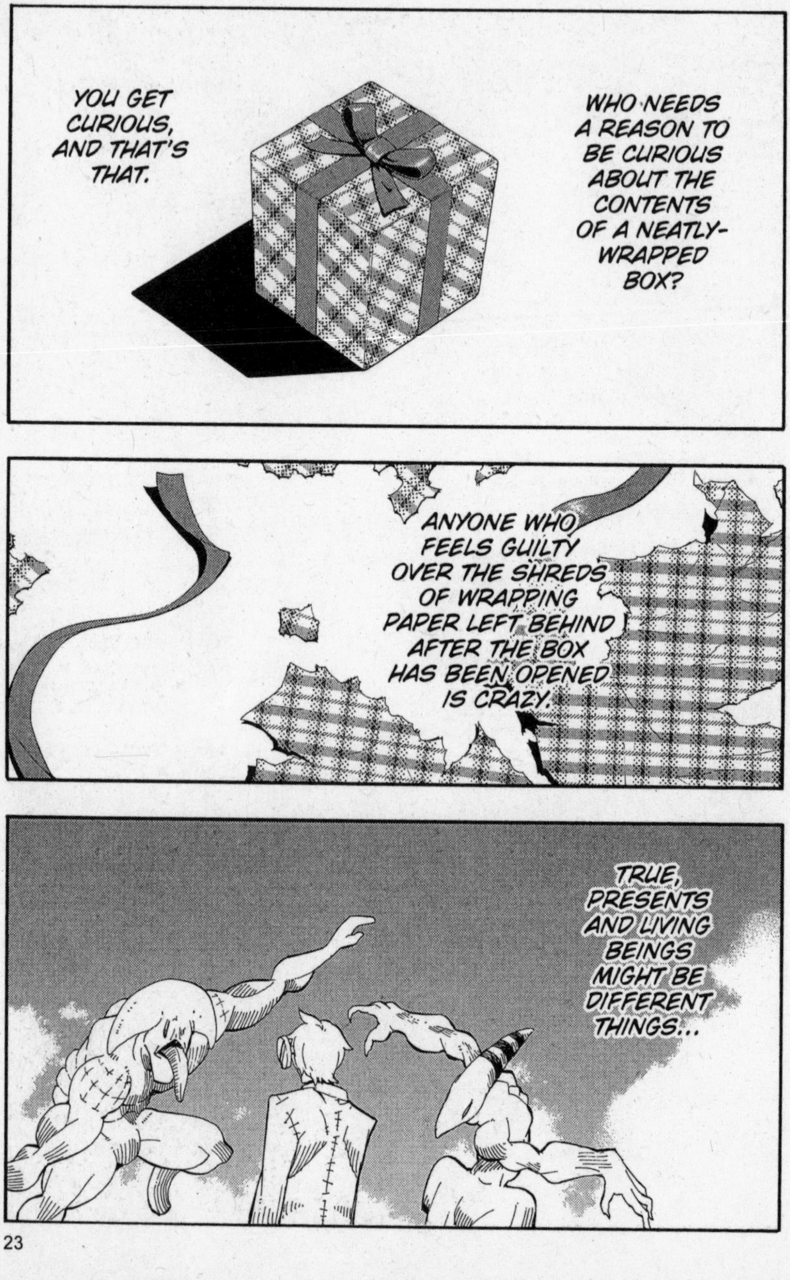
WHO NEEDS A REASON TO BE CURIOUS ABOUT THE CONTENTS OF A NEATLY-WRAPPED BOX?
YOU GET CURIOUS, AND THAT'S THAT.
ANYONE WHO FEELS GUILTY OVER THE SHREDS OF WRAPPING PAPER LEFT BEHIND AFTER THE BOX HAS BEEN OPENED IS CRAZY.
TRUE, PRESENTS AND LIVING BEINGS MIGHT BE DIFFERENT THINGS...

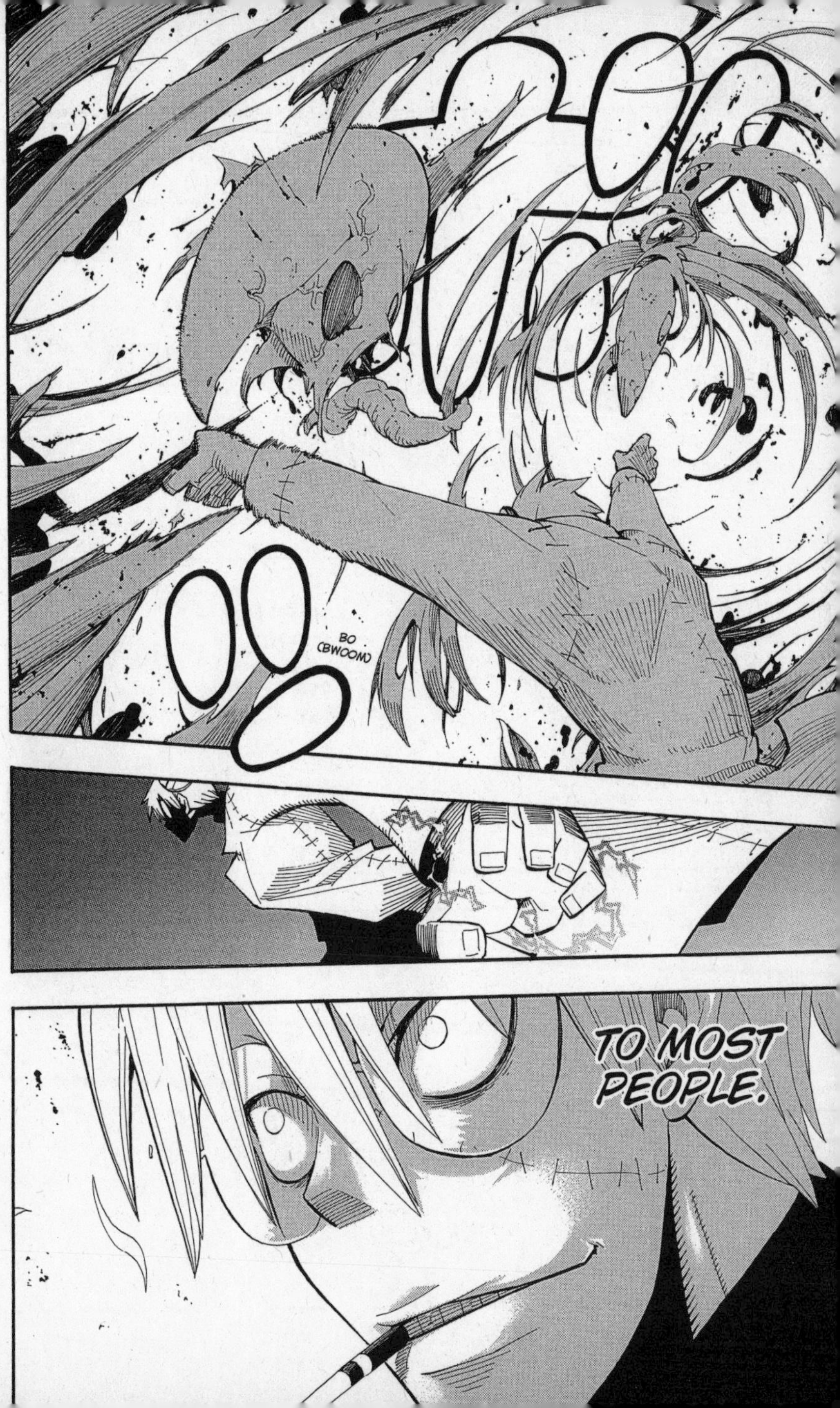
BO
(BWOOM)
TO MOST
PEOPLE.

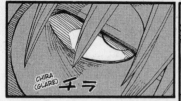

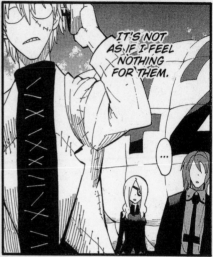

IT'S NOT AS IF I FEEL NOTHING FOR THEM.
...
CHIRA (GLARE)
チラ
ZOKU (CHILLS)
IT'S JUST THAT ANY FEELINGS I HAVE MERELY CHANGE THE ORDER THAT I DISSECT THEM...
SENPAI... MARIE... IT'S TIME FOR US TO JOIN THEM.
MARIE, TRANS-FORM.
SENPAI, BACK US UP.
WILL IT BE SOONER OR LATER? THAT'S THE ONLY QUESTION, HEH-HEH-HEH-HEH...

NOW, TO THE OPERATING ROOM...

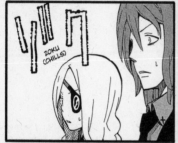

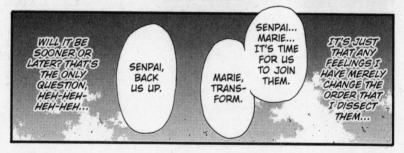

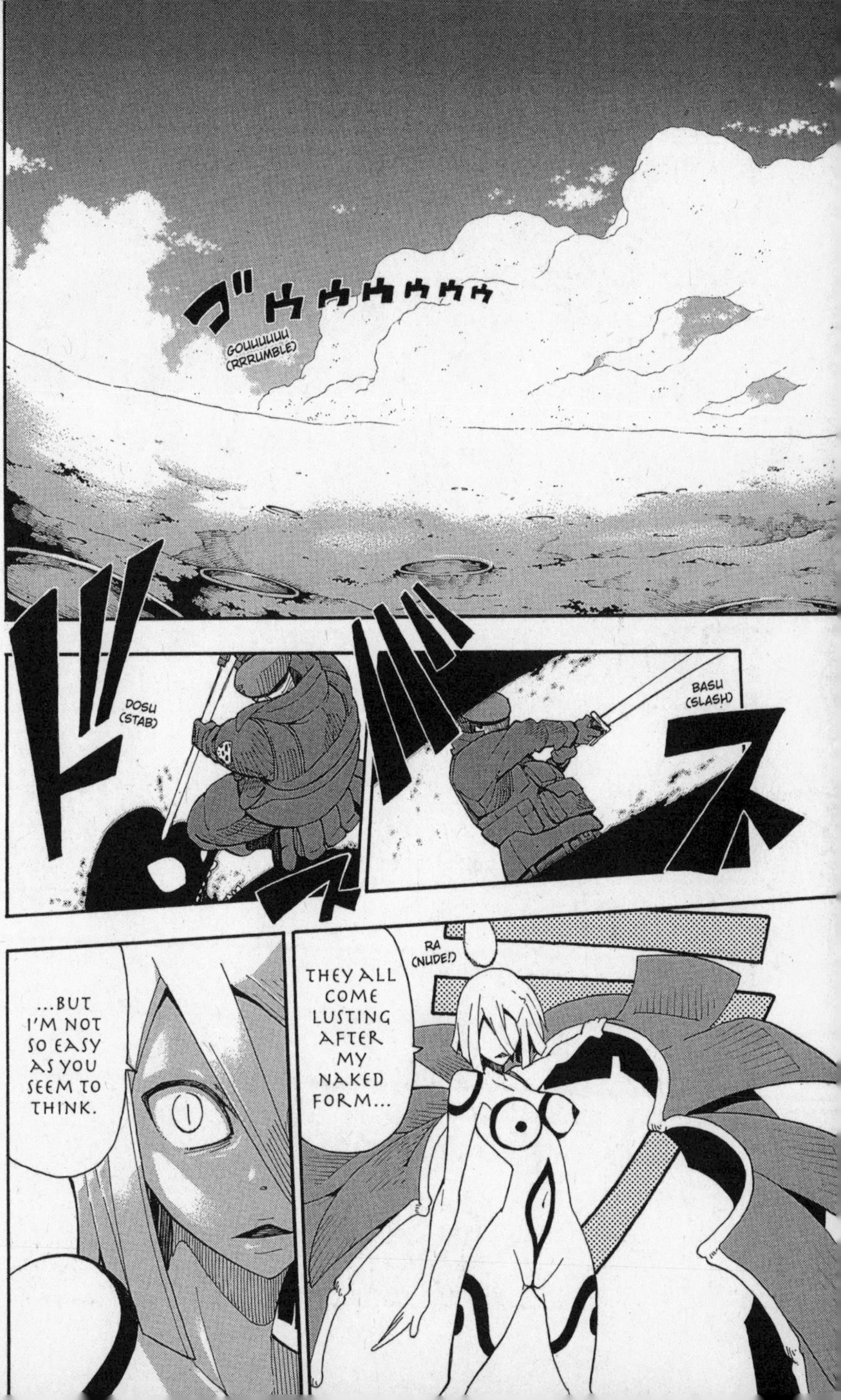

ゴウウウウウウ
GOUUUUUU (RRRUMBLE)
BASU (SLASH)
DOSU (STAB)
RA (NUDE!)
THEY ALL COME LUSTING AFTER MY NAKED FORM...
...BUT I'M NOT SO EASY AS YOU SEEM TO THINK.

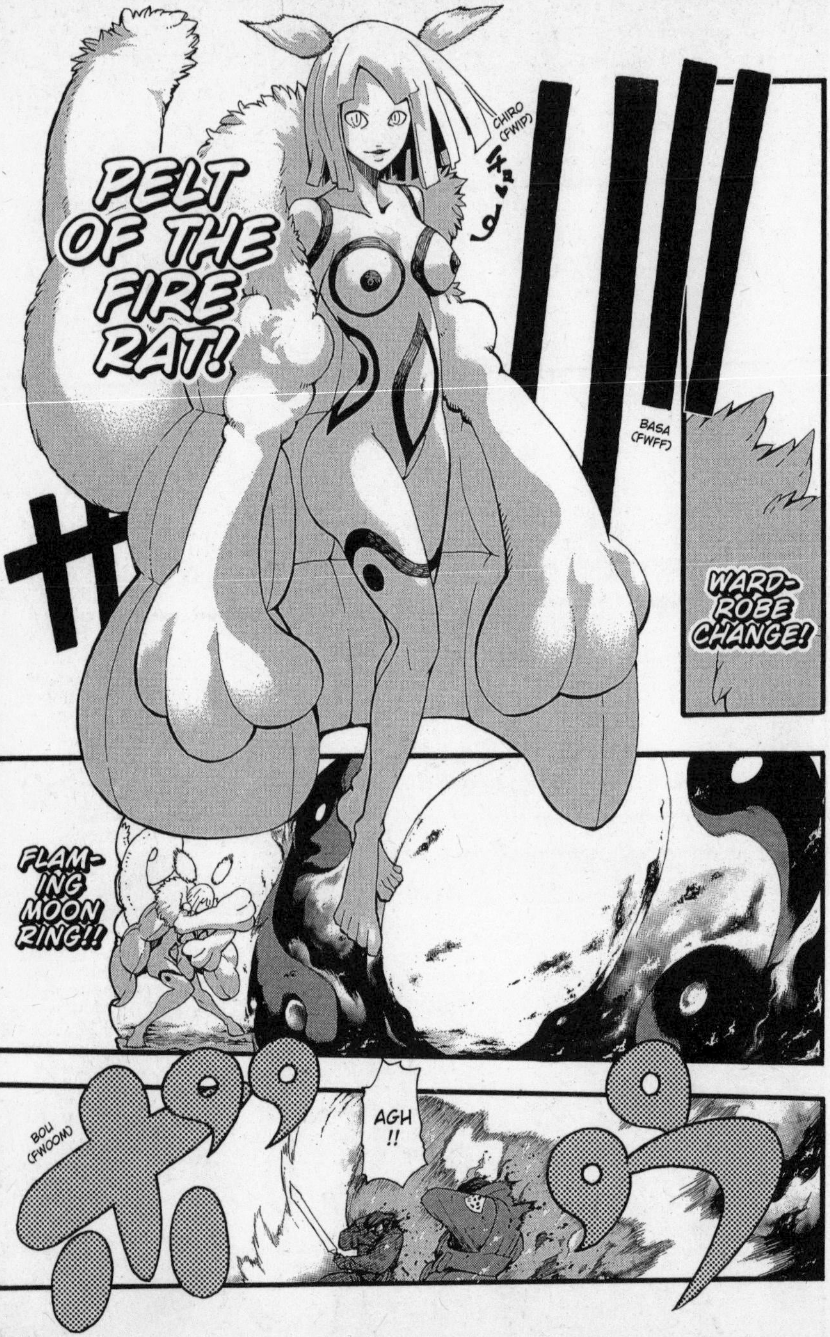
BASA (FWFF)
WARD-ROBE CHANGE!
CHIRO (FWIP)
PELT OF THE FIRE RAT!
FLAMING MOON RING!!
AGH !!
BOU (FWOOM)

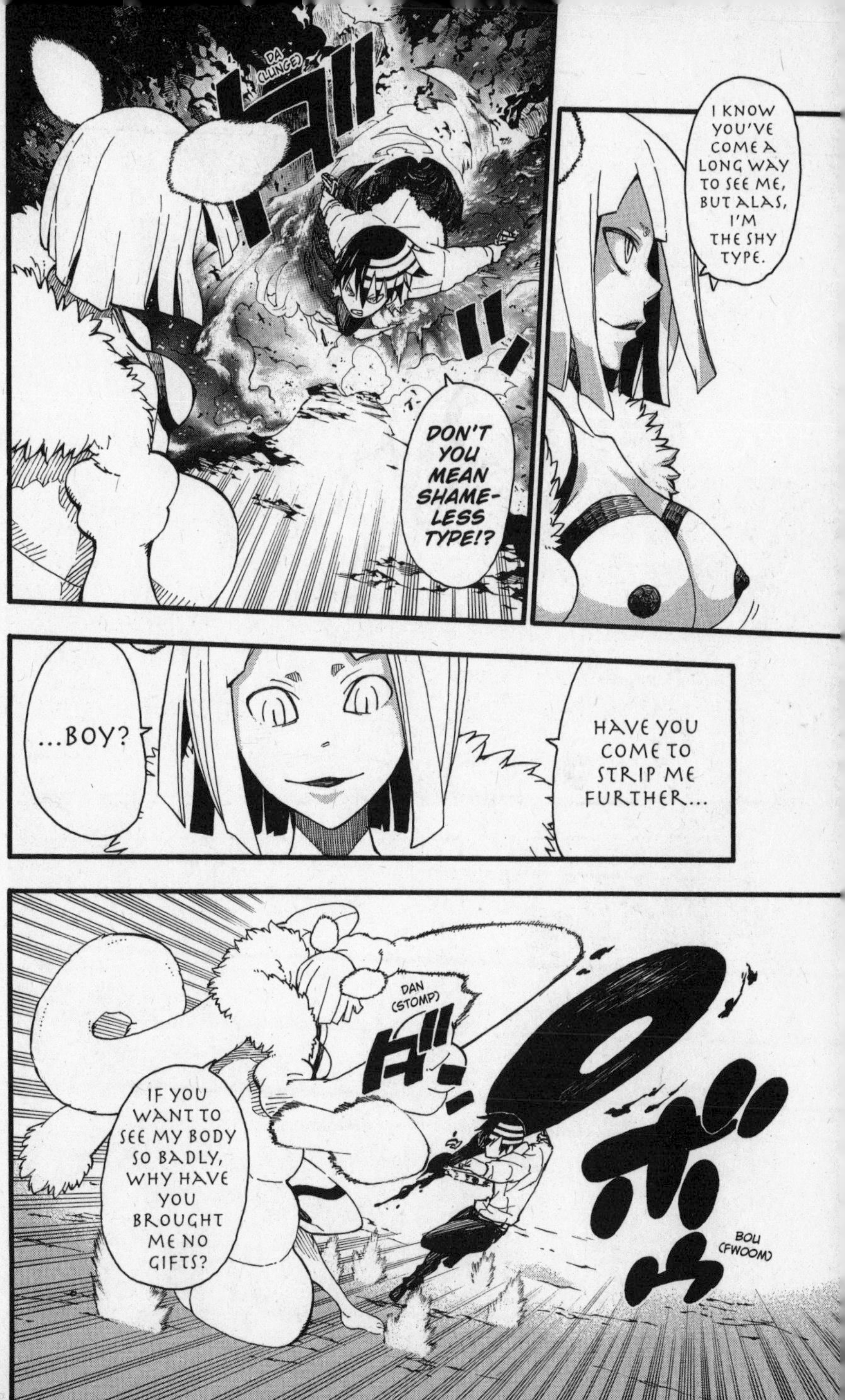
I KNOW YOU'VE COME A LONG WAY TO SEE ME, BUT ALAS, I'M THE SHY TYPE.
DA (LUNGE)
DON'T YOU MEAN SHAME-LESS TYPE!?
HAVE YOU COME TO STRIP ME FURTHER...
...BOY?
DAN (STOMP)
BOU (FWOOM)
IF YOU WANT TO SEE MY BODY SO BADLY, WHY HAVE YOU BROUGHT ME NO GIFTS?

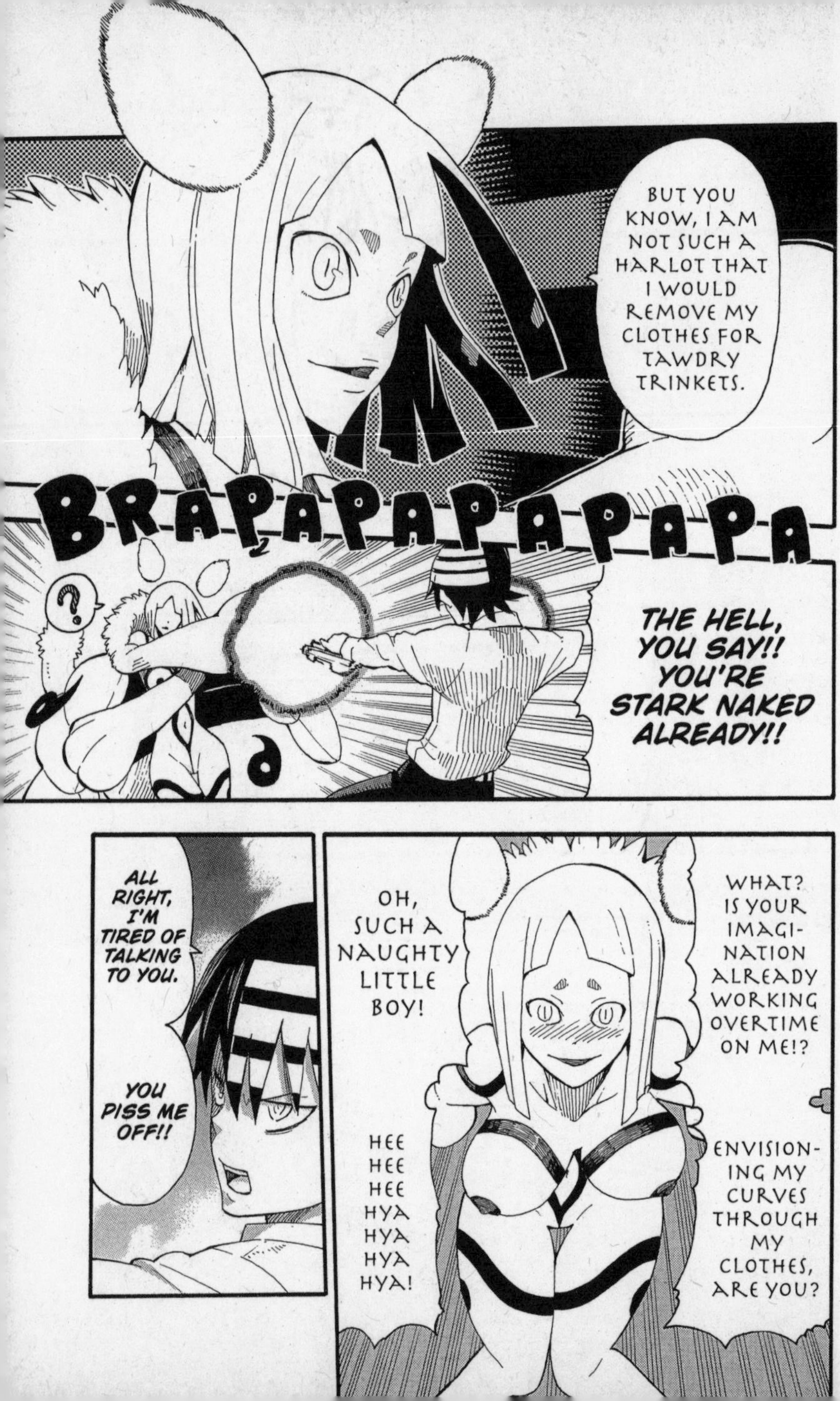
BUT YOU KNOW, I AM NOT SUCH A HARLOT THAT I WOULD REMOVE MY CLOTHES FOR TAWDRY TRINKETS.
BRAPAPAPAPAPAPA
?
THE HELL, YOU SAY!! YOU'RE STARK NAKED ALREADY!!
WHAT? IS YOUR IMAGI-NATION ALREADY WORKING OVERTIME ON ME!?
OH, SUCH A NAUGHTY LITTLE BOY!
ENVISION-ING MY CURVES THROUGH MY CLOTHES, ARE YOU?
HEE HEE HEE HYA HYA HYA HYA!
ALL RIGHT, I'M TIRED OF TALKING TO YOU.
YOU PISS ME OFF!!

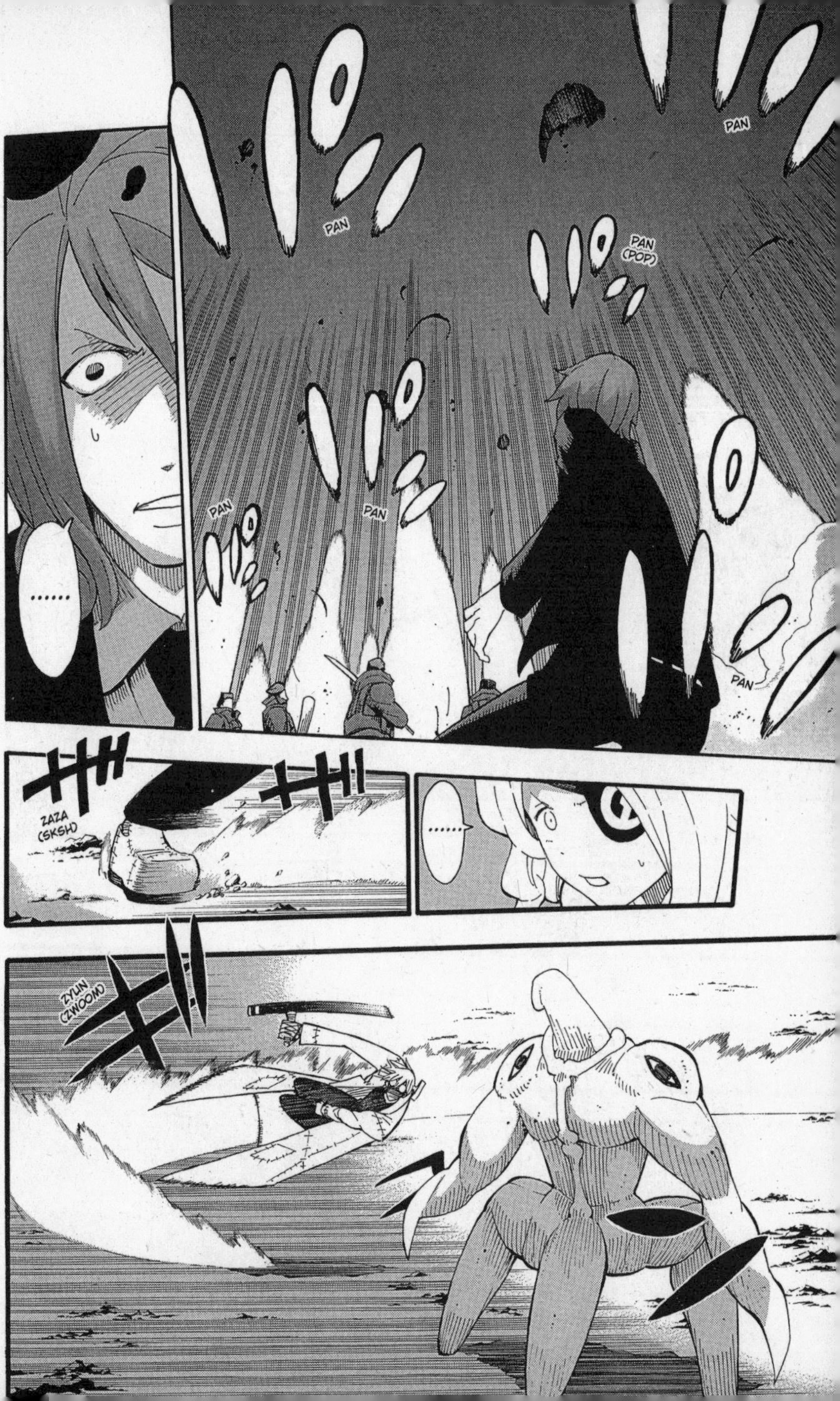
PAN
PAN
(POP)
PAN
PAN
PAN
PAN
PAN
......
......
ZAZA
(SKSH)
ZYUN
(ZWOOM)

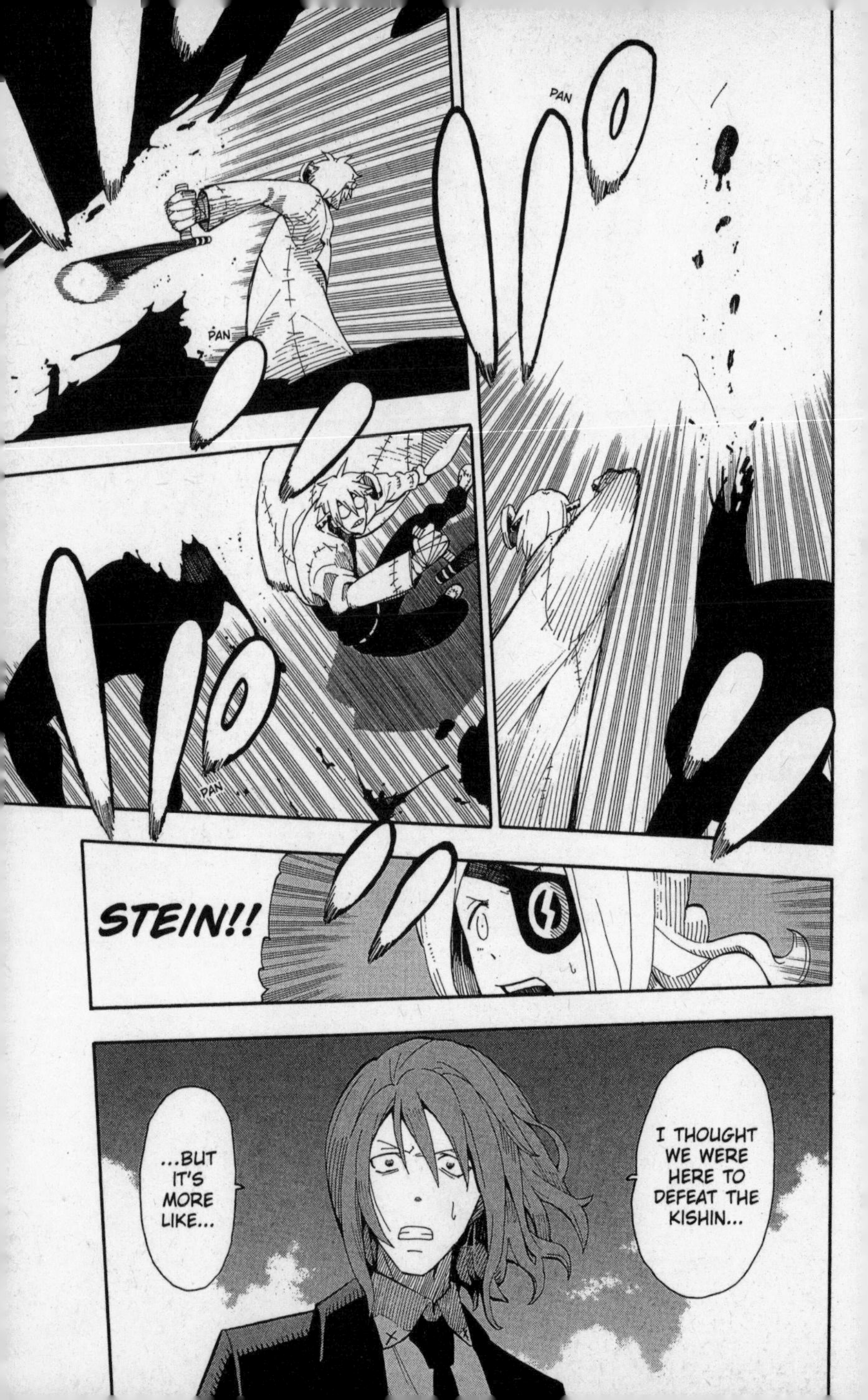
PAN
PAN
PAN
STEIN!!
I THOUGHT WE WERE HERE TO DEFEAT THE KISHIN...
...BUT IT'S MORE LIKE...

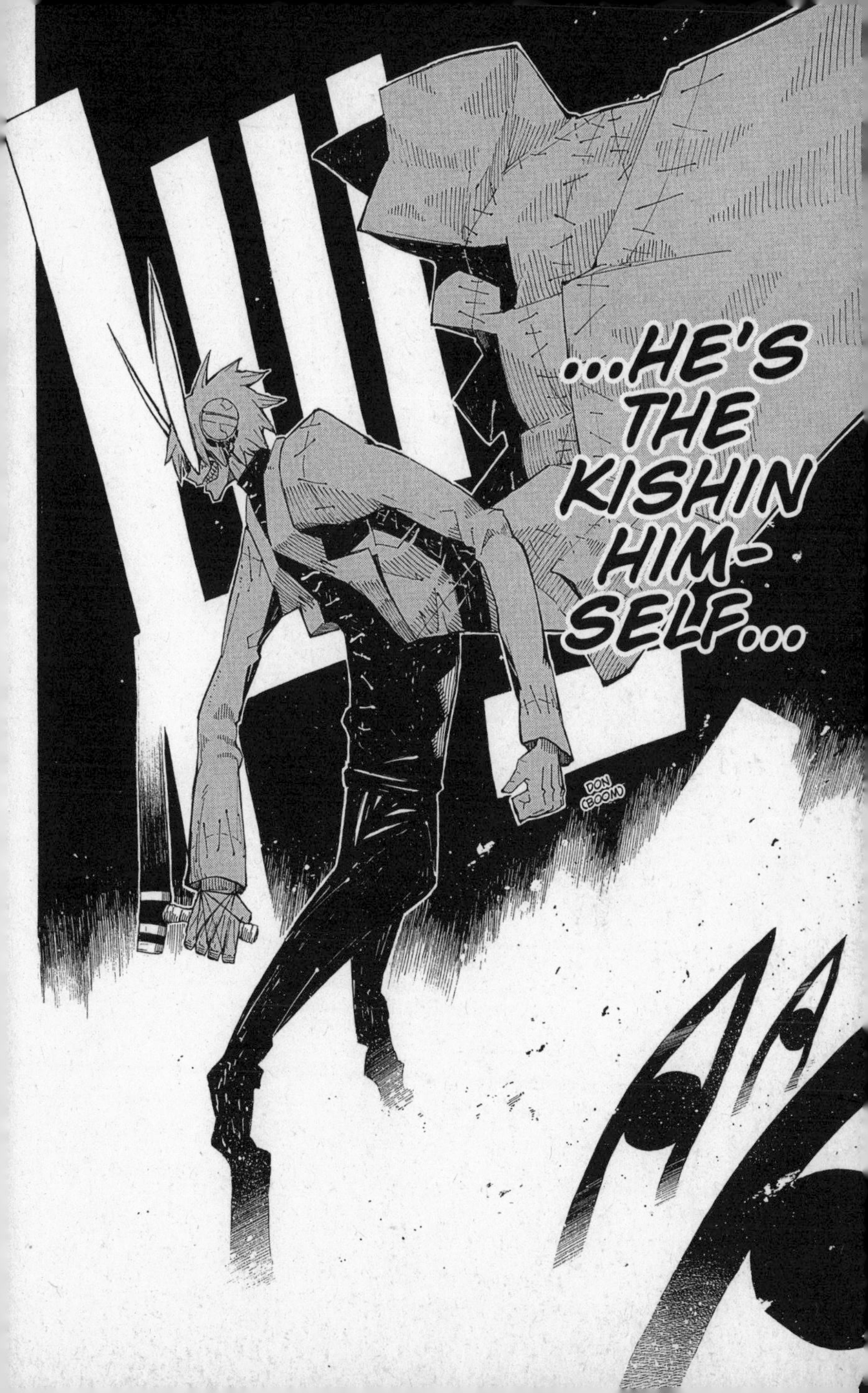
...HE'S THE KISHIN HIM-SELF...
DON (BOOM)

SOUL EATER

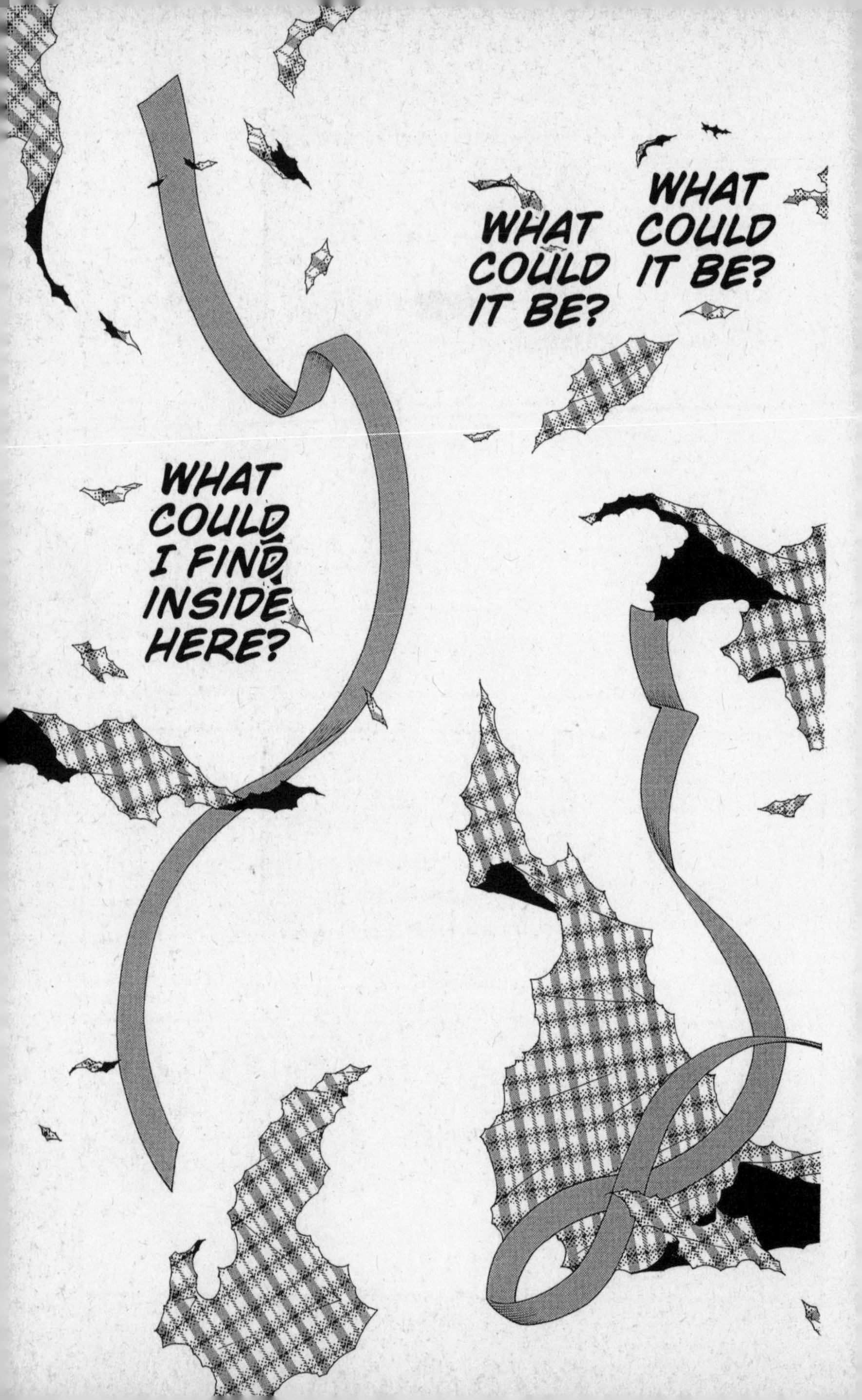
WHAT COULD IT BE?
WHAT COULD IT BE?
WHAT COULD I FIND INSIDE HERE?

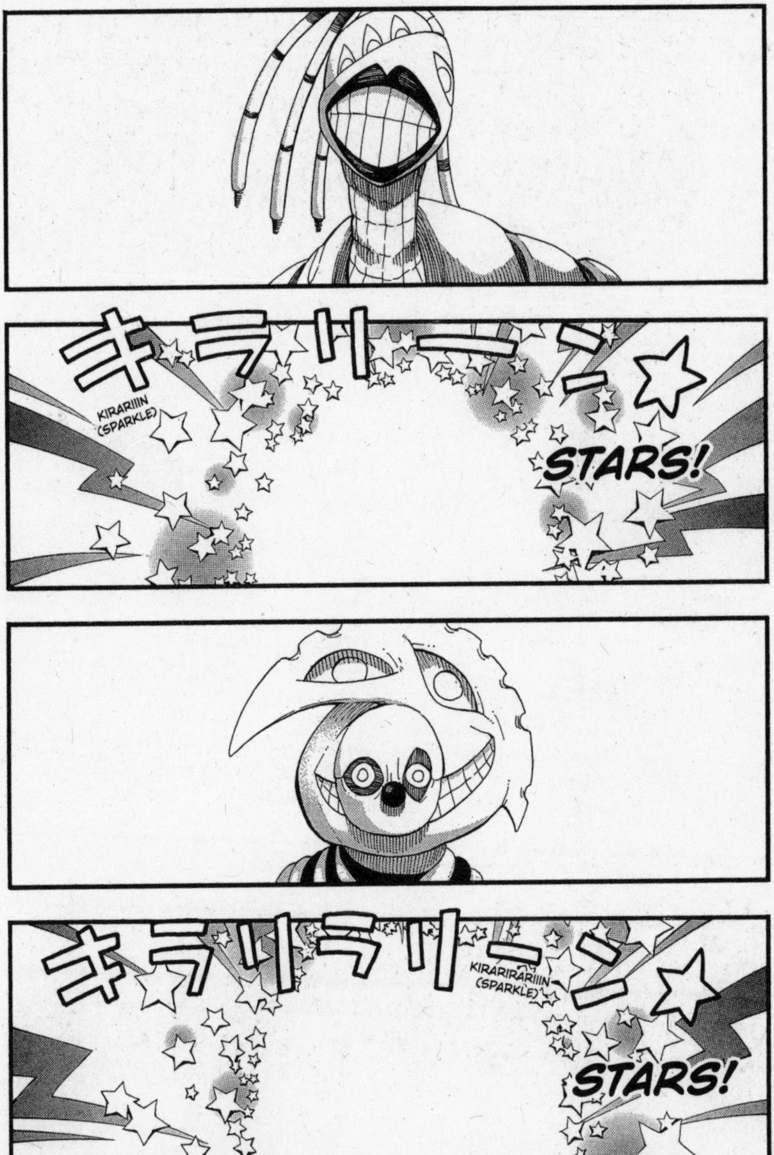
キラリーン☆
KIRARIIN (SPARKLE)
STARS!
キラリラリーン☆
KIRARIRARIIIN (SPARKLE)
STARS!

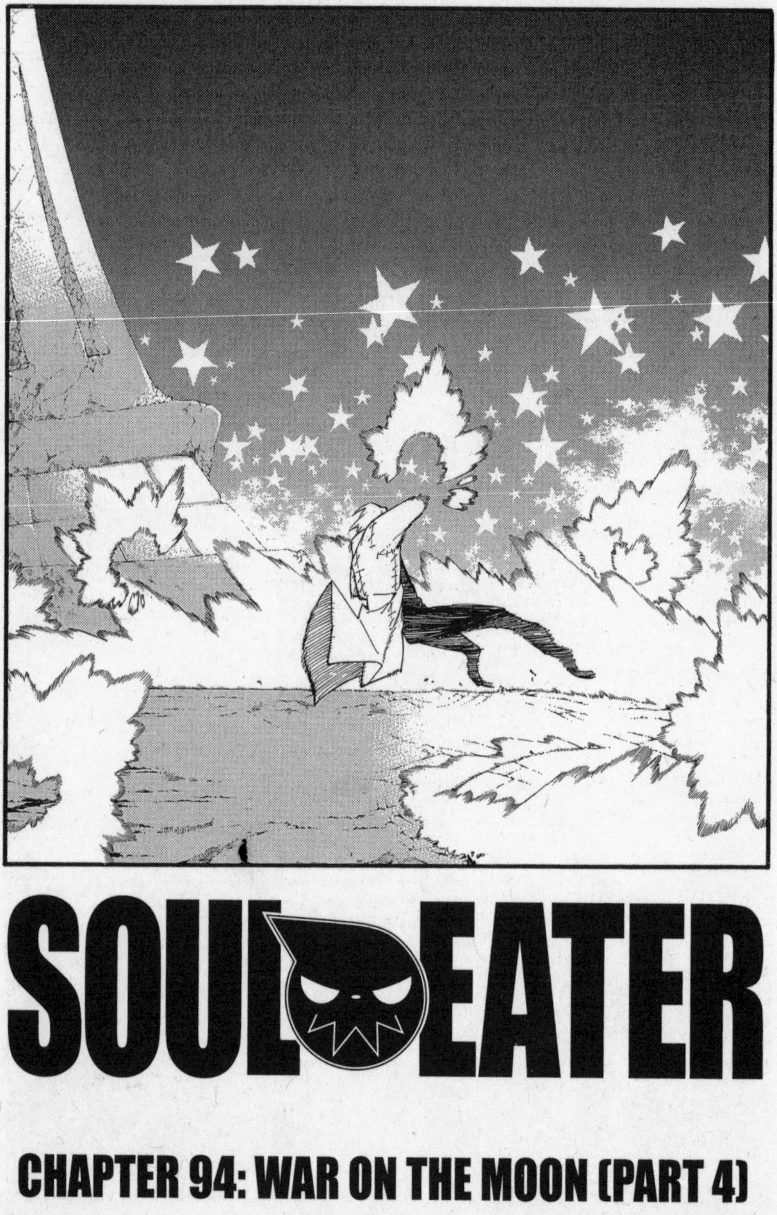

SOUL EATER

CHAPTER 94: WAR ON THE MOON (PART 4)

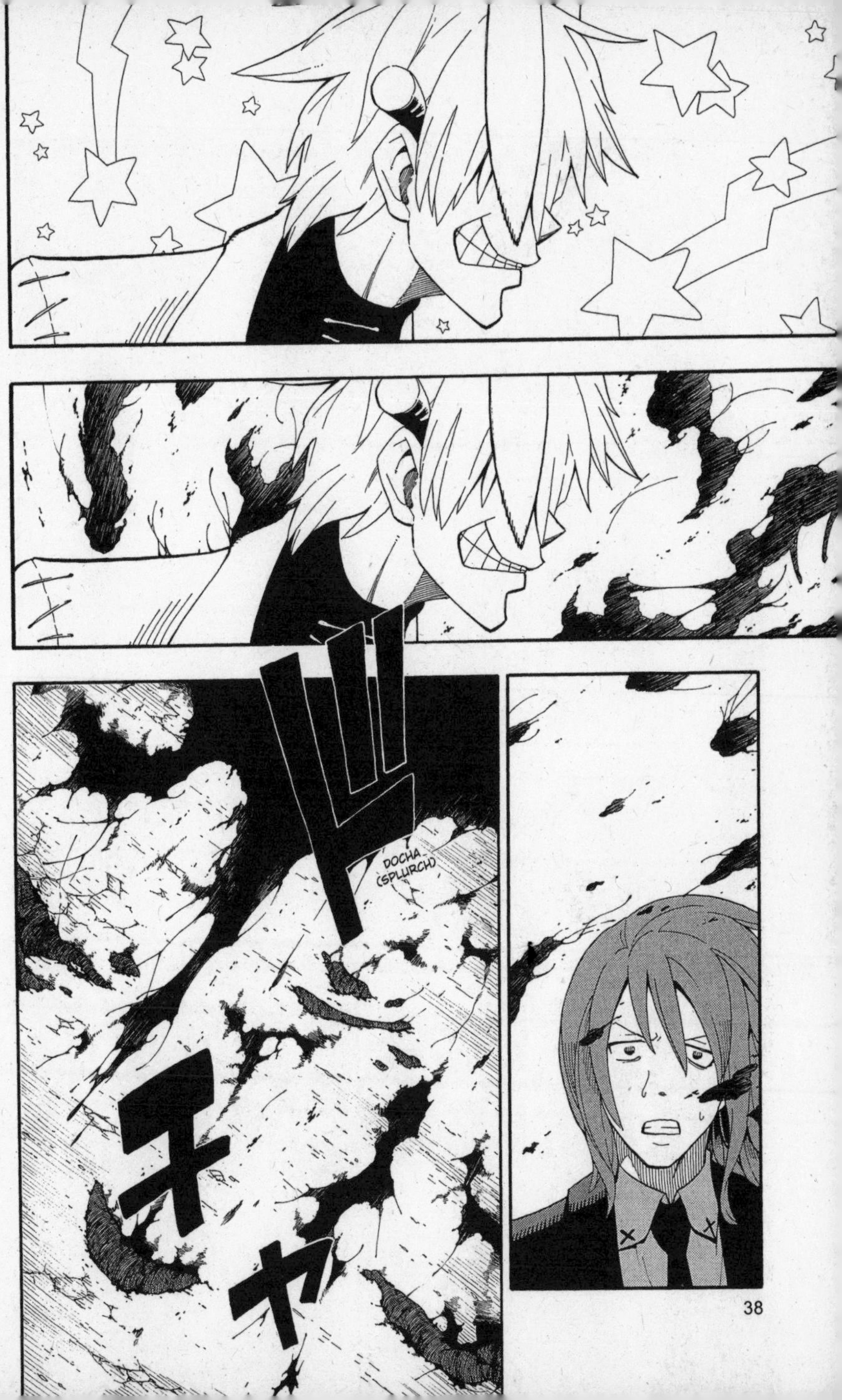

DOCHA
(SPLURCH)

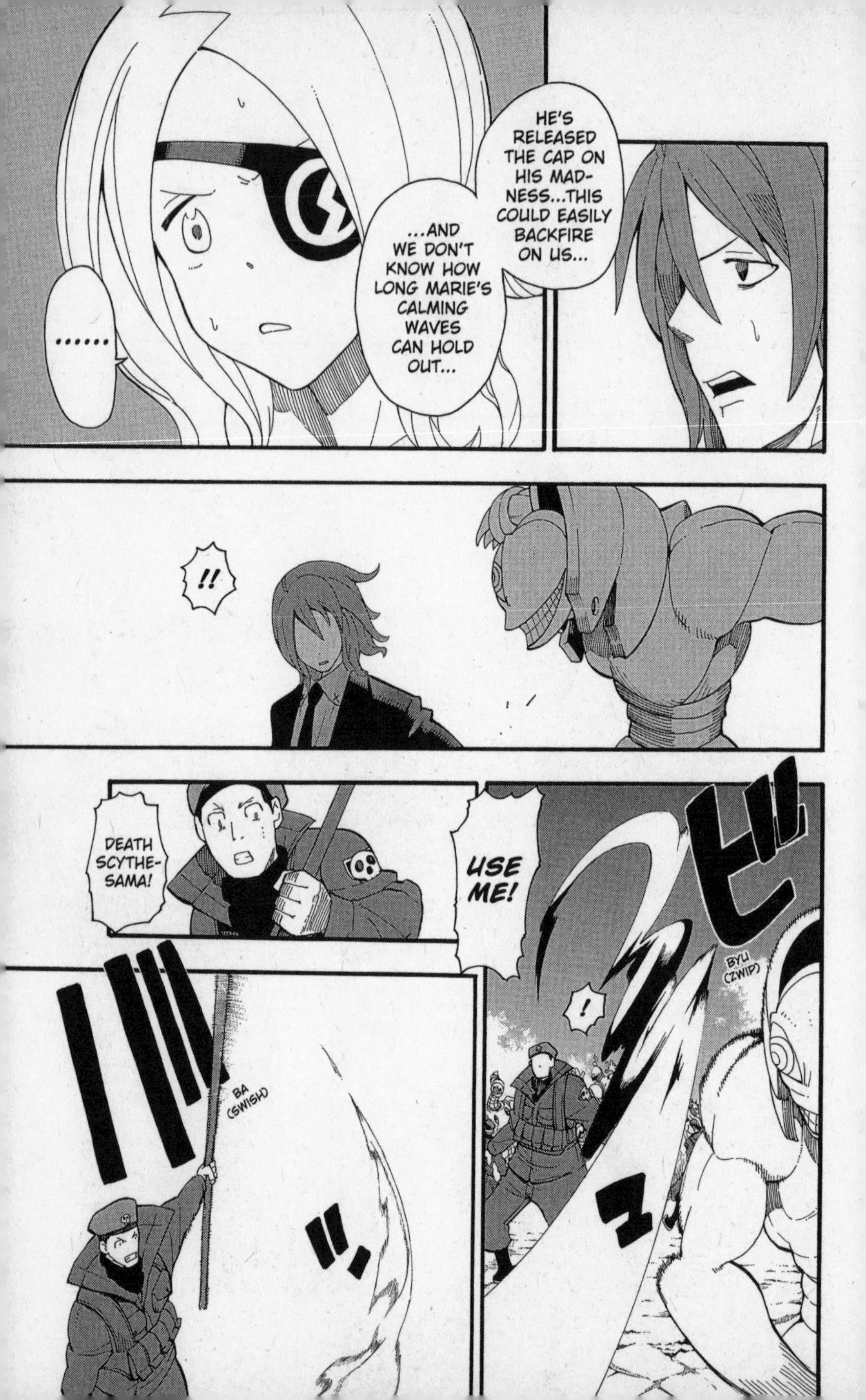

HE'S RELEASED THE CAP ON HIS MADNESS...THIS COULD EASILY BACKFIRE ON US...
...AND WE DON'T KNOW HOW LONG MARIE'S CALMING WAVES CAN HOLD OUT...
......
!!
DEATH SCYTHE-SAMA!
USE ME!
BA (SWISH)
BYU (ZWIP)
!

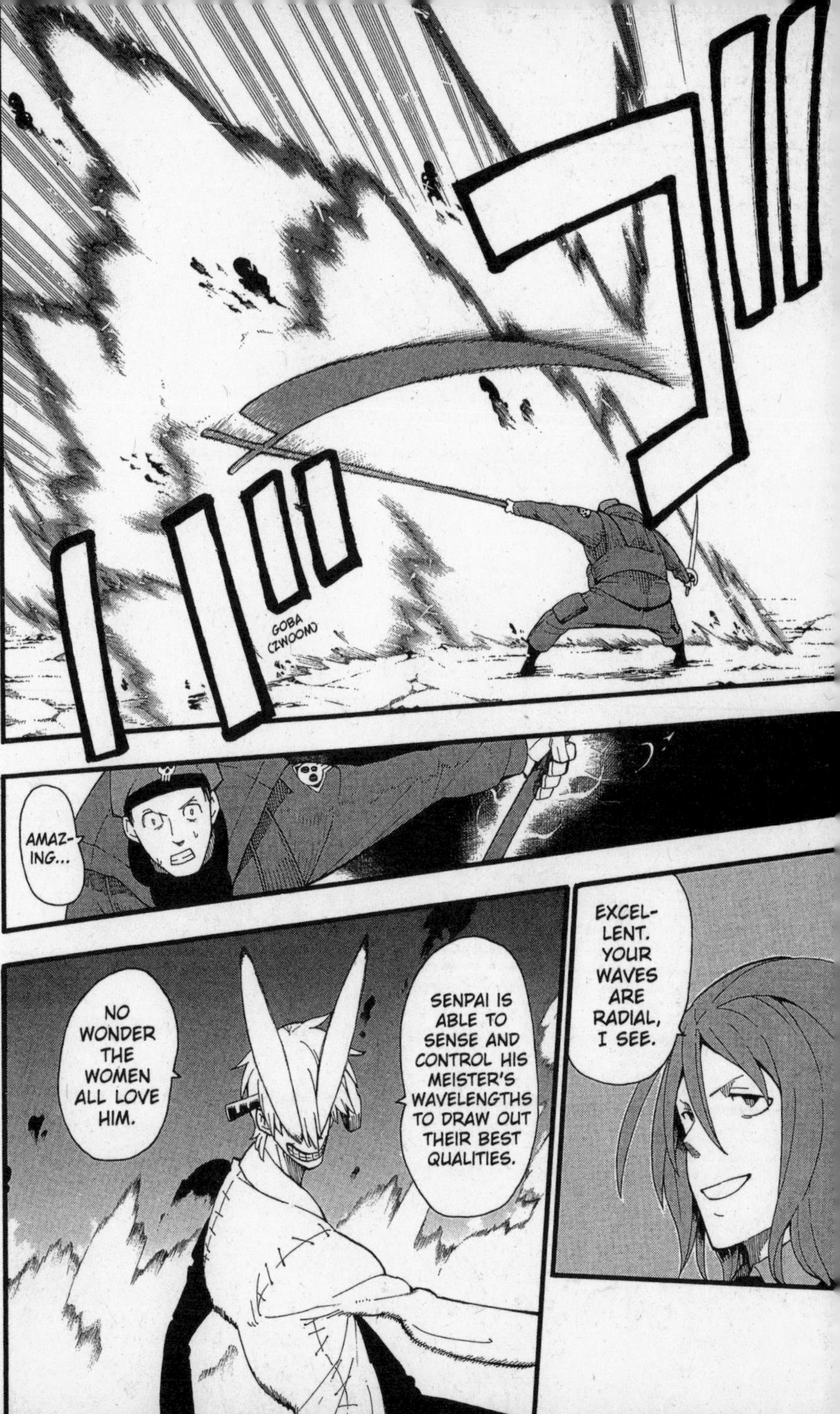
GOBA (ZWOOM)
AMAZ-ING...
EXCEL-LENT. YOUR WAVES ARE RADIAL, I SEE.
SENPAI IS ABLE TO SENSE AND CONTROL HIS MEISTER'S WAVELENGTHS TO DRAW OUT THEIR BEST QUALITIES.
NO WONDER THE WOMEN ALL LOVE HIM.

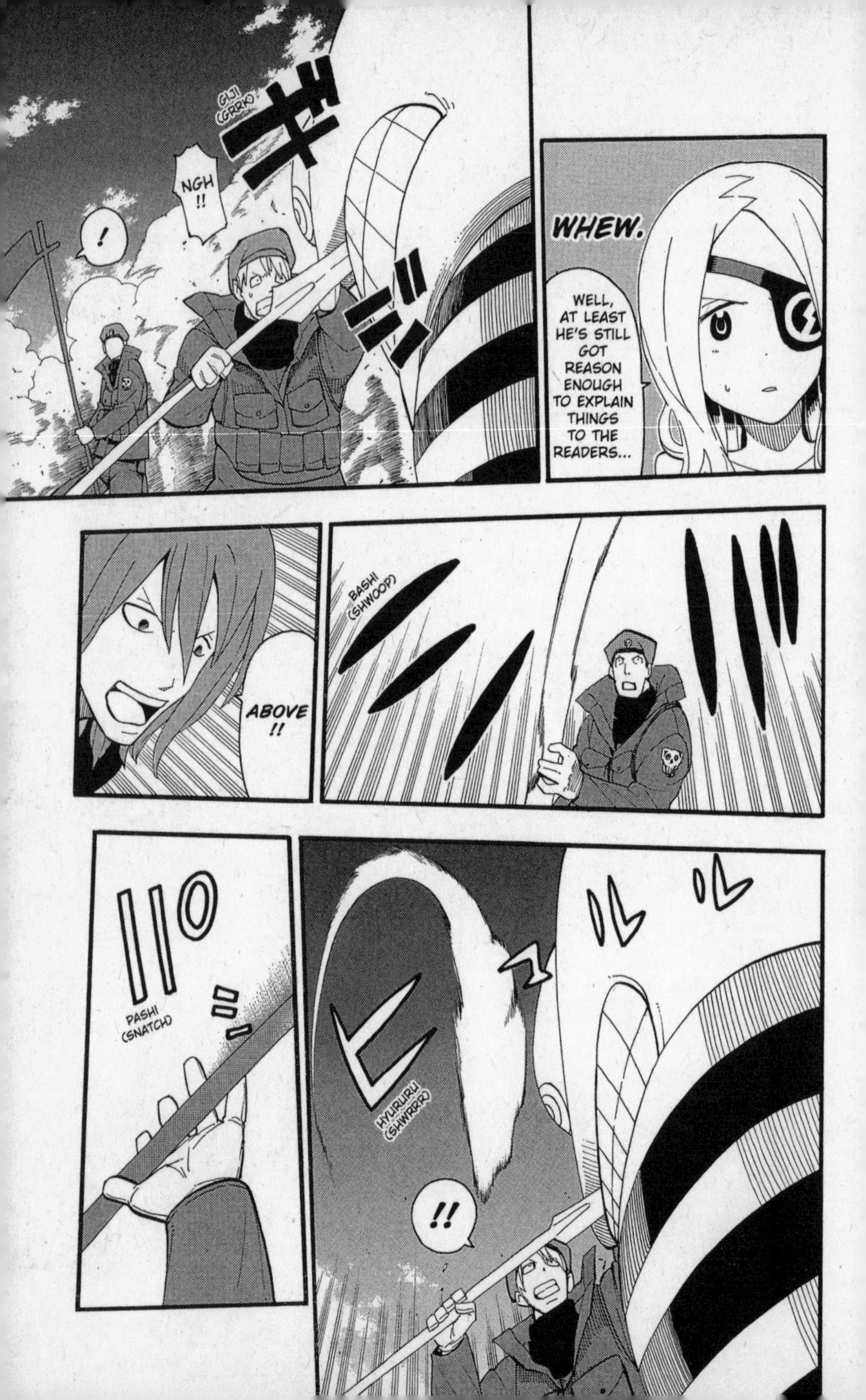
WHEW.
WELL, AT LEAST HE'S STILL GOT REASON ENOUGH TO EXPLAIN THINGS TO THE READERS...
GIJI (GRRK)
NGH !!
!
BASHI (SHWOOP)
ABOVE !!
HYURURU (SHWRRR)
!!
PASHI (SNATCH)

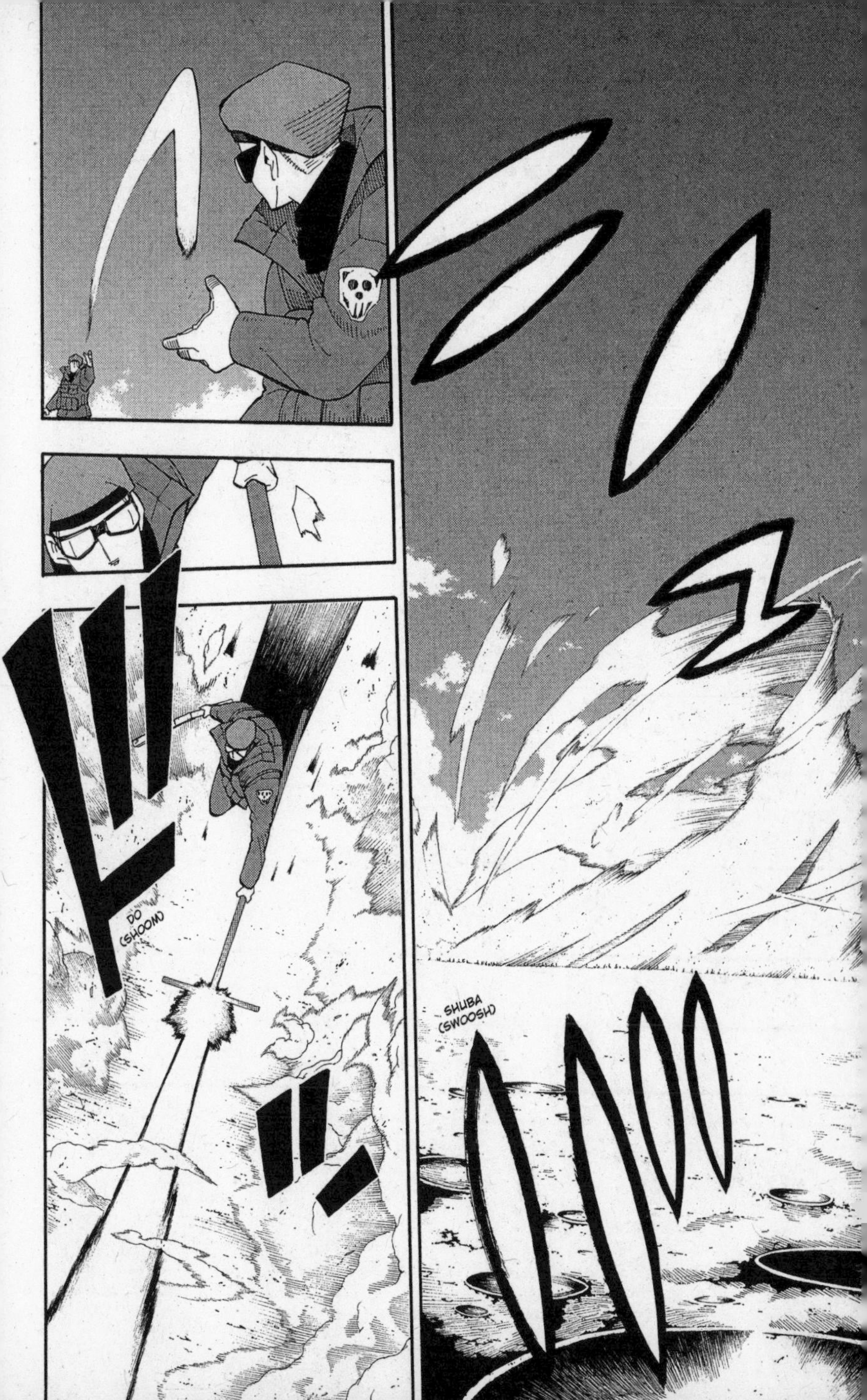
SHUBA
(SWOOSH)
DO
(SHOOM)

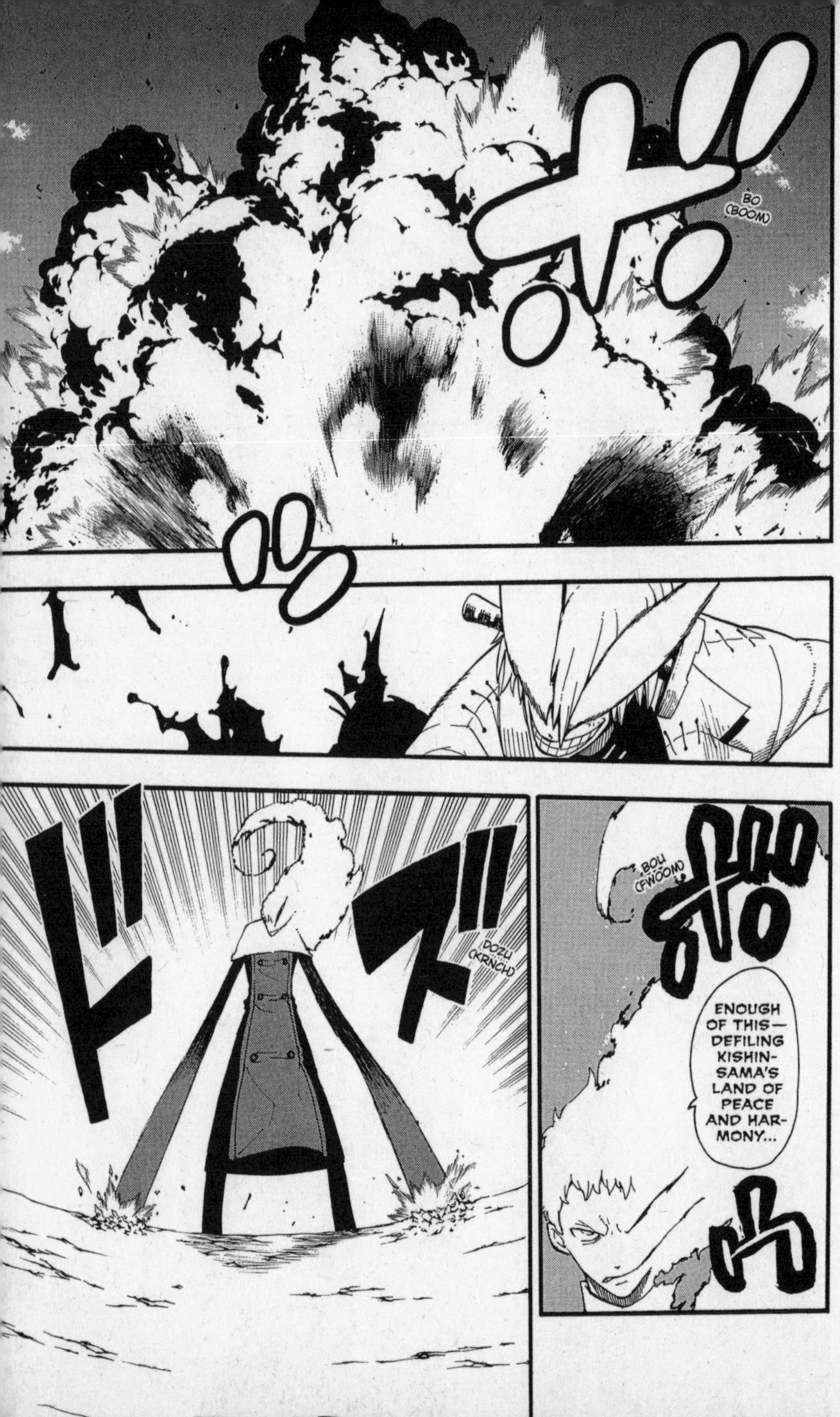
BO (BOOM)
BOU (FWOOM)
ENOUGH OF THIS— DEFILING KISHIN-SAMA'S LAND OF PEACE AND HARMONY...
DOZU (KRNCH)

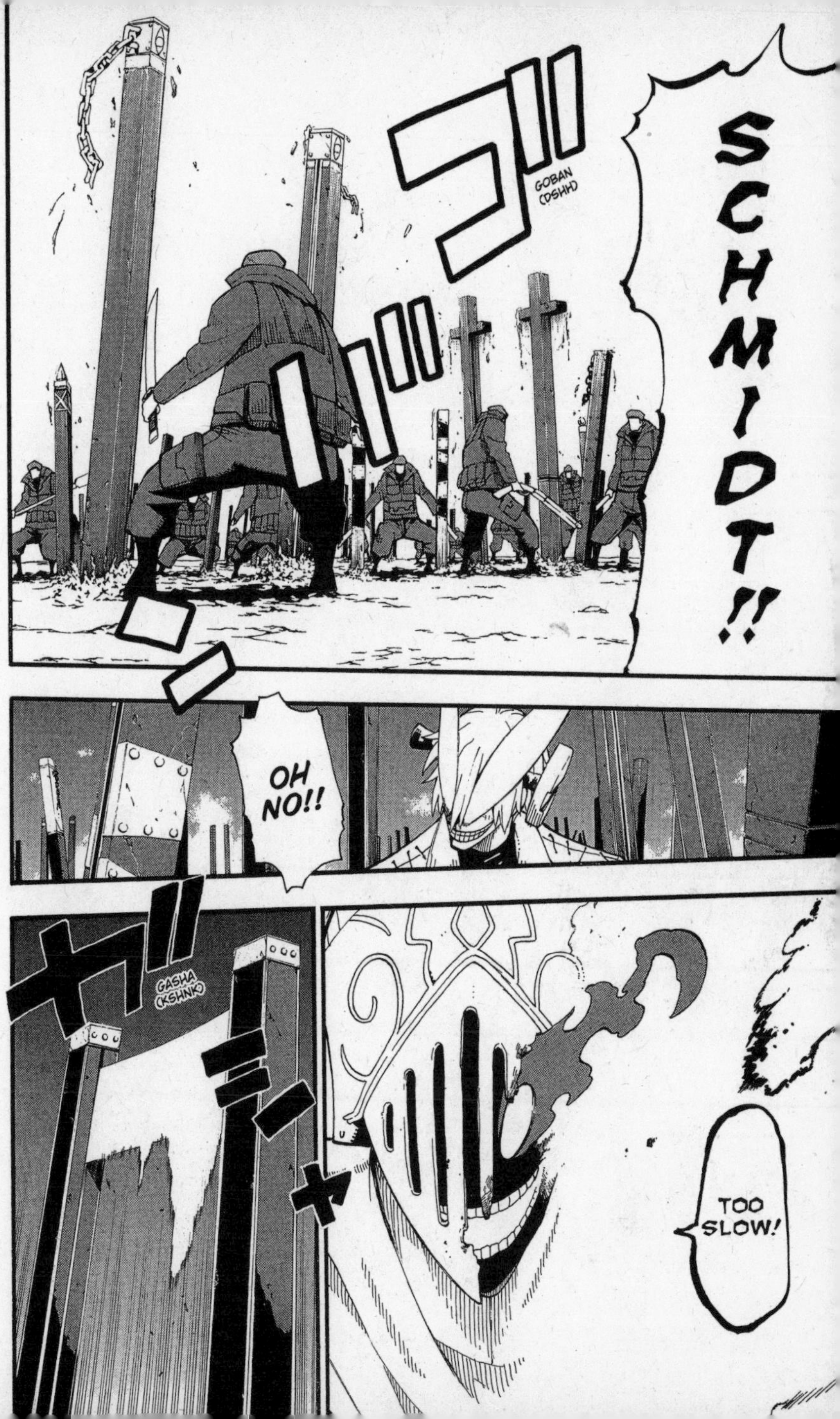
SCHMIDT!!
GOBAN (DSHH)
OH NO!!
TOO SLOW!
GASHA (KSHNK)

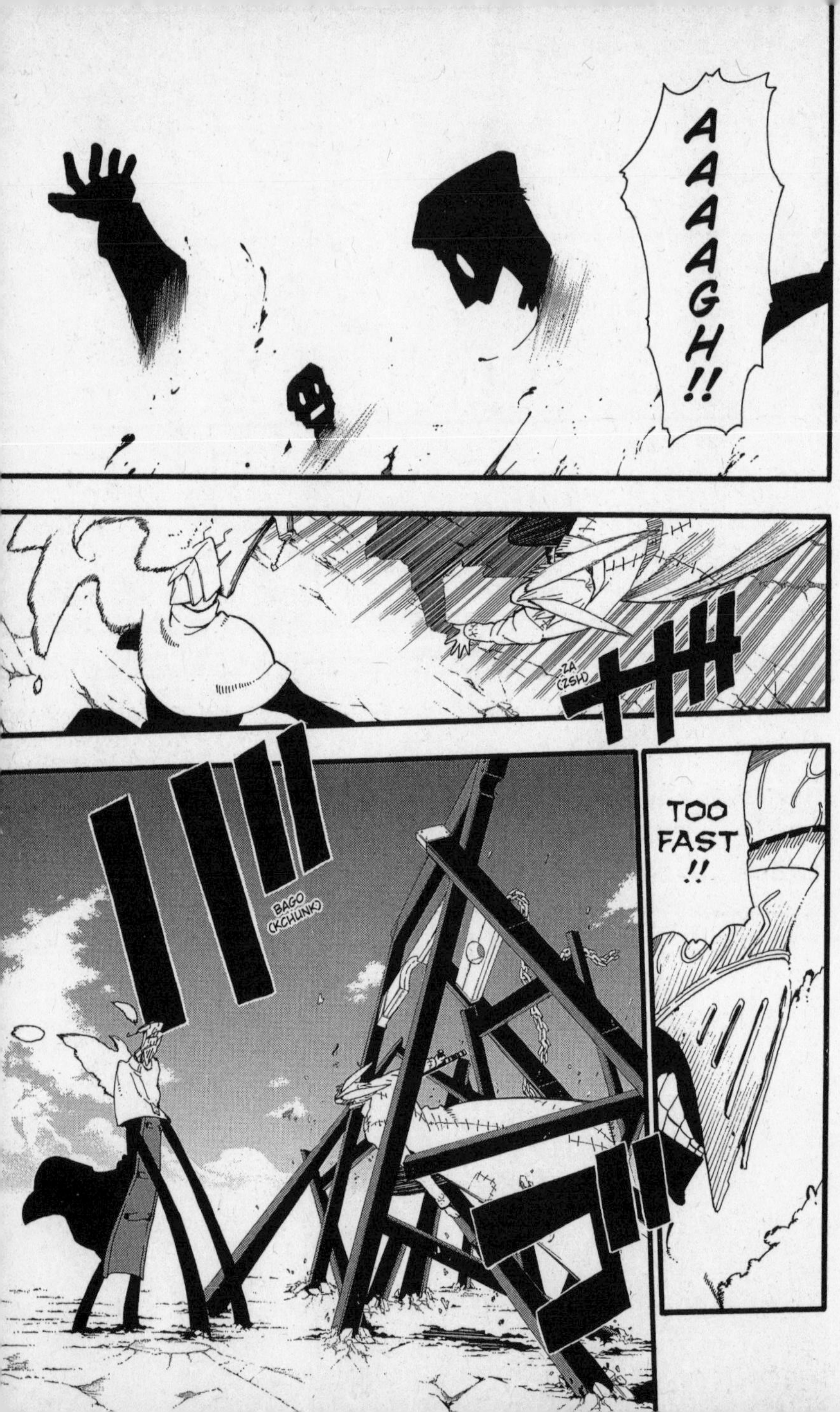
AAAAAGH!!
ZA (ZSH)
TOO FAST!!
BAGO (KCHUNK)

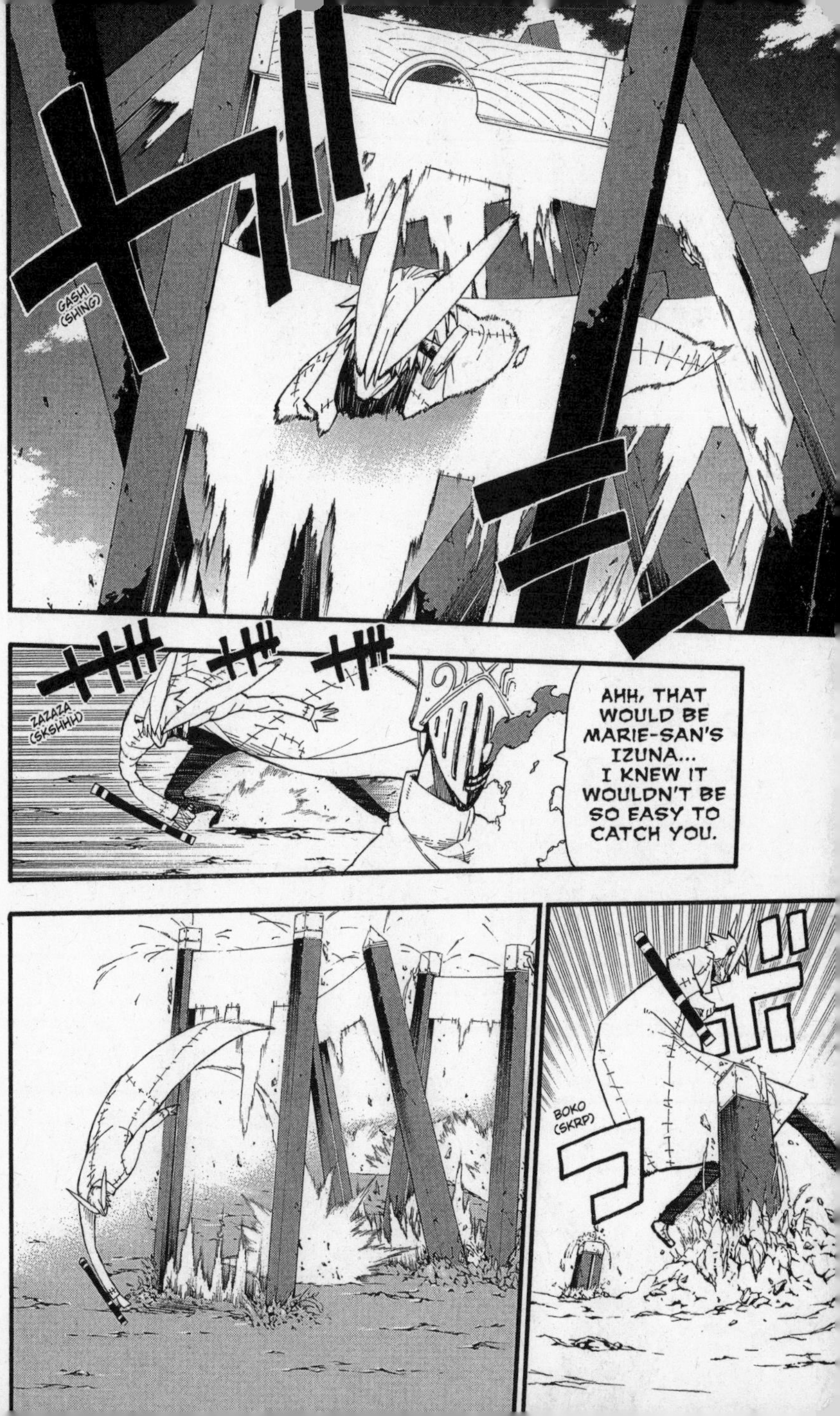
GASHI (SHING)
AHH, THAT WOULD BE MARIE-SAN'S IZUNA... I KNEW IT WOULDN'T BE SO EASY TO CATCH YOU.
ZAZAZA (SKSHHH)
BOKO (SKRP)

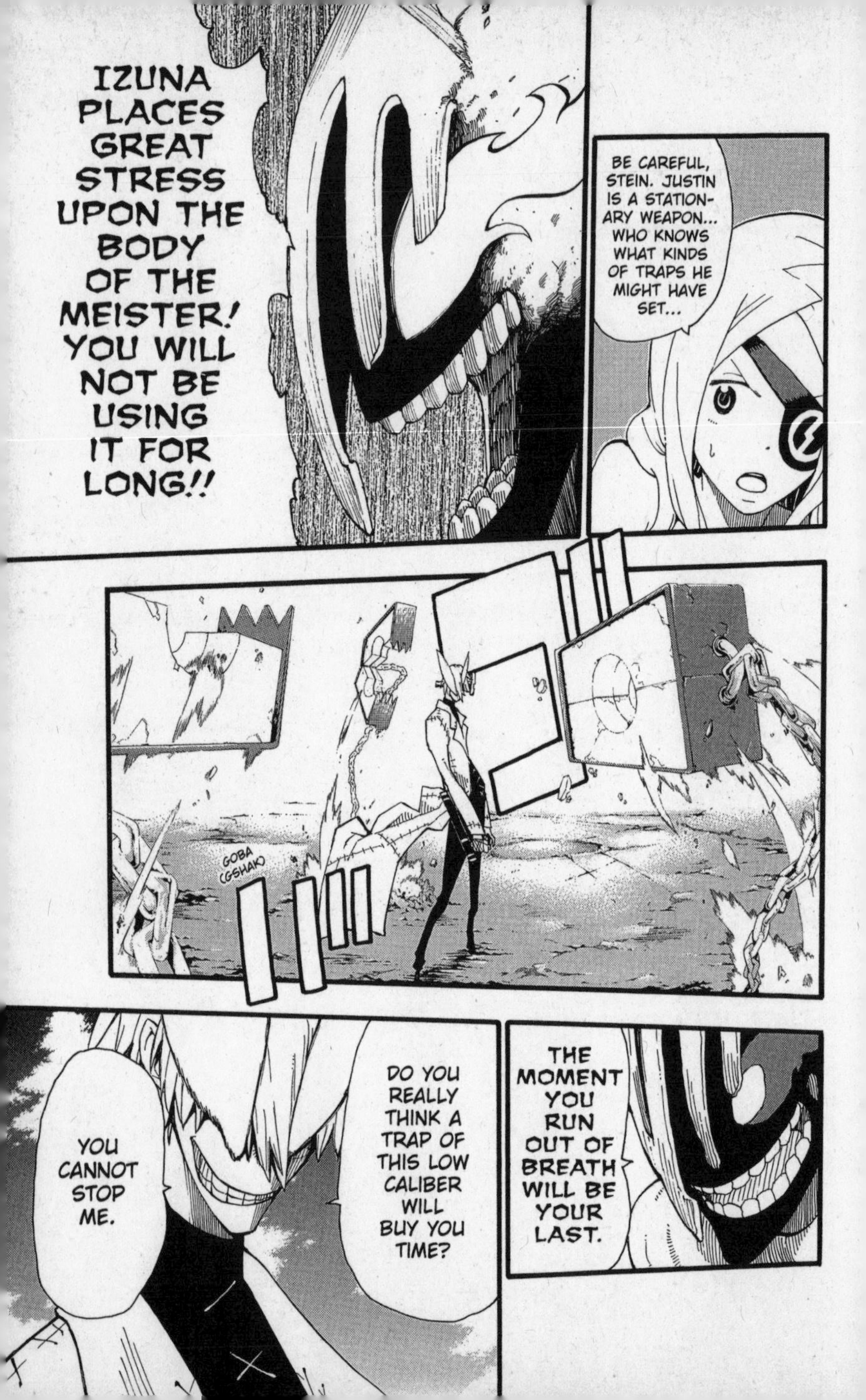
BE CAREFUL, STEIN. JUSTIN IS A STATIONARY WEAPON... WHO KNOWS WHAT KINDS OF TRAPS HE MIGHT HAVE SET...
IZUNA PLACES GREAT STRESS UPON THE BODY OF THE MEISTER! YOU WILL NOT BE USING IT FOR LONG!!
GOBA (GSHAK)
THE MOMENT YOU RUN OUT OF BREATH WILL BE YOUR LAST.
DO YOU REALLY THINK A TRAP OF THIS LOW CALIBER WILL BUY YOU TIME?
YOU CANNOT STOP ME.

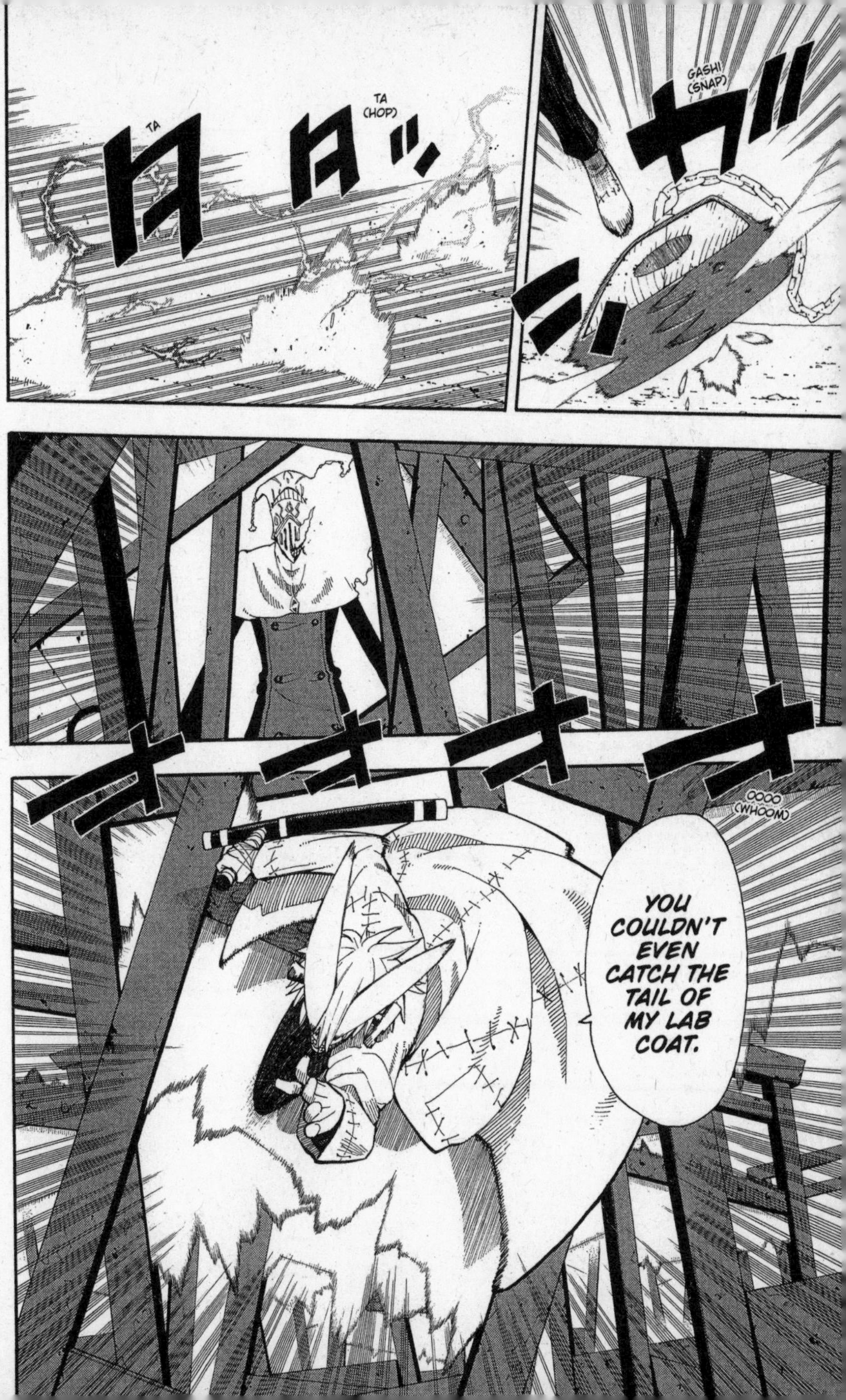
GASHI (SNAP)
TA (HOP)
TA
OOOO (WHOOM)
YOU COULDN'T EVEN CATCH THE TAIL OF MY LAB COAT.

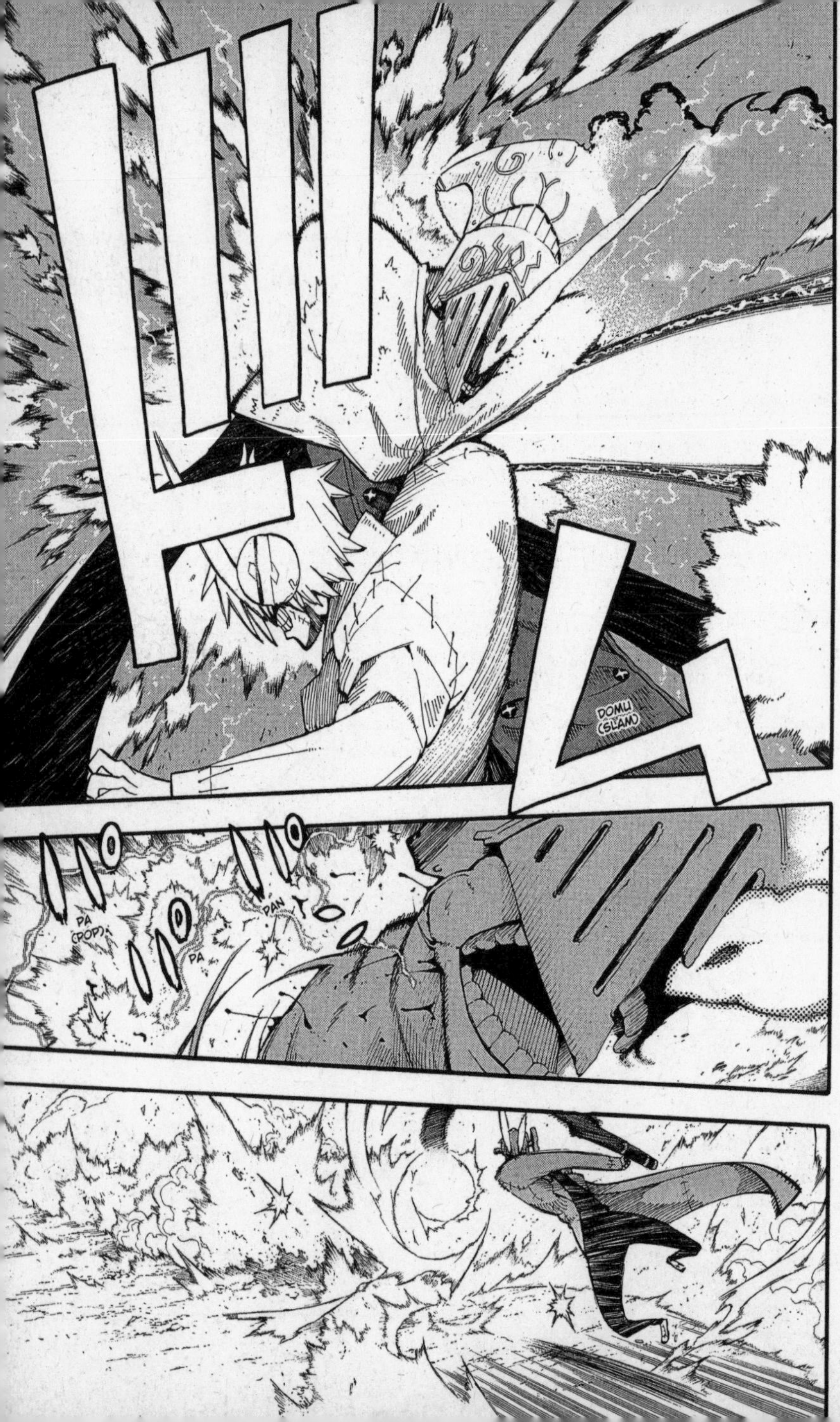
DOMU
(SLAM)
PAN
PA
PA
(POP)

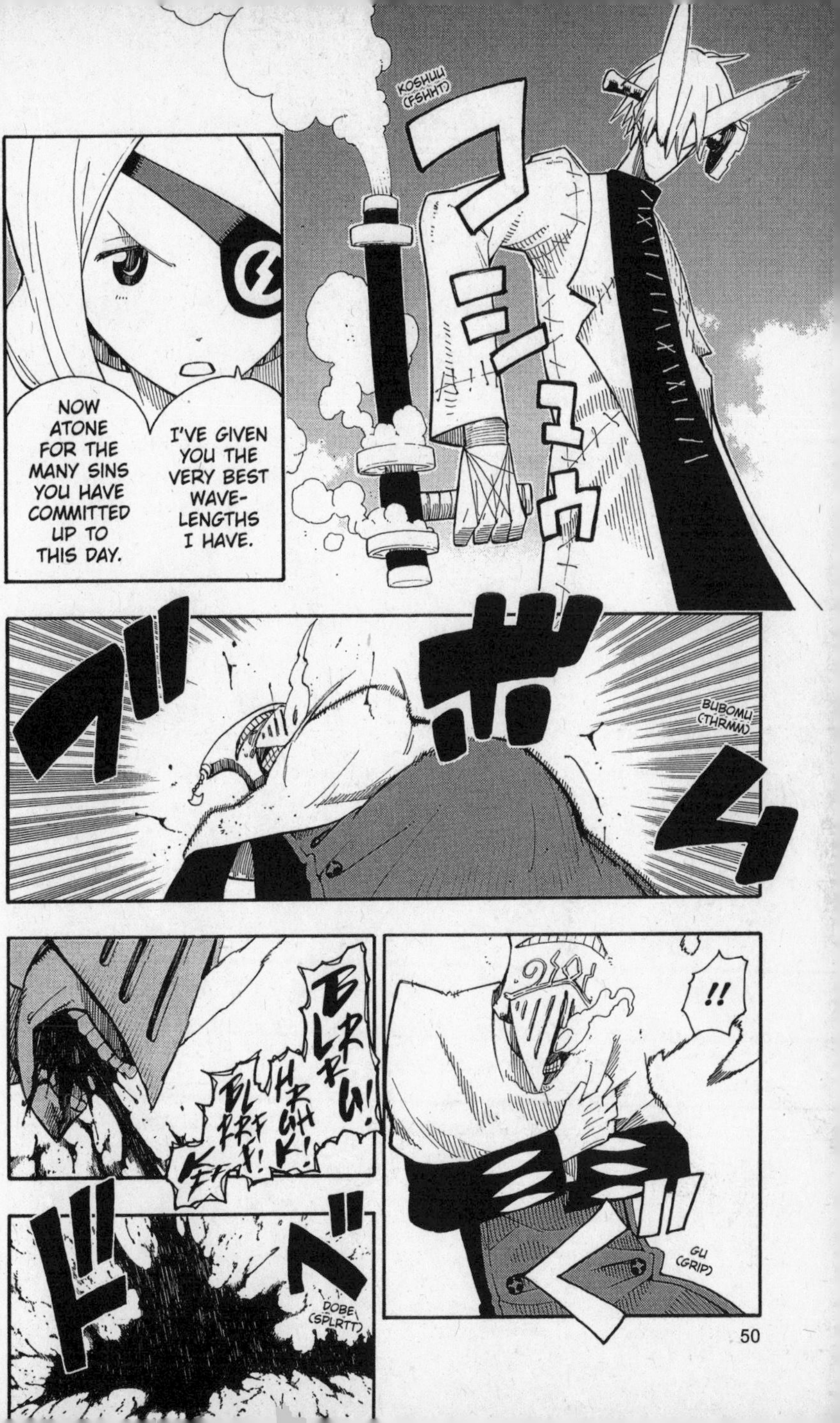
KOSHUU (FSHHT)
I'VE GIVEN YOU THE VERY BEST WAVE-LENGTHS I HAVE.
NOW ATONE FOR THE MANY SINS YOU HAVE COMMITTED UP TO THIS DAY.
BUBOMU (THRMM)
!!
GU (GRIP)
BLRRU!
HRGHK!
BLRRF! KEFF
DOBE (SPLRTT)

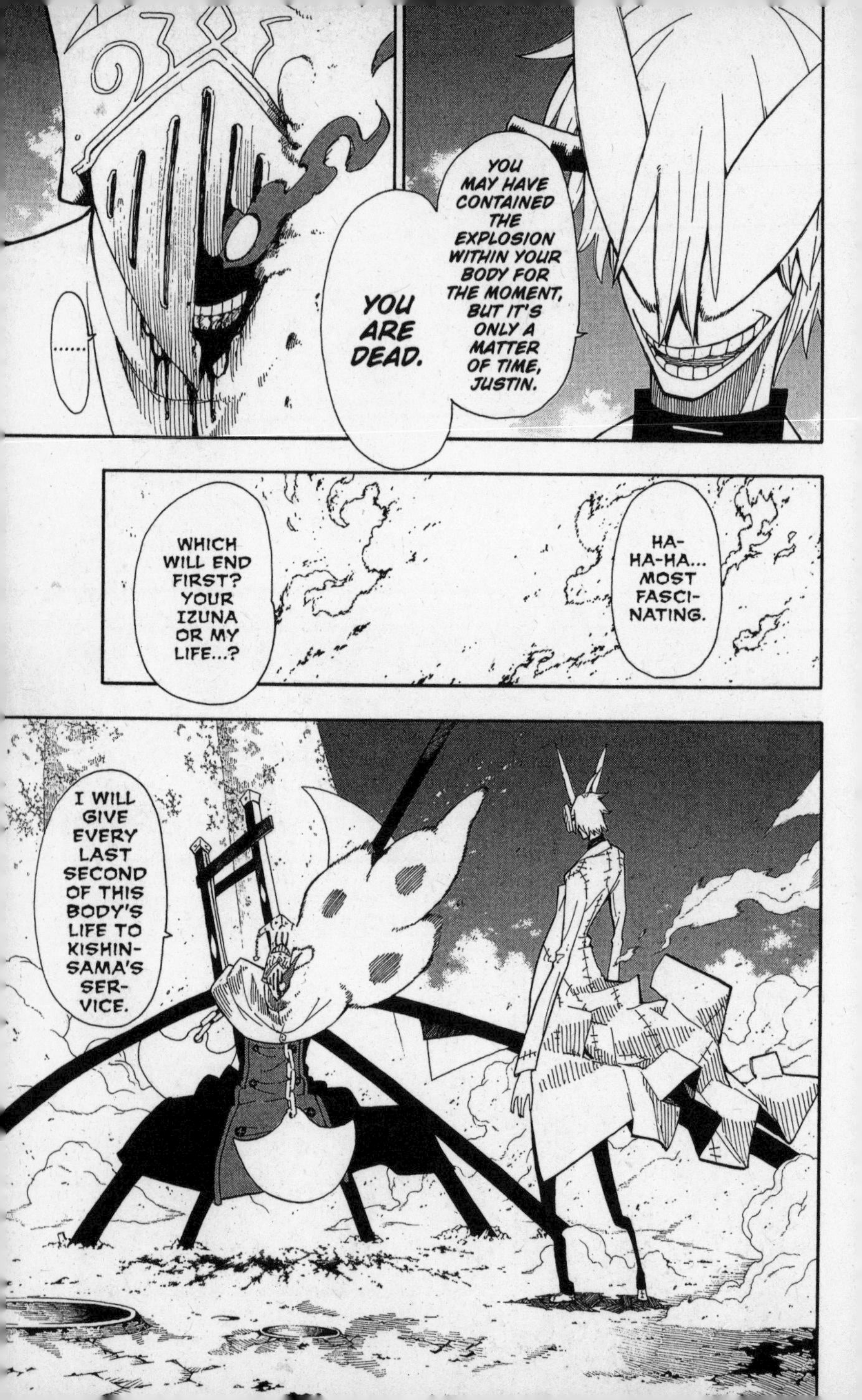
YOU MAY HAVE CONTAINED THE EXPLOSION WITHIN YOUR BODY FOR THE MOMENT, BUT IT'S ONLY A MATTER OF TIME, JUSTIN.
YOU ARE DEAD.
......
HA-HA-HA... MOST FASCI-NATING.
WHICH WILL END FIRST? YOUR IZUNA OR MY LIFE...?
I WILL GIVE EVERY LAST SECOND OF THIS BODY'S LIFE TO KISHIN-SAMA'S SER-VICE.

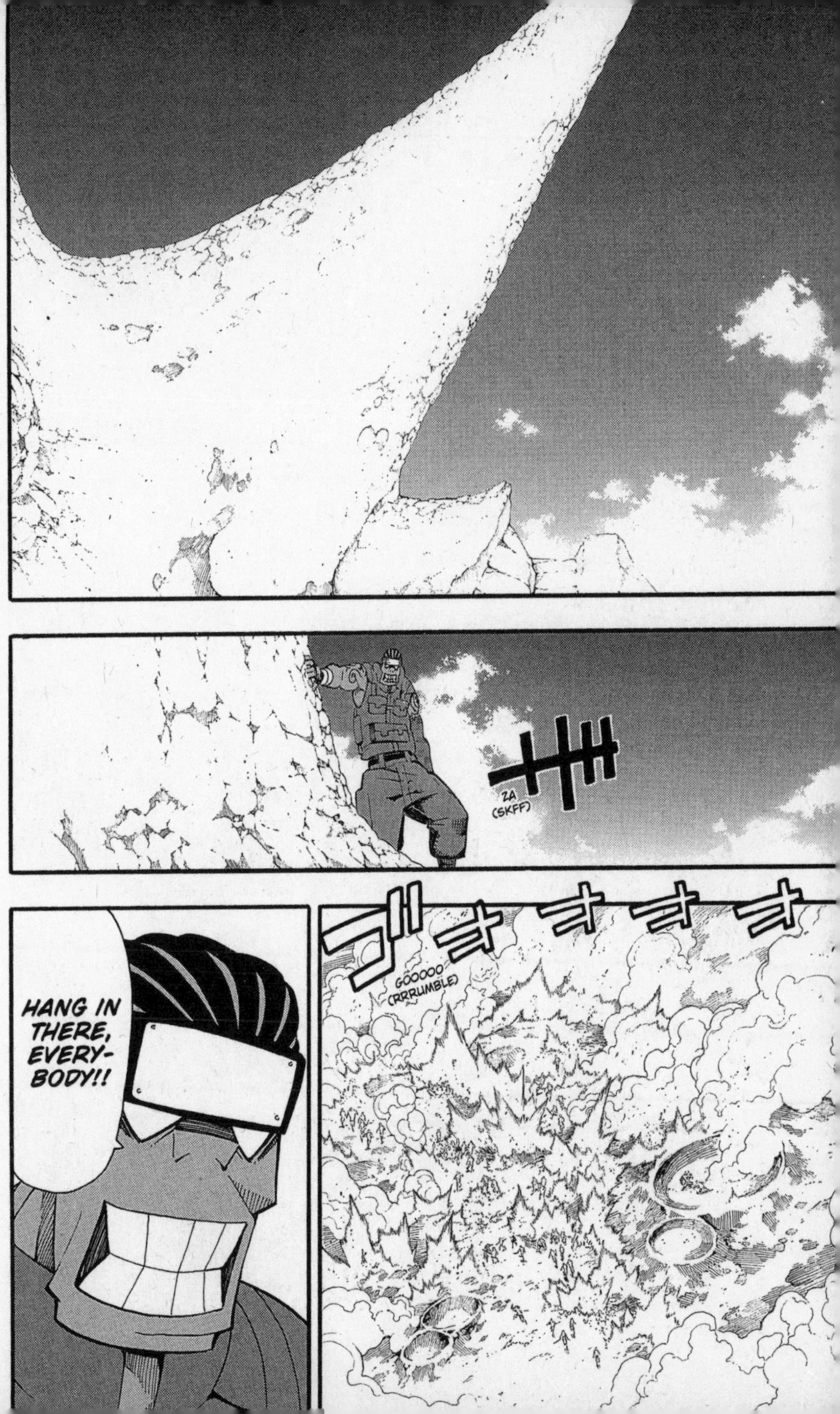
ZA
(SKFF)
GOOOOO
(RRRUMBLE)
HANG IN THERE, EVERY-BODY!!

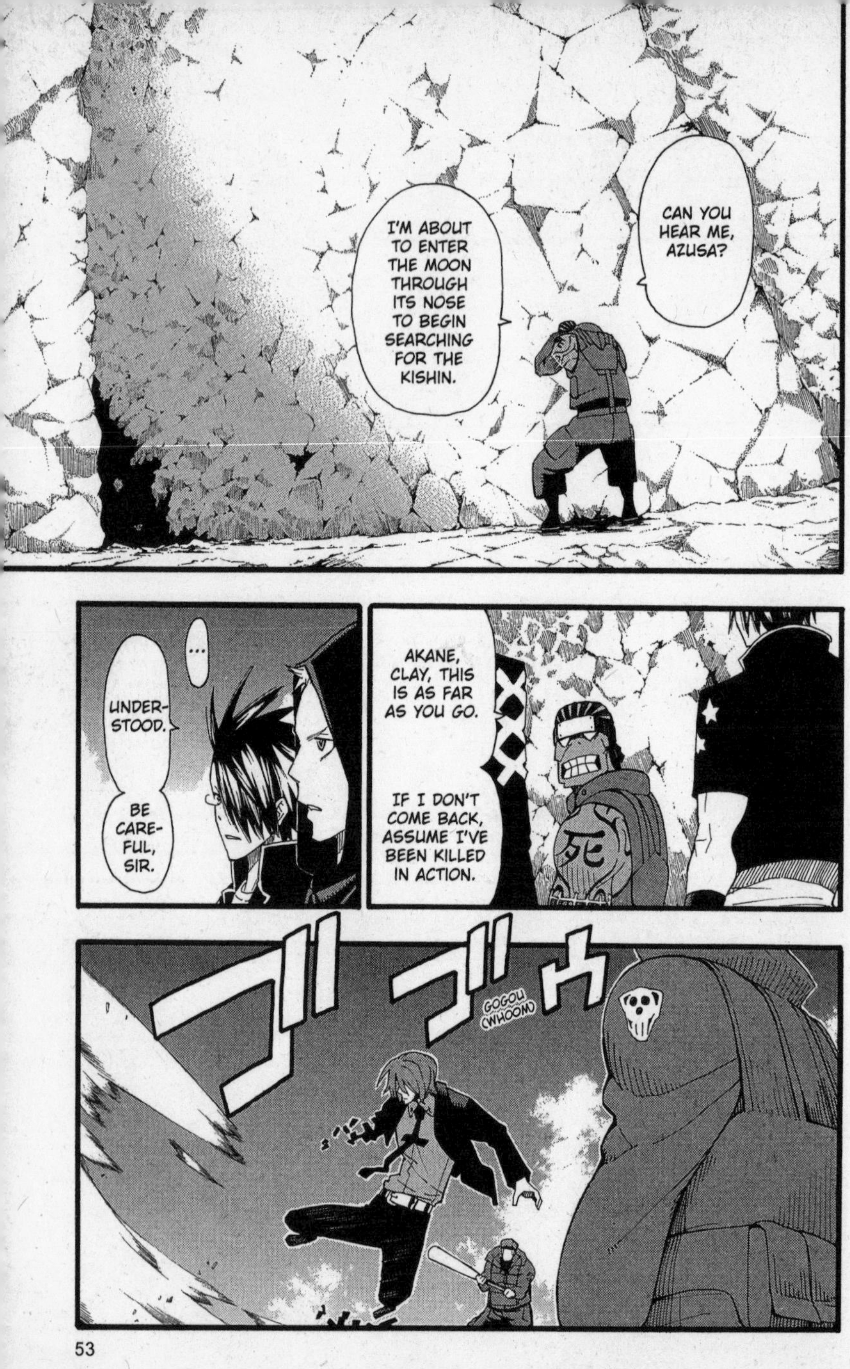
CAN YOU HEAR ME, AZUSA?
I'M ABOUT TO ENTER THE MOON THROUGH ITS NOSE TO BEGIN SEARCHING FOR THE KISHIN.
AKANE, CLAY, THIS IS AS FAR AS YOU GO.
IF I DON'T COME BACK, ASSUME I'VE BEEN KILLED IN ACTION.
...
UNDER-STOOD.
BE CARE-FUL, SIR.
ゴゴウ
GOGOU (WHOOM)

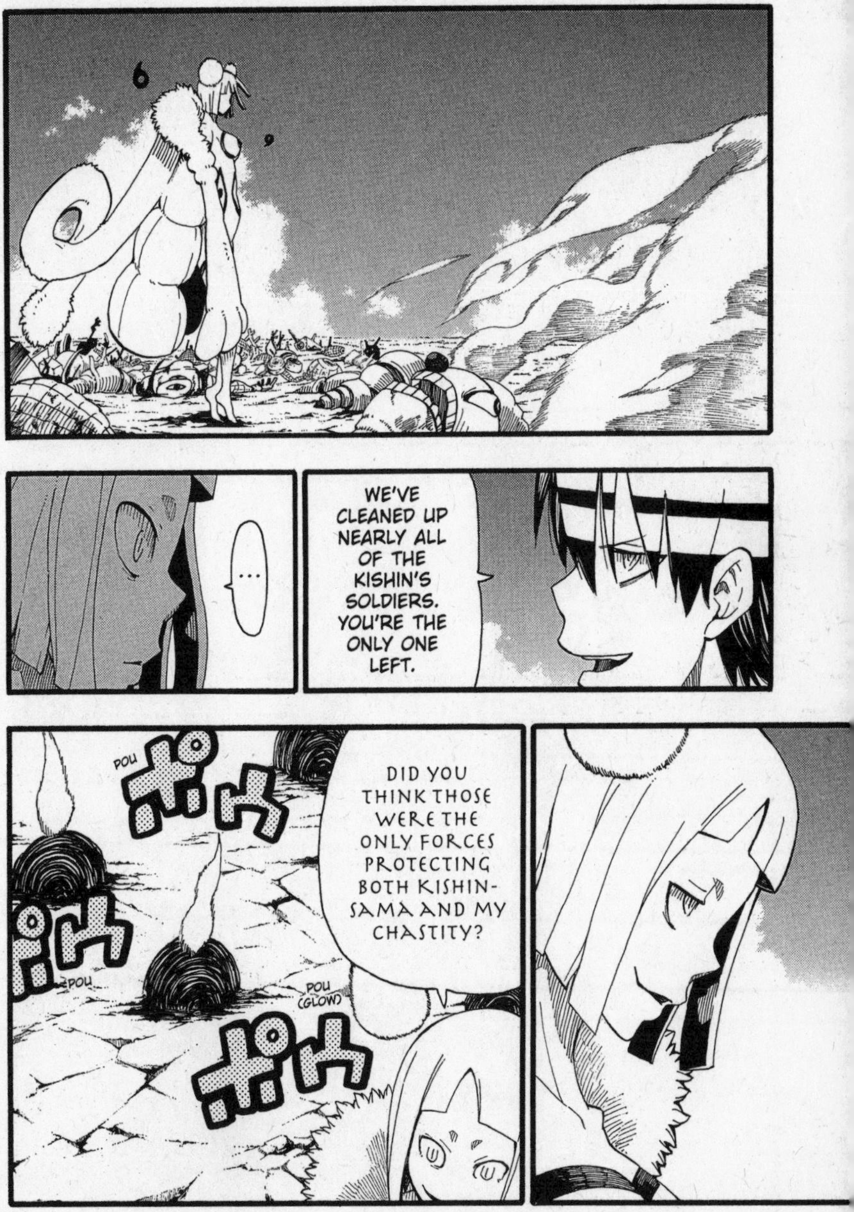
WE'VE CLEANED UP NEARLY ALL OF THE KISHIN'S SOLDIERS. YOU'RE THE ONLY ONE LEFT.
...
DID YOU THINK THOSE WERE THE ONLY FORCES PROTECTING BOTH KISHIN-SAMA AND MY CHASTITY?
POU
POU
POU (GLOW)

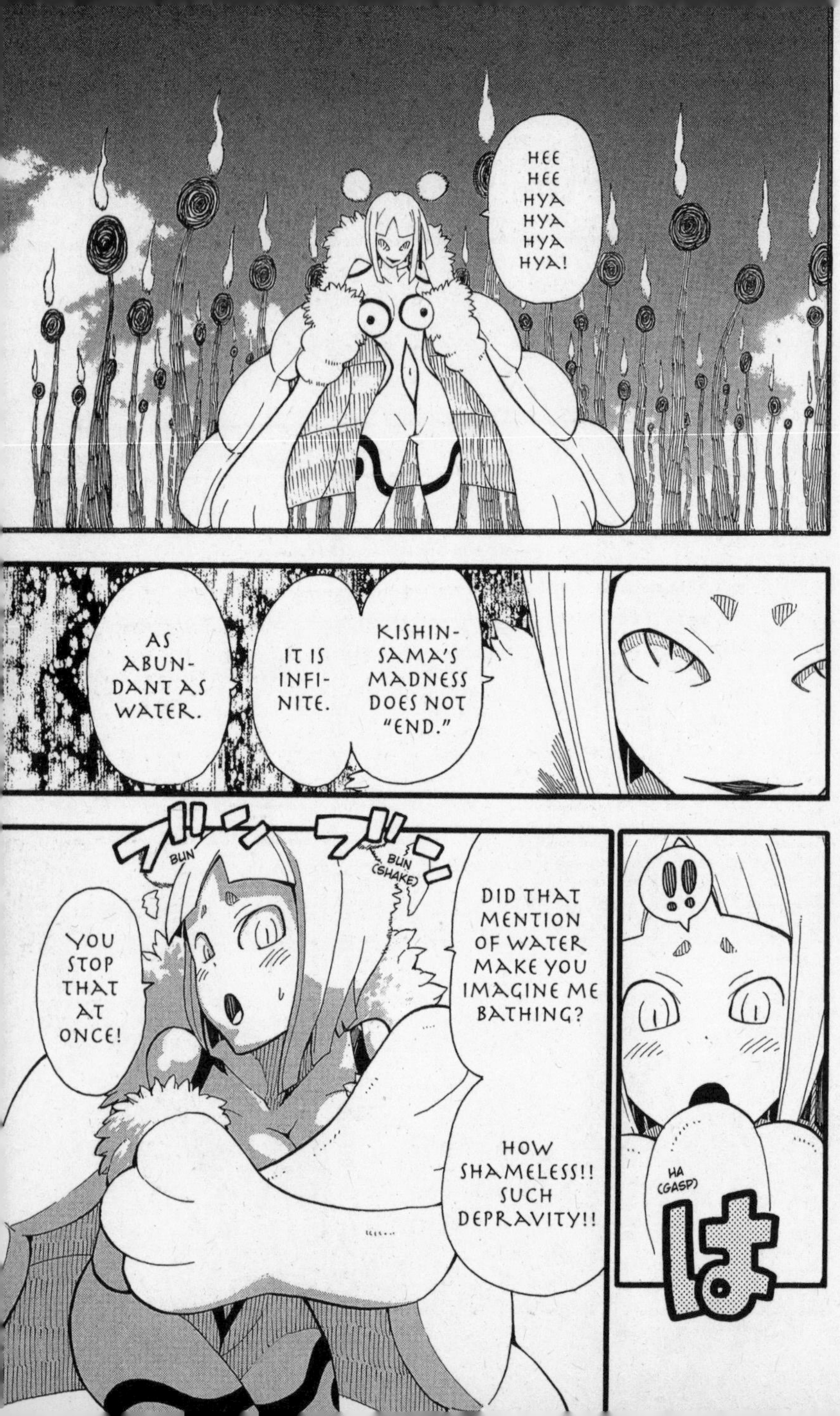
HEE HEE HYA HYA HYA HYA!
KISHIN-SAMA'S MADNESS DOES NOT "END."
IT IS INFINITE.
AS ABUNDANT AS WATER.
ha
HA (GASP)
BUN (SHAKE)
BUN
DID THAT MENTION OF WATER MAKE YOU IMAGINE ME BATHING?
HOW SHAMELESS!! SUCH DEPRAVITY!!
YOU STOP THAT AT ONCE!

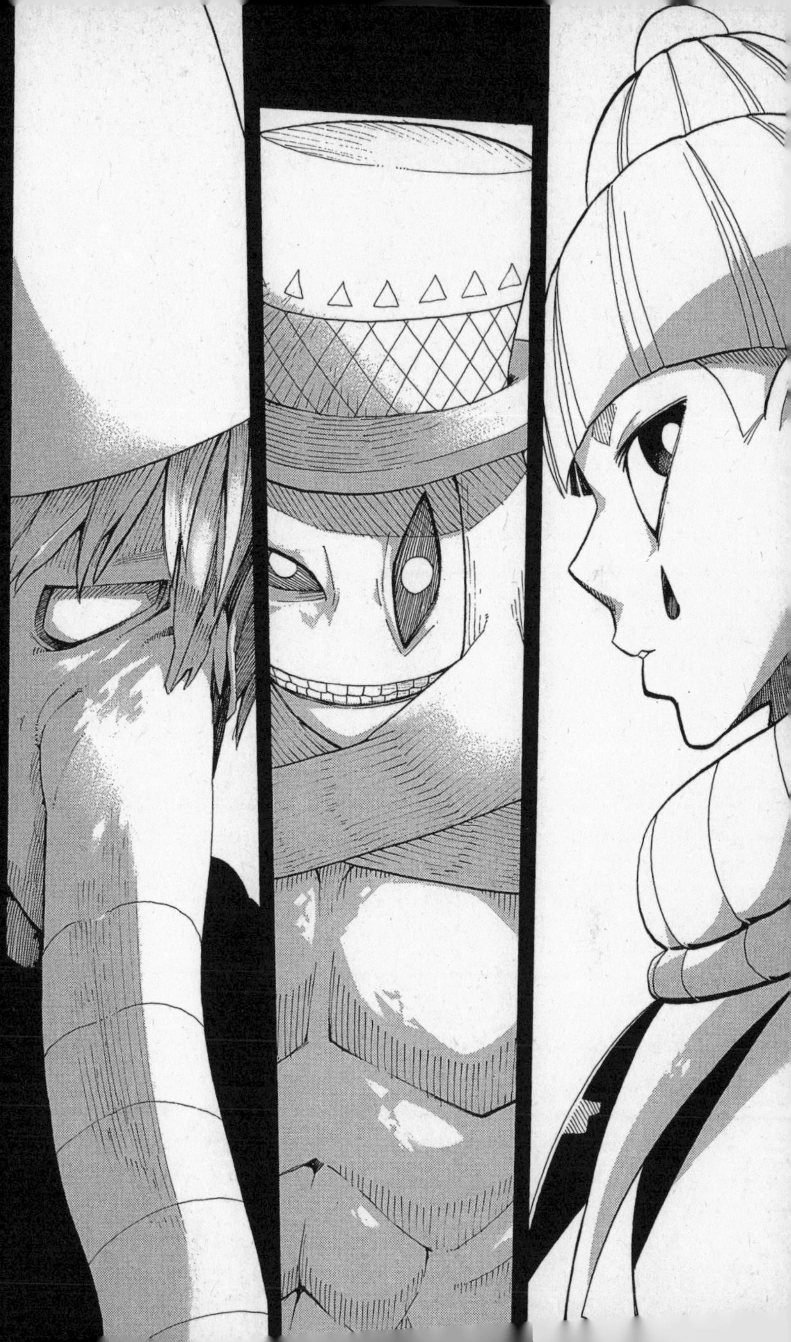

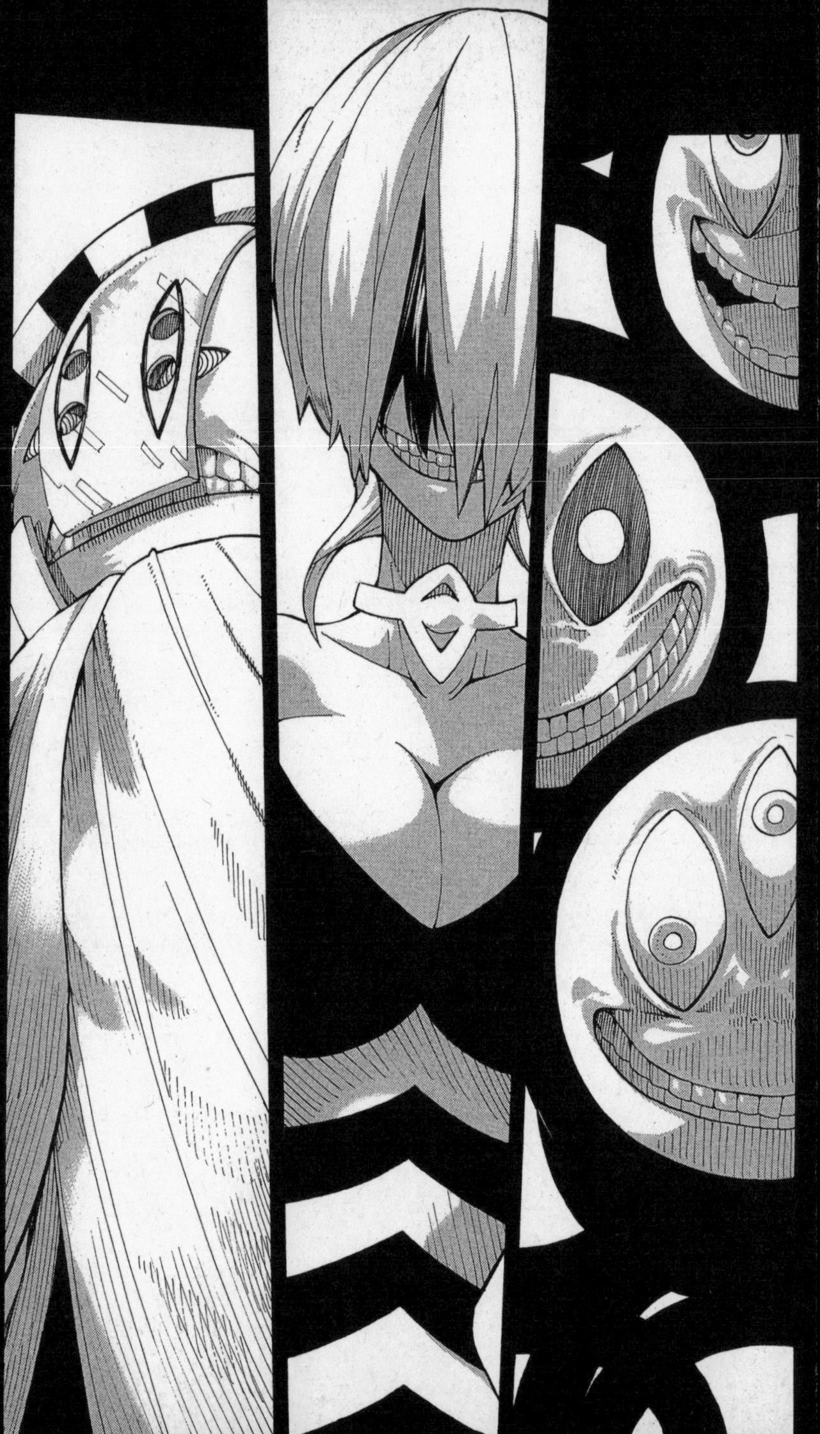

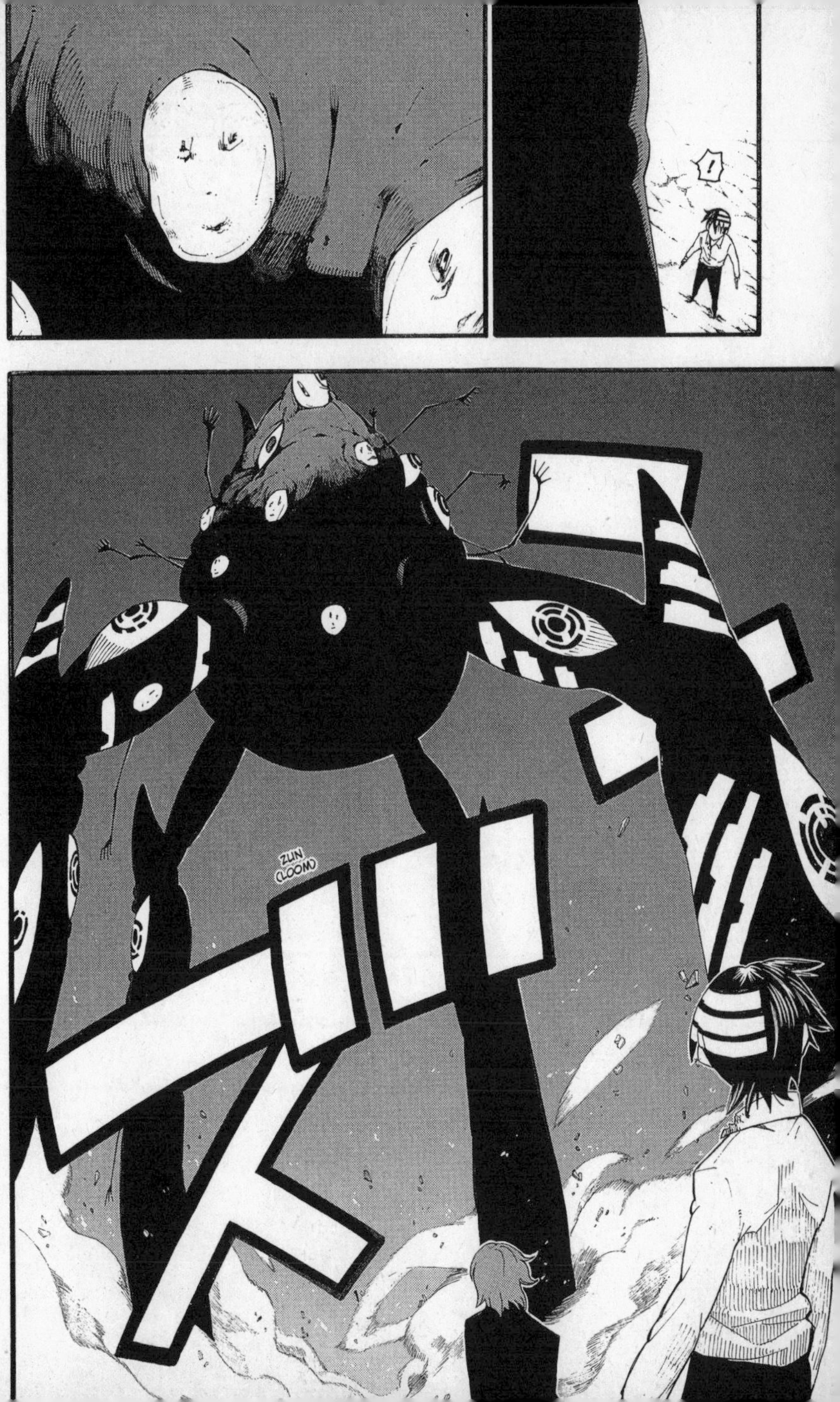
!
ZUN
(LOOM)

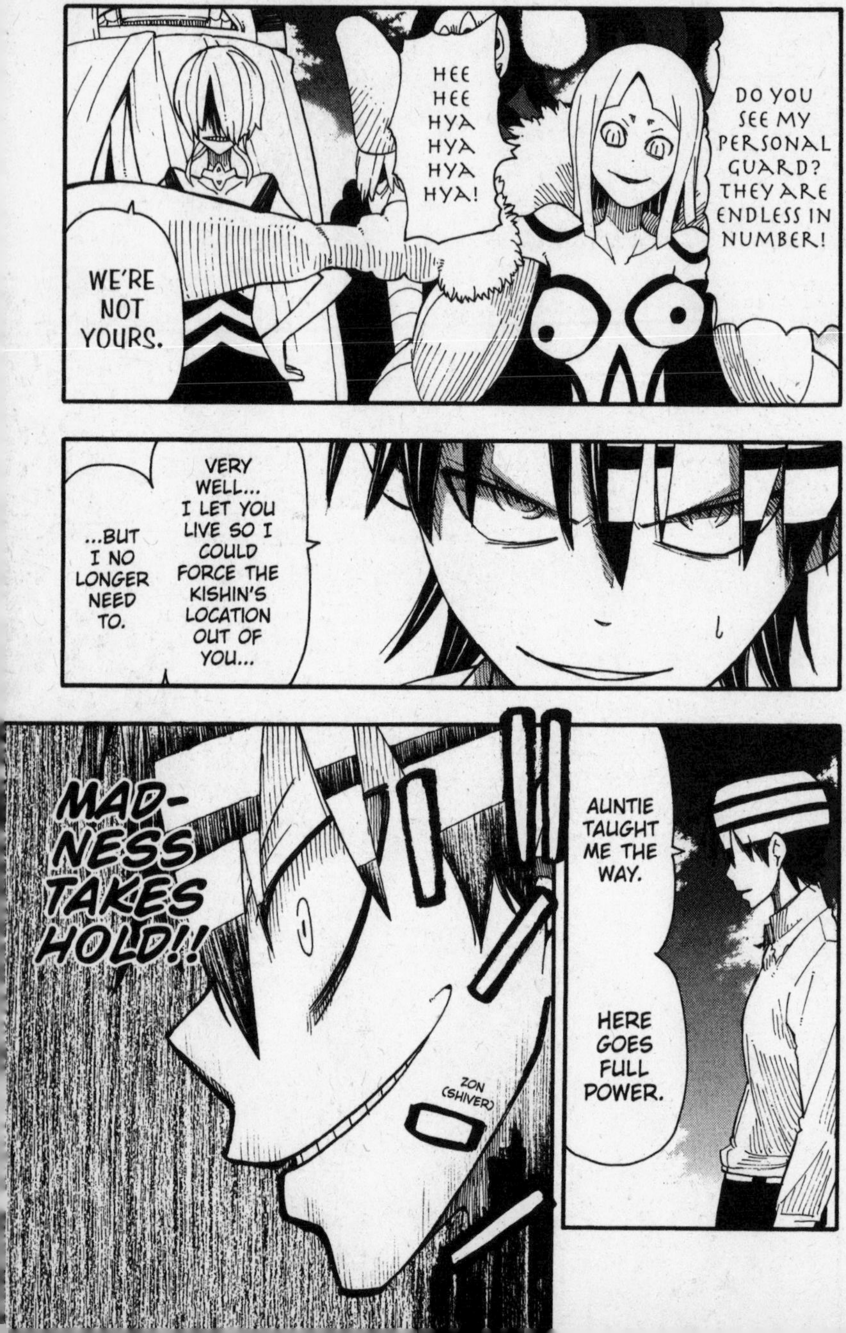
DO YOU SEE MY PERSONAL GUARD? THEY ARE ENDLESS IN NUMBER!
HEE HEE HYA HYA HYA HYA!
WE'RE NOT YOURS.
VERY WELL... I LET YOU LIVE SO I COULD FORCE THE KISHIN'S LOCATION OUT OF YOU...
...BUT I NO LONGER NEED TO.
AUNTIE TAUGHT ME THE WAY.
HERE GOES FULL POWER.
ZON (SHIVER)
MAD-NESS TAKES HOLD!!

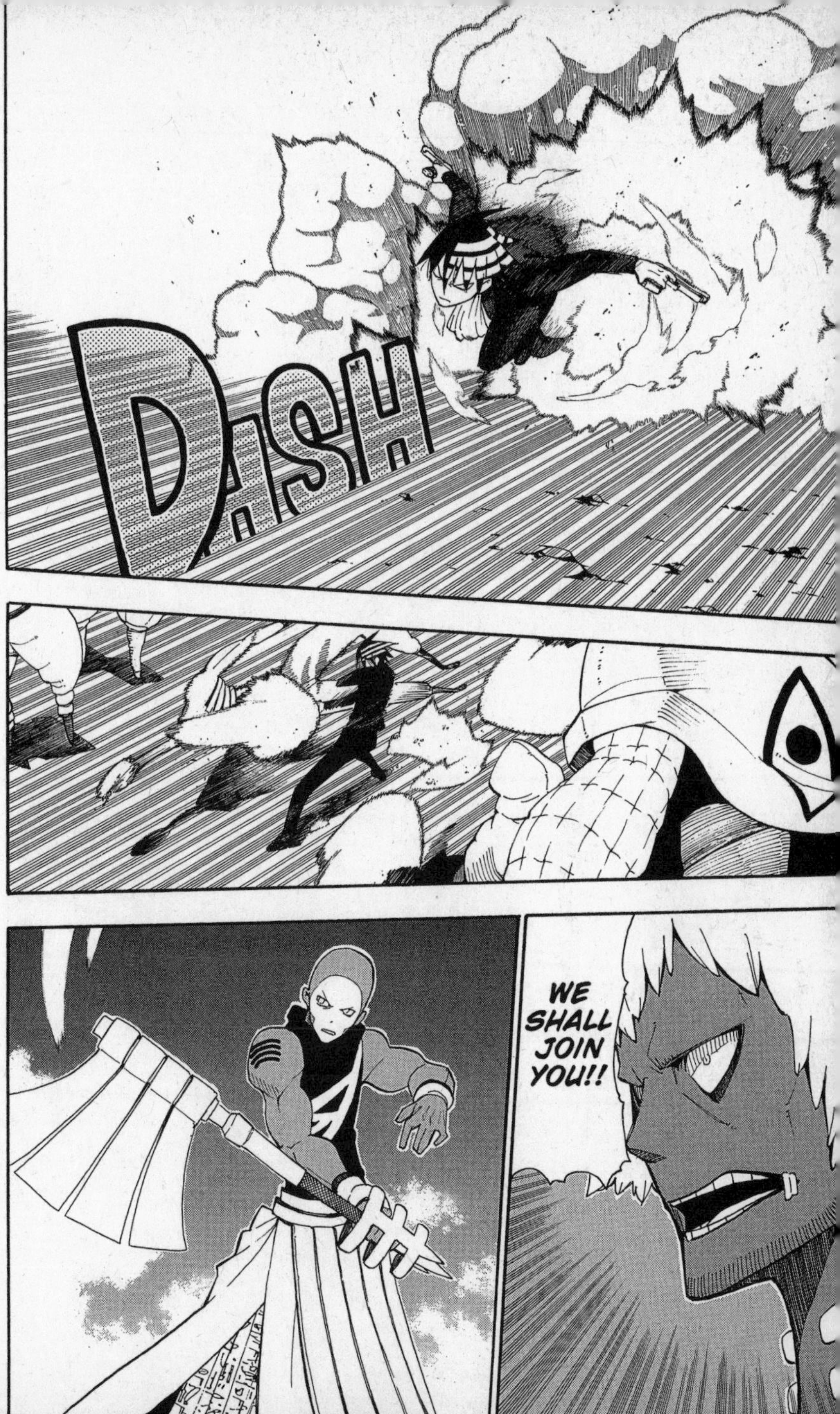
DASH
WE SHALL JOIN YOU!!

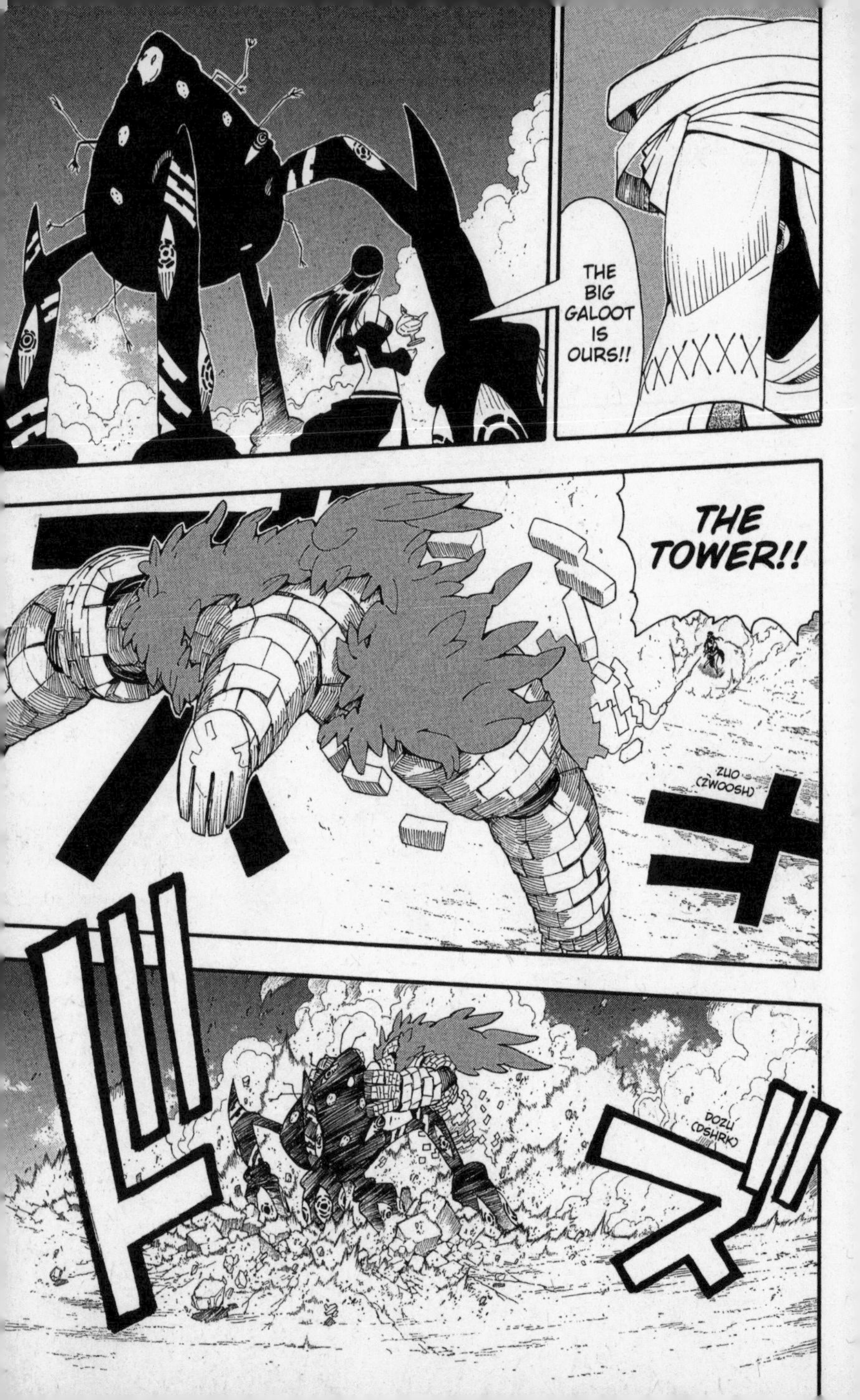
THE BIG GALOOT IS OURS!!
THE TOWER!!
ZUO (ZWOOSH)
ドズ
DOZU (DSHRK)

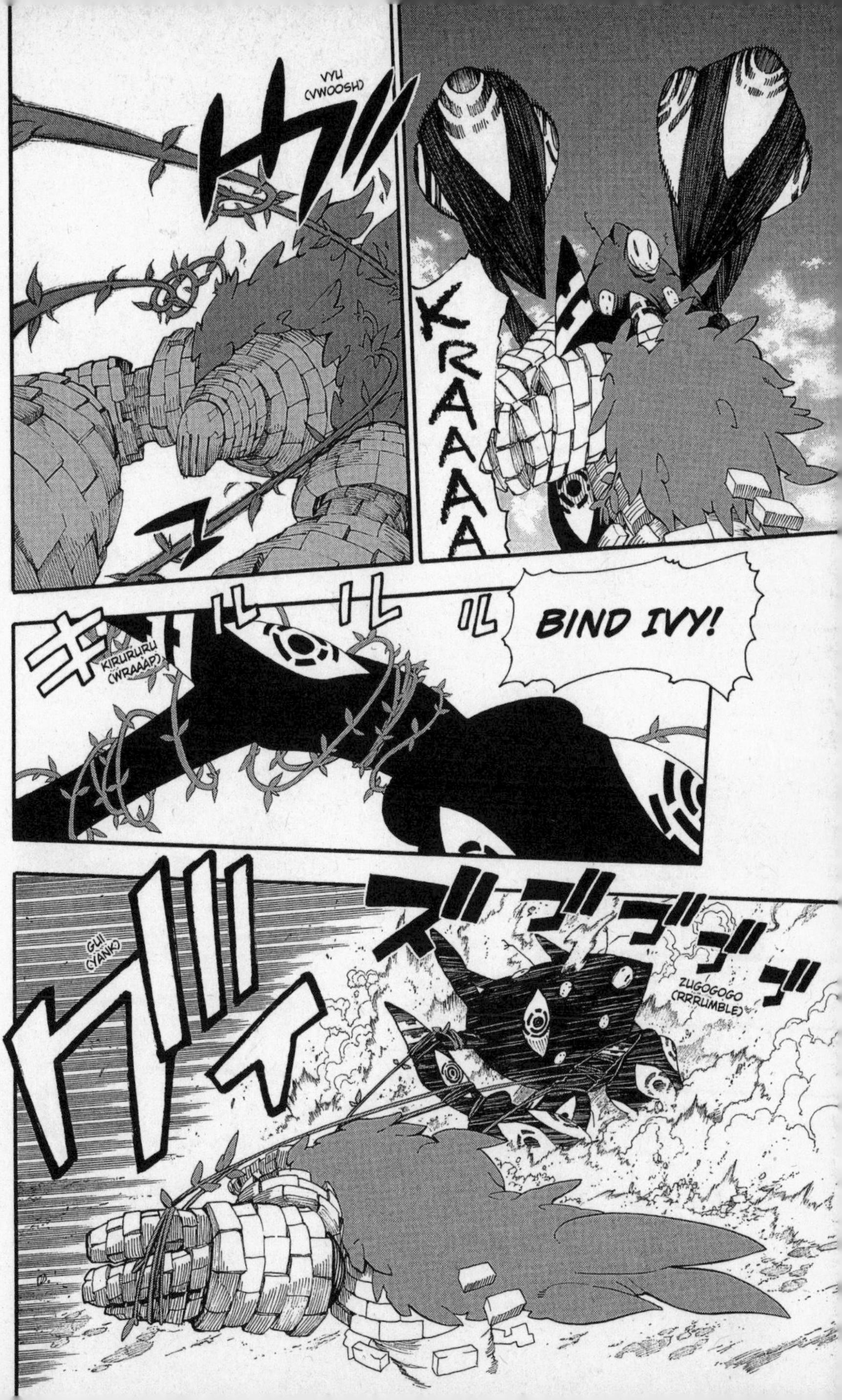
KRAAAA
VYU (VWOOSH)
BIND IVY!
KIRURURU (WRAAAP)
ZUGOGOGO (RRRUMBLE)
GUI (YANK)

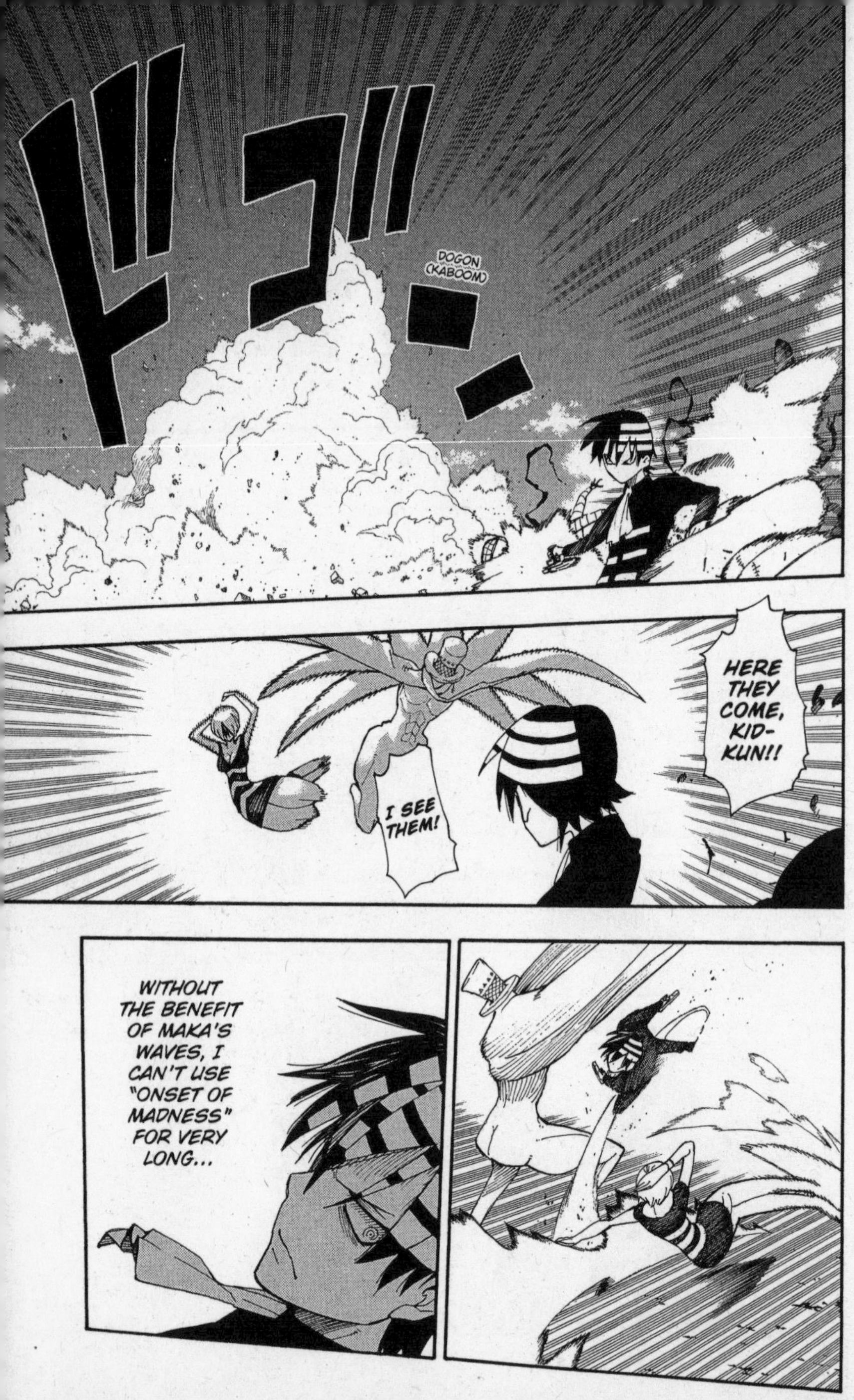
ドゴ
DOGON (KABOOM)
HERE THEY COME, KID-KUN!!
I SEE THEM!
WITHOUT THE BENEFIT OF MAKA'S WAVES, I CAN'T USE "ONSET OF MADNESS" FOR VERY LONG...

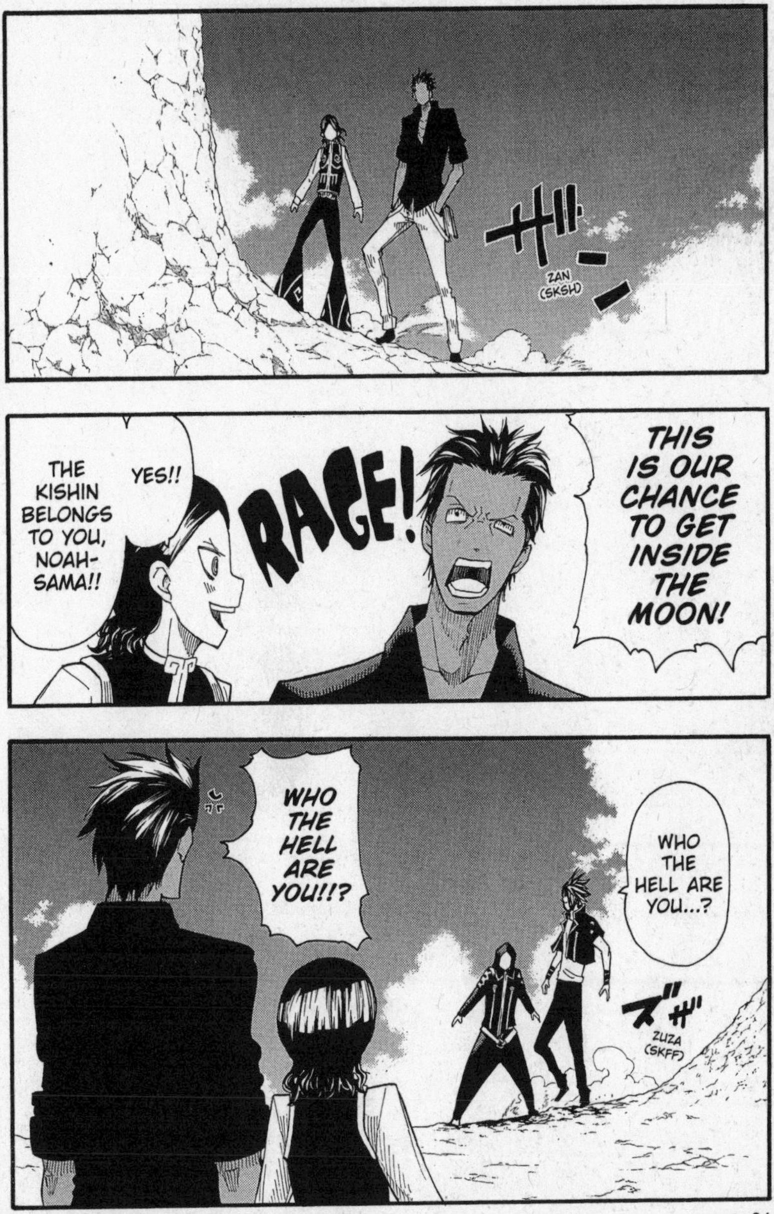
ZAN
(SKSH)
THIS IS OUR CHANCE TO GET INSIDE THE MOON!
RAGE!
YES!!
THE KISHIN BELONGS TO YOU, NOAH-SAMA!!
WHO THE HELL ARE YOU...?
WHO THE HELL ARE YOU!!?
ZUZA
(SKFF)

SOUL EATER

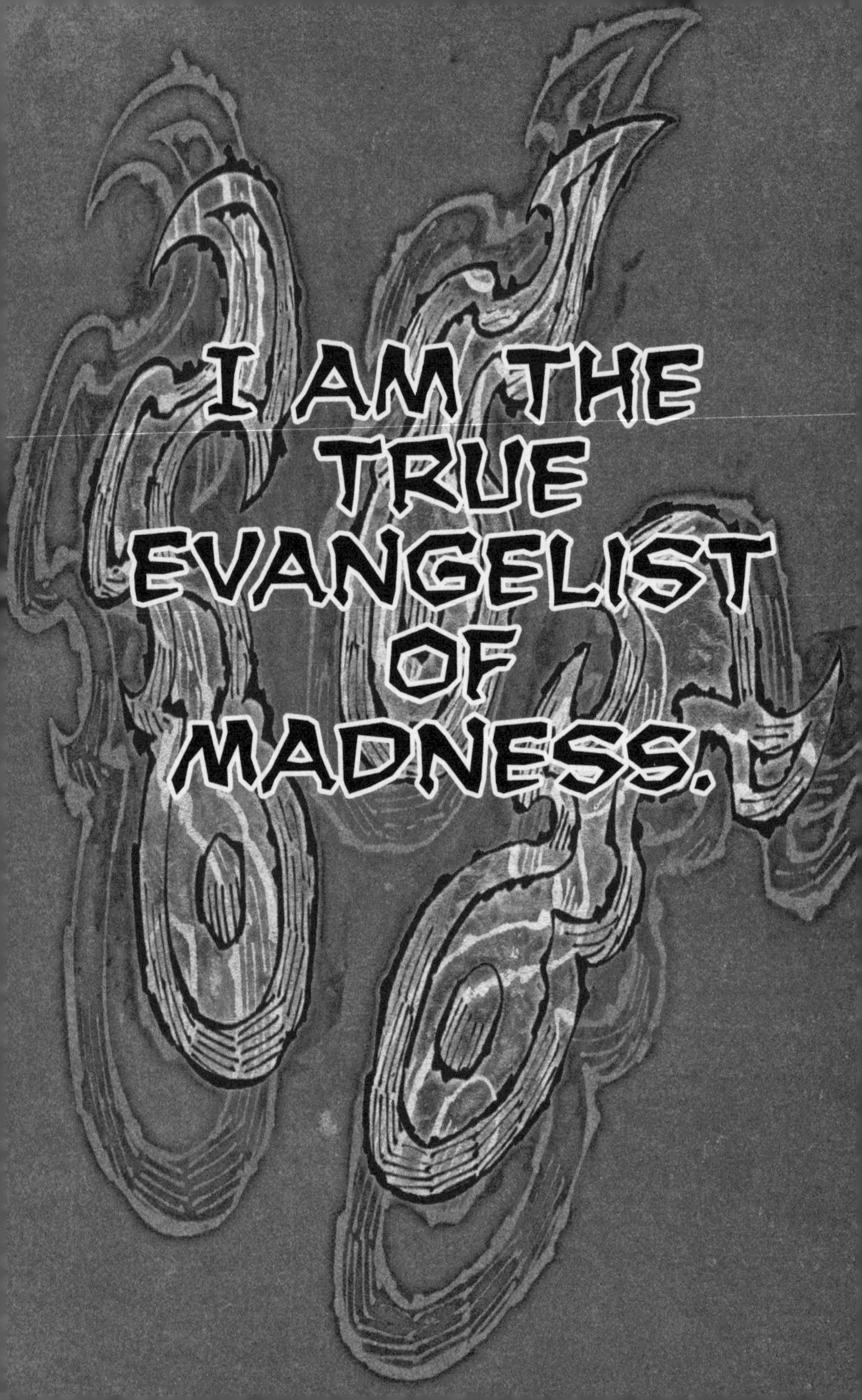
I AM THE TRUE EVANGELIST OF MADNESS.

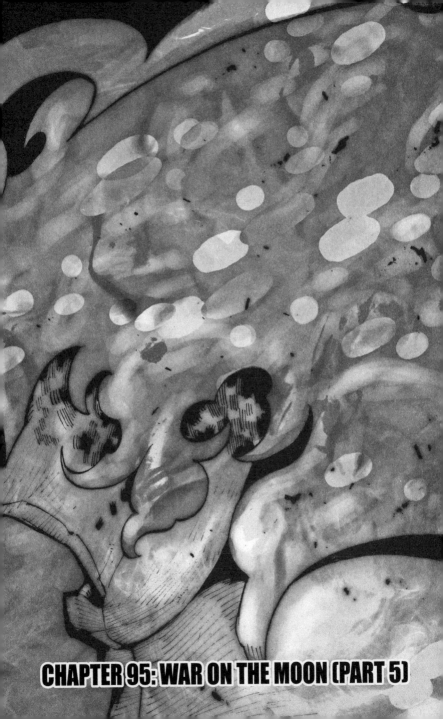

CHAPTER 95: WAR ON THE MOON (PART 5)

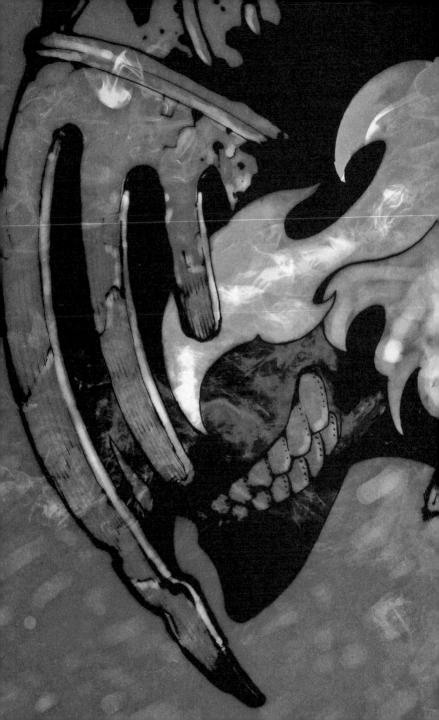

SOUL EATER

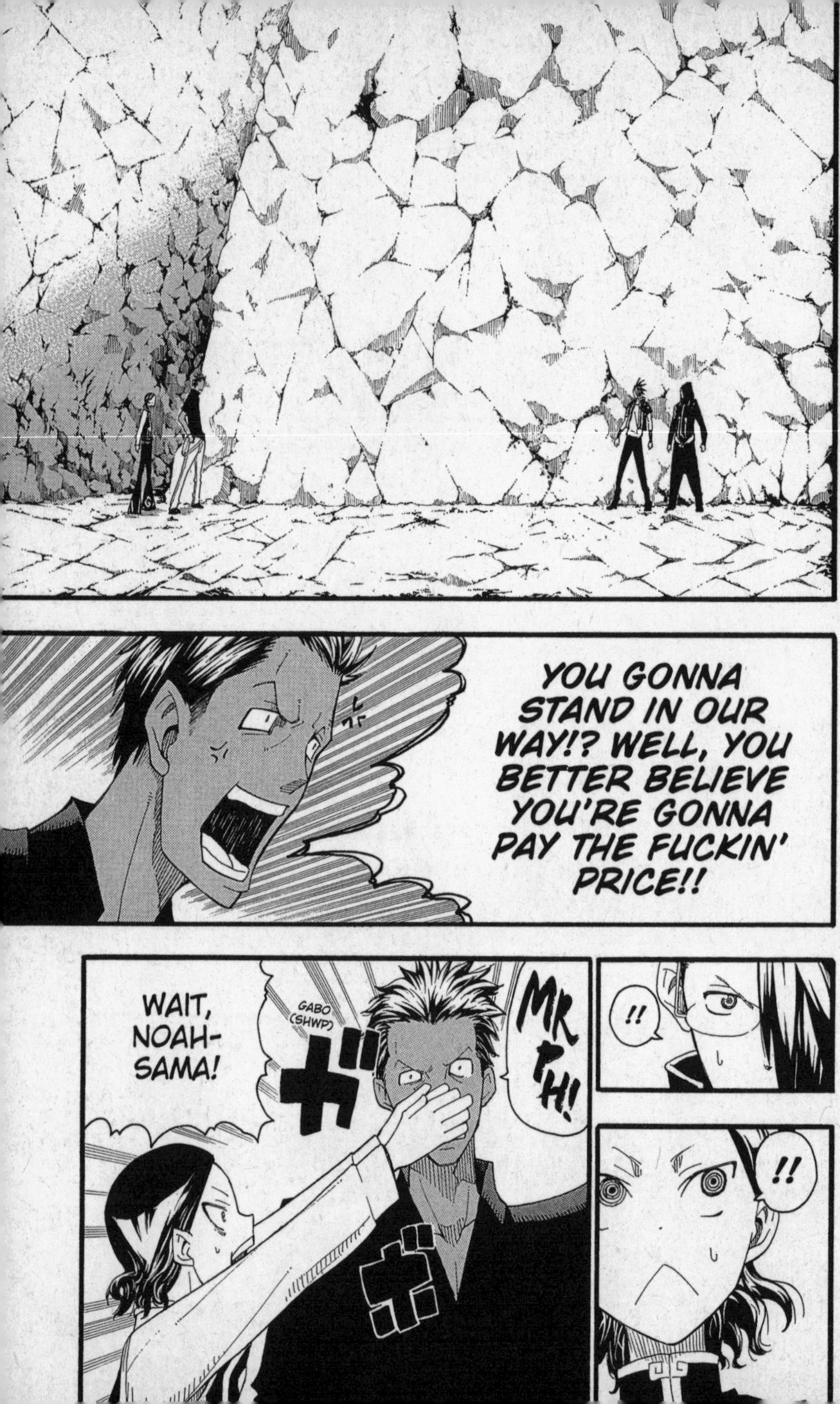
YOU GONNA STAND IN OUR WAY!? WELL, YOU BETTER BELIEVE YOU'RE GONNA PAY THE FUCKIN' PRICE!!
!!
!!
MRPH!
GABO (SHWP)
WAIT, NOAH-SAMA!

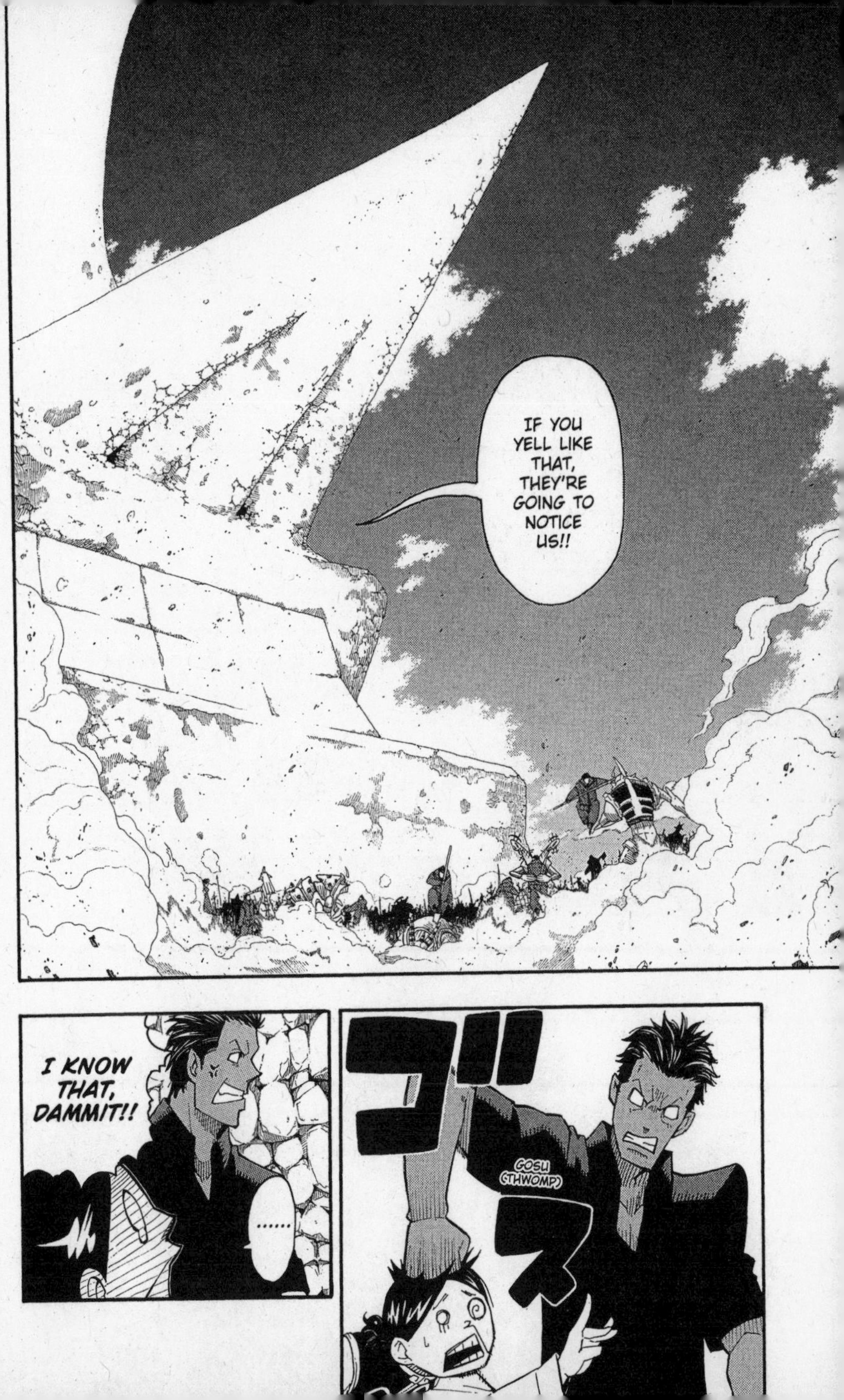
IF YOU YELL LIKE THAT, THEY'RE GOING TO NOTICE US!!
ゴス
GOSU (THWOMP)
I KNOW THAT, DAMMIT!!
......

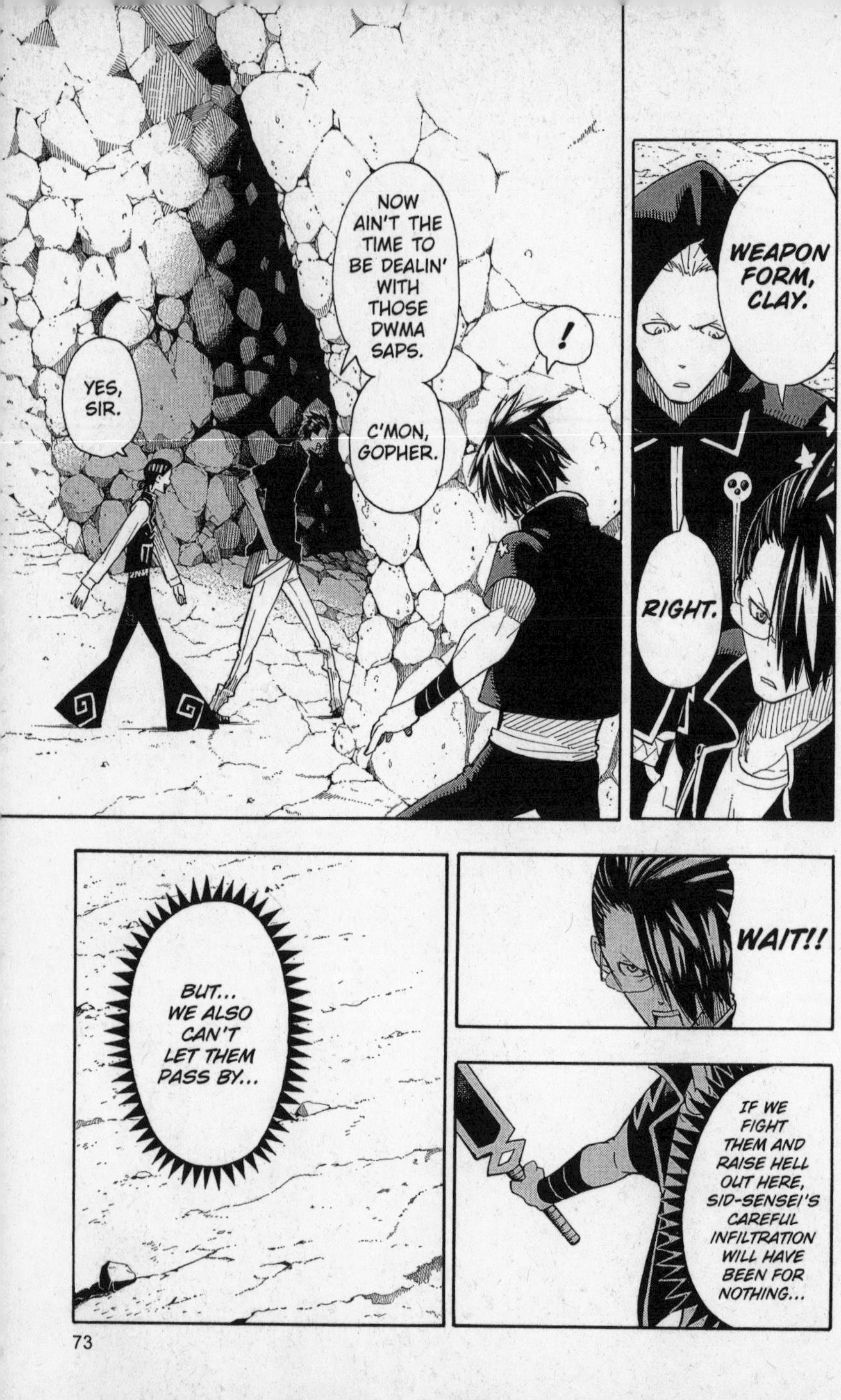
WEAPON FORM, CLAY.
RIGHT.
NOW AIN'T THE TIME TO BE DEALIN' WITH THOSE DWMA SAPS.
C'MON, GOPHER.
YES, SIR.
!
WAIT!!
IF WE FIGHT THEM AND RAISE HELL OUT HERE, SID-SENSEI'S CAREFUL INFILTRATION WILL HAVE BEEN FOR NOTHING...
BUT... WE ALSO CAN'T LET THEM PASS BY...

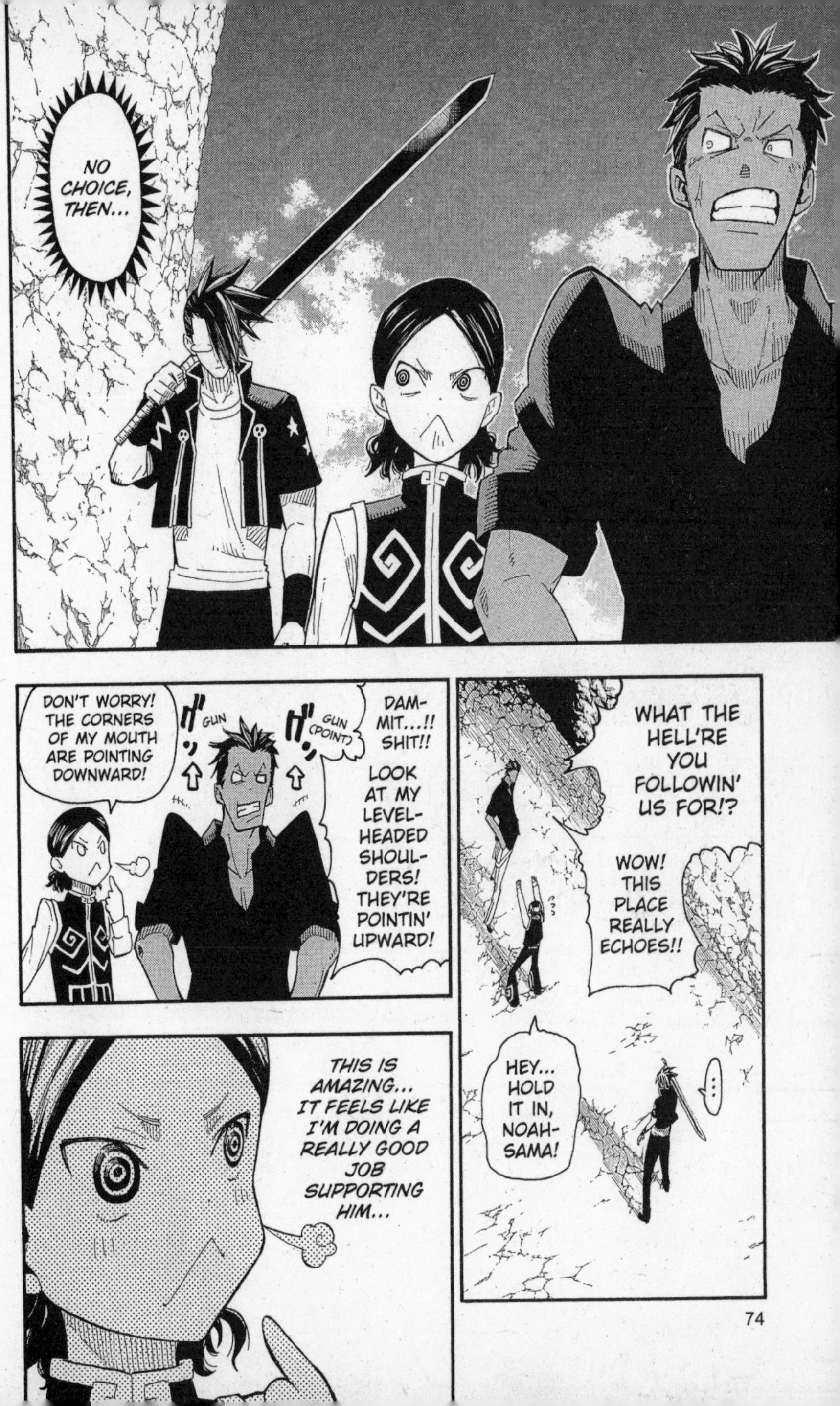
NO CHOICE, THEN...
WHAT THE HELL'RE YOU FOLLOWIN' US FOR!?
WOW! THIS PLACE REALLY ECHOES!!
HEY... HOLD IT IN, NOAH-SAMA!
...
DAM-MIT...!! SHIT!!
LOOK AT MY LEVEL-HEADED SHOULDERS! THEY'RE POINTIN' UPWARD!
GUN (POINT)
GUN
DON'T WORRY! THE CORNERS OF MY MOUTH ARE POINTING DOWNWARD!
THIS IS AMAZING... IT FEELS LIKE I'M DOING A REALLY GOOD JOB SUPPORTING HIM...

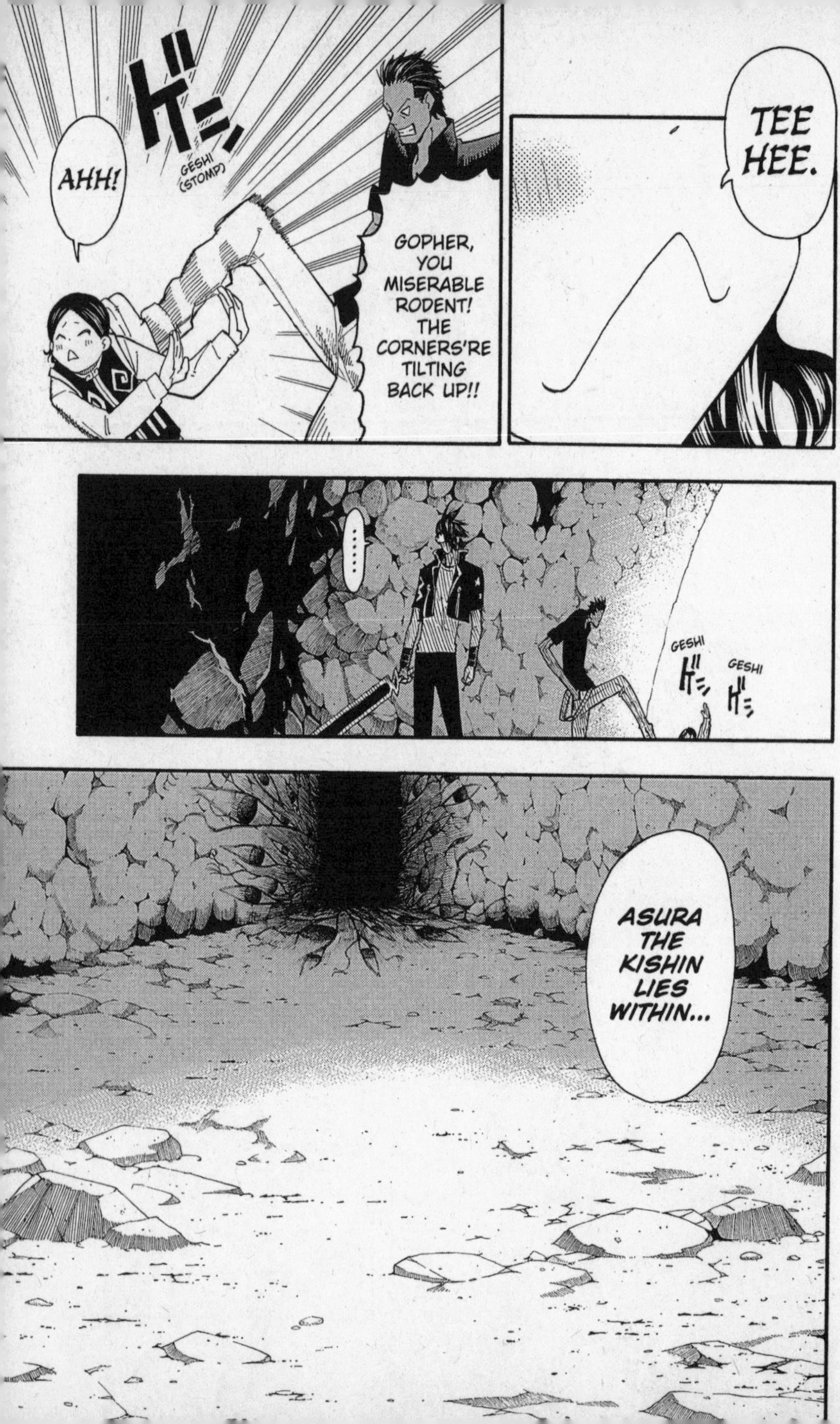
TEE HEE.
GOPHER, YOU MISERABLE RODENT! THE CORNERS'RE TILTING BACK UP!!
GESHI (STOMP)
AHH!
GESHI
GESHI
......
ASURA THE KISHIN LIES WITHIN...

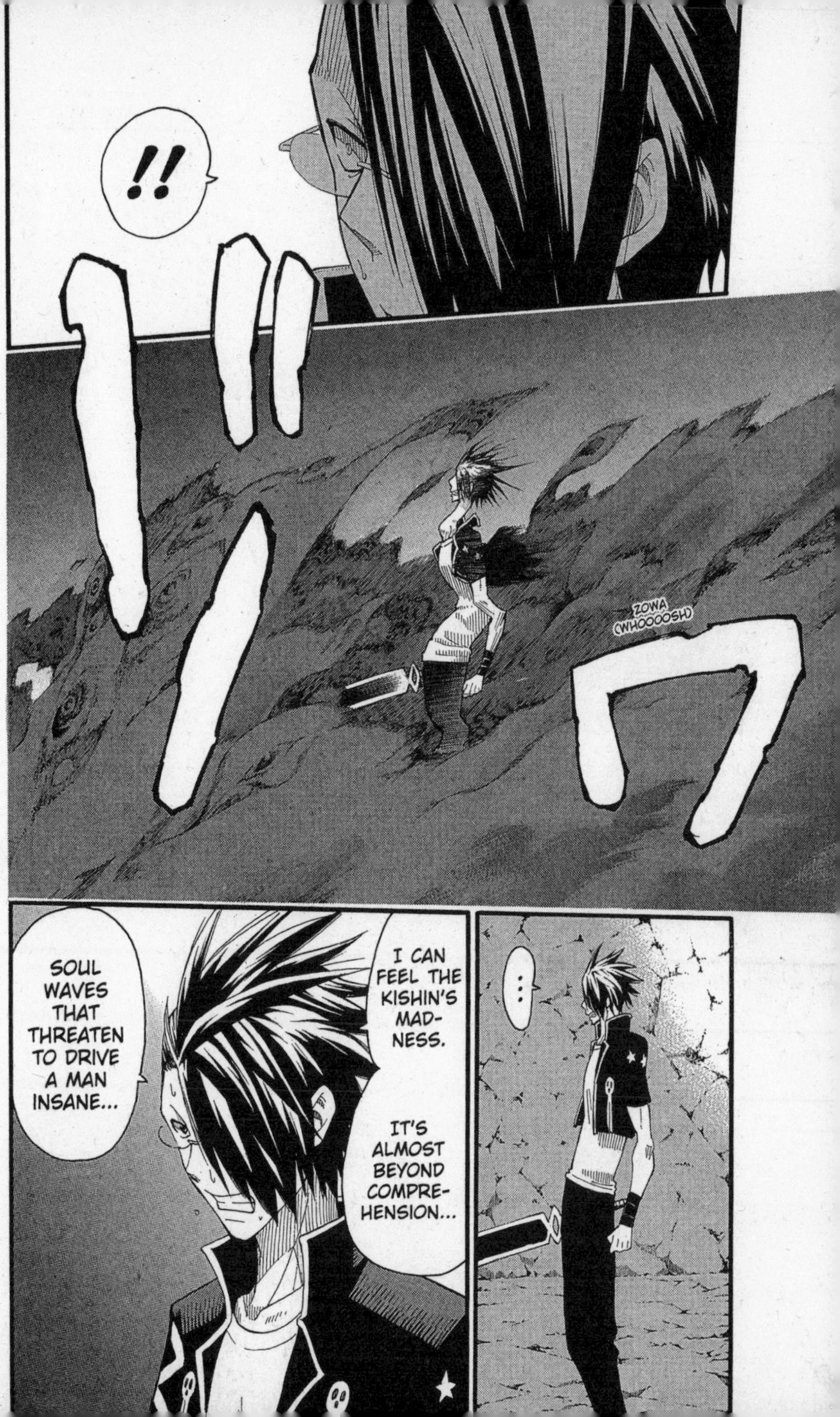
!!
ZOWA (WHOOOOSH)
...
I CAN FEEL THE KISHIN'S MAD-NESS.
IT'S ALMOST BEYOND COMPRE-HENSION...
SOUL WAVES THAT THREATEN TO DRIVE A MAN INSANE...

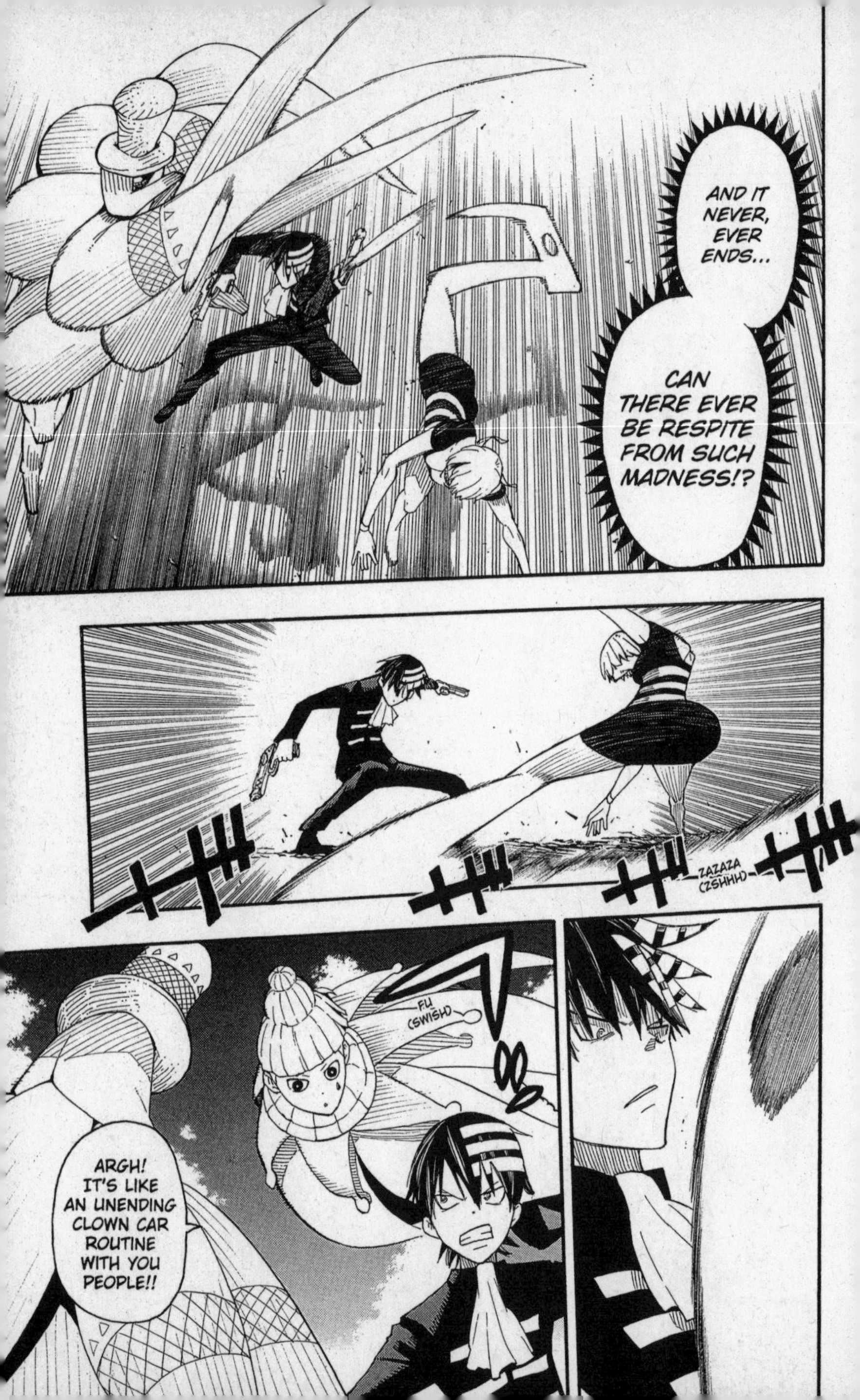
AND IT NEVER, EVER ENDS...
CAN THERE EVER BE RESPITE FROM SUCH MADNESS!?
ZAZAZA (ZSHHH)
FU (SWISH)
ARGH! IT'S LIKE AN UNENDING CLOWN CAR ROUTINE WITH YOU PEOPLE!!

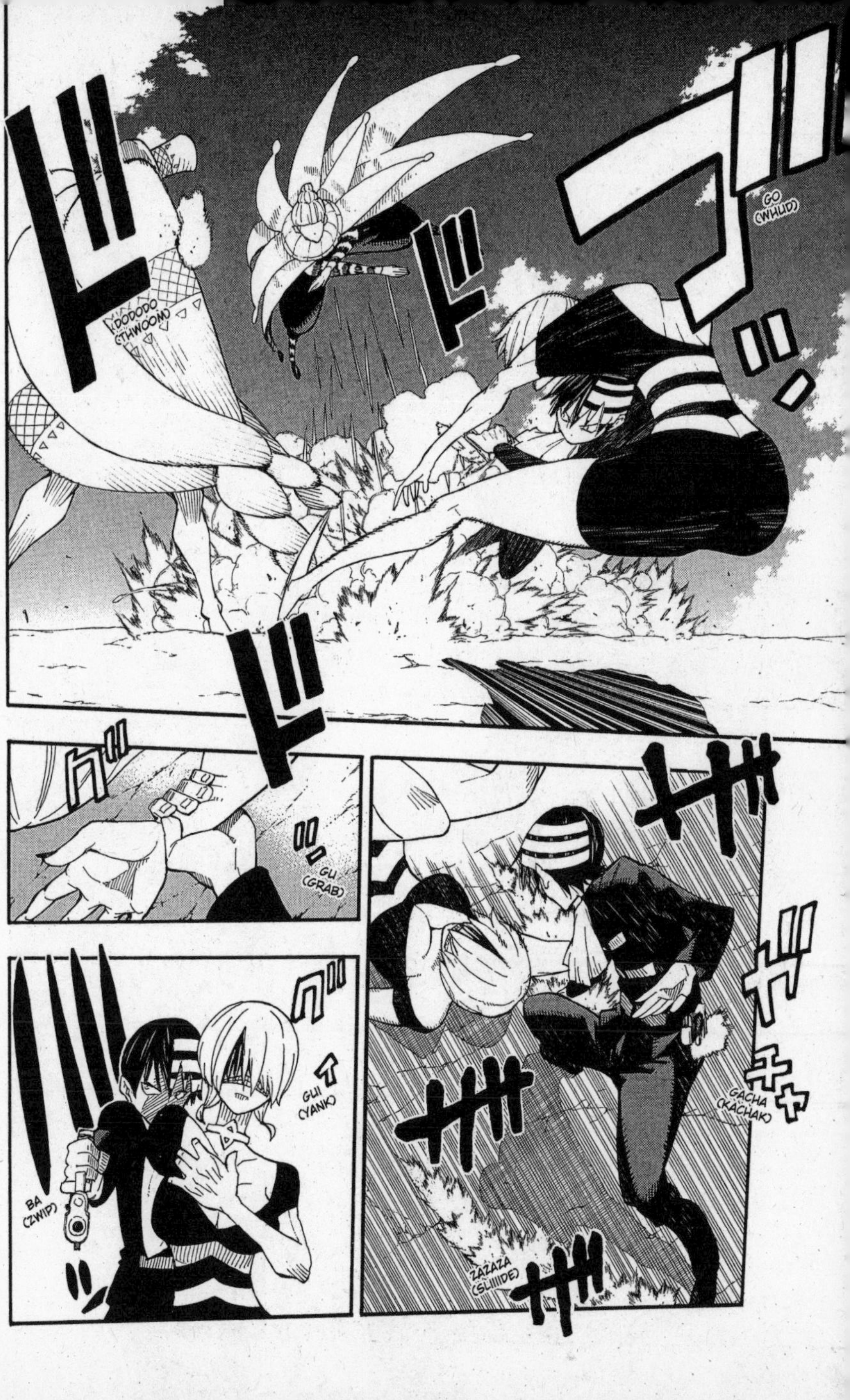
GO (WHUD)
DODODO (THWOOM)
GACHA (KACHAK)
ZAZAZA (SLIIIDE)
GU (GRAB)
GUI (YANK)
BA (ZWIP)

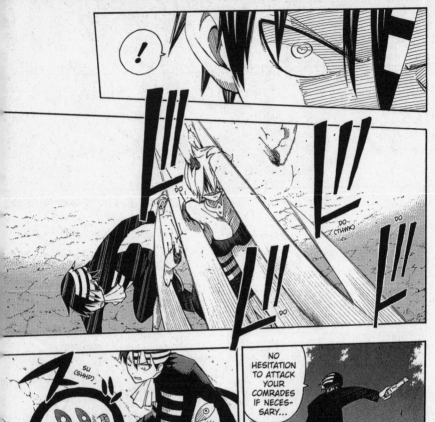

!

DO
(THWK)

DO

DO

DO

DO

SU
(SHHP)

NO
HESITATION
TO ATTACK
YOUR
COMRADES
IF NECES-
SARY...

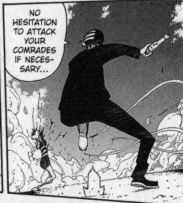

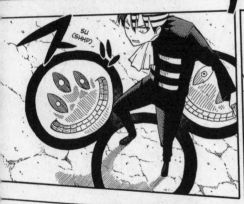

LOSING
ONE OF
THEM IS
HARDLY
AN ISSUE.

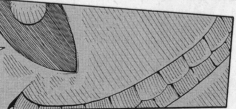

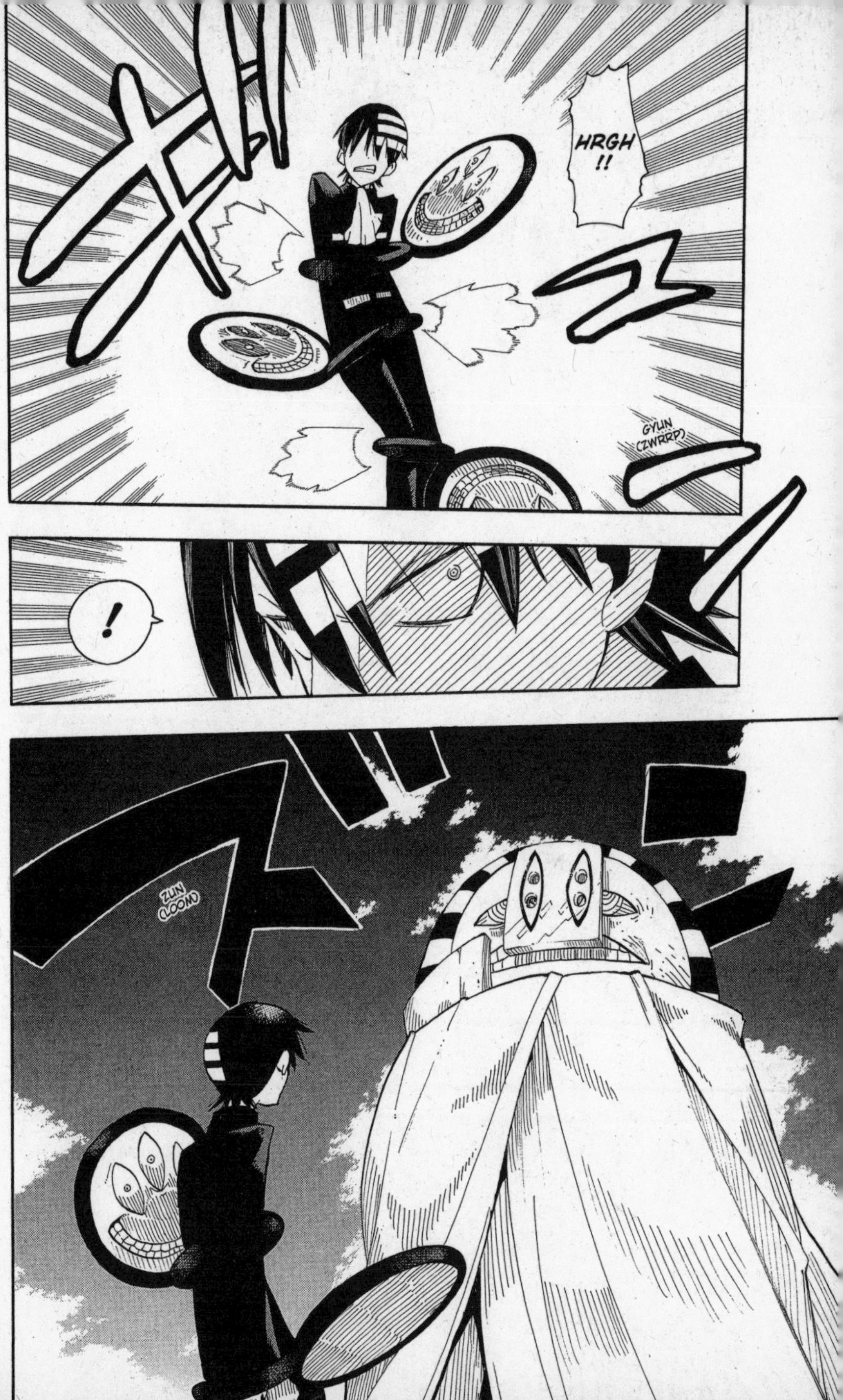
HRGH !!
GYUN (ZWRRP)
!
ZUN (LOOM)

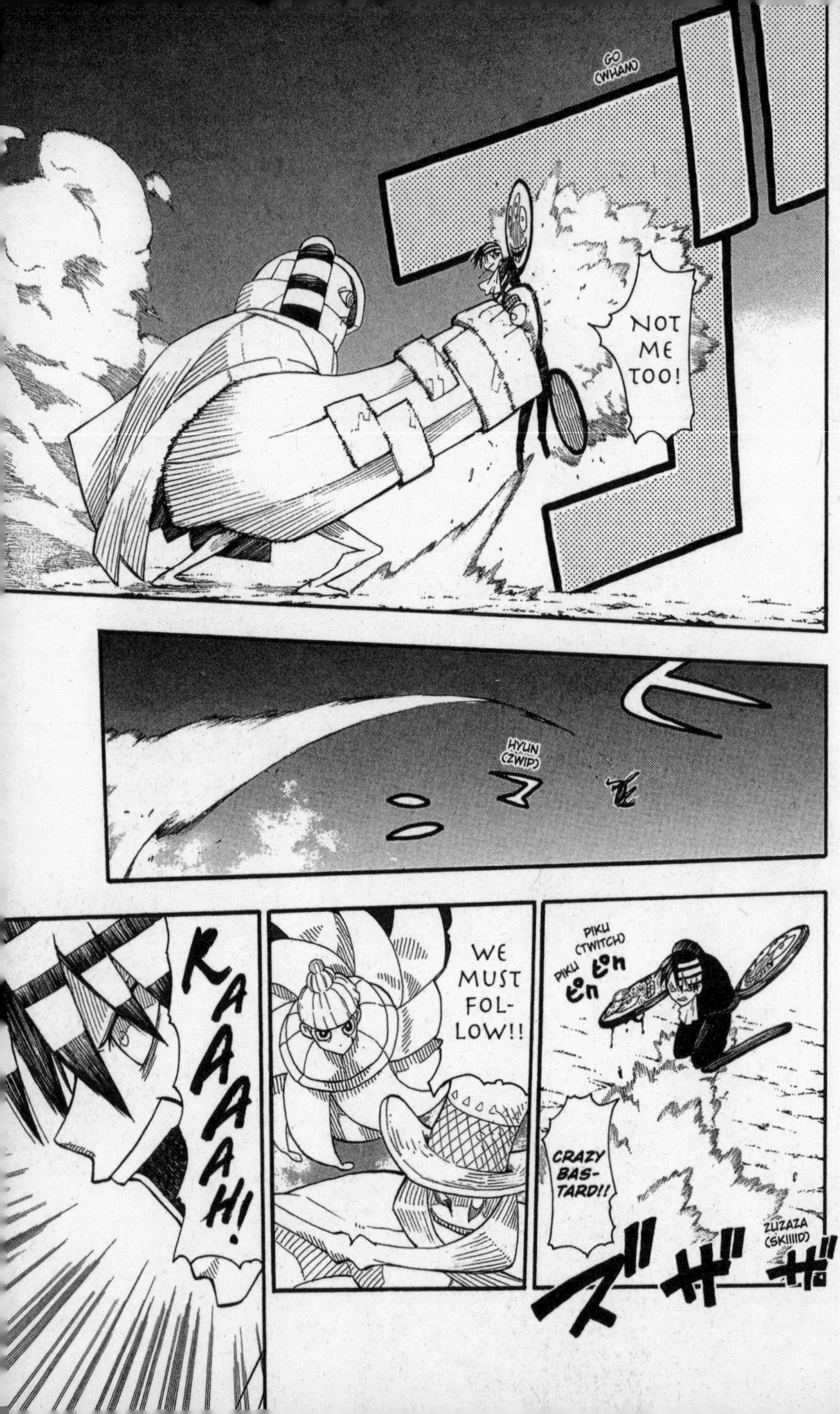
GO (WHAM)
NOT ME TOO!
HYUN (ZWIP)
PIKU PIKU (TWITCH)
CRAZY BAS-TARD!!
ZUZAZA (SKIIIID)
WE MUST FOL-LOW!!
KAAAAAH!

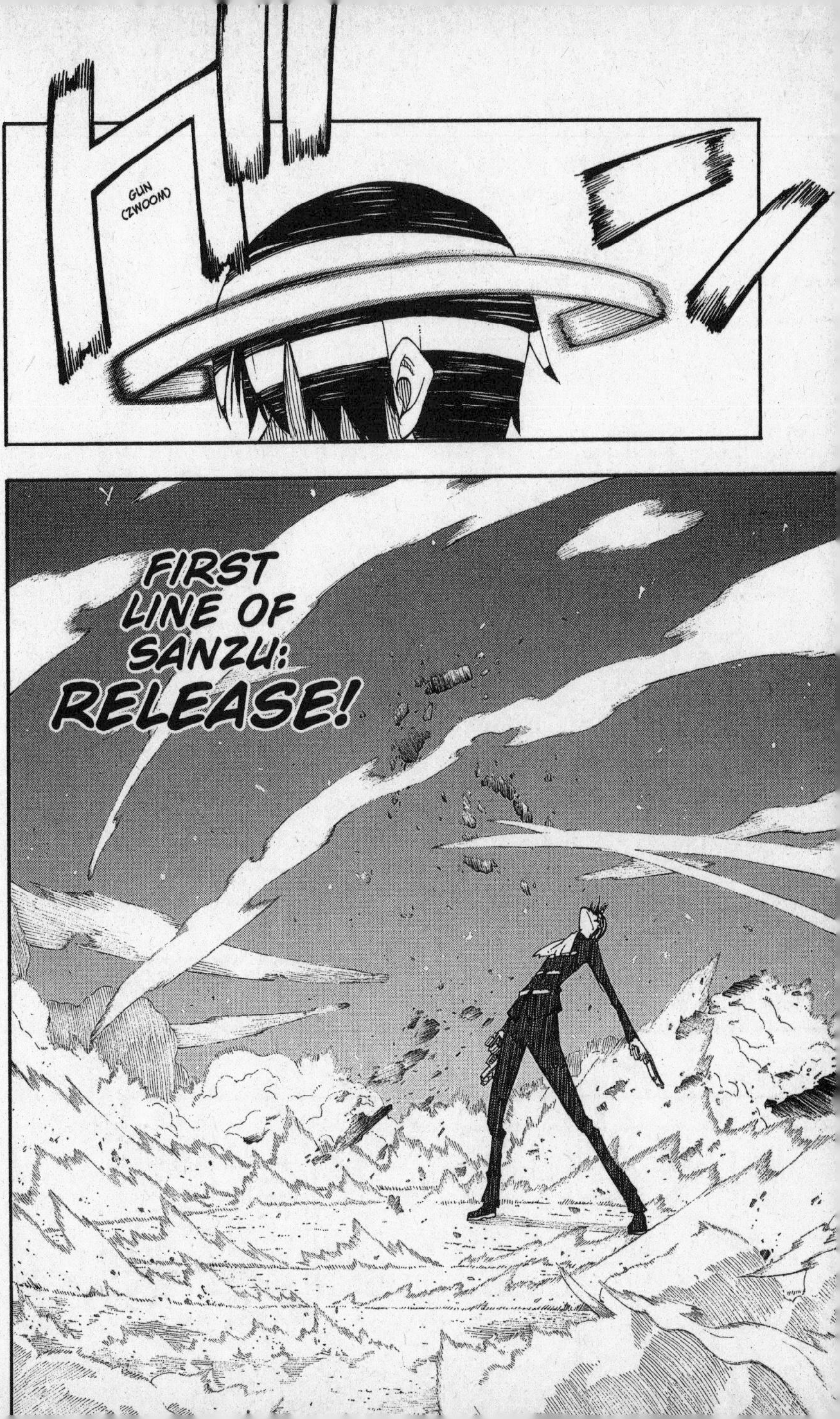
GUN (ZWOOM)
FIRST LINE OF SANZU: RELEASE!

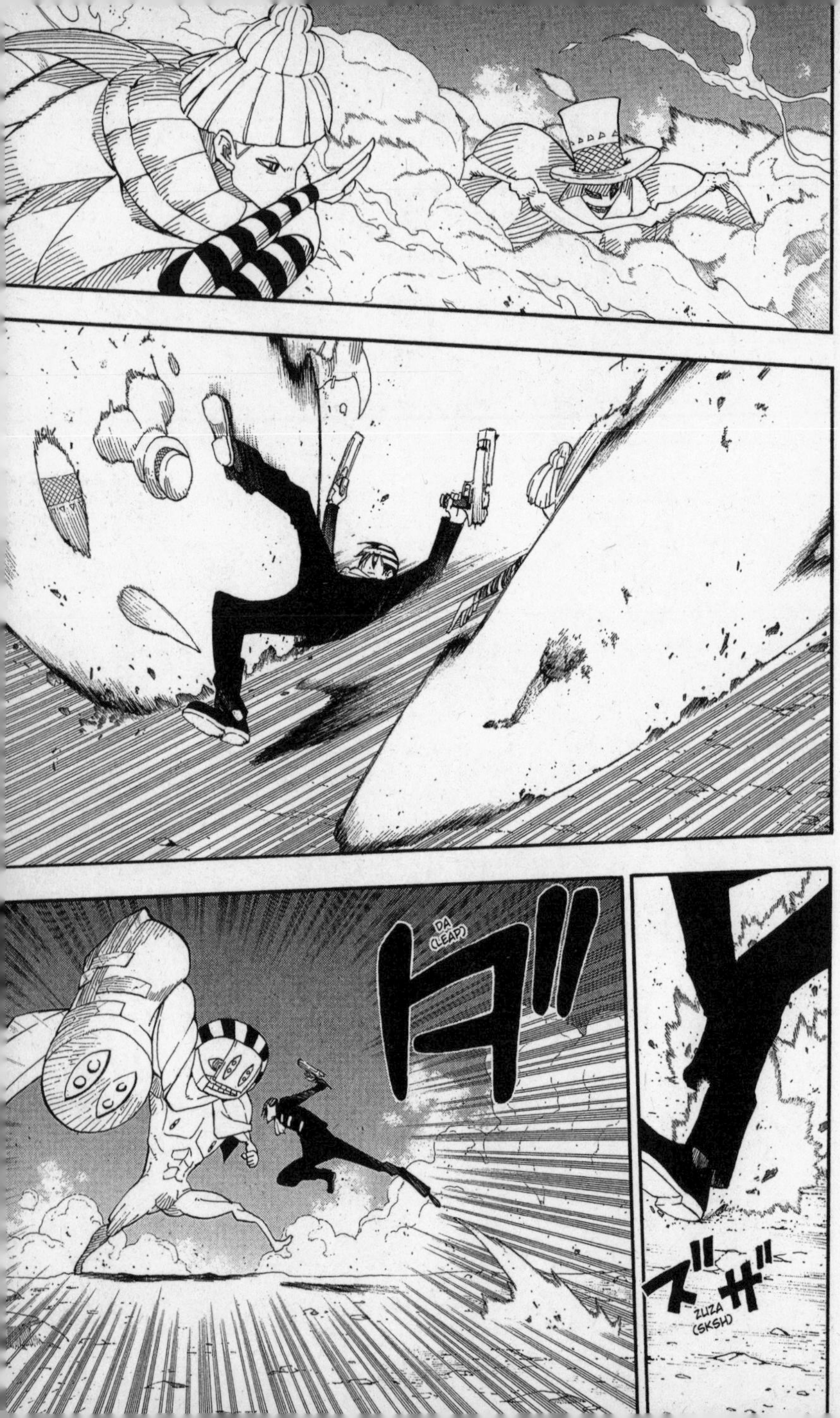
DA (LEAP)
ZUZA (SKSH)

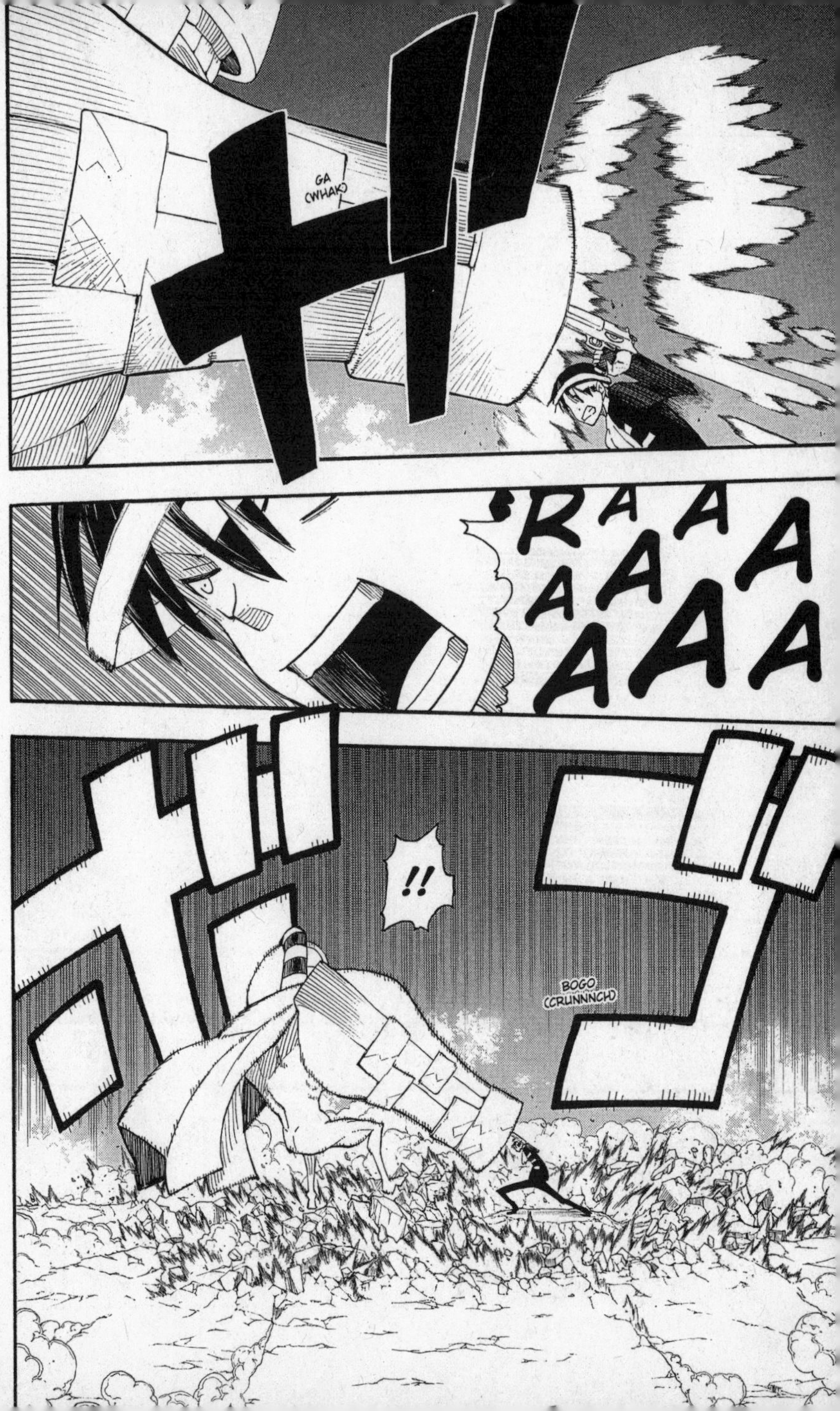
GA (WHAK)
RAAAAAAAAAA
!!
BOGO (CRUNNNCH)

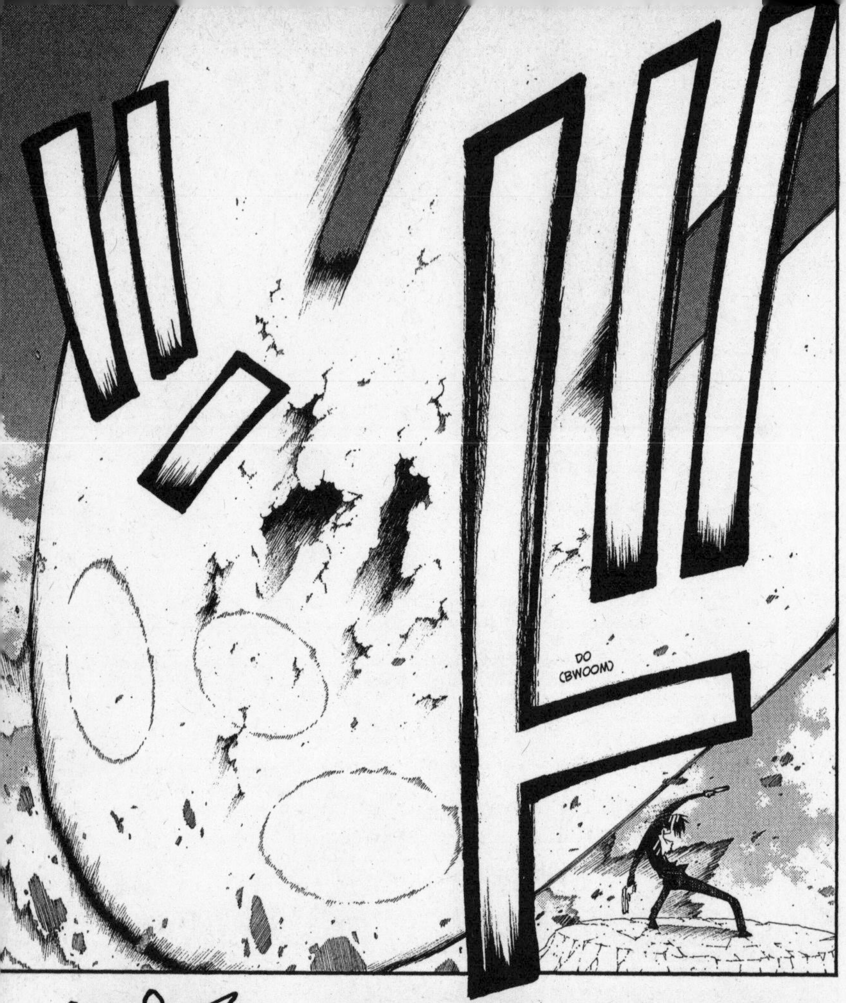
DO
(BWOOM)

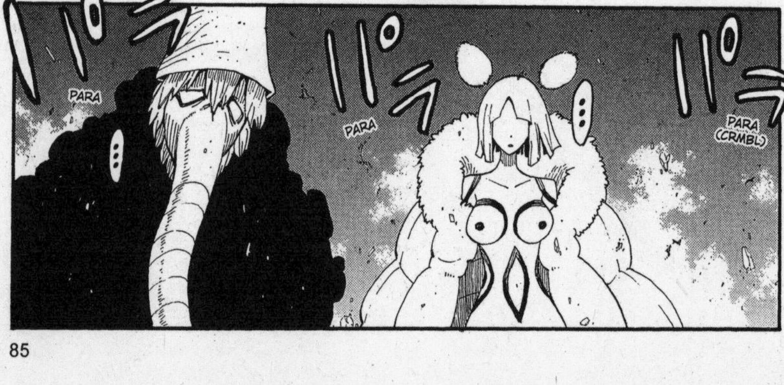
PARA
(CRMBL)
...
PARA
PARA
...

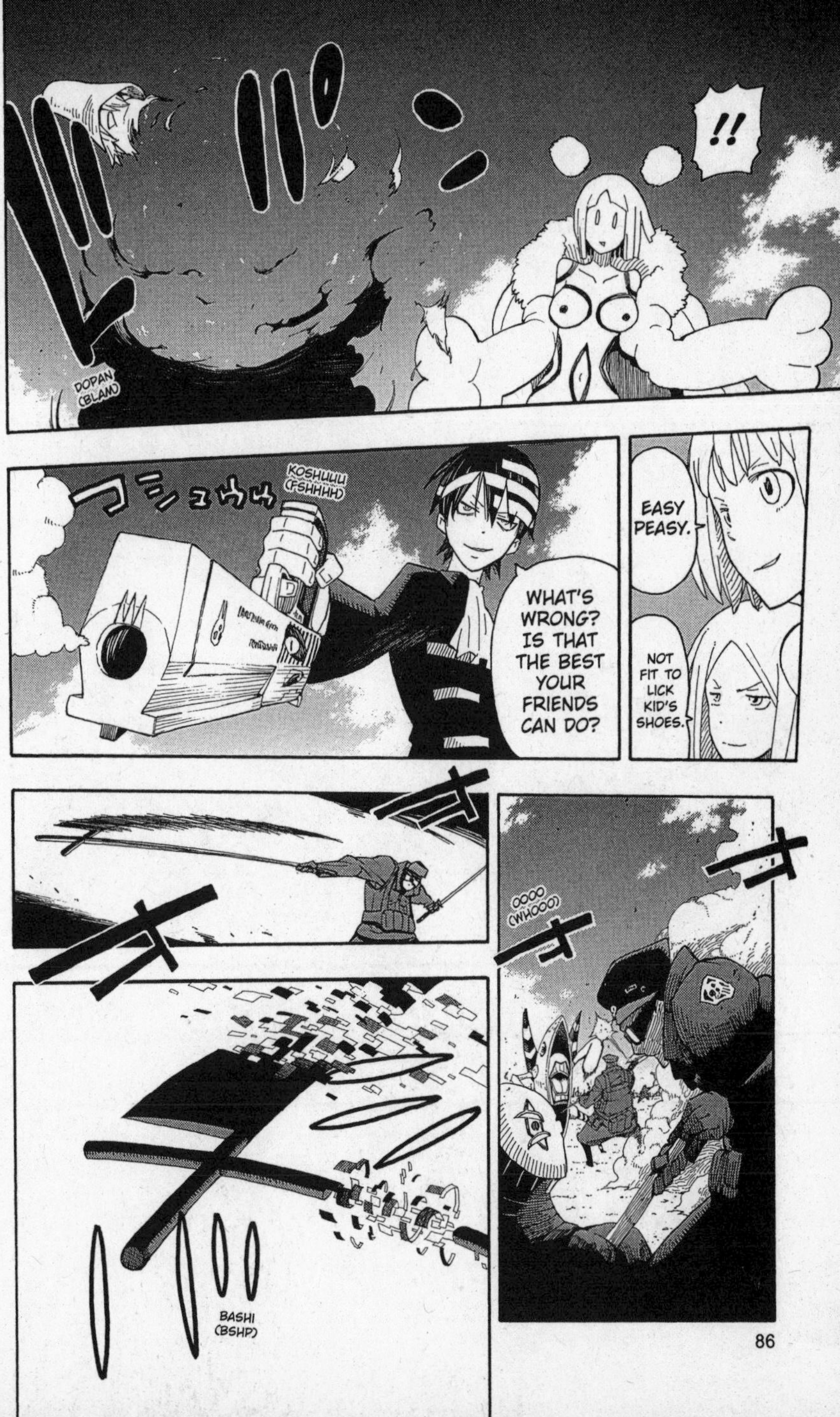
!!
DOPAN (BLAM)
EASY PEASY.
NOT FIT TO LICK KID'S SHOES.
KOSHUUU (FSHHHH)
WHAT'S WRONG? IS THAT THE BEST YOUR FRIENDS CAN DO?
OOOO (WHOOO)
BASHI (BSHP)

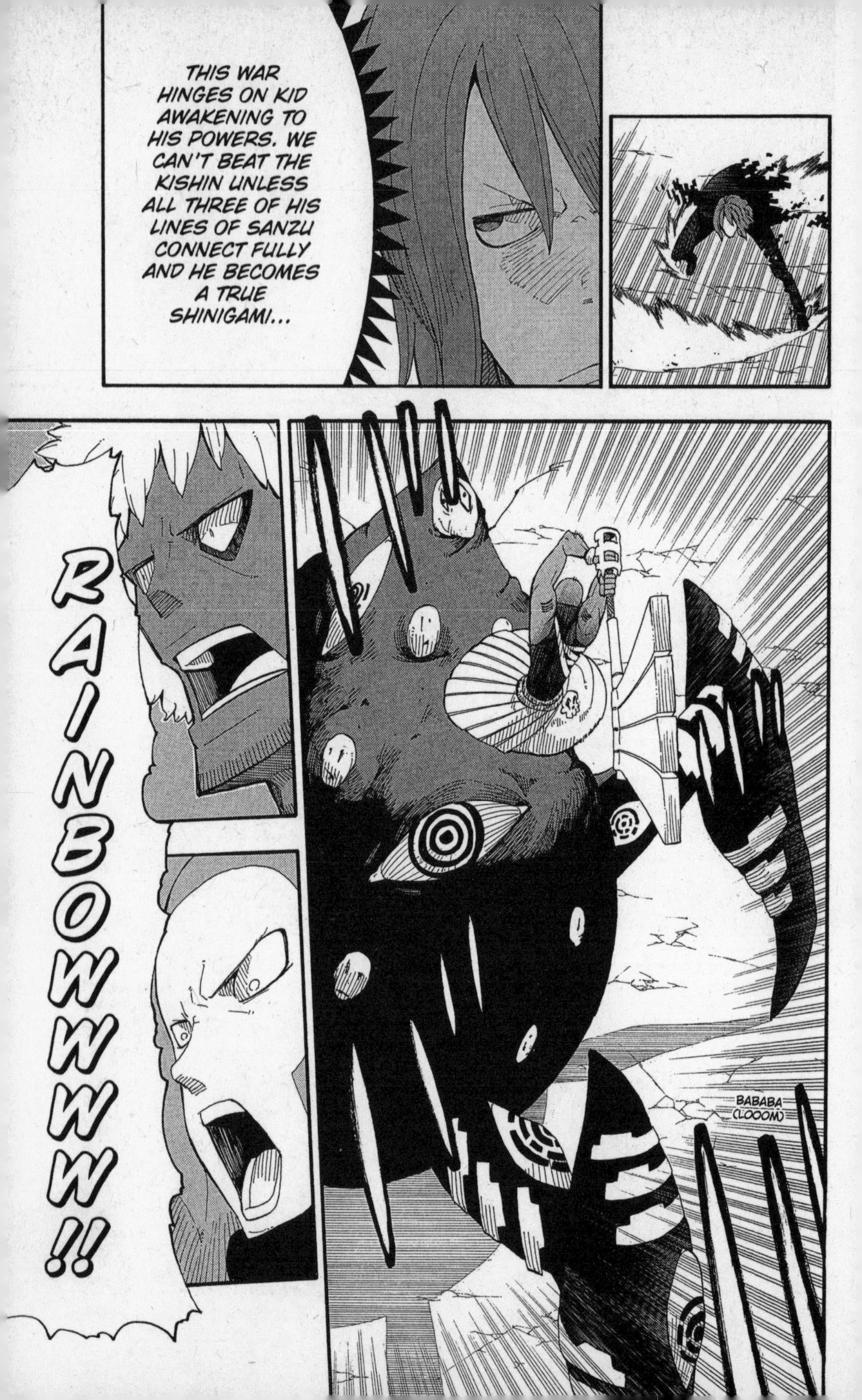
THIS WAR HINGES ON KID AWAKENING TO HIS POWERS. WE CAN'T BEAT THE KISHIN UNLESS ALL THREE OF HIS LINES OF SANZU CONNECT FULLY AND HE BECOMES A TRUE SHINIGAMI...
BABABA (LOOOM)
RAINBOWWWWW!!

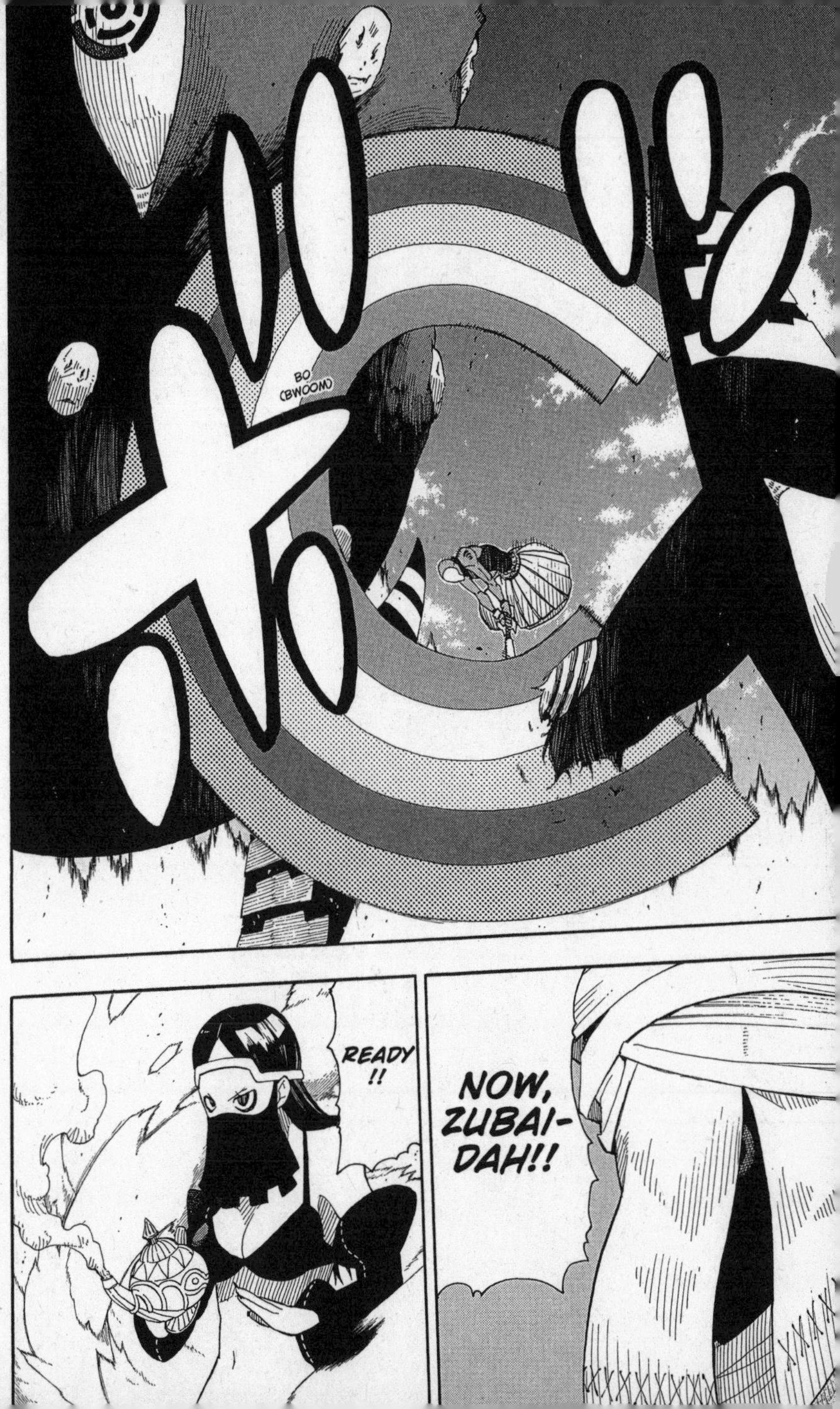
BO (BWOOM)
NOW, ZUBAIDAH!!
READY!!

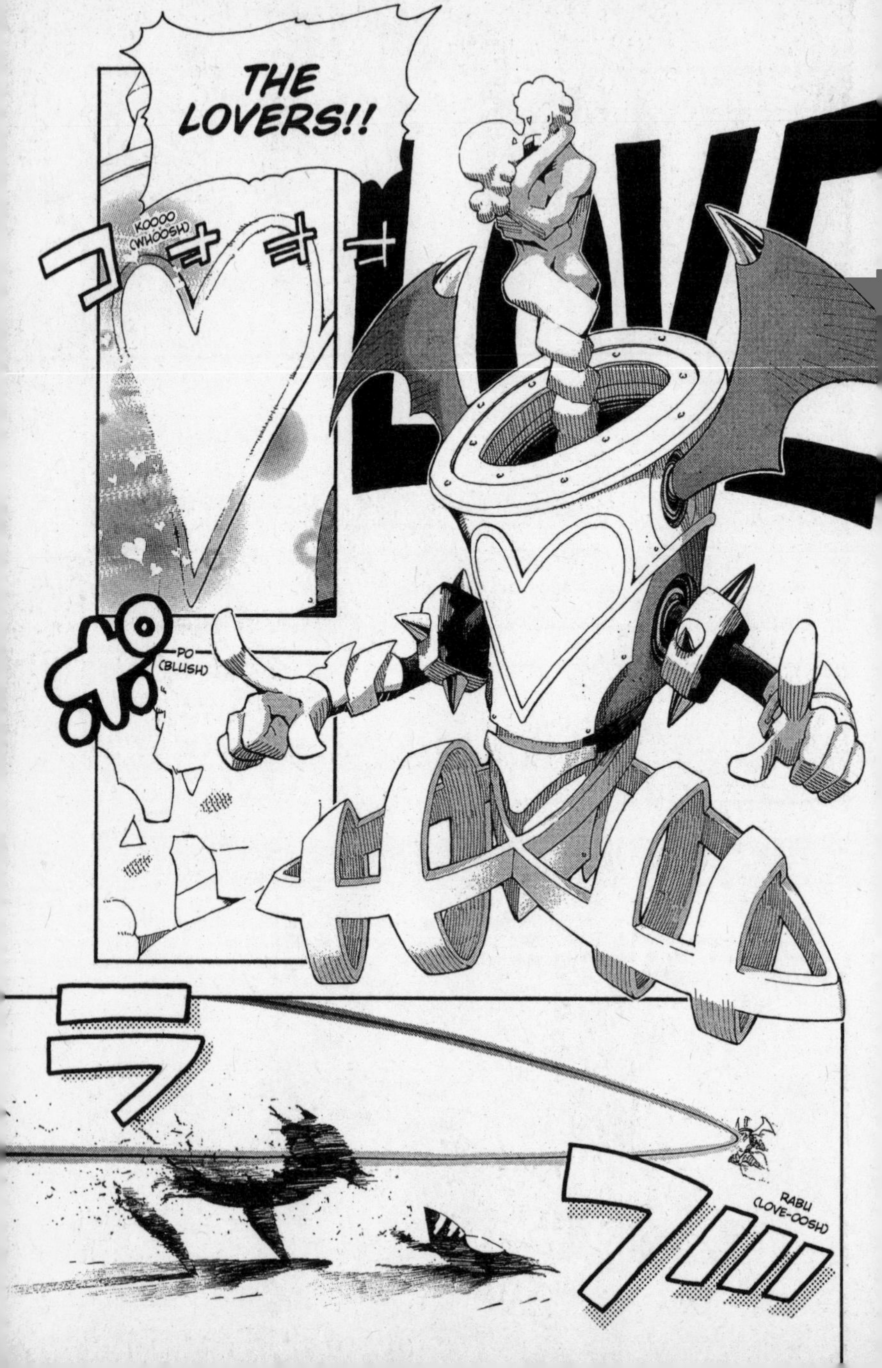
THE LOVERS!!
KOOOO (WHOOSH)
PO (BLUSH)
RABU (LOVE-OOSH)

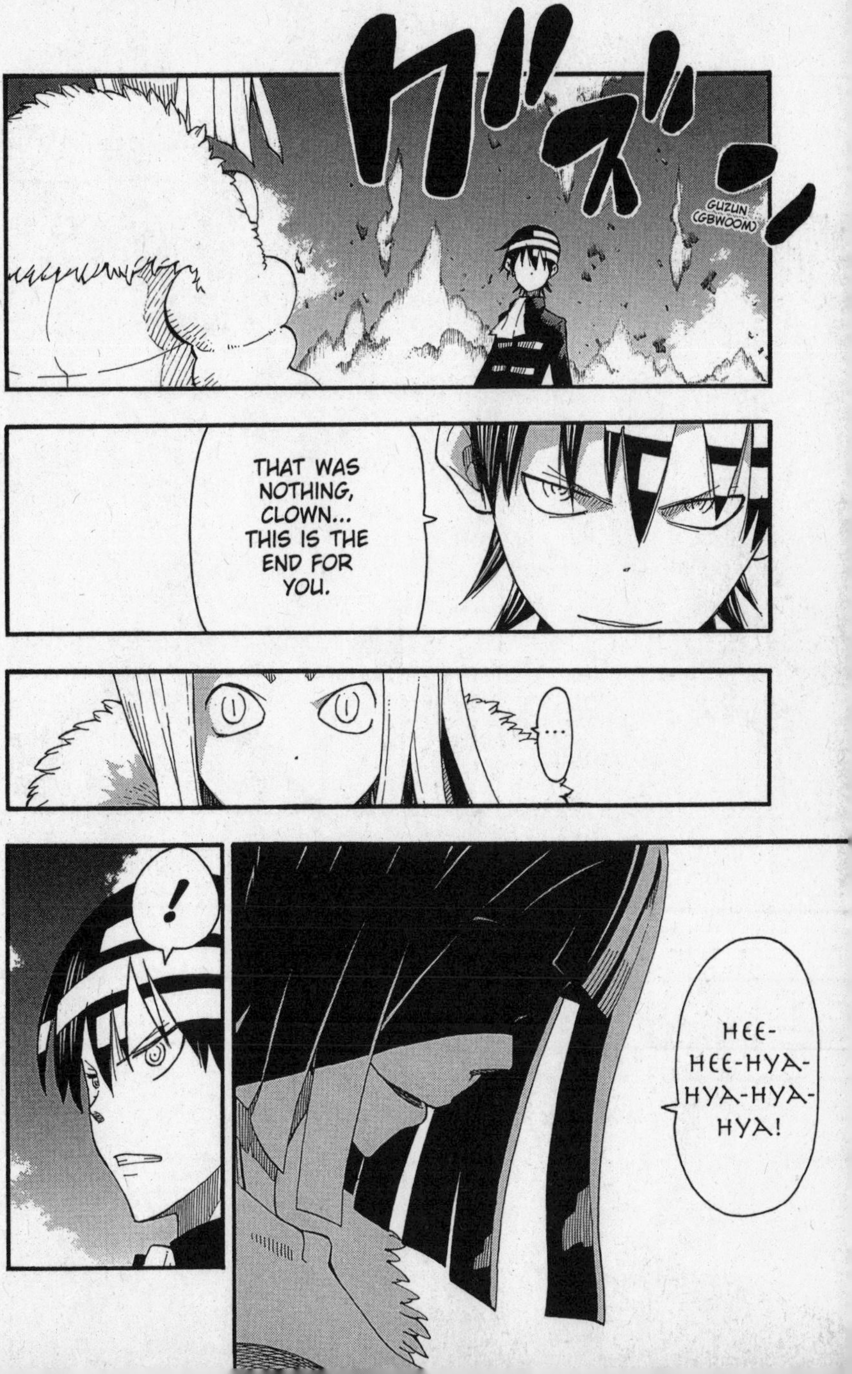
GUZUN (GBWOOM)
THAT WAS NOTHING, CLOWN... THIS IS THE END FOR YOU.
...
HEE-HEE-HYA-HYA-HYA-HYA!
!

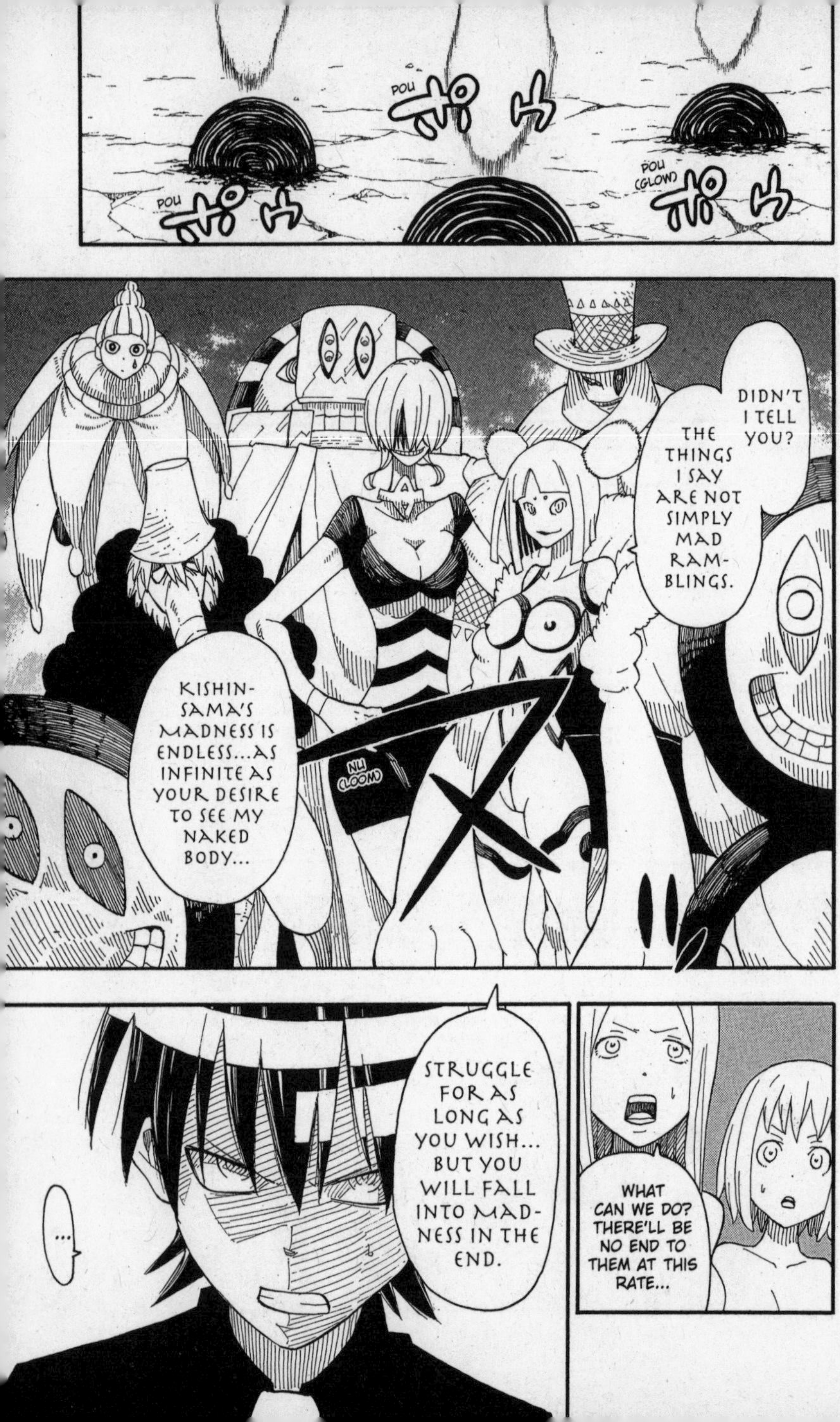
POU
POU (GLOW)
POU
DIDN'T I TELL YOU? THE THINGS I SAY ARE NOT SIMPLY MAD RAMBLINGS.
NU (LOOM)
KISHIN-SAMA'S MADNESS IS ENDLESS...AS INFINITE AS YOUR DESIRE TO SEE MY NAKED BODY...
WHAT CAN WE DO? THERE'LL BE NO END TO THEM AT THIS RATE...
STRUGGLE FOR AS LONG AS YOU WISH... BUT YOU WILL FALL INTO MADNESS IN THE END.
...

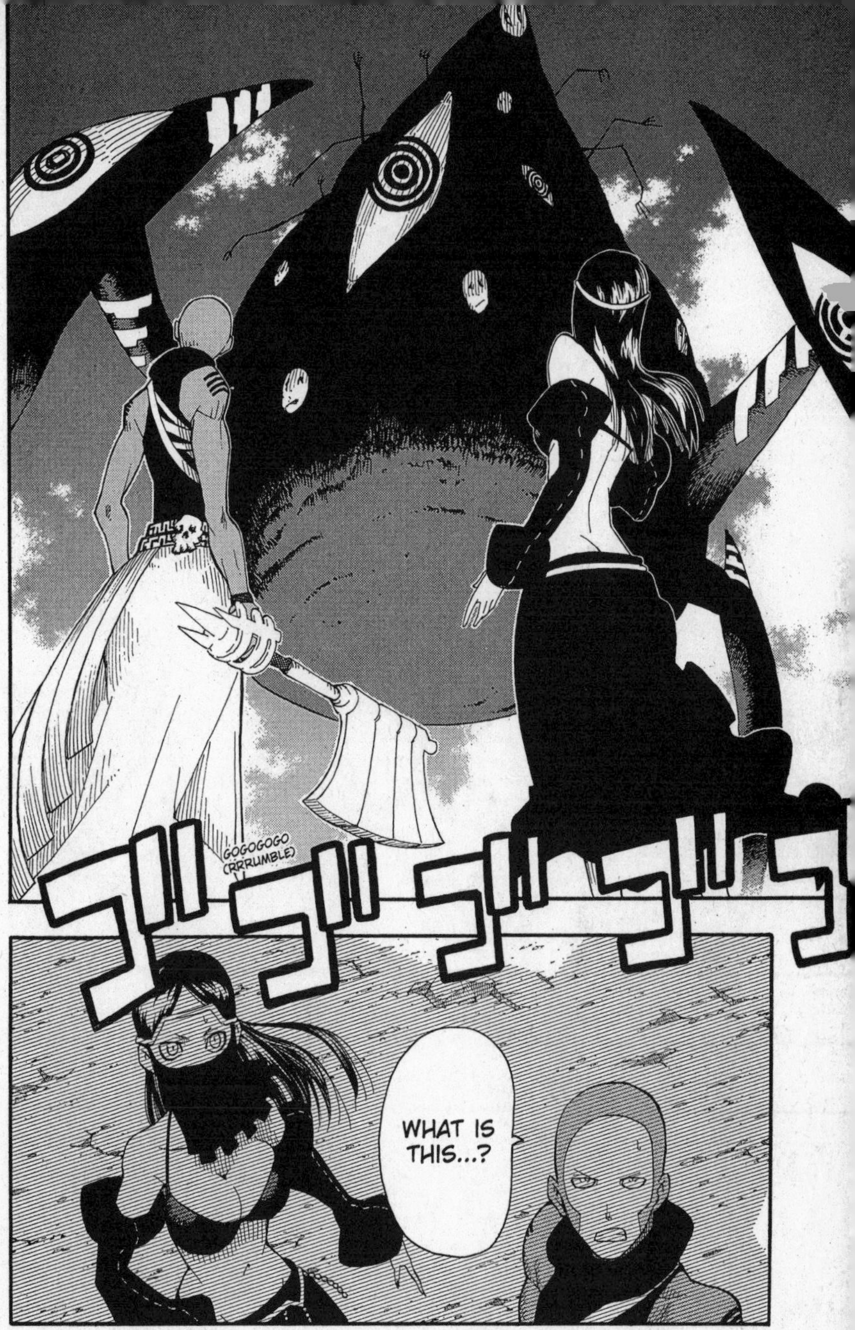
GOGOGOGO
(RRRUMBLE)
ゴゴゴゴ
WHAT IS THIS...?

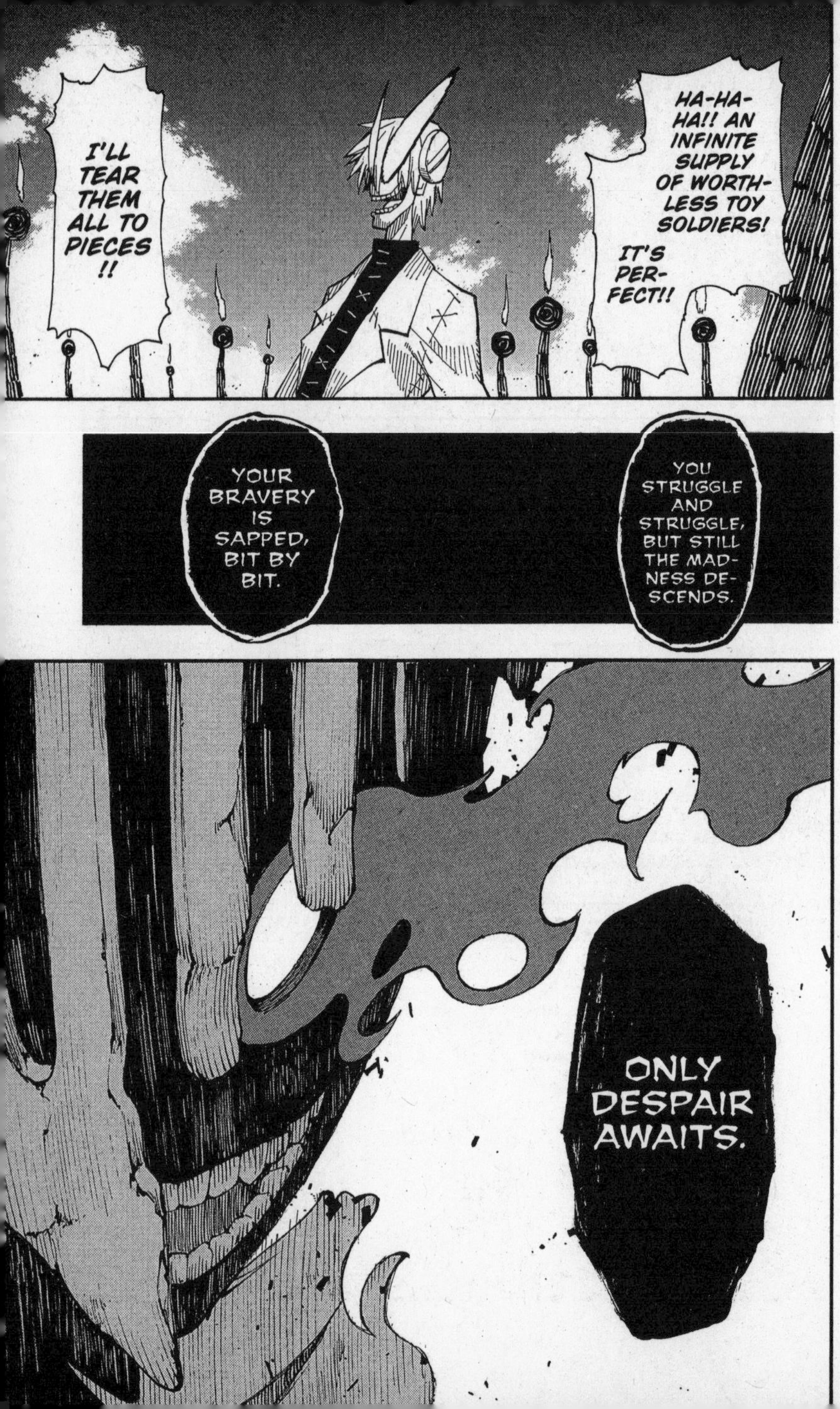
HA-HA-HA!! AN INFINITE SUPPLY OF WORTHLESS TOY SOLDIERS!
IT'S PERFECT!!
I'LL TEAR THEM ALL TO PIECES!!
YOU STRUGGLE AND STRUGGLE, BUT STILL THE MADNESS DESCENDS.
YOUR BRAVERY IS SAPPED, BIT BY BIT.
ONLY DESPAIR AWAITS.

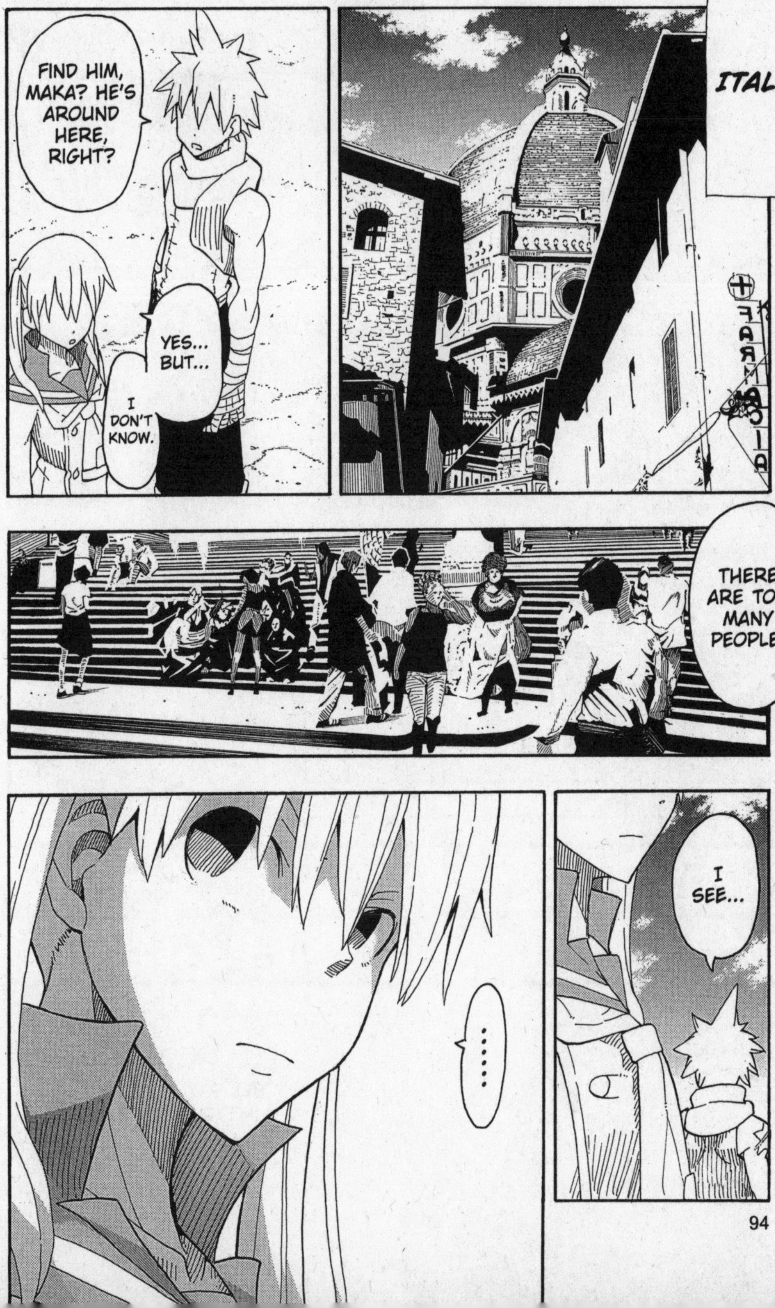
ITALY
FARMACIA
FIND HIM, MAKA? HE'S AROUND HERE, RIGHT?
YES... BUT...
I DON'T KNOW.
THERE ARE TOO MANY PEOPLE.
I SEE...
......

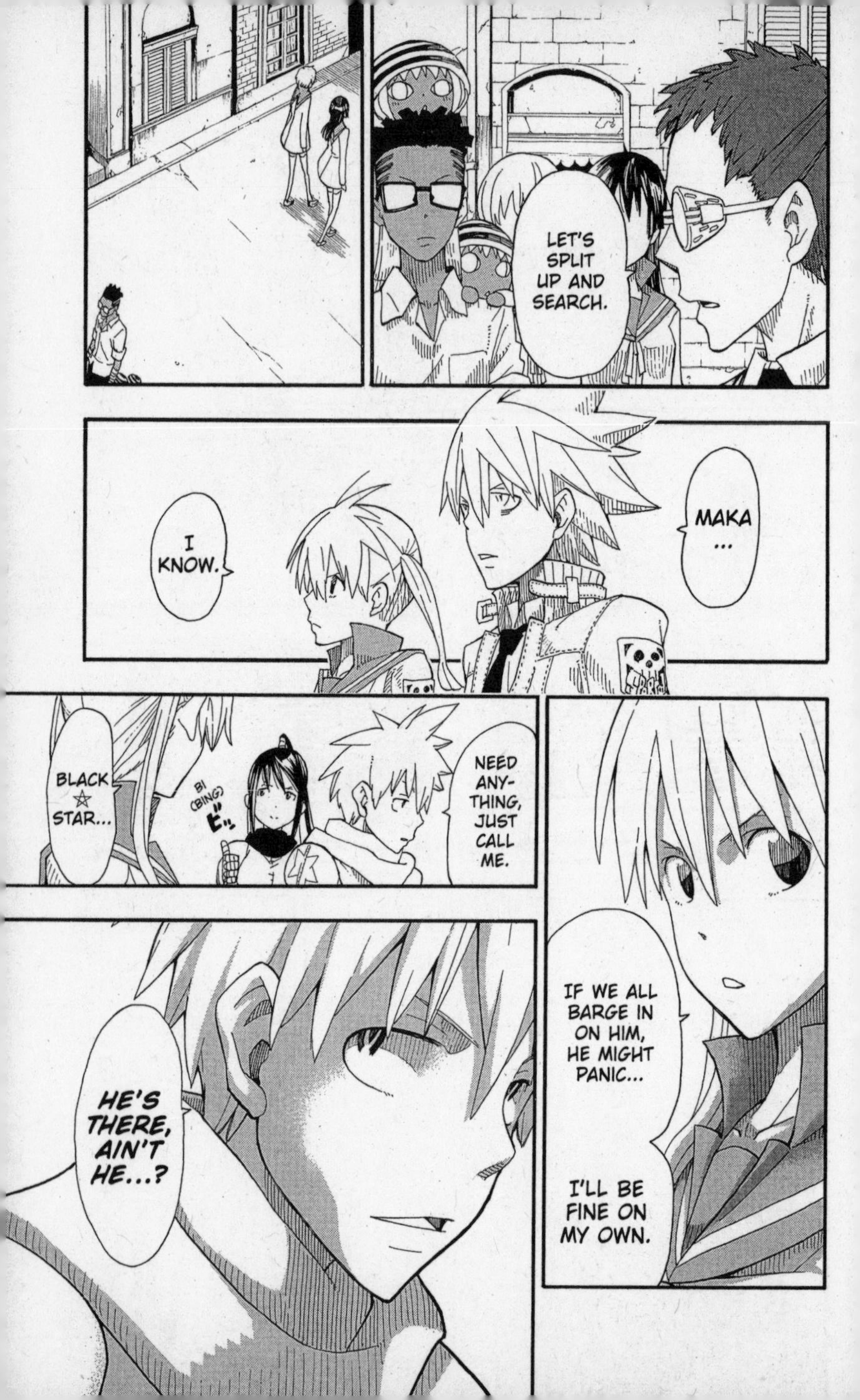
LET'S SPLIT UP AND SEARCH.
MAKA ...
I KNOW.
IF WE ALL BARGE IN ON HIM, HE MIGHT PANIC...
I'LL BE FINE ON MY OWN.
NEED ANY-THING, JUST CALL ME.
BI (BING)
BLACK ☆ STAR...
HE'S THERE, AIN'T HE...?

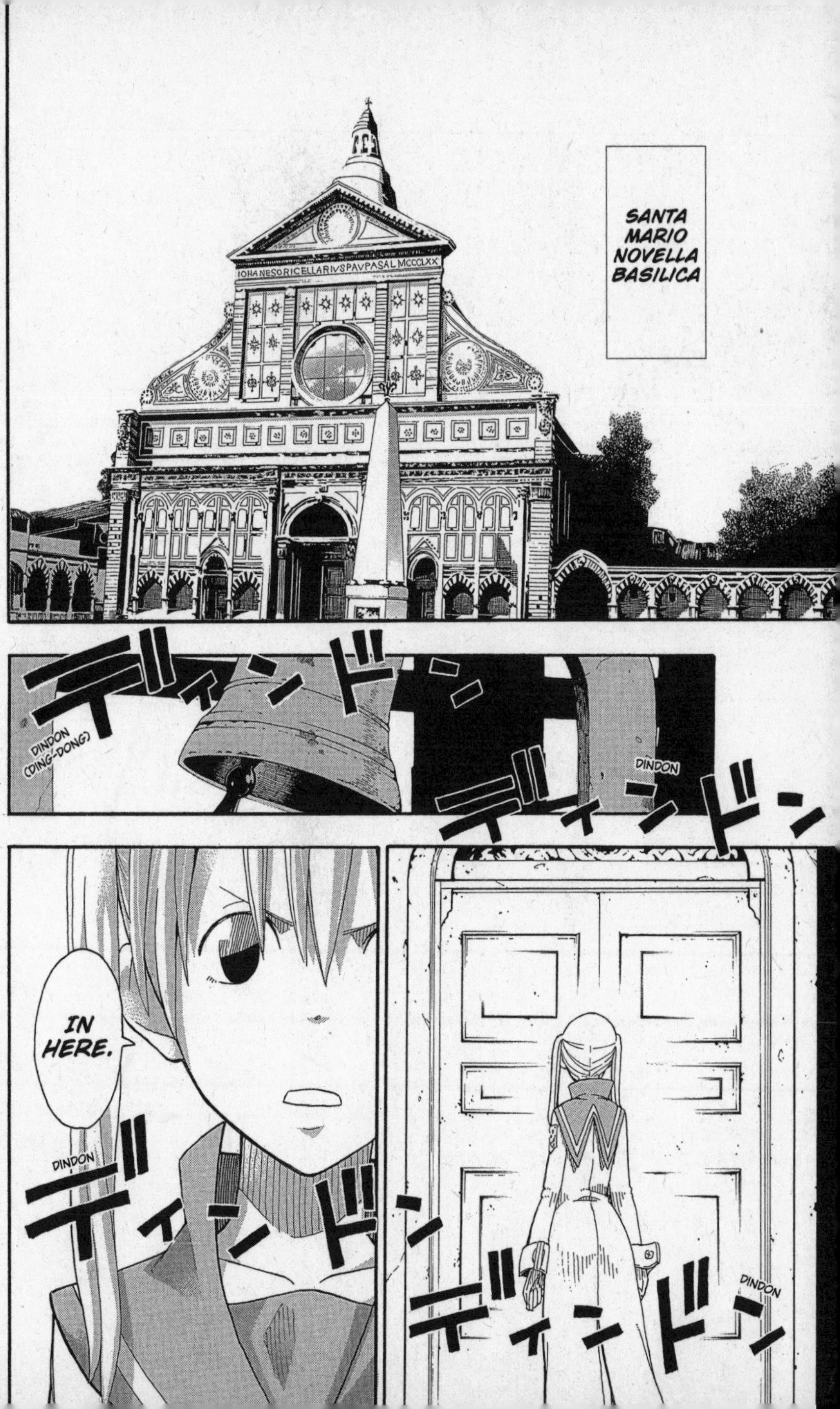
SANTA MARIO NOVELLA BASILICA
ディンドーン
DINDON (DING-DONG)
ディンドーン
DINDON
ディンドーン
DINDON
IN HERE.
ディーンドーン
DINDON

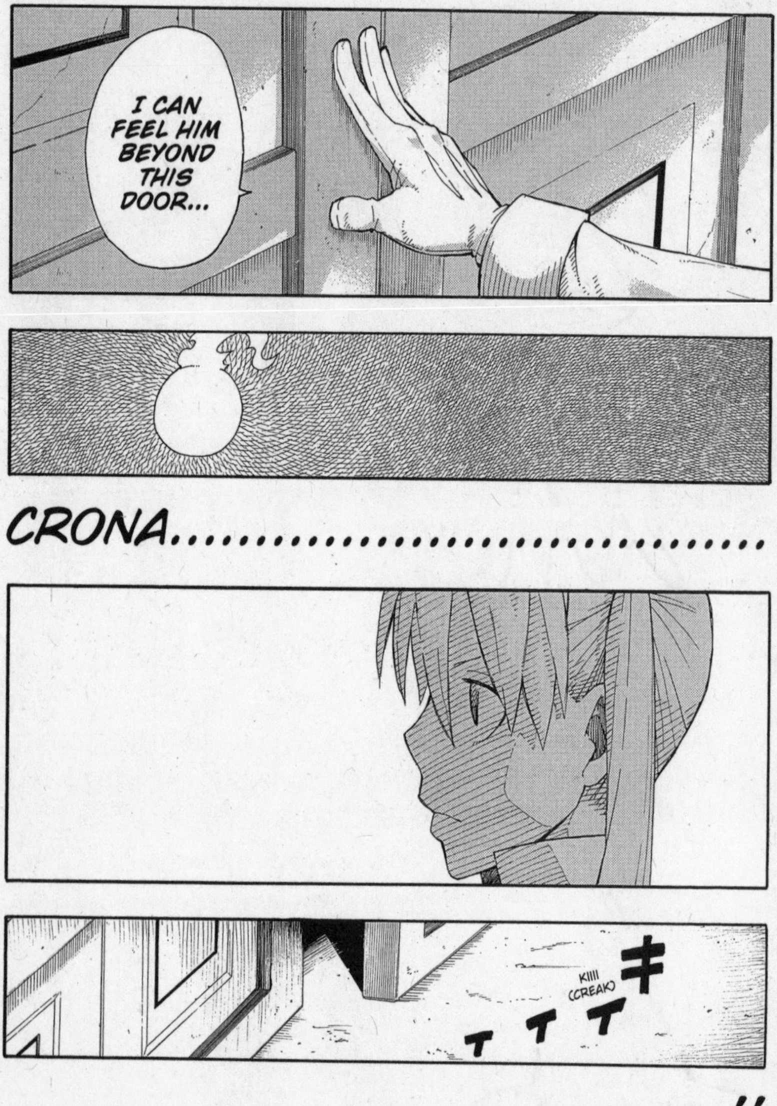
I CAN FEEL HIM BEYOND THIS DOOR...
CRONA..................................
キィィィ
KIIII (CREAK)
......................................!!

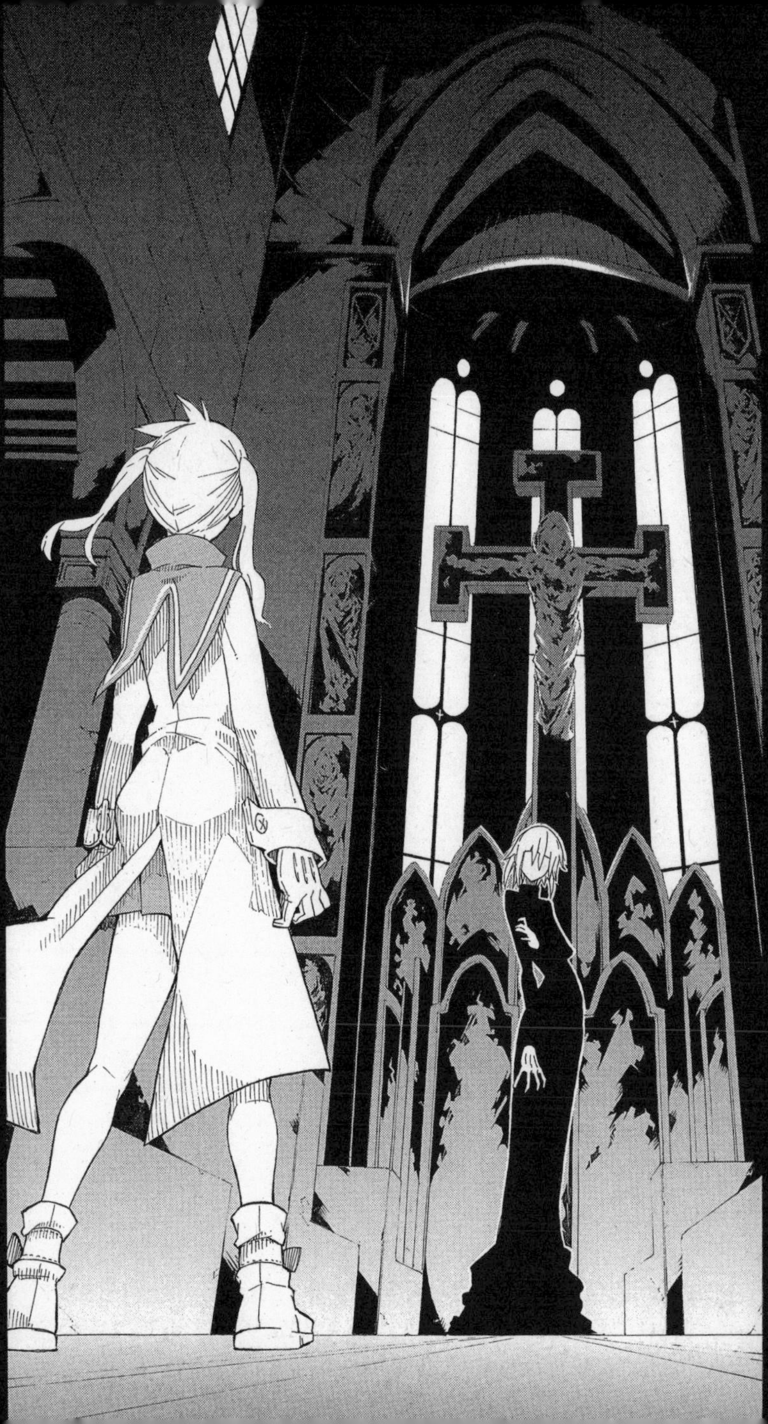

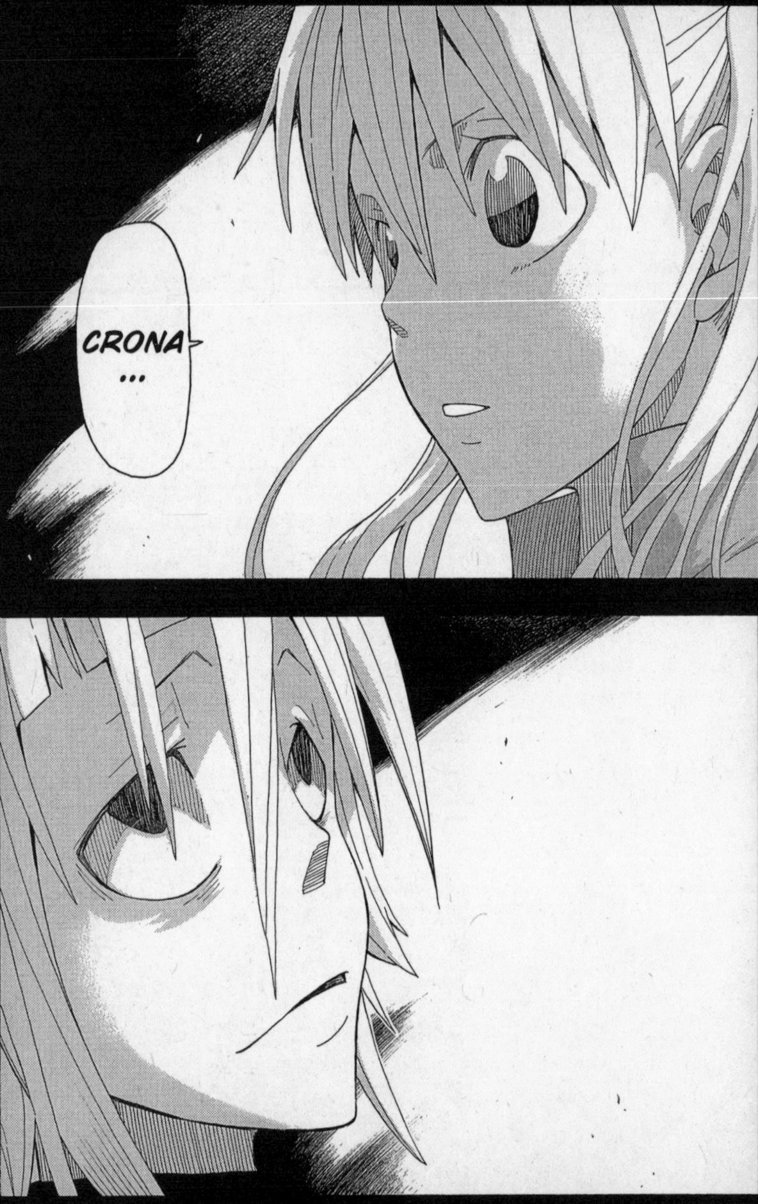
CRONA ...

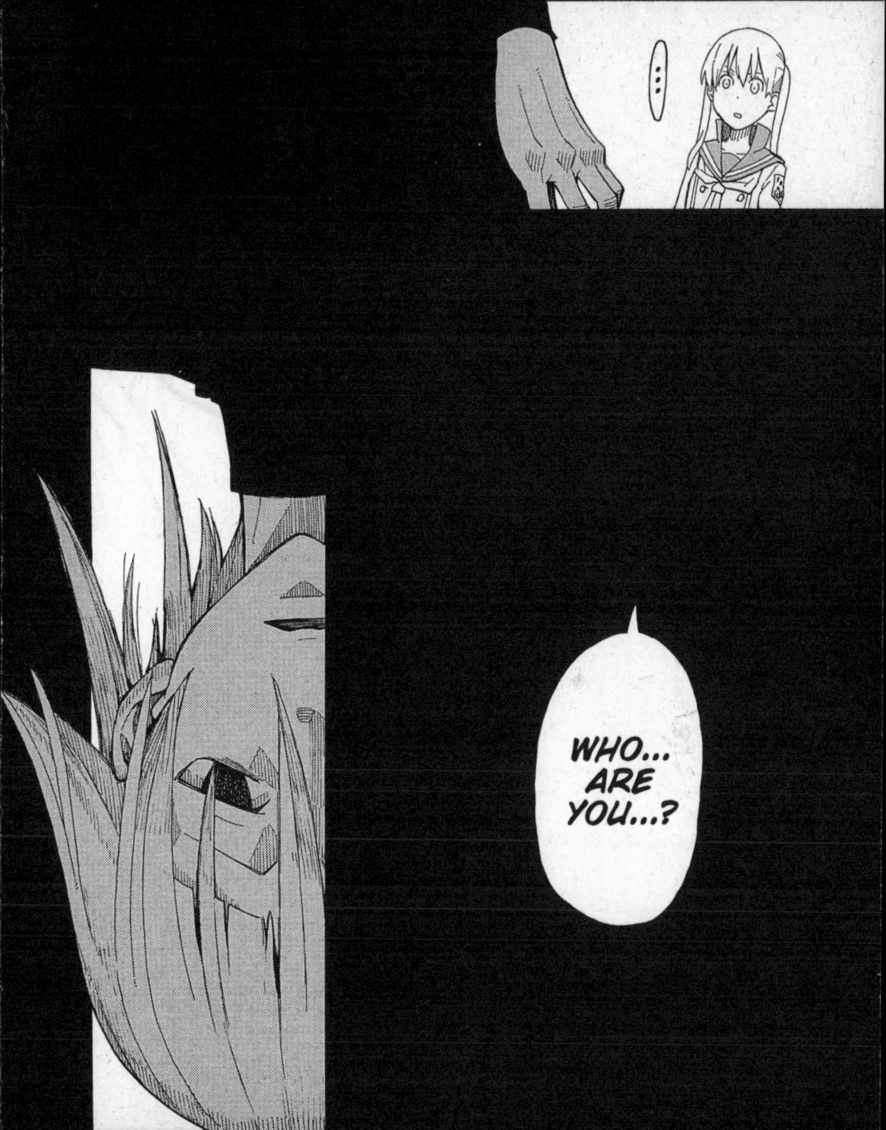
...
WHO... ARE YOU...?

SOUL EATER

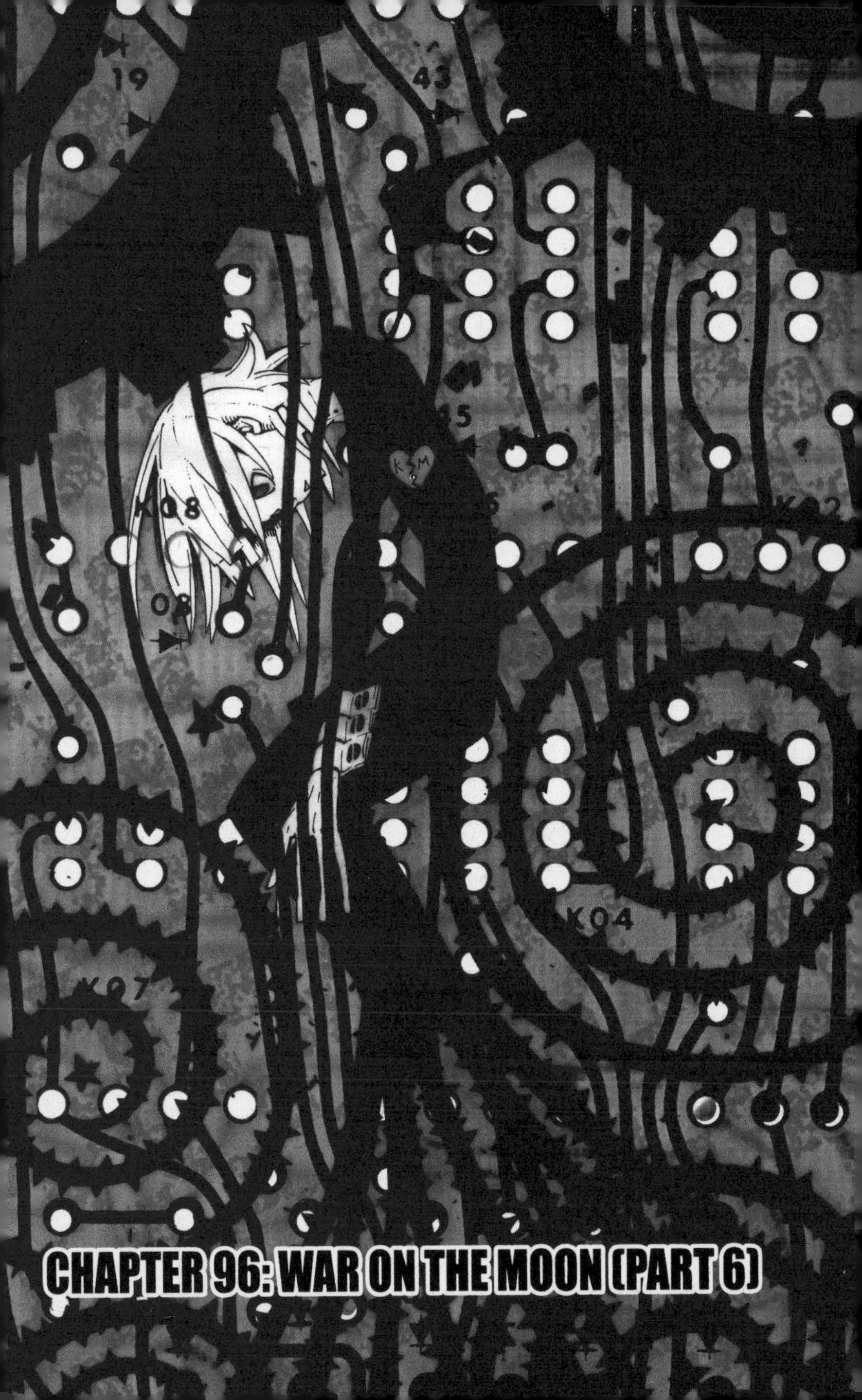
CHAPTER 96: WAR ON THE MOON (PART 6)

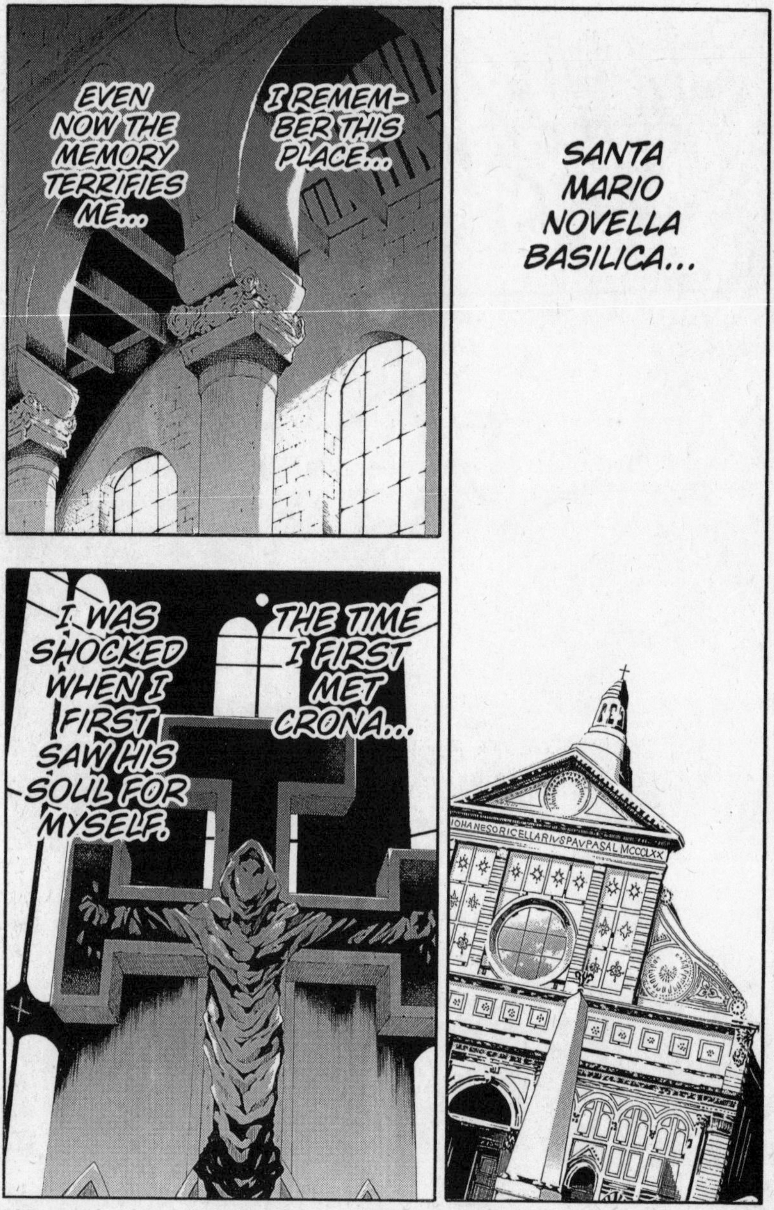
SANTA MARIO NOVELLA BASILICA...
IOHANESORICELLARIVSPAVPASAL MCCCLXX
I REMEMBER THIS PLACE...
EVEN NOW THE MEMORY TERRIFIES ME...
THE TIME I FIRST MET CRONA...
I WAS SHOCKED WHEN I FIRST SAW HIS SOUL FOR MYSELF.

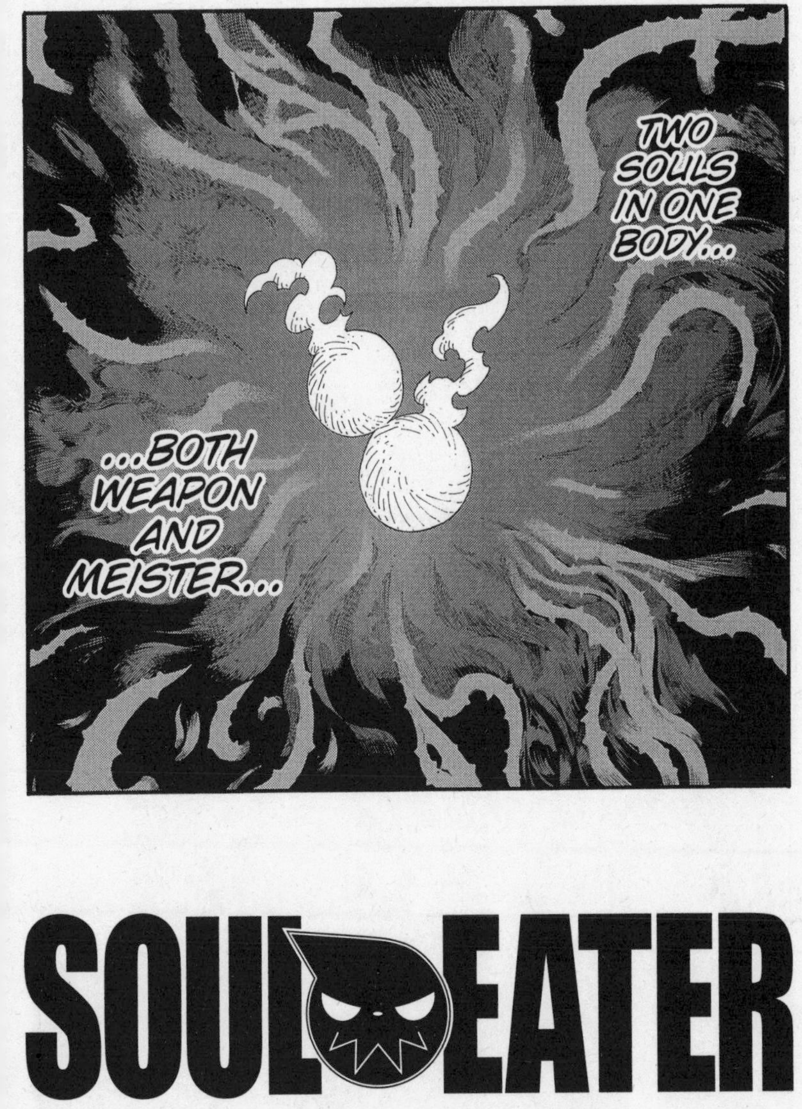
TWO SOULS IN ONE BODY...
...BOTH WEAPON AND MEISTER...

SOUL EATER

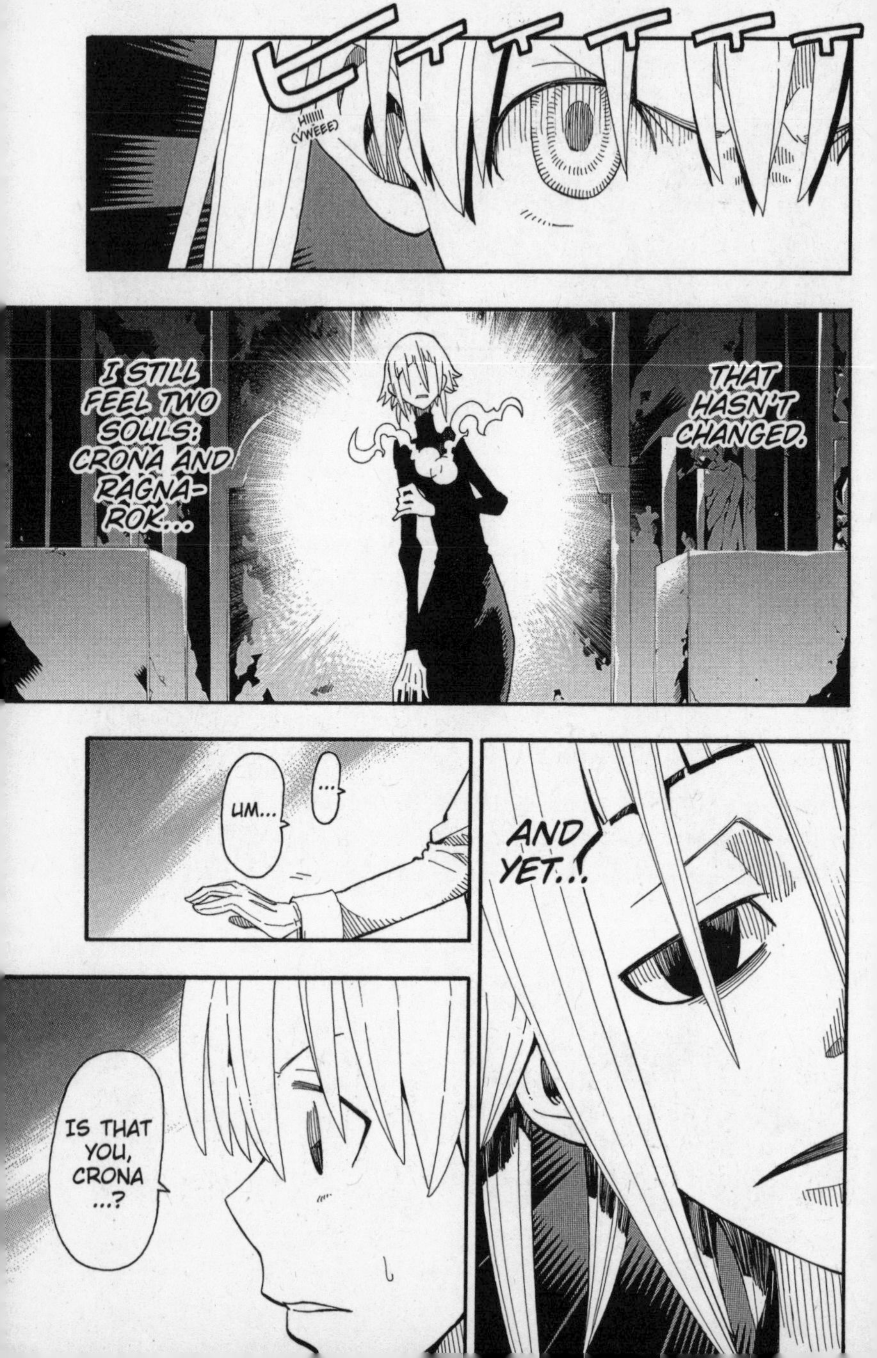

ビイイイイイイ
HIIIII (VWEEE)
I STILL FEEL TWO SOULS: CRONA AND RAGNA-ROK...
THAT HASN'T CHANGED.
AND YET...
...
UM...
IS THAT YOU, CRONA ...?

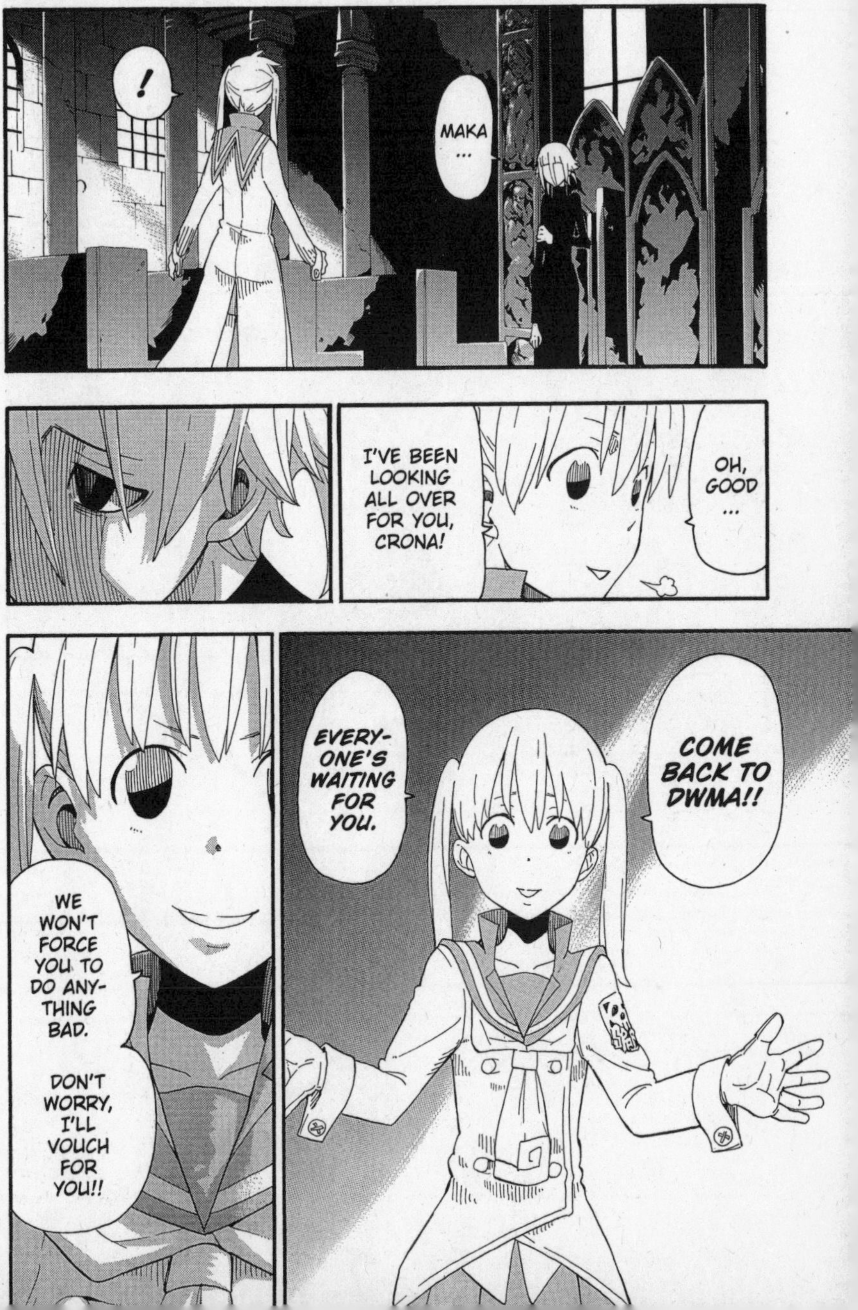
MAKA ...
!
OH, GOOD ...
I'VE BEEN LOOKING ALL OVER FOR YOU, CRONA!
COME BACK TO DWMA!!
EVERY-ONE'S WAITING FOR YOU.
WE WON'T FORCE YOU TO DO ANY-THING BAD.
DON'T WORRY, I'LL VOUCH FOR YOU!!

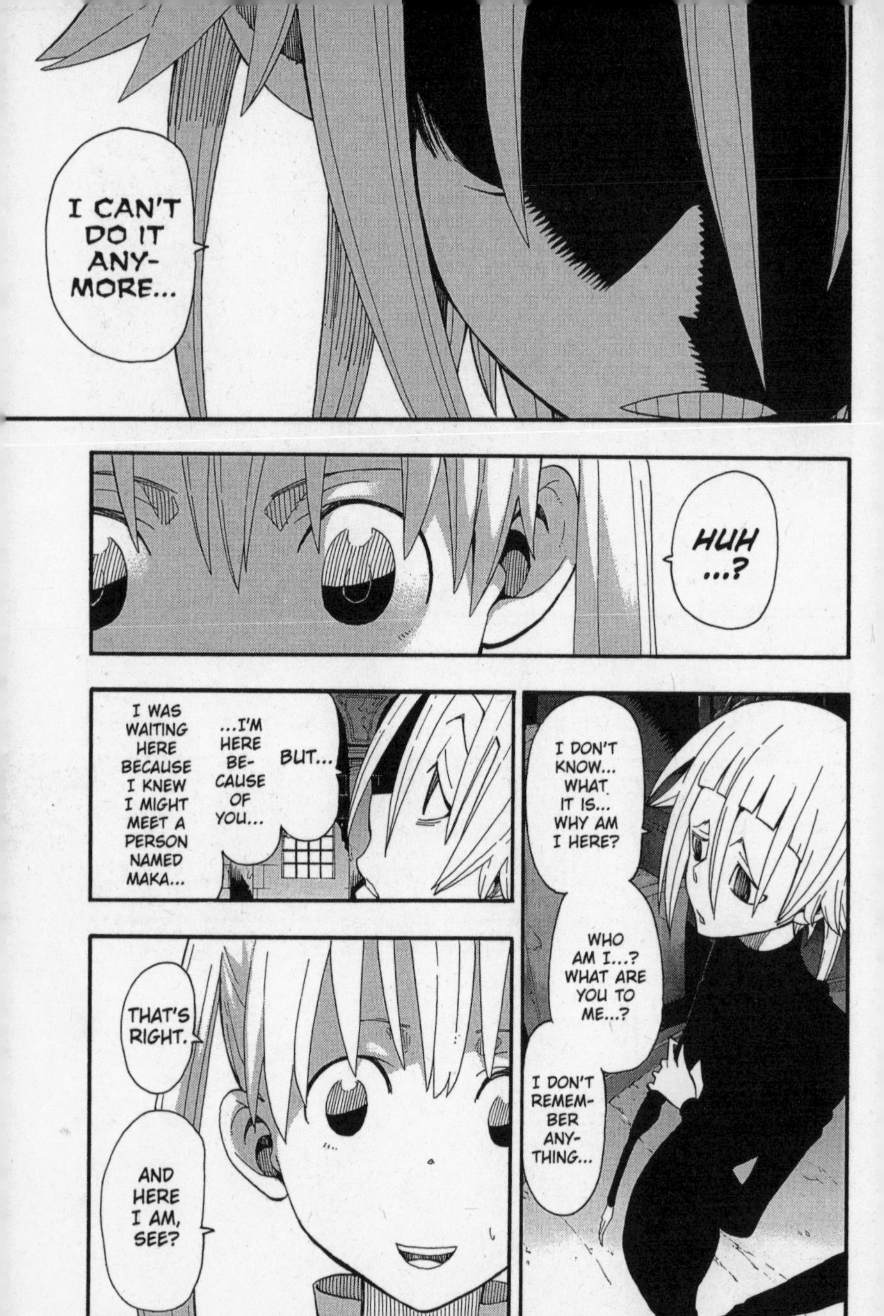
I CAN'T DO IT ANY-MORE...
HUH ...?
I DON'T KNOW... WHAT IT IS... WHY AM I HERE?
WHO AM I...? WHAT ARE YOU TO ME...?
I DON'T REMEM-BER ANY-THING...
BUT...
...I'M HERE BE-CAUSE OF YOU...
I WAS WAITING HERE BECAUSE I KNEW I MIGHT MEET A PERSON NAMED MAKA...
THAT'S RIGHT.
AND HERE I AM, SEE?

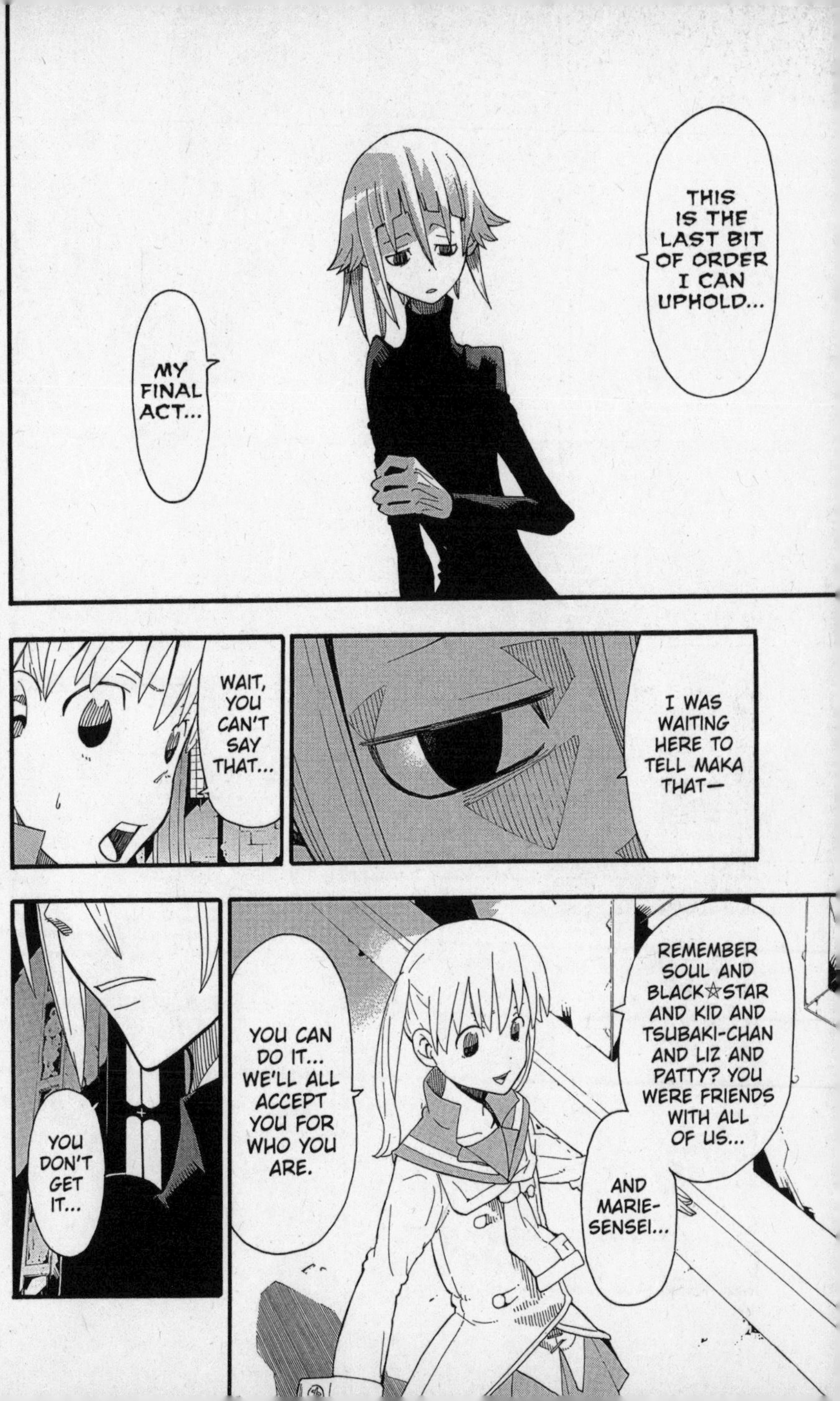
THIS IS THE LAST BIT OF ORDER I CAN UPHOLD...
MY FINAL ACT...
I WAS WAITING HERE TO TELL MAKA THAT—
WAIT, YOU CAN'T SAY THAT...
REMEMBER SOUL AND BLACK☆STAR AND KID AND TSUBAKI-CHAN AND LIZ AND PATTY? YOU WERE FRIENDS WITH ALL OF US...
AND MARIE-SENSEI...
YOU CAN DO IT... WE'LL ALL ACCEPT YOU FOR WHO YOU ARE.
YOU DON'T GET IT...

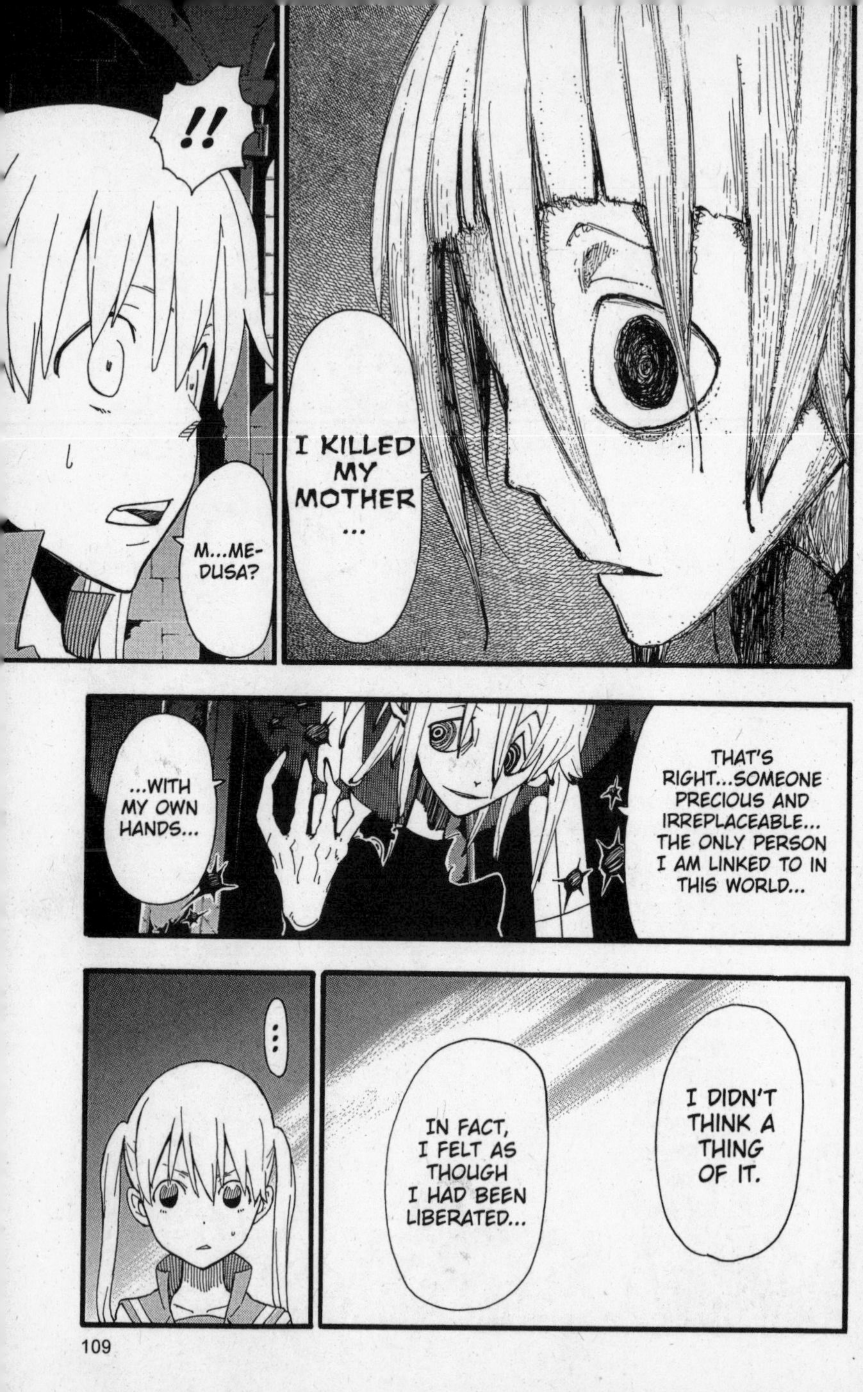
I KILLED MY MOTHER...
!!
M...ME-DUSA?
THAT'S RIGHT...SOMEONE PRECIOUS AND IRREPLACEABLE... THE ONLY PERSON I AM LINKED TO IN THIS WORLD...
...WITH MY OWN HANDS...
I DIDN'T THINK A THING OF IT.
IN FACT, I FELT AS THOUGH I HAD BEEN LIBERATED...
...

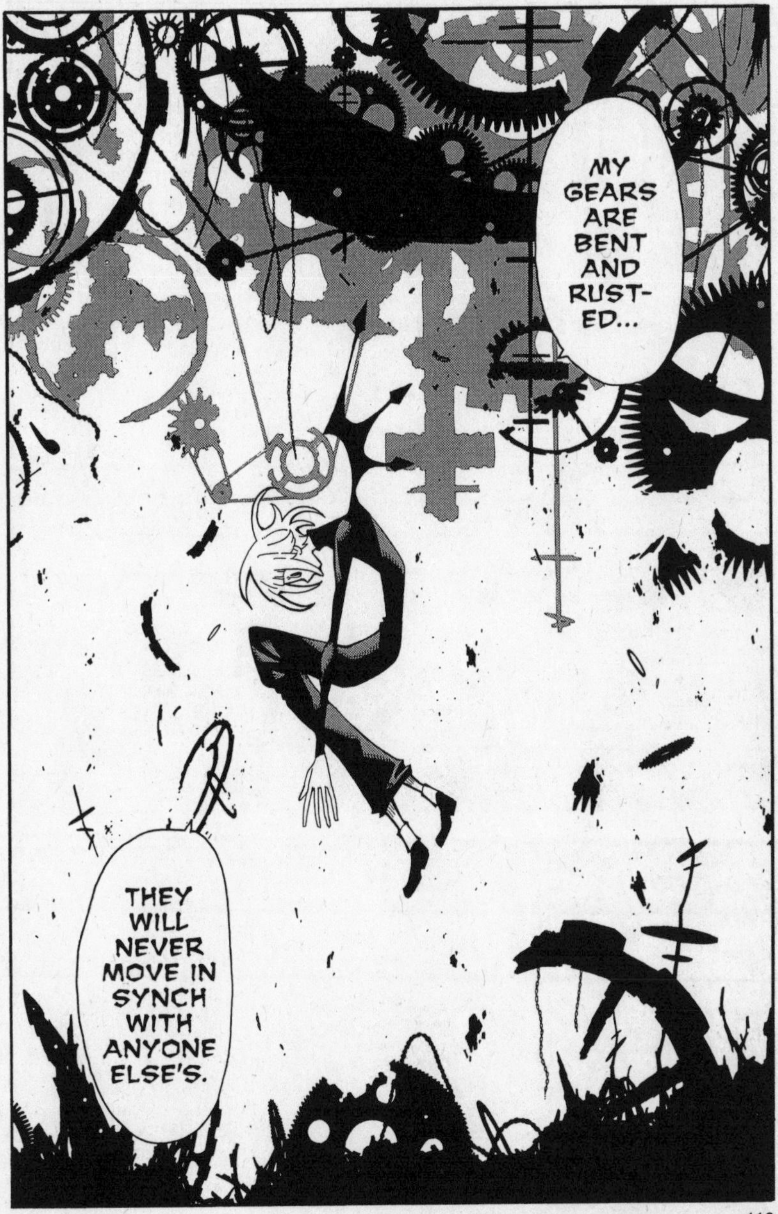
MY GEARS ARE BENT AND RUST-ED...
THEY WILL NEVER MOVE IN SYNCH WITH ANYONE ELSE'S.

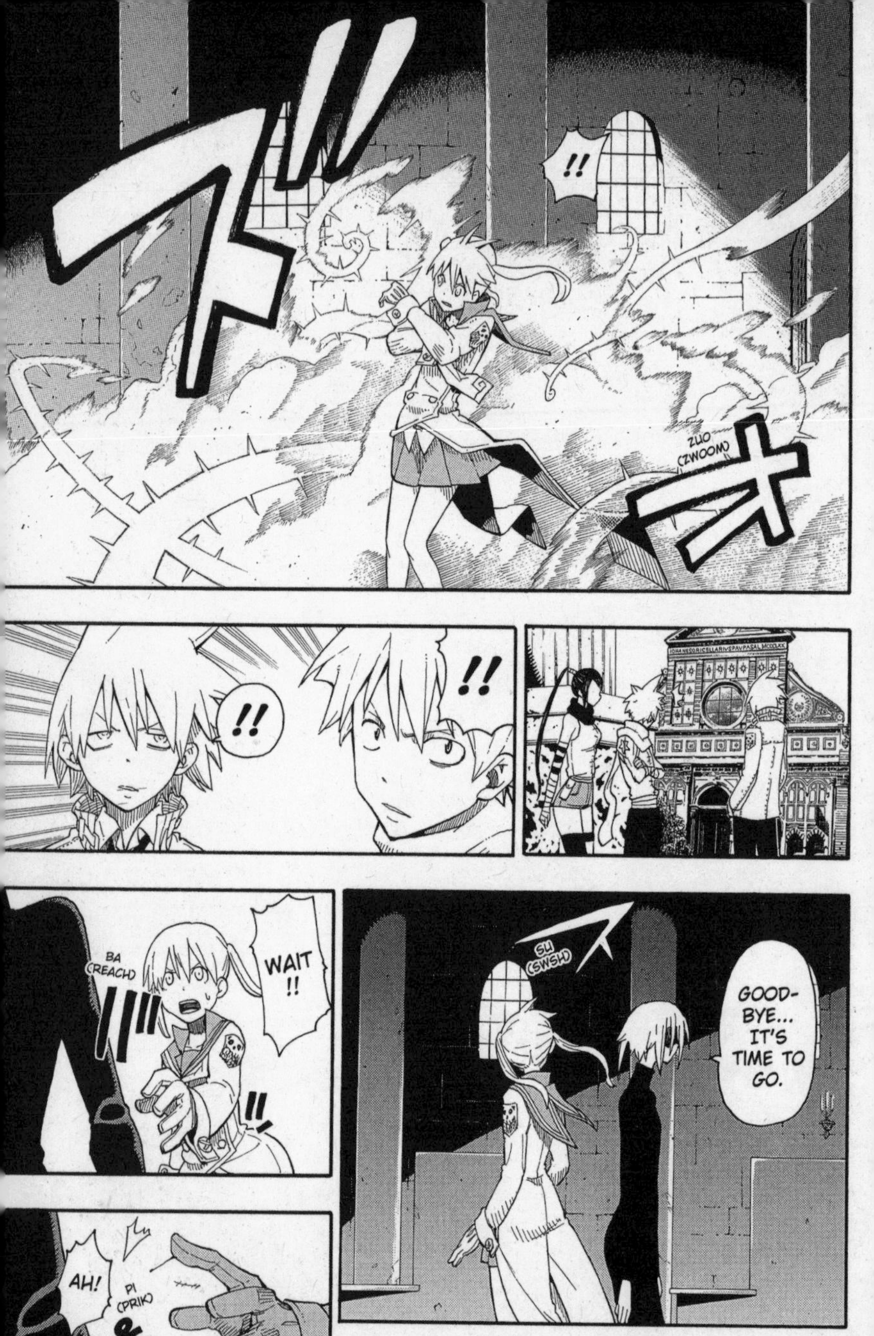
!!
ZUO
(ZWOOM)
!!
!!
SU
(SWSH)
GOOD-BYE... IT'S TIME TO GO.
BA
(REACH)
WAIT !!
AH!
PI
(PRIK)

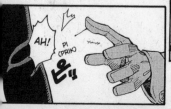

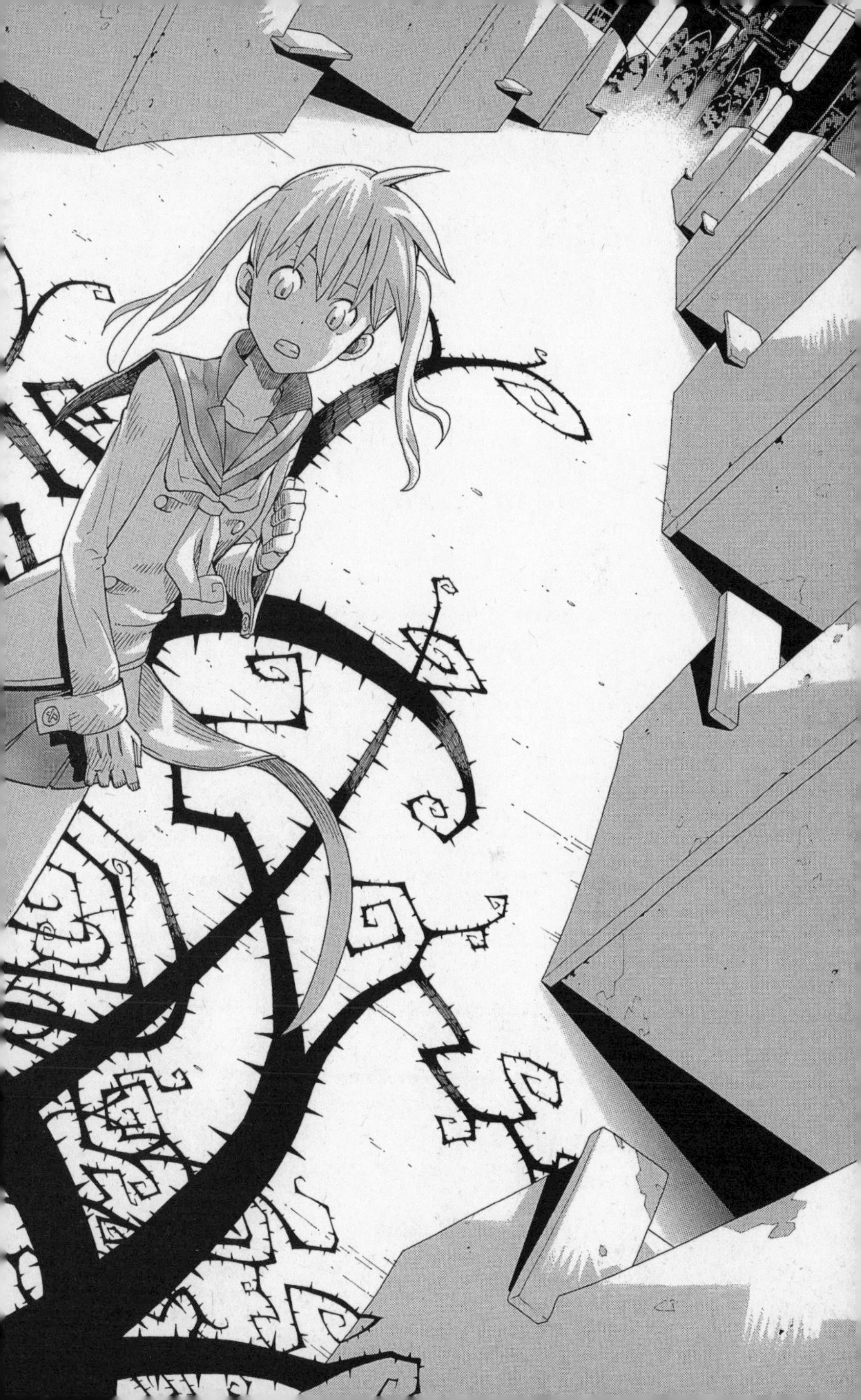

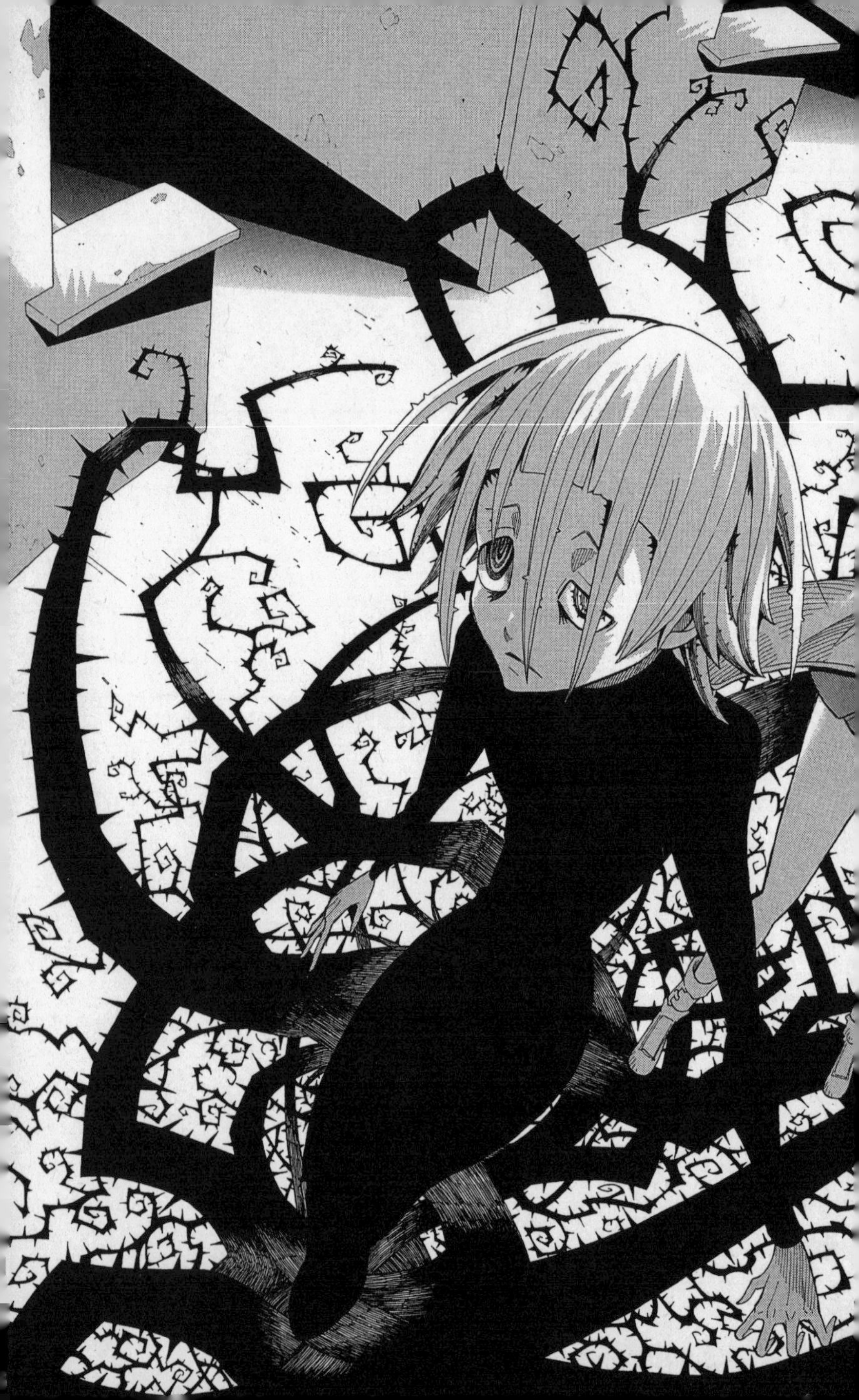

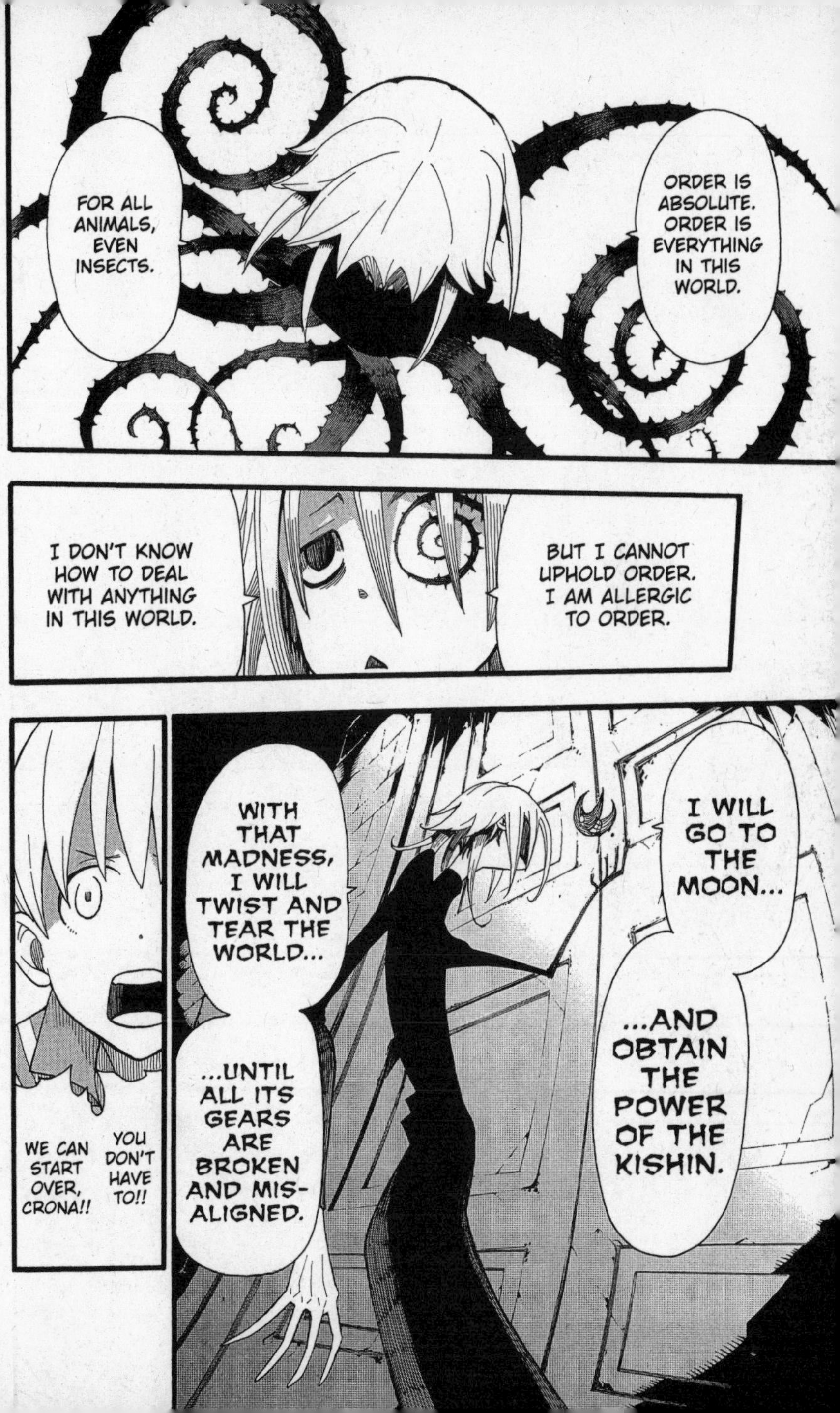
ORDER IS ABSOLUTE. ORDER IS EVERYTHING IN THIS WORLD.
FOR ALL ANIMALS, EVEN INSECTS.
BUT I CANNOT UPHOLD ORDER. I AM ALLERGIC TO ORDER.
I DON'T KNOW HOW TO DEAL WITH ANYTHING IN THIS WORLD.
I WILL GO TO THE MOON...
...AND OBTAIN THE POWER OF THE KISHIN.
WITH THAT MADNESS, I WILL TWIST AND TEAR THE WORLD...
...UNTIL ALL ITS GEARS ARE BROKEN AND MIS-ALIGNED.
YOU DON'T HAVE TO!!
WE CAN START OVER, CRONA!!

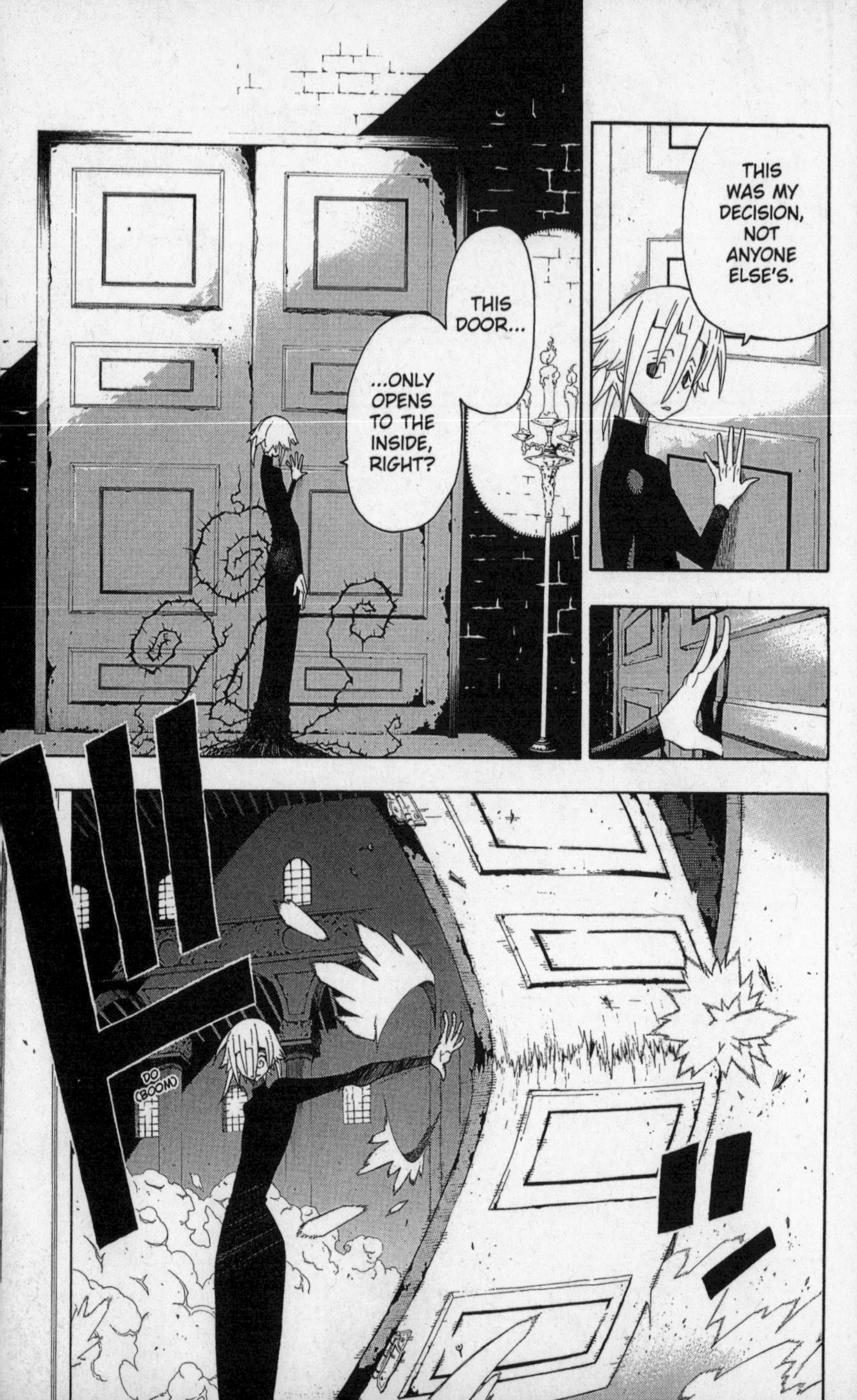
THIS WAS MY DECISION, NOT ANYONE ELSE'S.
THIS DOOR...
...ONLY OPENS TO THE INSIDE, RIGHT?
DO (BOOM)

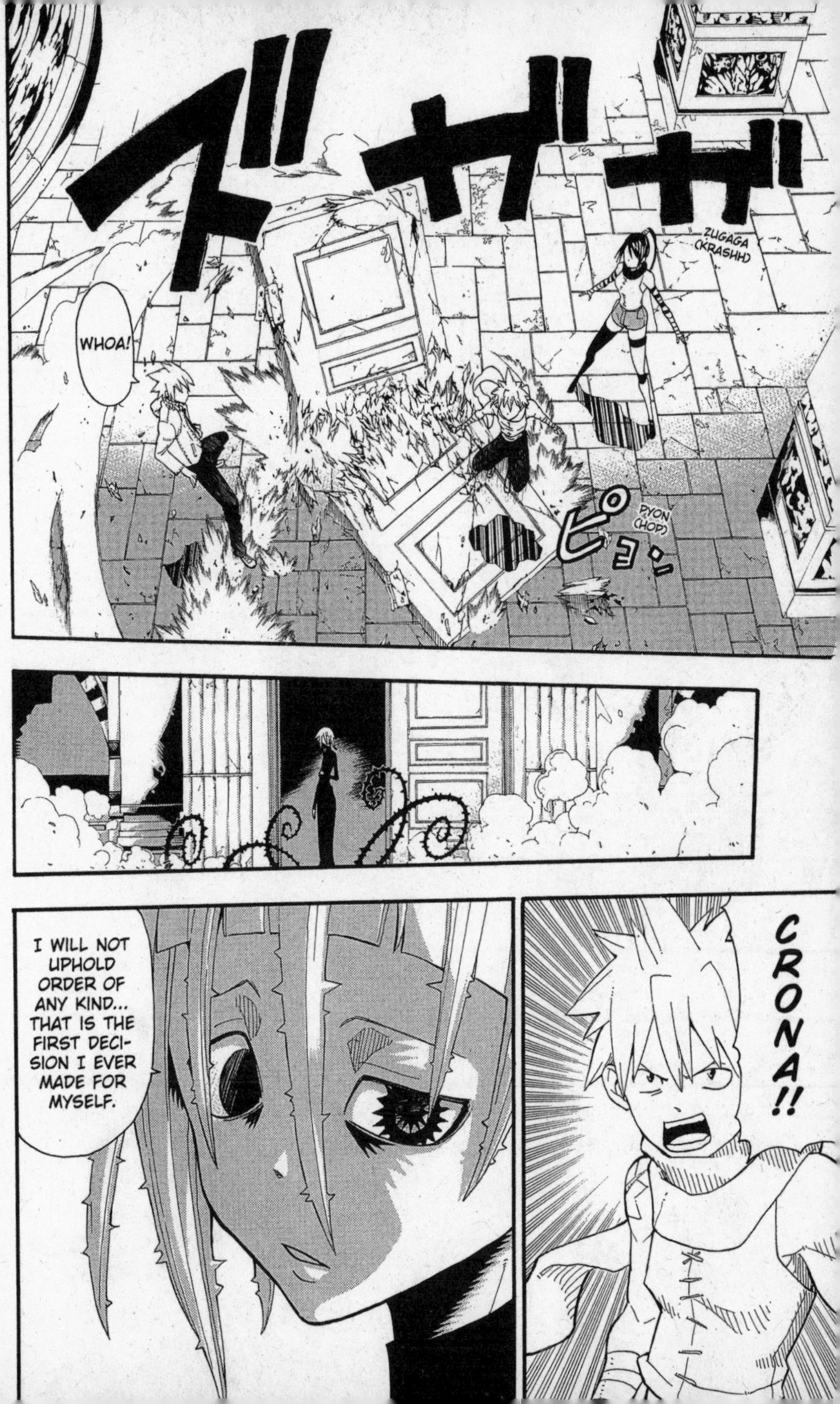
ズガガ
ZUGAGA (KRASHH)
WHOA!
ピョン
PYON (HOP)
CRONA!!
I WILL NOT UPHOLD ORDER OF ANY KIND... THAT IS THE FIRST DECISION I EVER MADE FOR MYSELF.

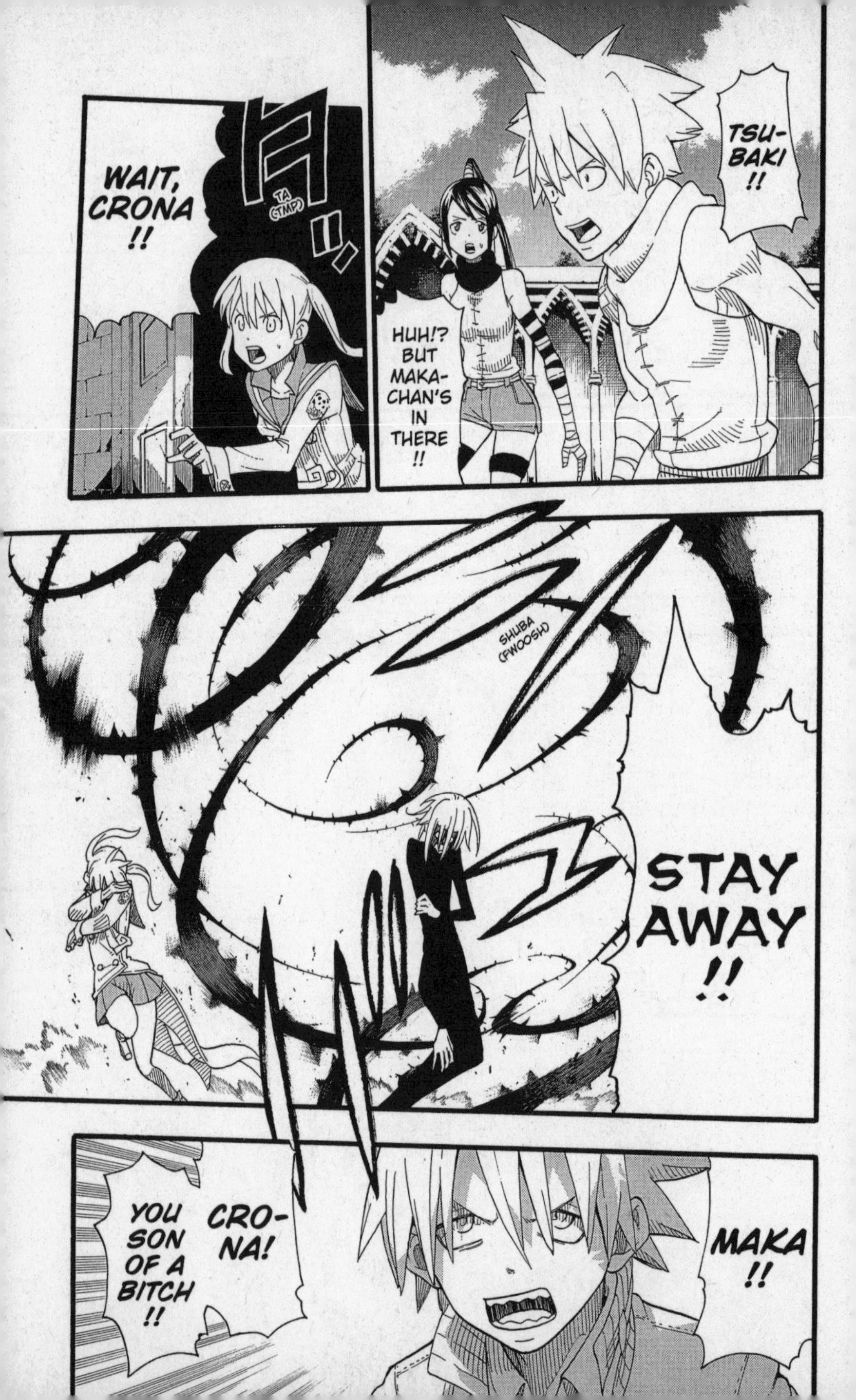
TSU-BAKI !!
HUH!? BUT MAKA-CHAN'S IN THERE !!
TA (TMP)
WAIT, CRONA !!
SHUBA (FWOOSH)
STAY AWAY !!
MAKA !!
CRO-NA!
YOU SON OF A BITCH !!

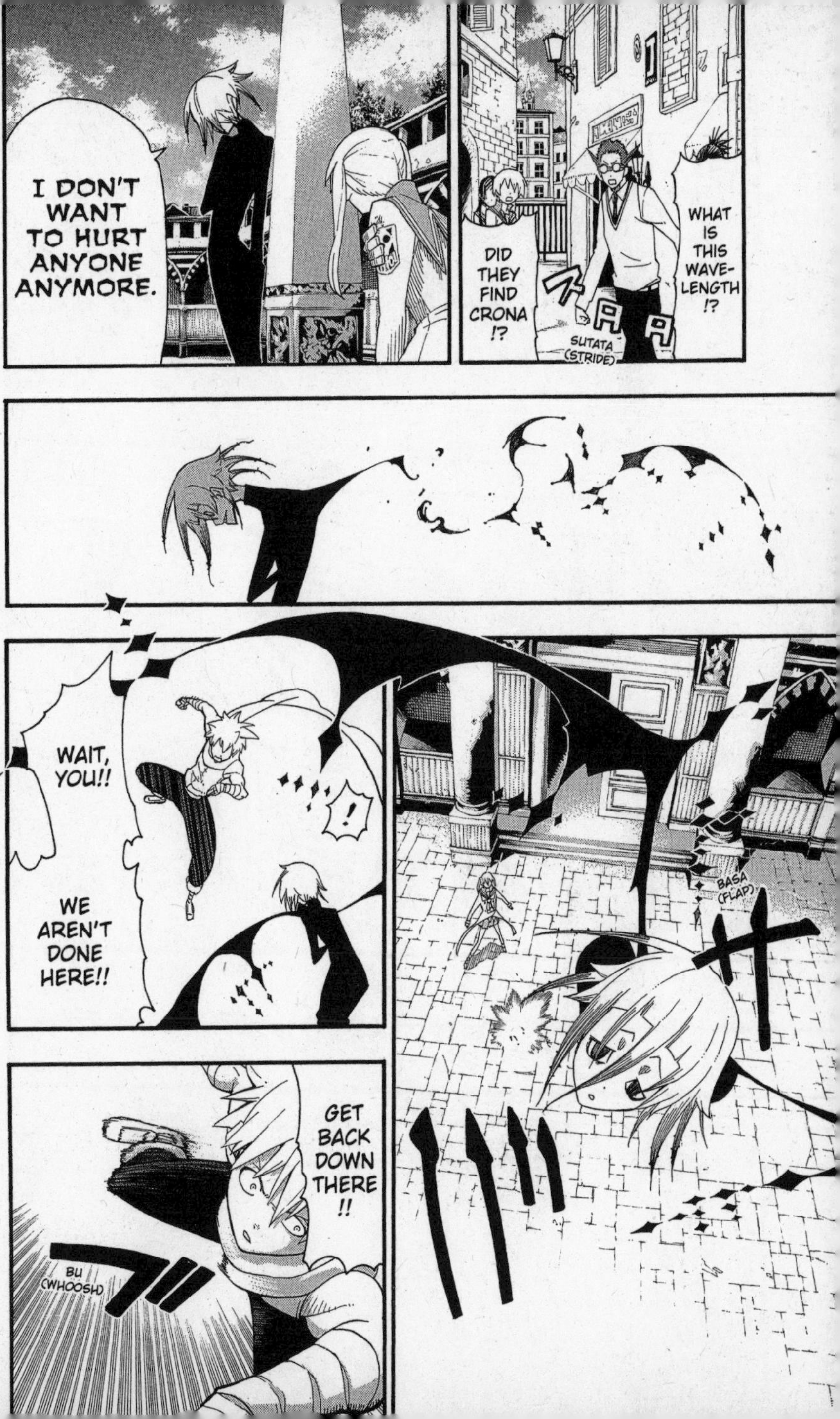
WHAT IS THIS WAVE-LENGTH!?
DID THEY FIND CRONA!?
SUTATA (STRIDE)
I DON'T WANT TO HURT ANYONE ANYMORE.
BASA (FLAP)
WAIT, YOU!!
WE AREN'T DONE HERE!!
!
GET BACK DOWN THERE!!
BU (WHOOSH)

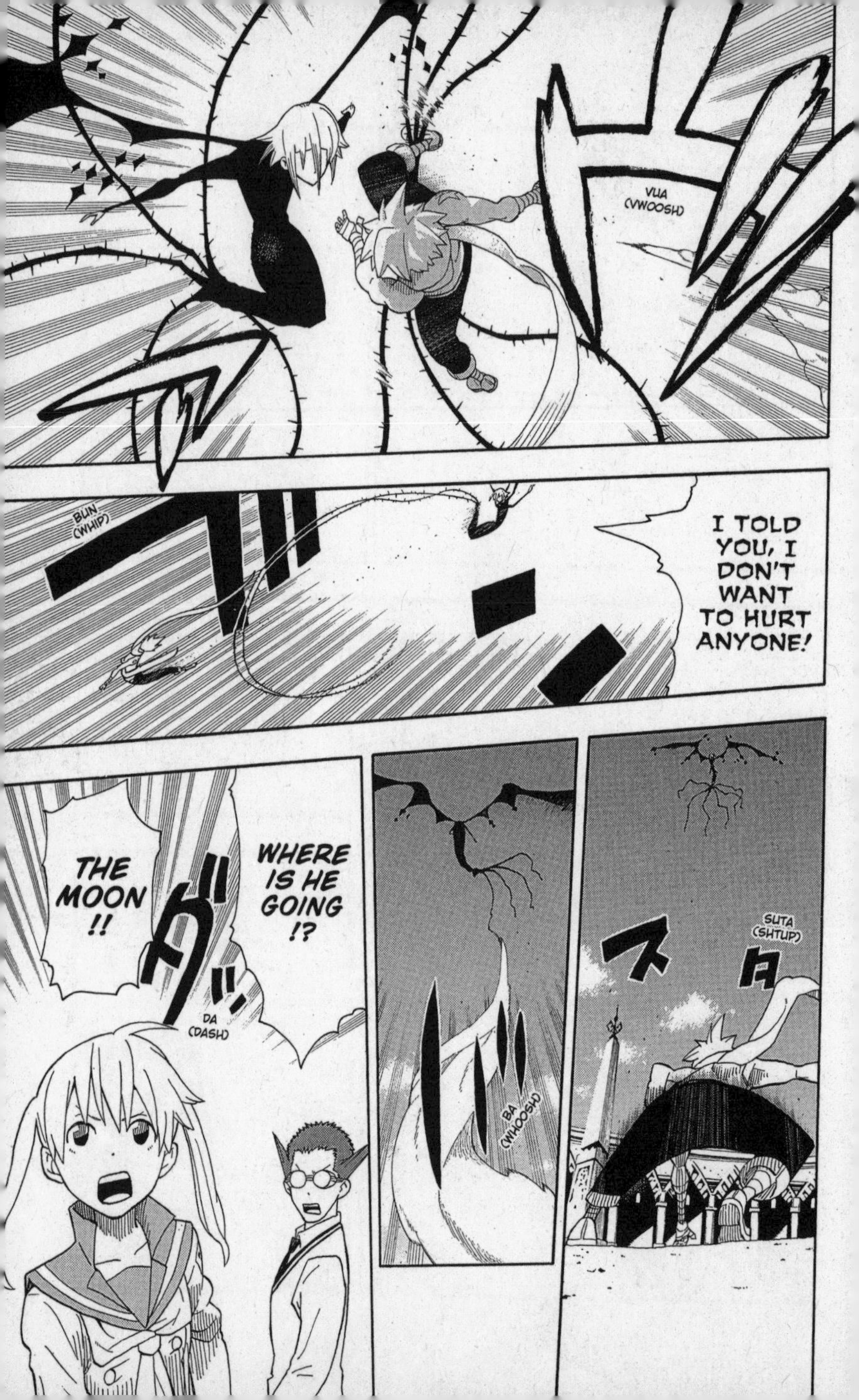
VUA (VWOOSH)
I TOLD YOU, I DON'T WANT TO HURT ANYONE!
BUN (WHIP)
SUTA (SHTUP)
BA (WHOOSH)
WHERE IS HE GOING !?
THE MOON !!
DA (DASH)

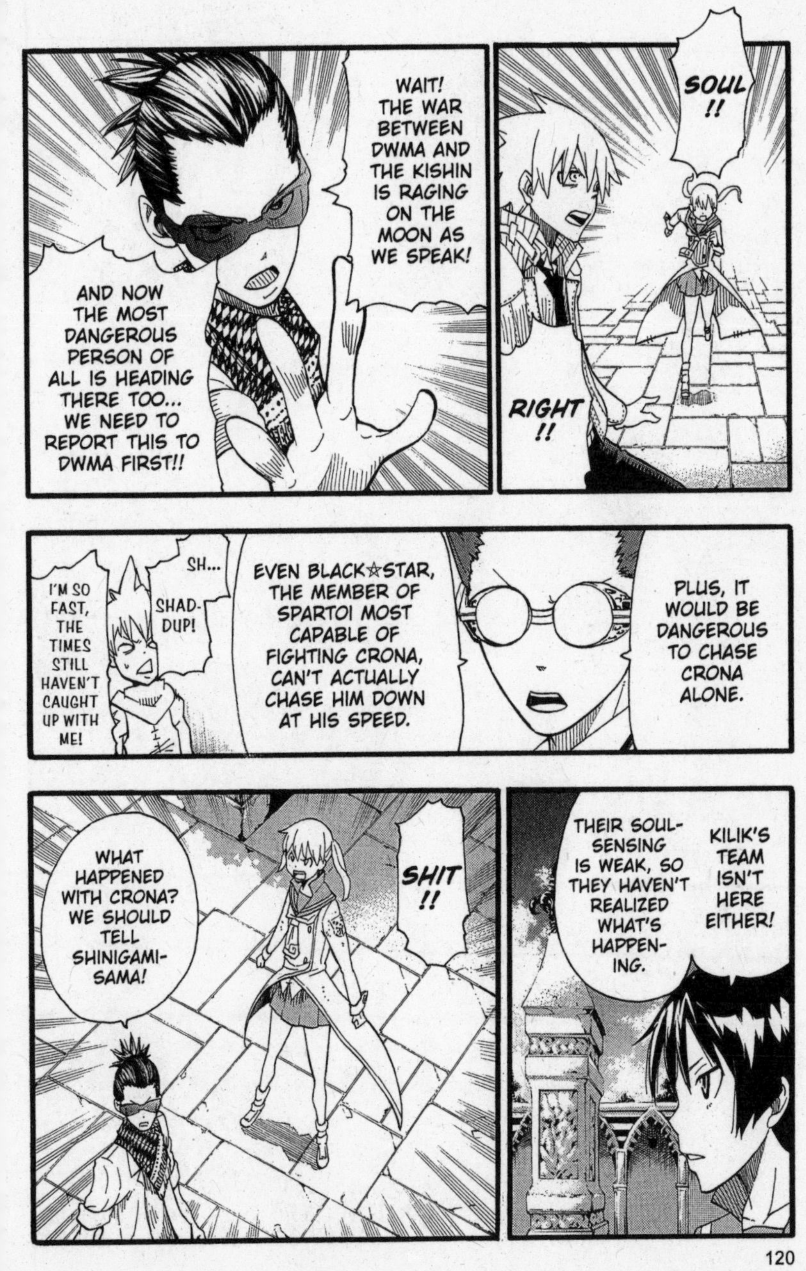
SOUL!!
RIGHT!!
WAIT! THE WAR BETWEEN DWMA AND THE KISHIN IS RAGING ON THE MOON AS WE SPEAK!
AND NOW THE MOST DANGEROUS PERSON OF ALL IS HEADING THERE TOO... WE NEED TO REPORT THIS TO DWMA FIRST!!
PLUS, IT WOULD BE DANGEROUS TO CHASE CRONA ALONE.
EVEN BLACK☆STAR, THE MEMBER OF SPARTOI MOST CAPABLE OF FIGHTING CRONA, CAN'T ACTUALLY CHASE HIM DOWN AT HIS SPEED.
SH...
SHAD-DUP!
I'M SO FAST, THE TIMES STILL HAVEN'T CAUGHT UP WITH ME!
KILIK'S TEAM ISN'T HERE EITHER!
THEIR SOUL-SENSING IS WEAK, SO THEY HAVEN'T REALIZED WHAT'S HAPPEN-ING.
SHIT!!
WHAT HAPPENED WITH CRONA? WE SHOULD TELL SHINIGAMI-SAMA!

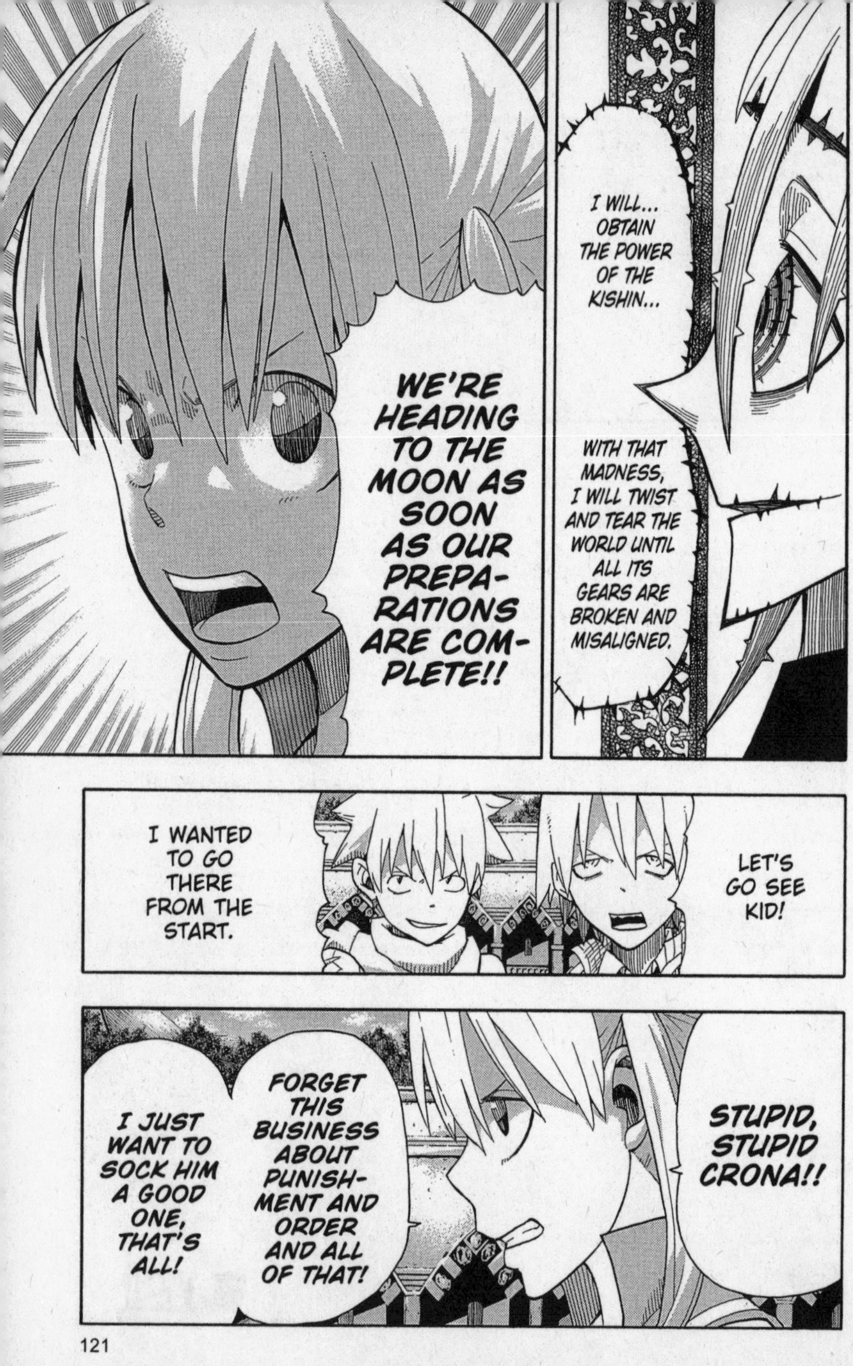
I WILL... OBTAIN THE POWER OF THE KISHIN...
WITH THAT MADNESS, I WILL TWIST AND TEAR THE WORLD UNTIL ALL ITS GEARS ARE BROKEN AND MISALIGNED.
WE'RE HEADING TO THE MOON AS SOON AS OUR PREPARATIONS ARE COMPLETE!!
LET'S GO SEE KID!
I WANTED TO GO THERE FROM THE START.
STUPID, STUPID CRONA!!
FORGET THIS BUSINESS ABOUT PUNISHMENT AND ORDER AND ALL OF THAT!
I JUST WANT TO SOCK HIM A GOOD ONE, THAT'S ALL!

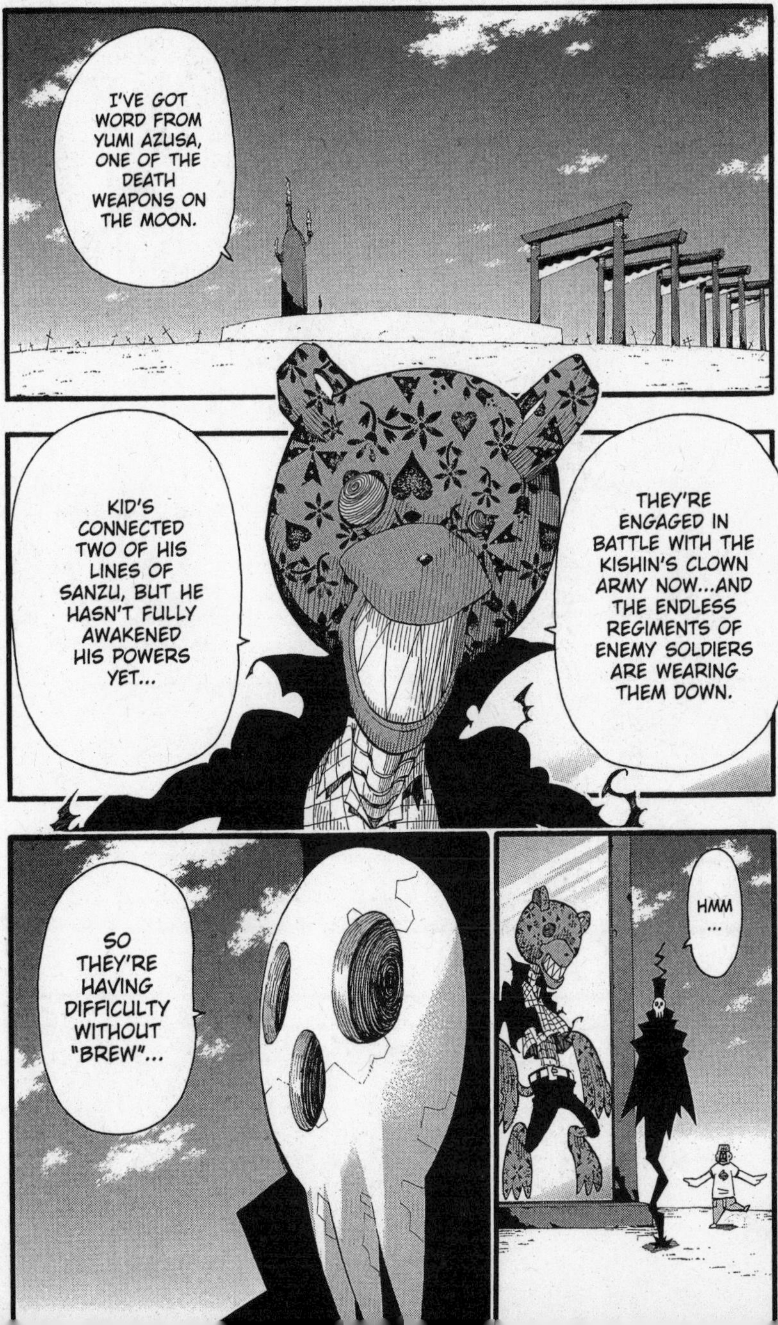
I'VE GOT WORD FROM YUMI AZUSA, ONE OF THE DEATH WEAPONS ON THE MOON.
THEY'RE ENGAGED IN BATTLE WITH THE KISHIN'S CLOWN ARMY NOW...AND THE ENDLESS REGIMENTS OF ENEMY SOLDIERS ARE WEARING THEM DOWN.
KID'S CONNECTED TWO OF HIS LINES OF SANZU, BUT HE HASN'T FULLY AWAKENED HIS POWERS YET...
HMM ...
SO THEY'RE HAVING DIFFICULTY WITHOUT "BREW"...

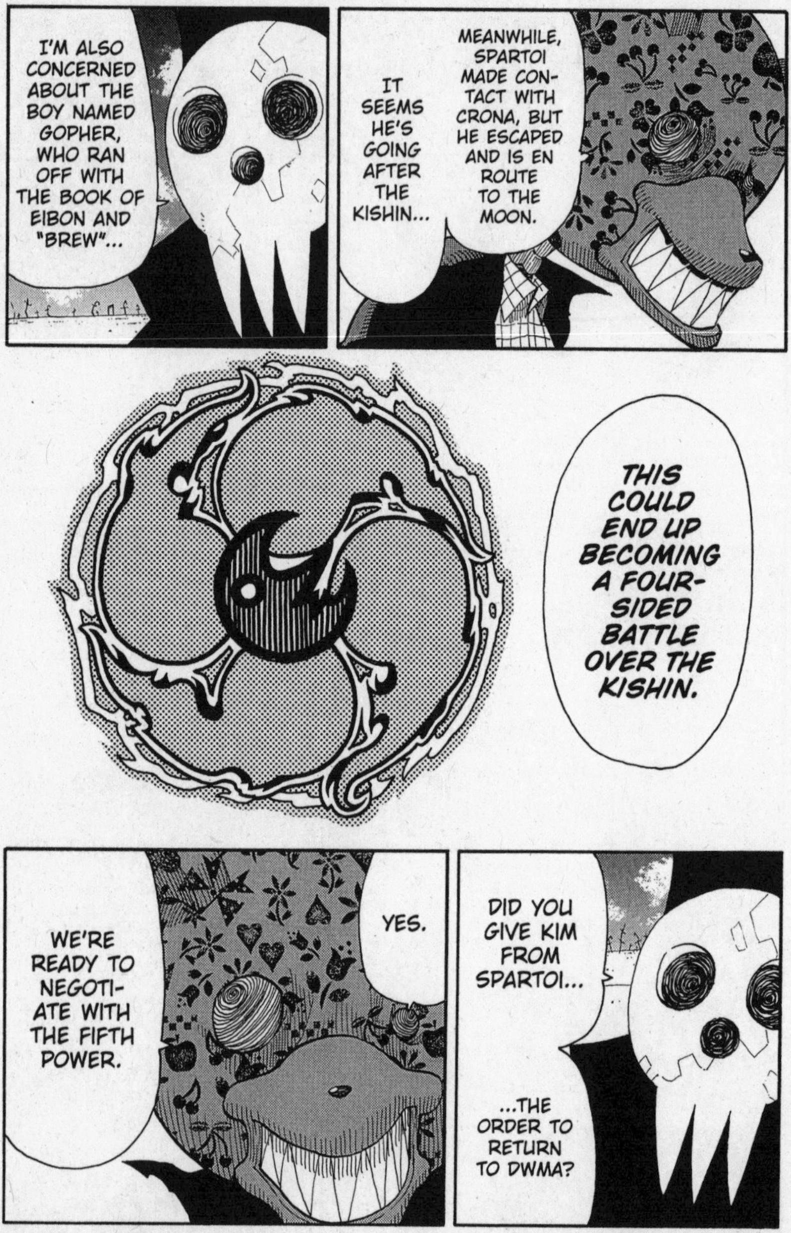
MEANWHILE, SPARTOI MADE CONTACT WITH CRONA, BUT HE ESCAPED AND IS EN ROUTE TO THE MOON.
IT SEEMS HE'S GOING AFTER THE KISHIN...
I'M ALSO CONCERNED ABOUT THE BOY NAMED GOPHER, WHO RAN OFF WITH THE BOOK OF EIBON AND "BREW"...
THIS COULD END UP BECOMING A FOUR-SIDED BATTLE OVER THE KISHIN.
DID YOU GIVE KIM FROM SPARTOI...
...THE ORDER TO RETURN TO DWMA?
YES.
WE'RE READY TO NEGOTIATE WITH THE FIFTH POWER.

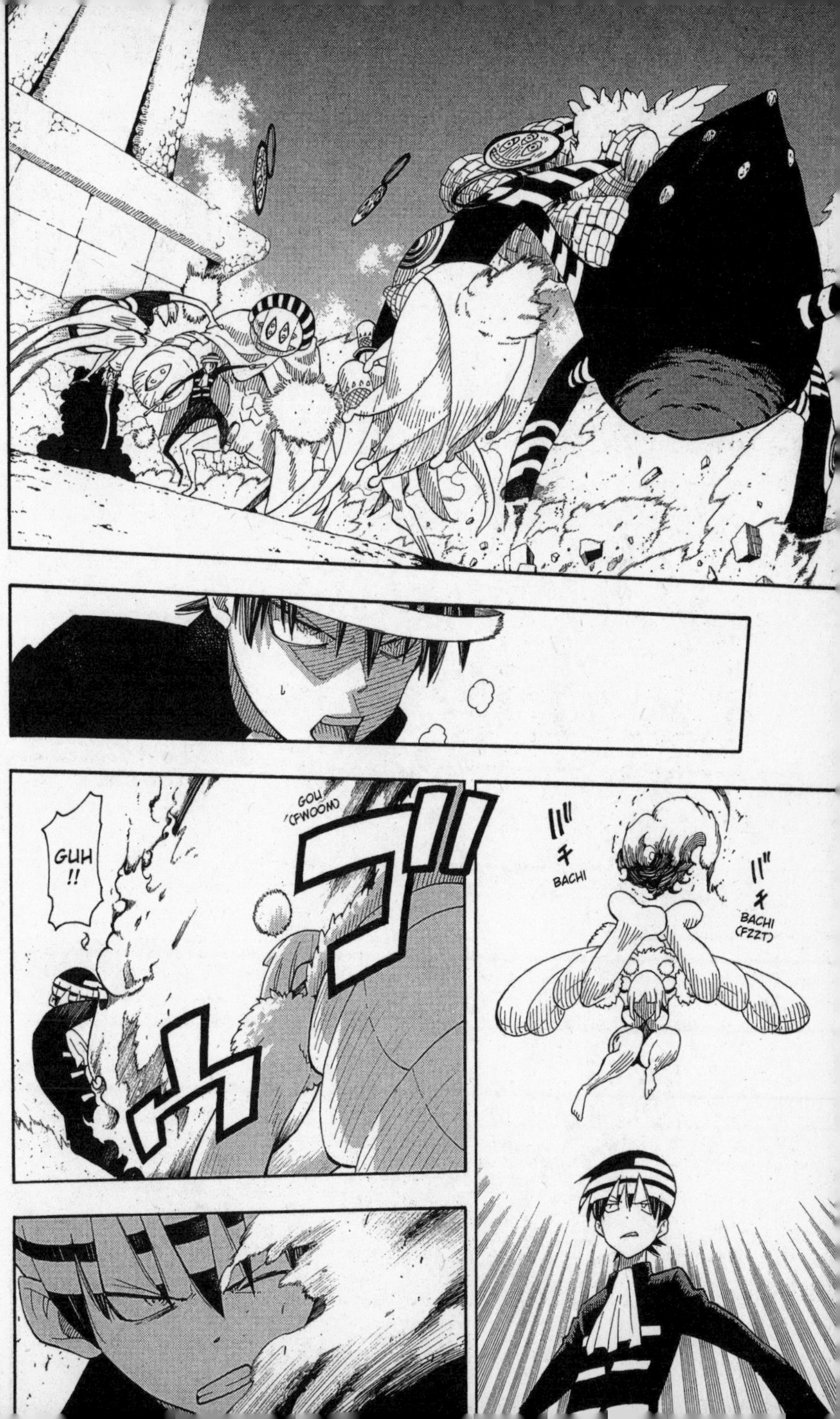
BACHI
BACHI (FZZT)
GOU (FWOOM)
GUH !!

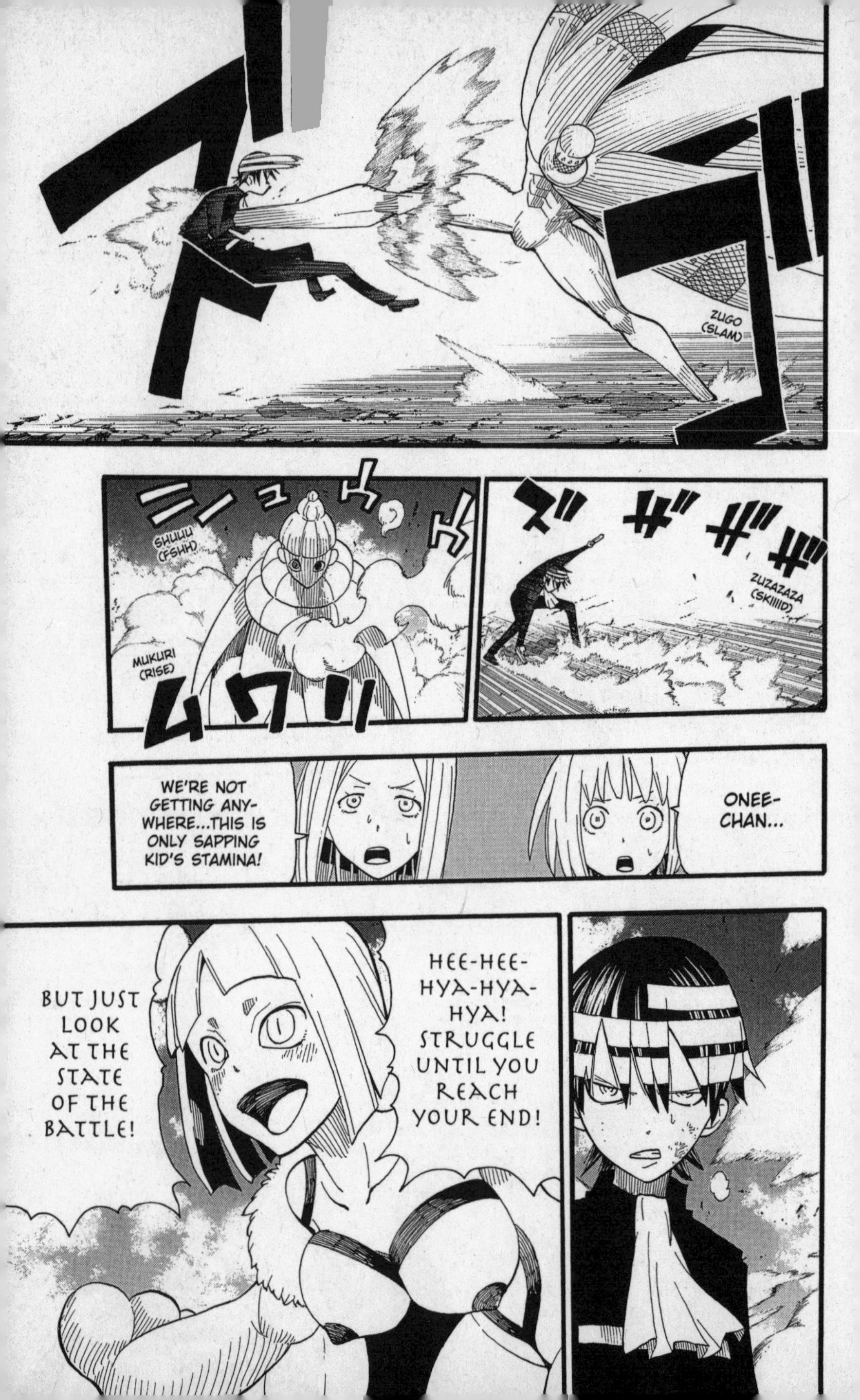

ZUGO
(SLAM)
ZUZAZAZA
(SKIIIID)
SHUUU
(FSHH)
MUKURI
(RISE)
ONEE-CHAN...
WE'RE NOT GETTING ANYWHERE...THIS IS ONLY SAPPING KID'S STAMINA!
HEE-HEE-HYA-HYA-HYA! STRUGGLE UNTIL YOU REACH YOUR END!
BUT JUST LOOK AT THE STATE OF THE BATTLE!

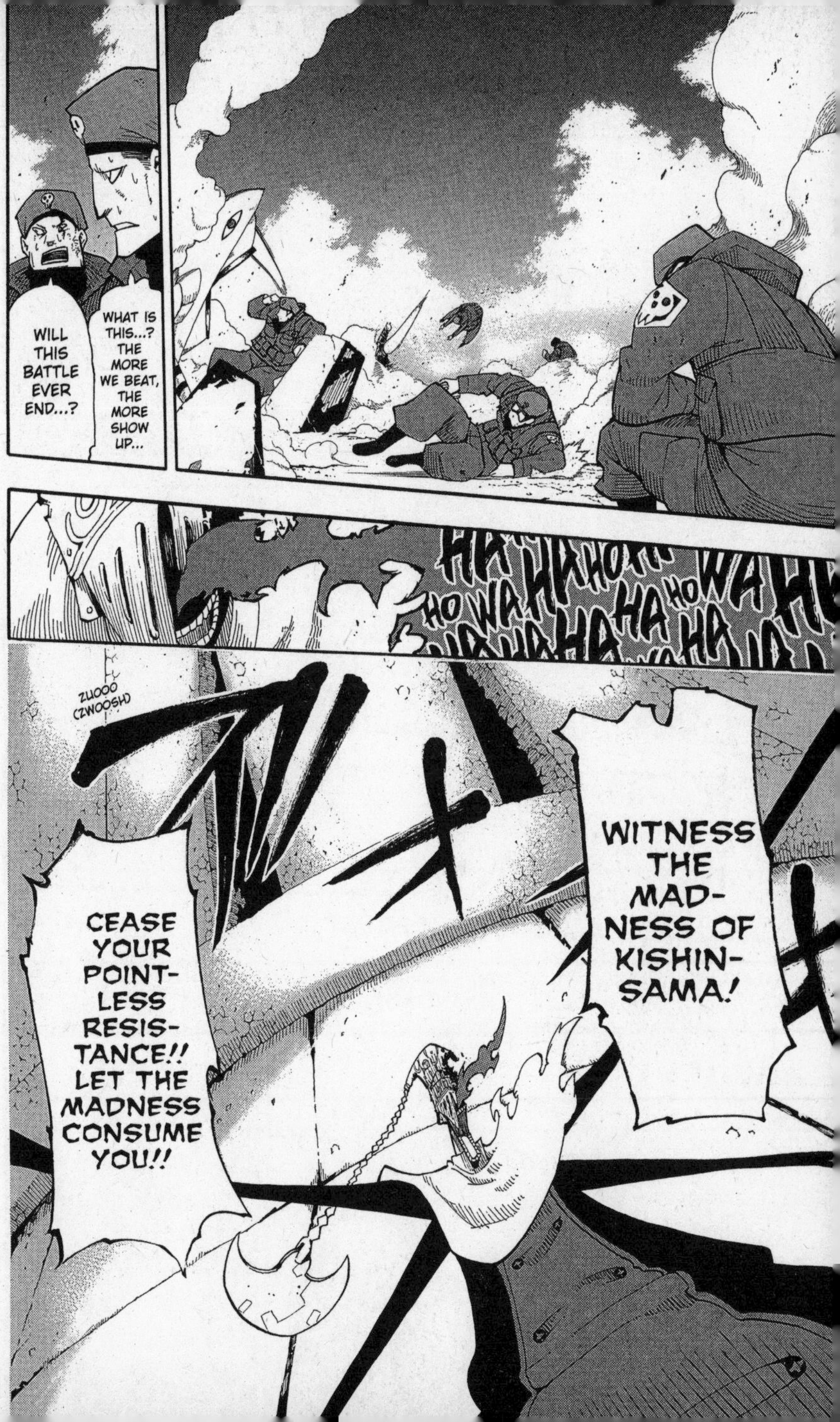
WHAT IS THIS...? THE MORE WE BEAT, THE MORE SHOW UP...
WILL THIS BATTLE EVER END...?
ZUOOO (ZWOOSH)
WITNESS THE MAD-NESS OF KISHIN-SAMA!
CEASE YOUR POINT-LESS RESIS-TANCE!! LET THE MADNESS CONSUME YOU!!

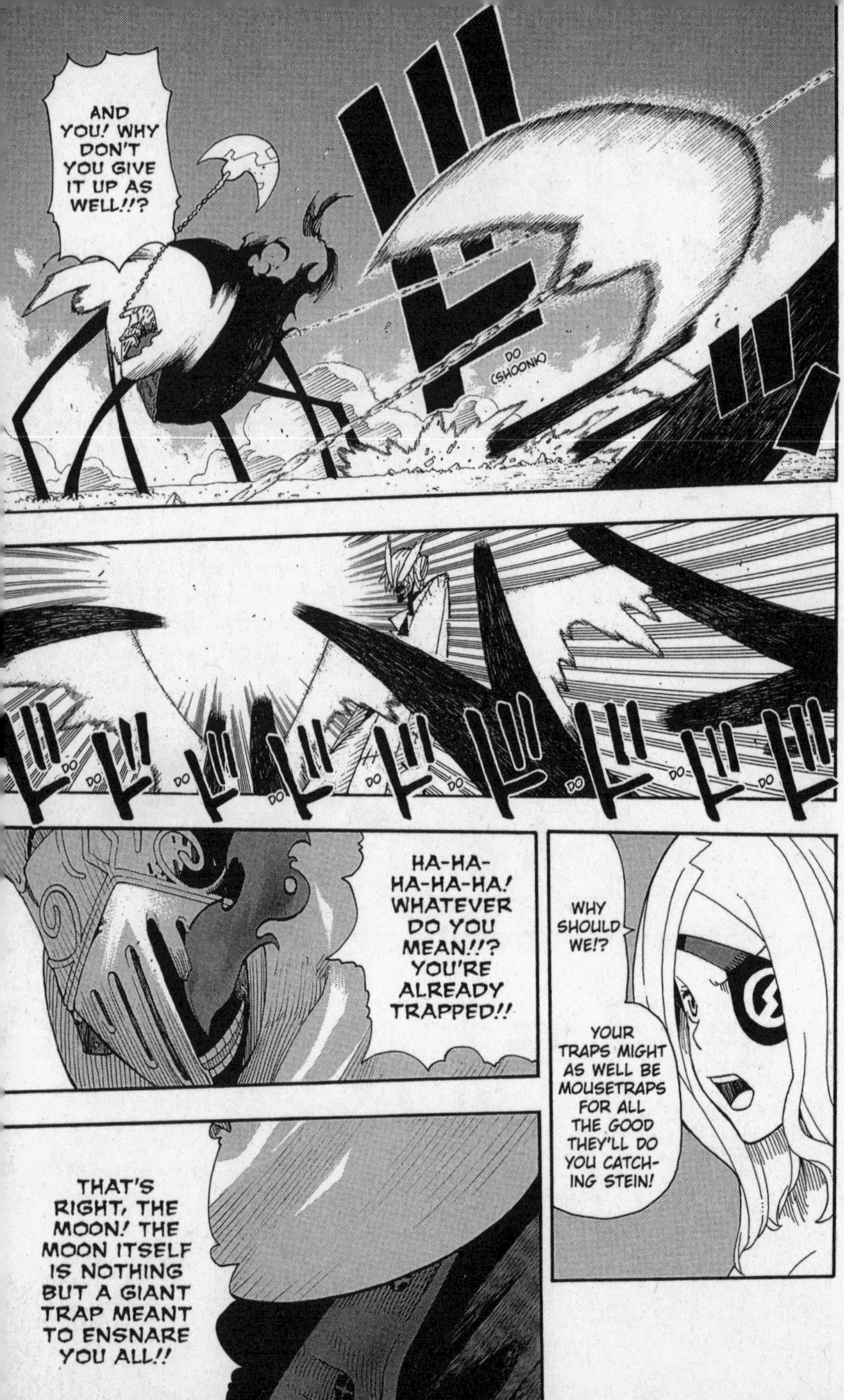
AND YOU! WHY DON'T YOU GIVE IT UP AS WELL!!?
DO (SHOONK)
DO DO DO DO DO DO DO DO
WHY SHOULD WE!?
YOUR TRAPS MIGHT AS WELL BE MOUSETRAPS FOR ALL THE GOOD THEY'LL DO YOU CATCH-ING STEIN!
HA-HA-HA-HA-HA! WHATEVER DO YOU MEAN!!? YOU'RE ALREADY TRAPPED!!
THAT'S RIGHT, THE MOON! THE MOON ITSELF IS NOTHING BUT A GIANT TRAP MEANT TO ENSNARE YOU ALL!!

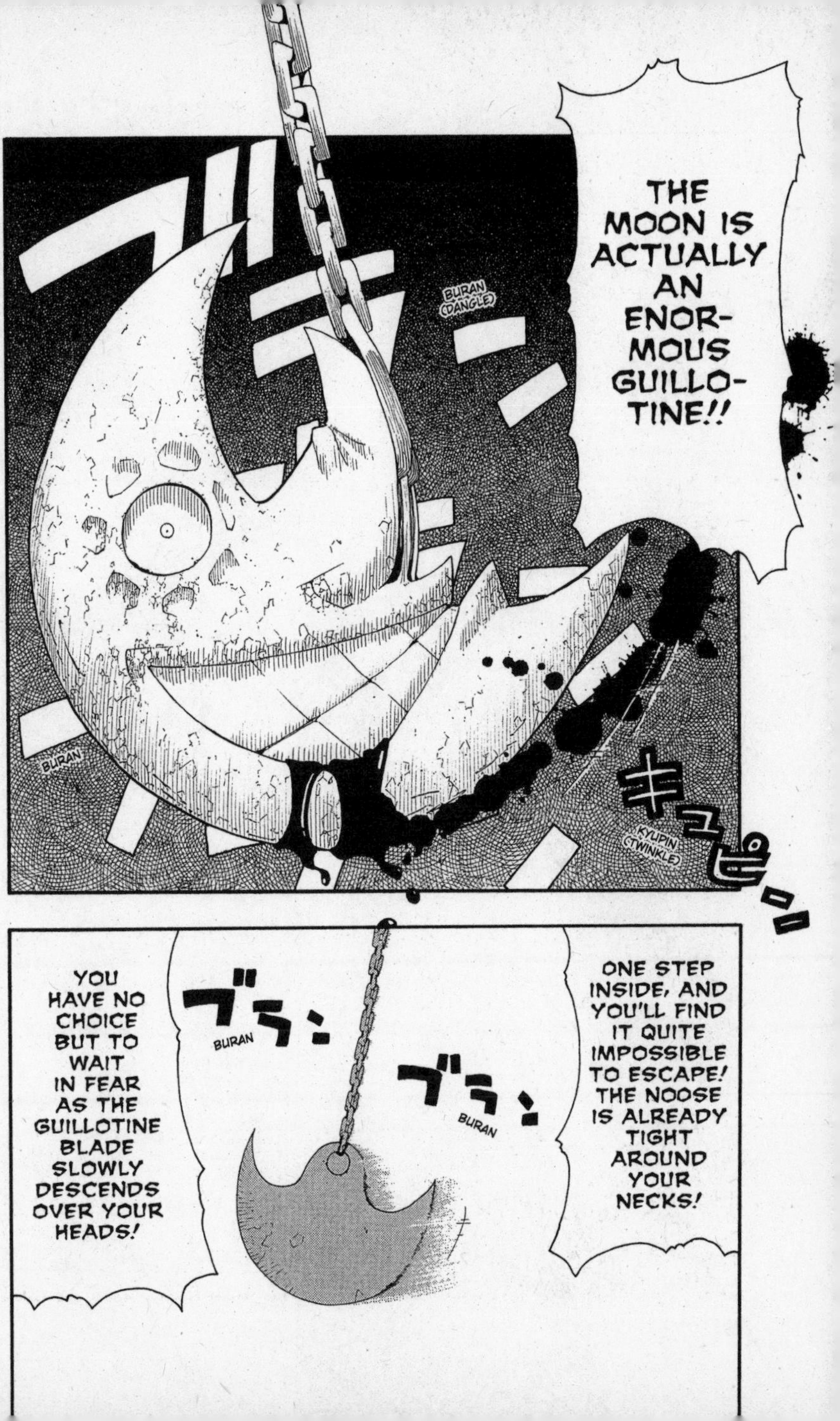
THE MOON IS ACTUALLY AN ENORMOUS GUILLOTINE!!
BURAN (DANGLE)
BURAN
KYUPIN (TWINKLE)
ONE STEP INSIDE, AND YOU'LL FIND IT QUITE IMPOSSIBLE TO ESCAPE! THE NOOSE IS ALREADY TIGHT AROUND YOUR NECKS!
BURAN
BURAN
YOU HAVE NO CHOICE BUT TO WAIT IN FEAR AS THE GUILLOTINE BLADE SLOWLY DESCENDS OVER YOUR HEADS!

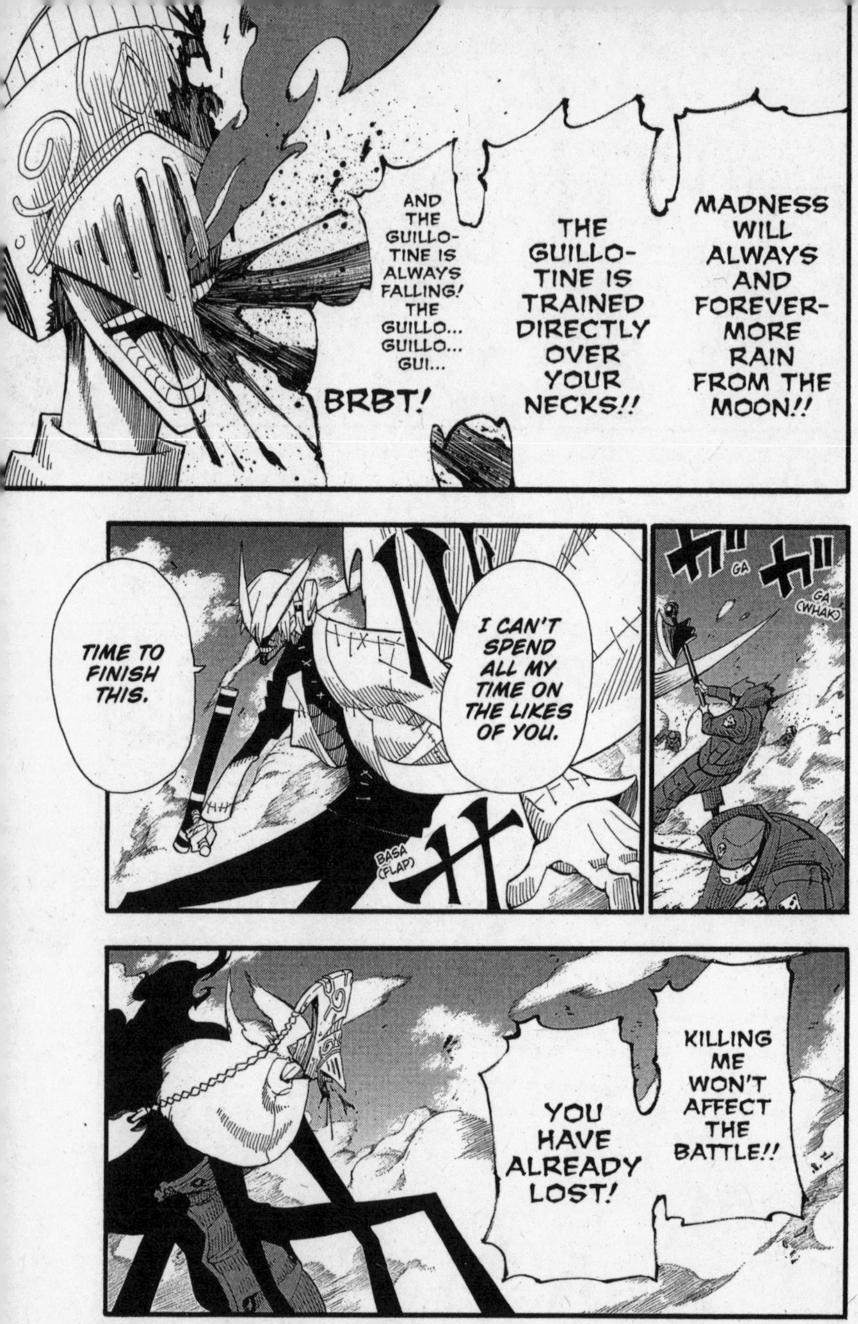
MADNESS WILL ALWAYS AND FOREVER-MORE RAIN FROM THE MOON!!
THE GUILLO-TINE IS TRAINED DIRECTLY OVER YOUR NECKS!!
AND THE GUILLO-TINE IS ALWAYS FALLING! THE GUILLO... GUILLO... GUI...
BRBT!
GA
GA (WHAK)
I CAN'T SPEND ALL MY TIME ON THE LIKES OF YOU.
TIME TO FINISH THIS.
BASA (FLAP)
KILLING ME WON'T AFFECT THE BATTLE!!
YOU HAVE ALREADY LOST!

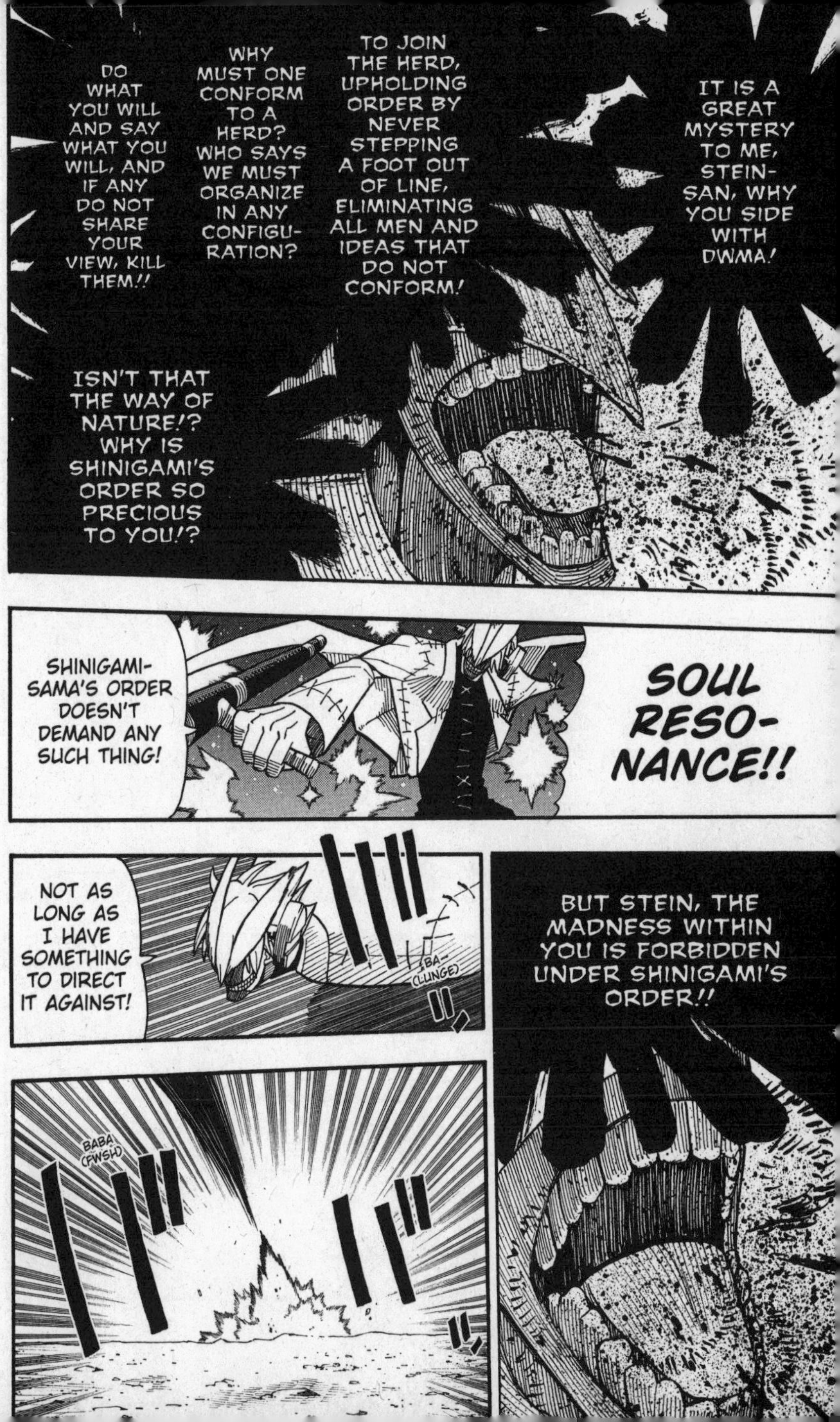
IT IS A GREAT MYSTERY TO ME, STEIN-SAN, WHY YOU SIDE WITH DWMA!
TO JOIN THE HERD, UPHOLDING ORDER BY NEVER STEPPING A FOOT OUT OF LINE, ELIMINATING ALL MEN AND IDEAS THAT DO NOT CONFORM!
WHY MUST ONE CONFORM TO A HERD? WHO SAYS WE MUST ORGANIZE IN ANY CONFIGU-RATION?
DO WHAT YOU WILL AND SAY WHAT YOU WILL, AND IF ANY DO NOT SHARE YOUR VIEW, KILL THEM!!
ISN'T THAT THE WAY OF NATURE!? WHY IS SHINIGAMI'S ORDER SO PRECIOUS TO YOU!?
SOUL RESO-NANCE!!
SHINIGAMI-SAMA'S ORDER DOESN'T DEMAND ANY SUCH THING!
BUT STEIN, THE MADNESS WITHIN YOU IS FORBIDDEN UNDER SHINIGAMI'S ORDER!!
NOT AS LONG AS I HAVE SOMETHING TO DIRECT IT AGAINST!
BA (LUNGE)
BABA (FWSH)

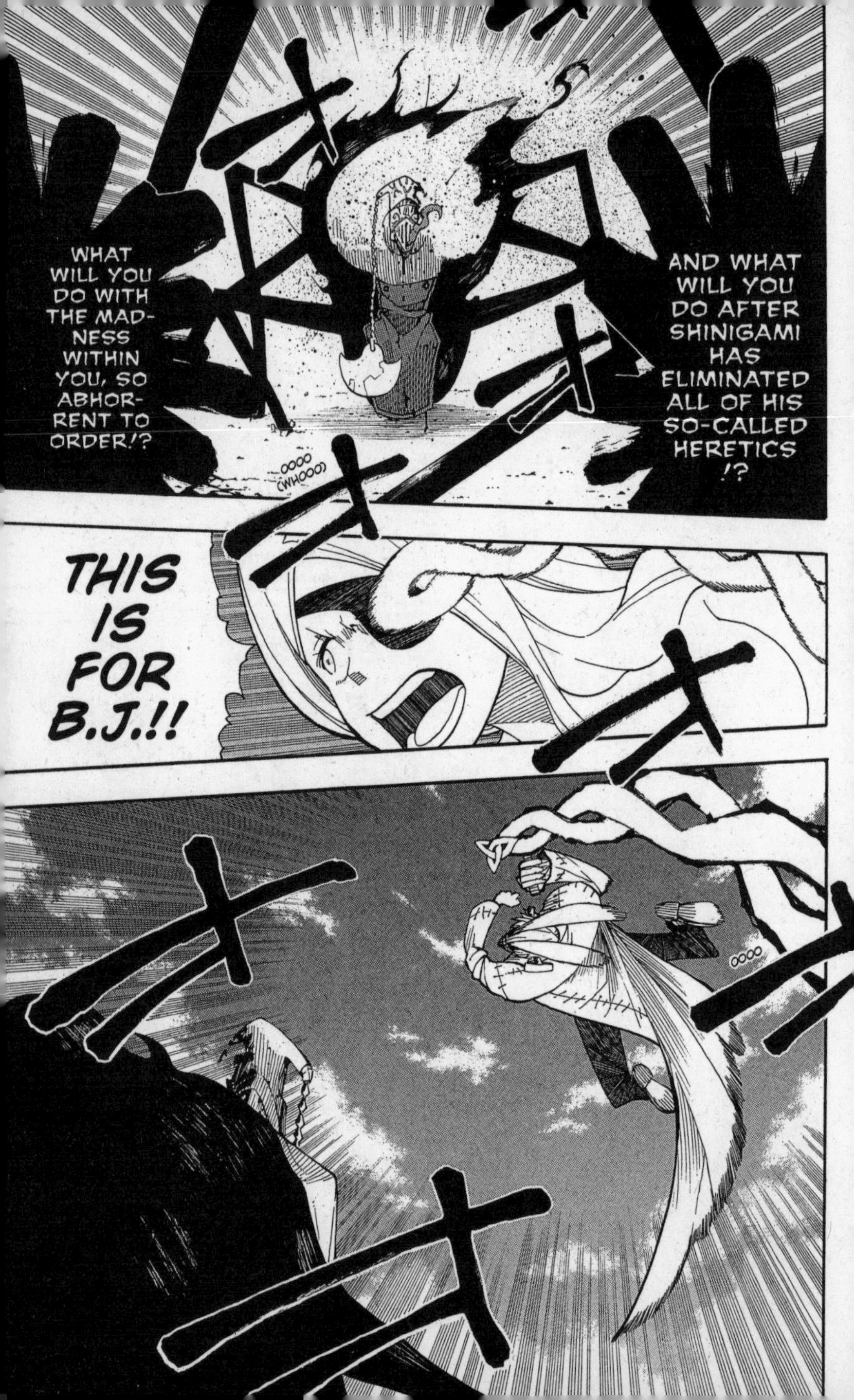
AND WHAT WILL YOU DO AFTER SHINIGAMI HAS ELIMINATED ALL OF HIS SO-CALLED HERETICS !?
WHAT WILL YOU DO WITH THE MADNESS WITHIN YOU, SO ABHORRENT TO ORDER!?
OOOO (WHOOO)
THIS IS FOR B.J.!!
OOOO

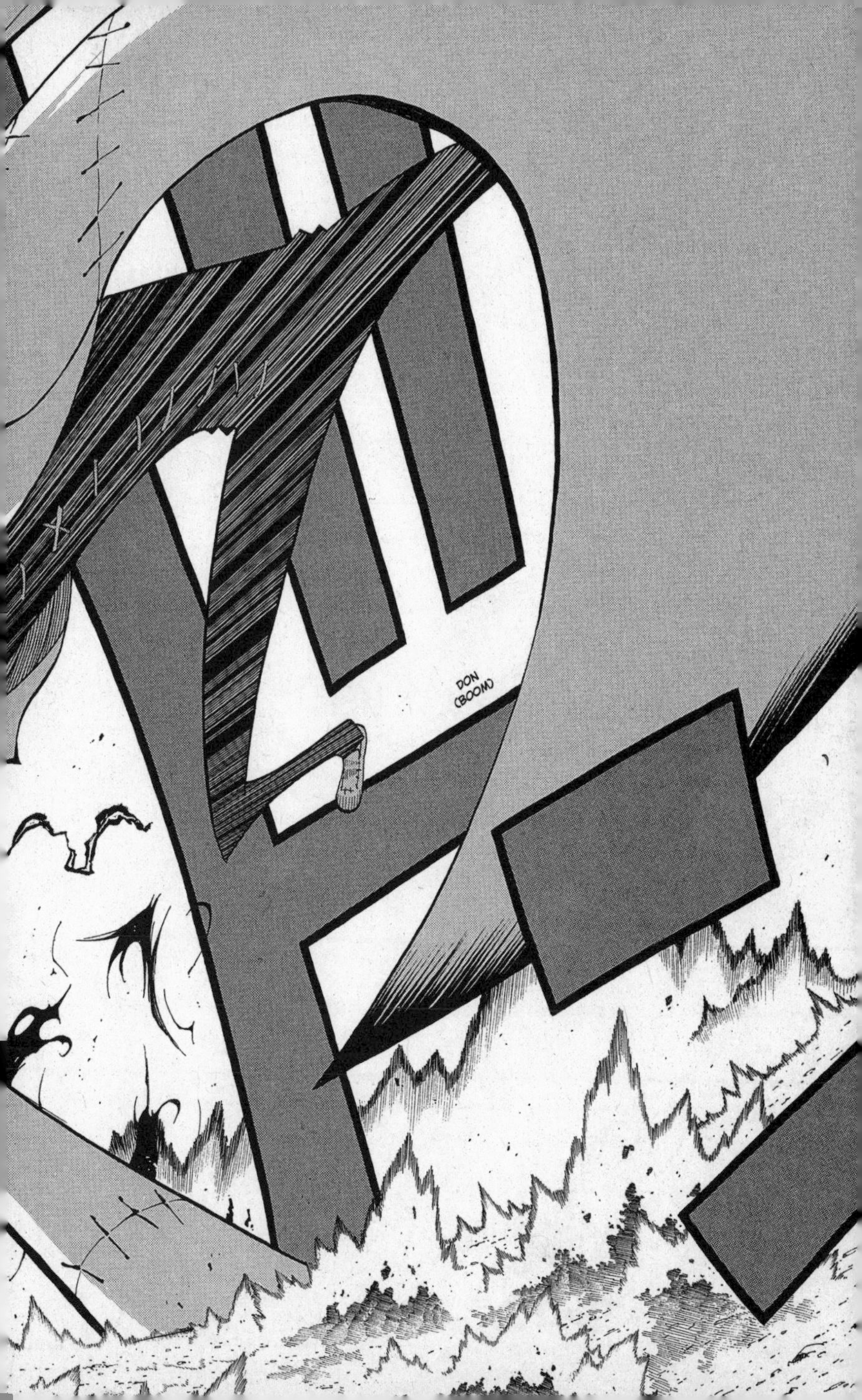
DON
(BOOM)

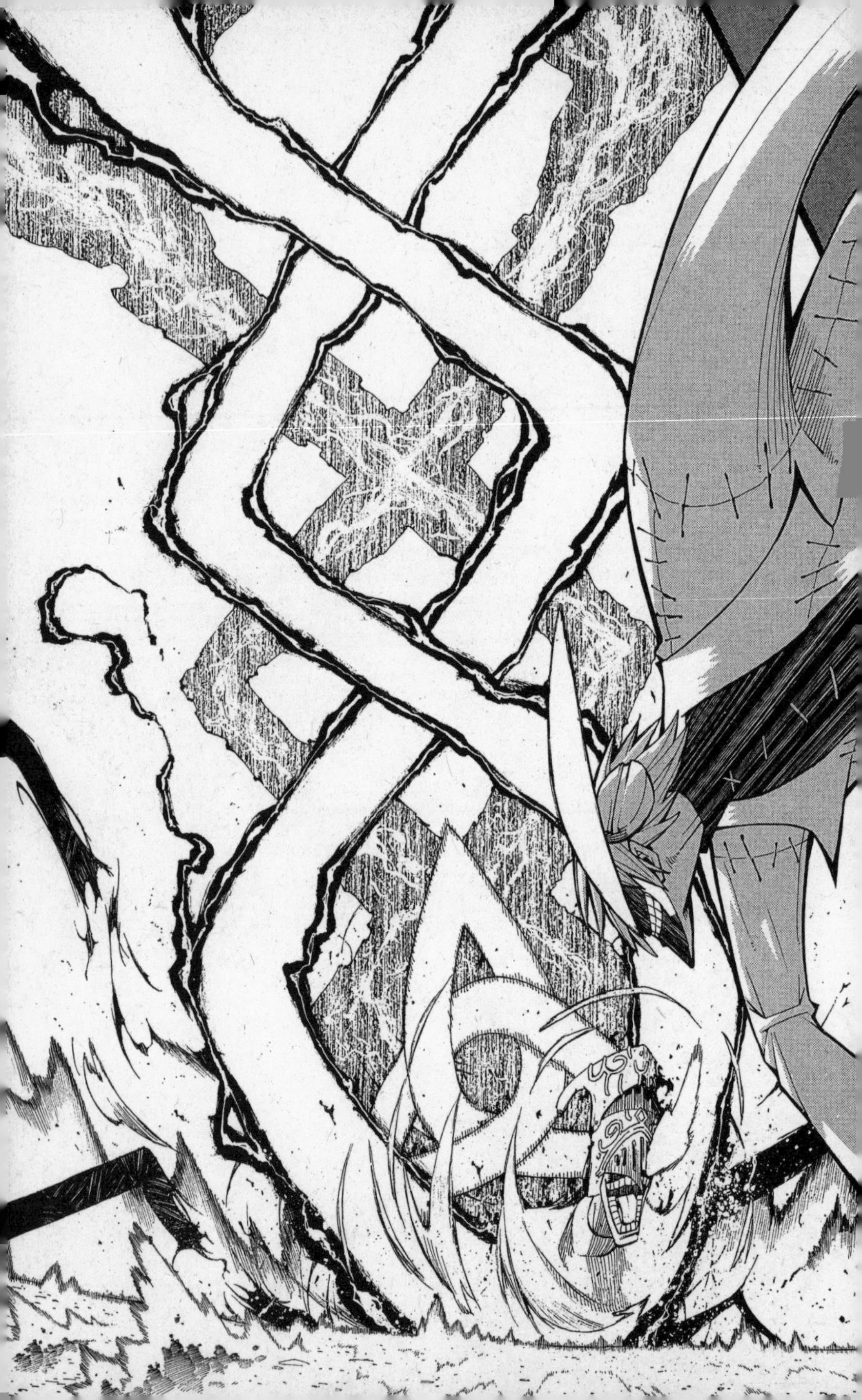

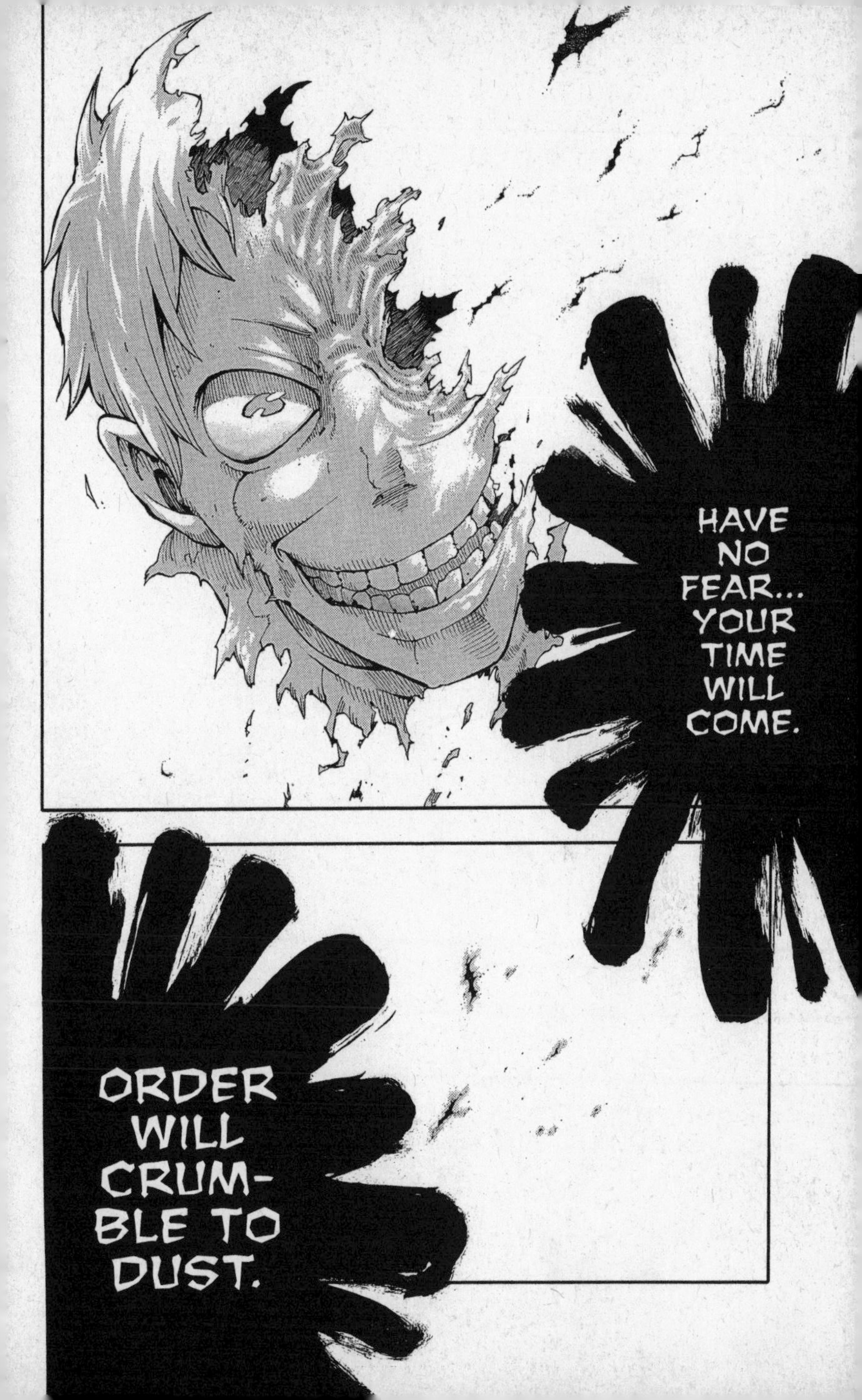
HAVE NO FEAR... YOUR TIME WILL COME.
ORDER WILL CRUMBLE TO DUST.

SOUL EATER

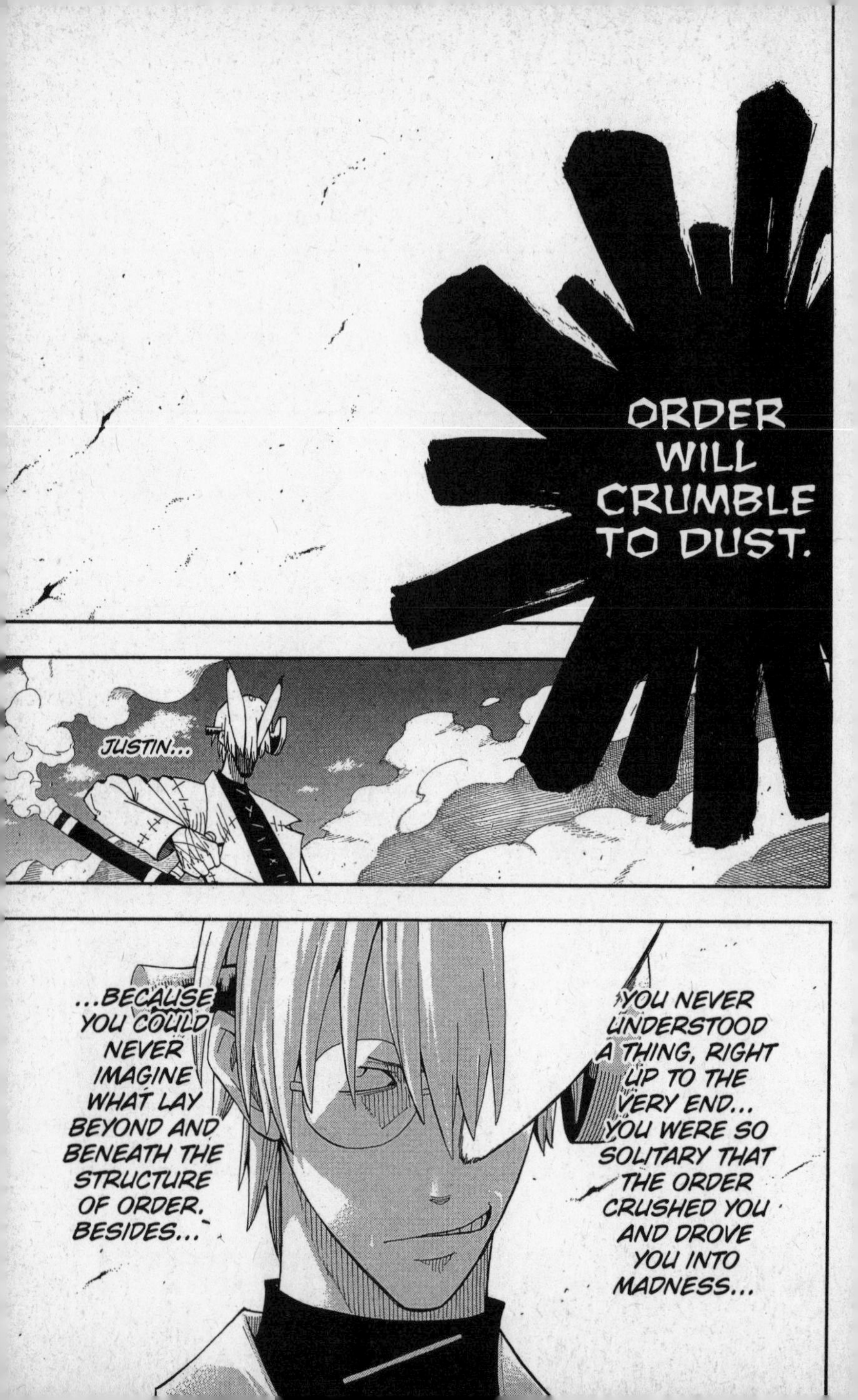

ORDER WILL CRUMBLE TO DUST.
JUSTIN...
YOU NEVER UNDERSTOOD A THING, RIGHT UP TO THE VERY END... YOU WERE SO SOLITARY THAT THE ORDER CRUSHED YOU AND DROVE YOU INTO MADNESS...
...BECAUSE YOU COULD NEVER IMAGINE WHAT LAY BEYOND AND BENEATH THE STRUCTURE OF ORDER. BESIDES...

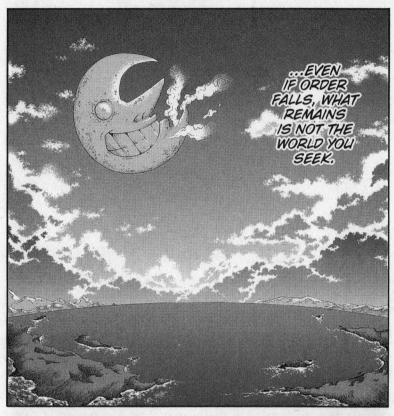

...EVEN IF ORDER FALLS, WHAT REMAINS IS NOT THE WORLD YOU SEEK.

SOUL EATER

CHAPTER 97: WAR ON THE MOON (PART 7)

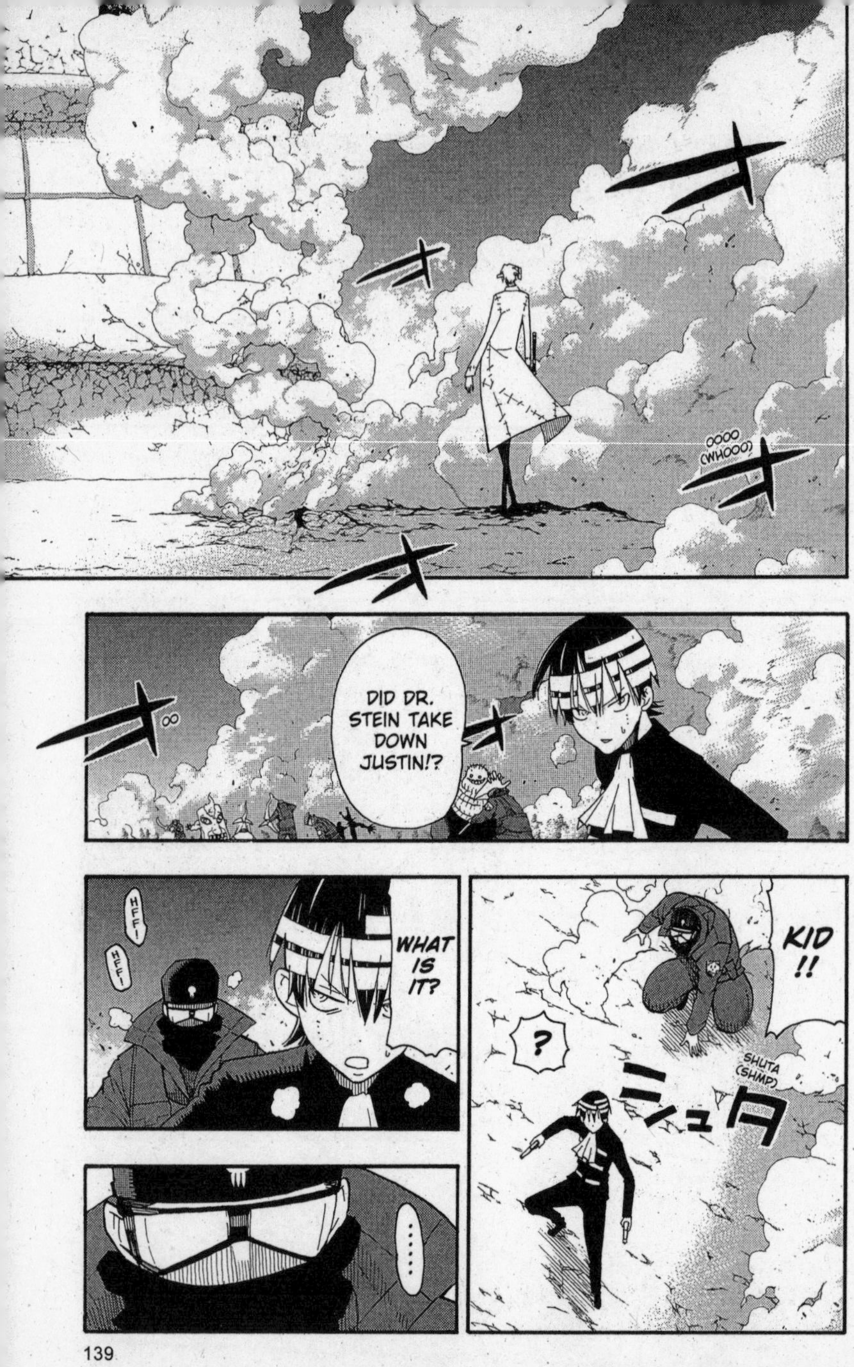
OOOO
(WHOOO)
DID DR. STEIN TAKE DOWN JUSTIN!?
KID !!
?
SHUTA
(SHMP)
WHAT IS IT?
HFF!
HFF!
......

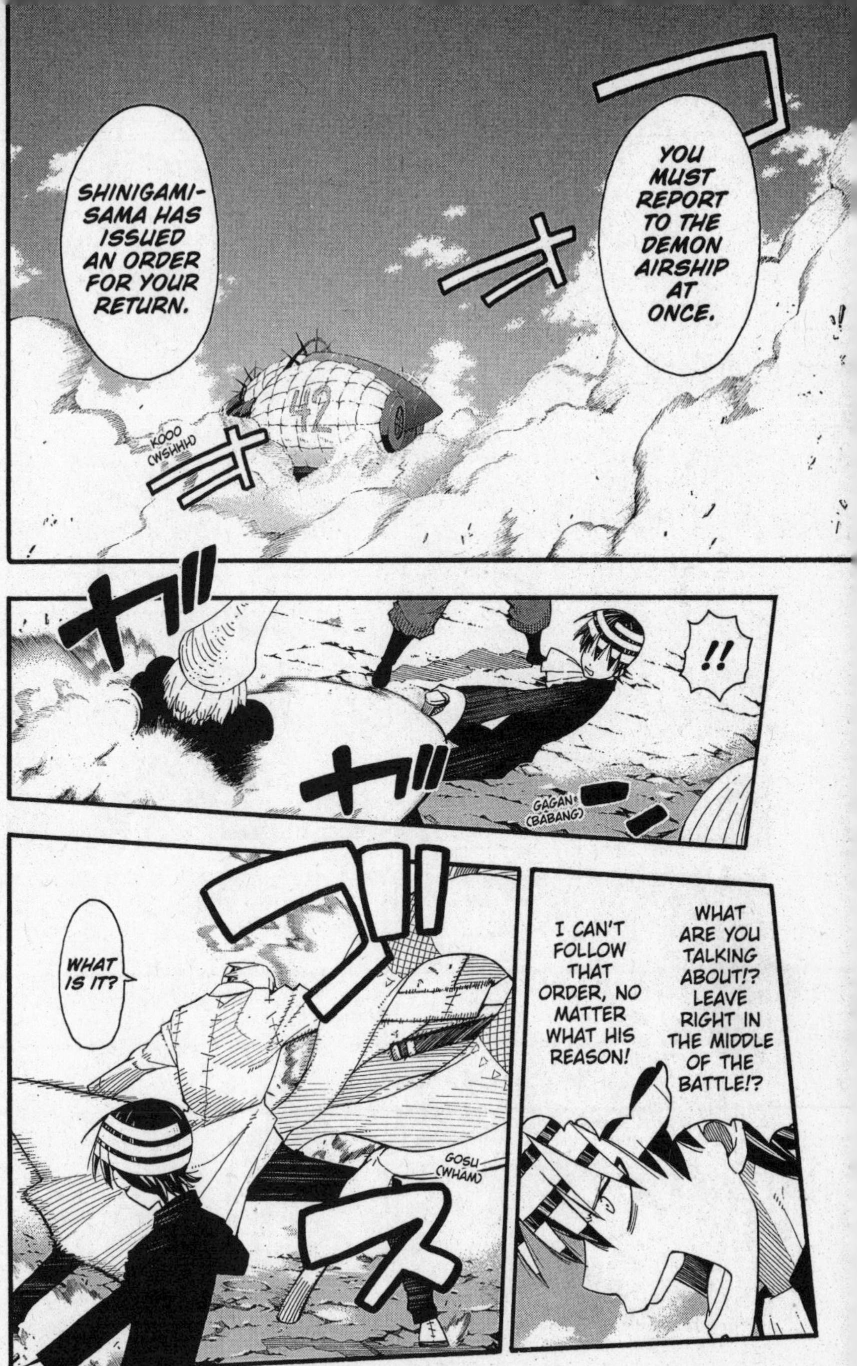
YOU MUST REPORT TO THE DEMON AIRSHIP AT ONCE.
SHINIGAMI-SAMA HAS ISSUED AN ORDER FOR YOUR RETURN.
KOOO (WSHHH)
!!
GAGAN (BABANG)
WHAT ARE YOU TALKING ABOUT!? LEAVE RIGHT IN THE MIDDLE OF THE BATTLE!?
I CAN'T FOLLOW THAT ORDER, NO MATTER WHAT HIS REASON!
WHAT IS IT?
GOSU (WHAM)

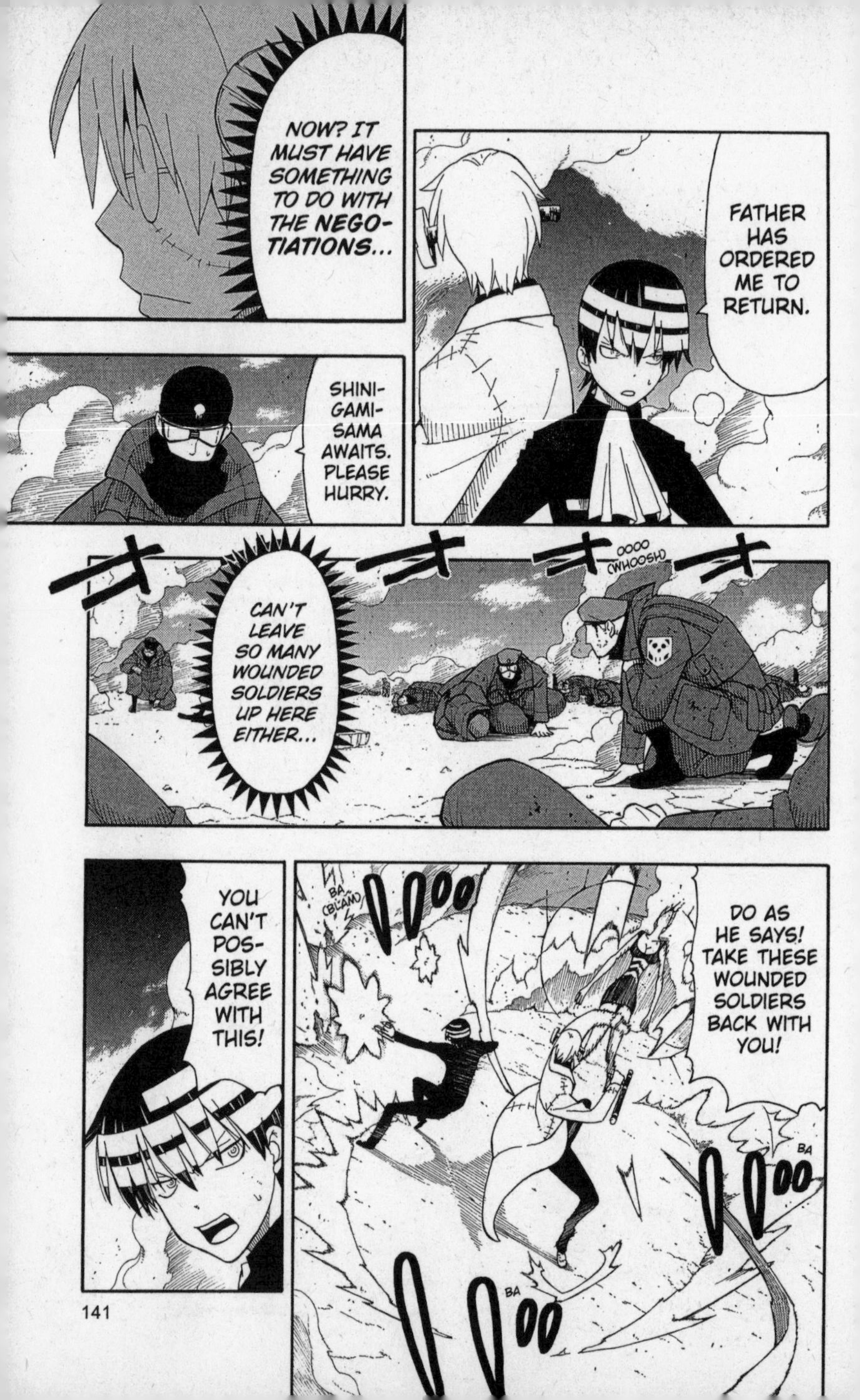
FATHER HAS ORDERED ME TO RETURN.
NOW? IT MUST HAVE SOMETHING TO DO WITH THE **NEGO-TIATIONS**...
SHINI-GAMI-SAMA AWAITS. PLEASE HURRY.
OOOO (WHOOSH)
CAN'T LEAVE SO MANY WOUNDED SOLDIERS UP HERE EITHER...
DO AS HE SAYS! TAKE THESE WOUNDED SOLDIERS BACK WITH YOU!
BA (BLAM)
BA
BA
YOU CAN'T POS-SIBLY AGREE WITH THIS!

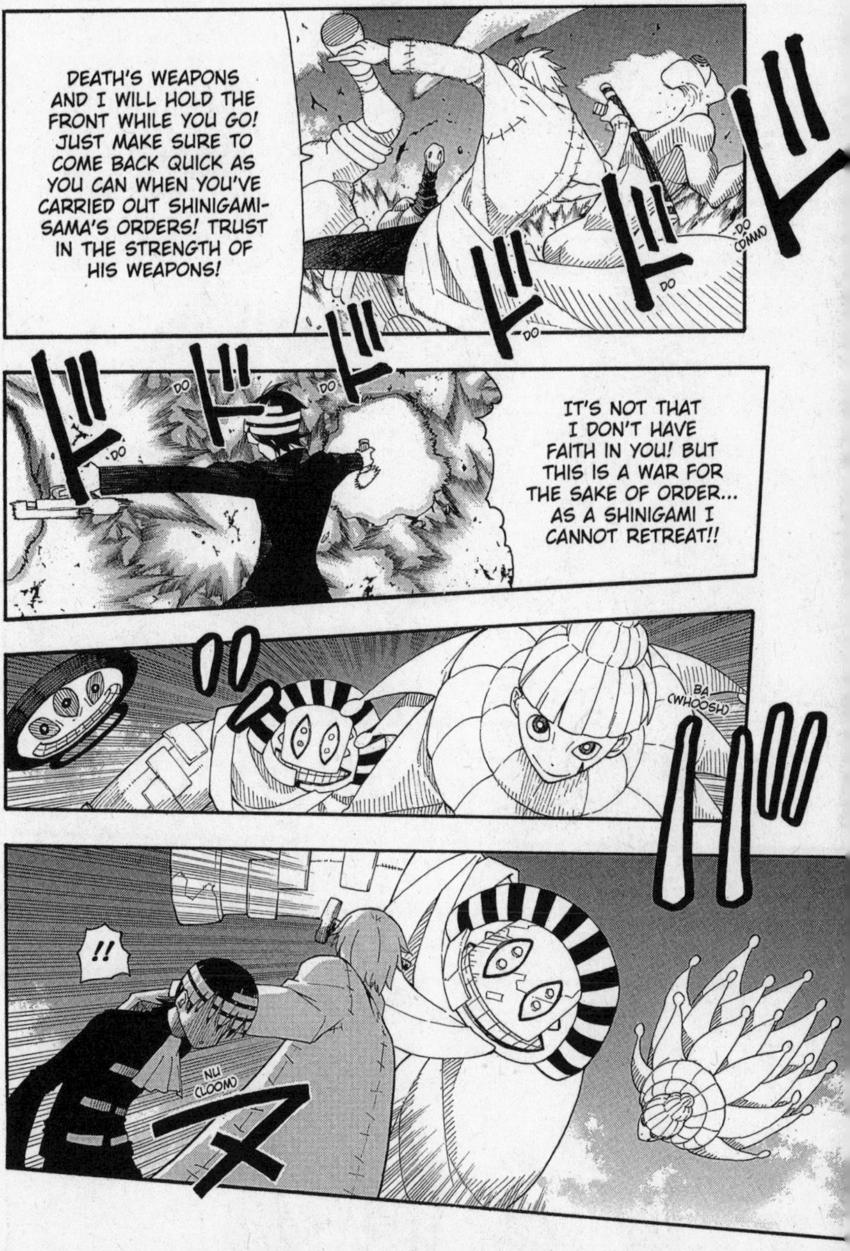
DO (DMM)
DO
DO
DEATH'S WEAPONS AND I WILL HOLD THE FRONT WHILE YOU GO! JUST MAKE SURE TO COME BACK QUICK AS YOU CAN WHEN YOU'VE CARRIED OUT SHINIGAMI-SAMA'S ORDERS! TRUST IN THE STRENGTH OF HIS WEAPONS!
IT'S NOT THAT I DON'T HAVE FAITH IN YOU! BUT THIS IS A WAR FOR THE SAKE OF ORDER... AS A SHINIGAMI I CANNOT RETREAT!!
DO
DO
DO
BA (WHOOSH)
!!
NU (LOOM)

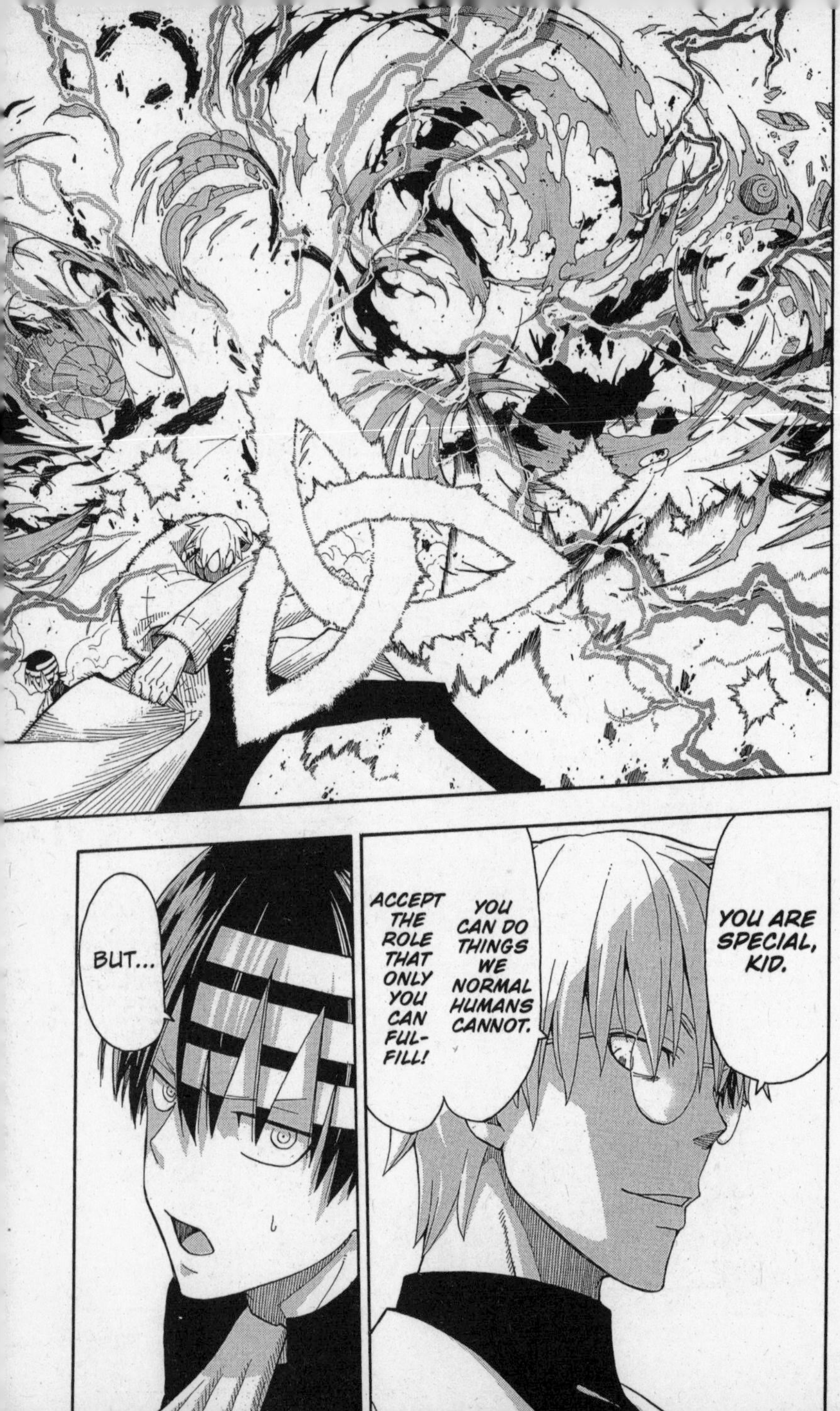
YOU ARE SPECIAL, KID.
YOU CAN DO THINGS WE NORMAL HUMANS CANNOT.
ACCEPT THE ROLE THAT ONLY YOU CAN FUL-FILL!
BUT...

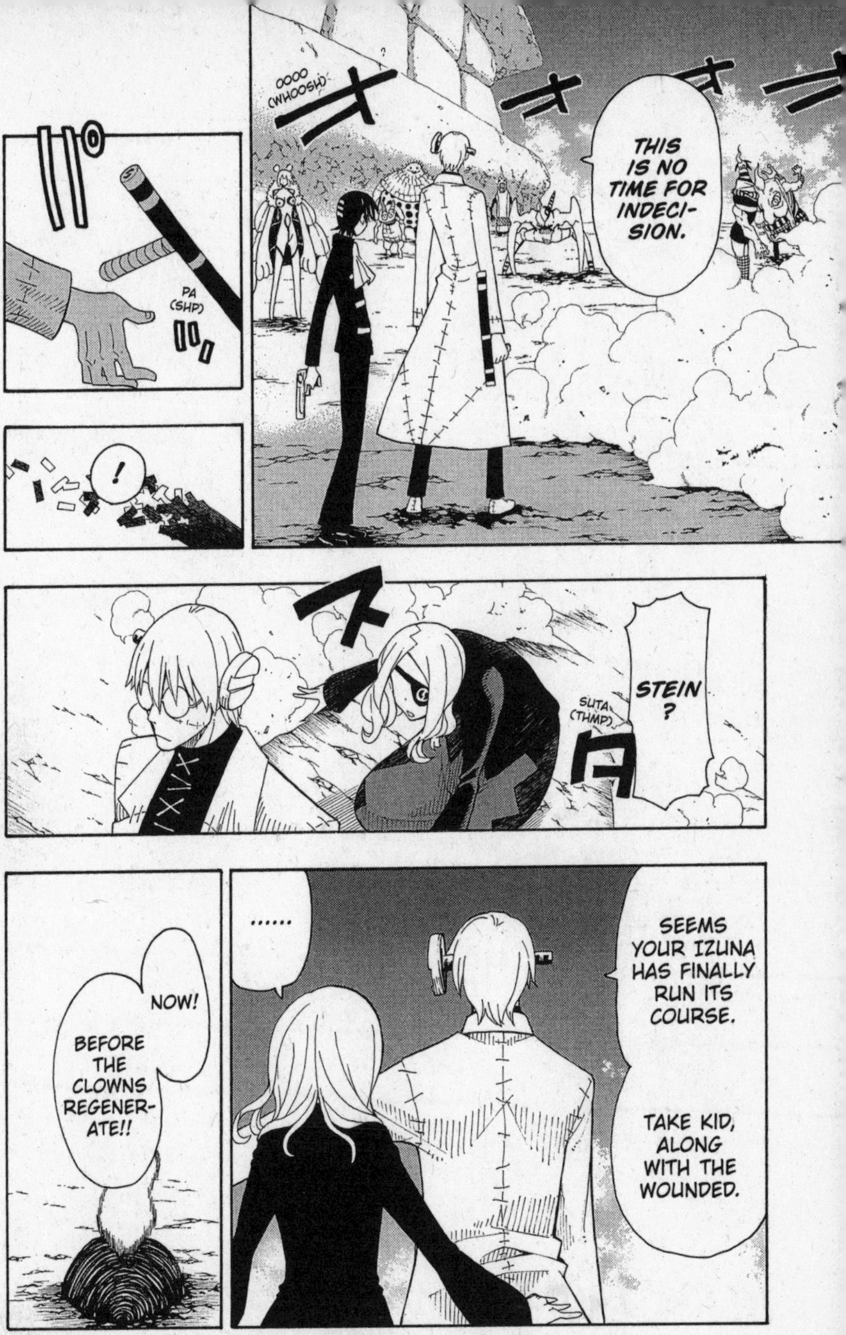
OOOO (WHOOSH)
THIS IS NO TIME FOR INDECI-SION.
PA (SHP)
!
STEIN ?
SUTA (THMP)
SEEMS YOUR IZUNA HAS FINALLY RUN ITS COURSE.
TAKE KID, ALONG WITH THE WOUNDED.
......
NOW!
BEFORE THE CLOWNS REGENER-ATE!!

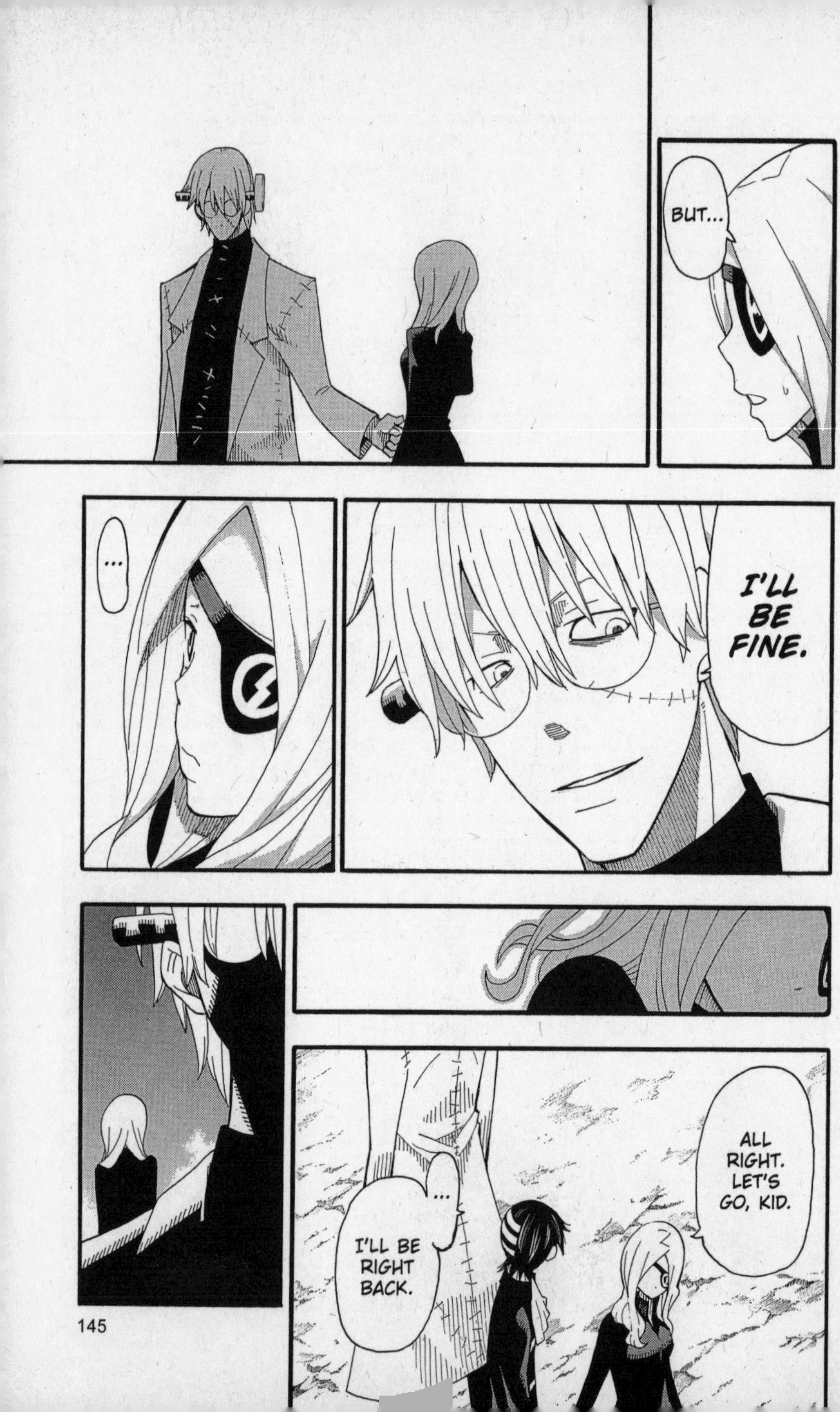
BUT...
I'LL BE FINE.
...
ALL RIGHT. LET'S GO, KID.
...
I'LL BE RIGHT BACK.

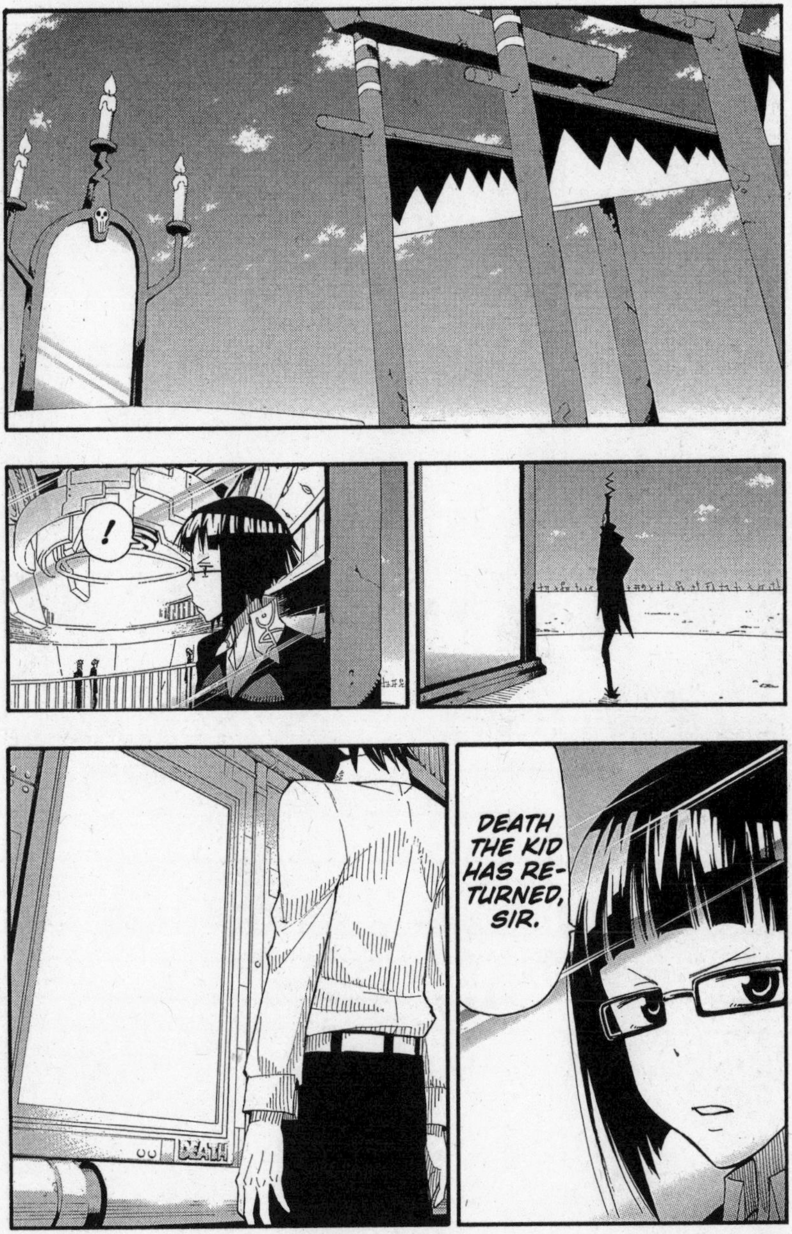
!
DEATH THE KID HAS RE- TURNED, SIR.

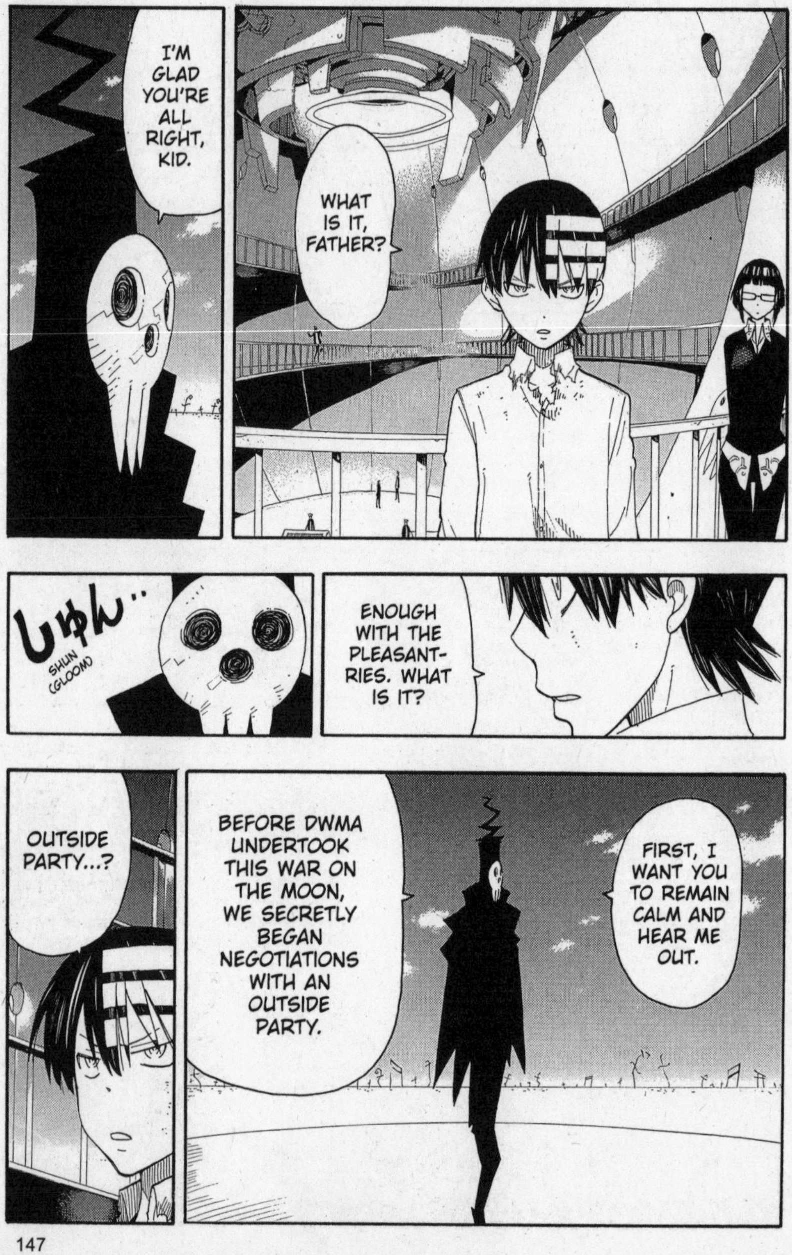
WHAT IS IT, FATHER?
I'M GLAD YOU'RE ALL RIGHT, KID.
ENOUGH WITH THE PLEASANT-RIES. WHAT IS IT?
しゅん..
SHUN (GLOOM)
FIRST, I WANT YOU TO REMAIN CALM AND HEAR ME OUT.
BEFORE DWMA UNDERTOOK THIS WAR ON THE MOON, WE SECRETLY BEGAN NEGOTIATIONS WITH AN OUTSIDE PARTY.
OUTSIDE PARTY...?

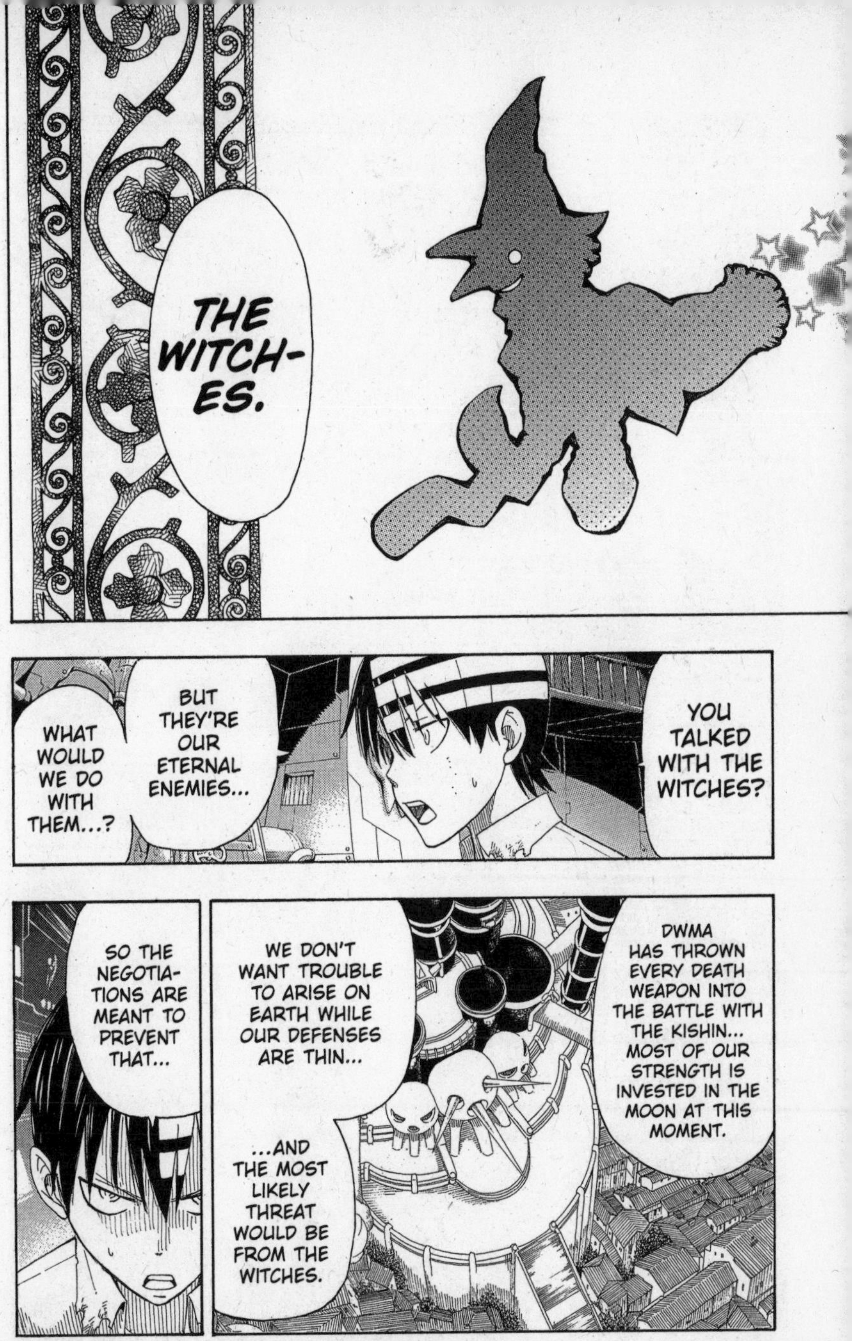
THE WITCH-ES.
YOU TALKED WITH THE WITCHES?
BUT THEY'RE OUR ETERNAL ENEMIES...
WHAT WOULD WE DO WITH THEM...?
DWMA HAS THROWN EVERY DEATH WEAPON INTO THE BATTLE WITH THE KISHIN... MOST OF OUR STRENGTH IS INVESTED IN THE MOON AT THIS MOMENT.
WE DON'T WANT TROUBLE TO ARISE ON EARTH WHILE OUR DEFENSES ARE THIN...
...AND THE MOST LIKELY THREAT WOULD BE FROM THE WITCHES.
SO THE NEGOTIA-TIONS ARE MEANT TO PREVENT THAT...

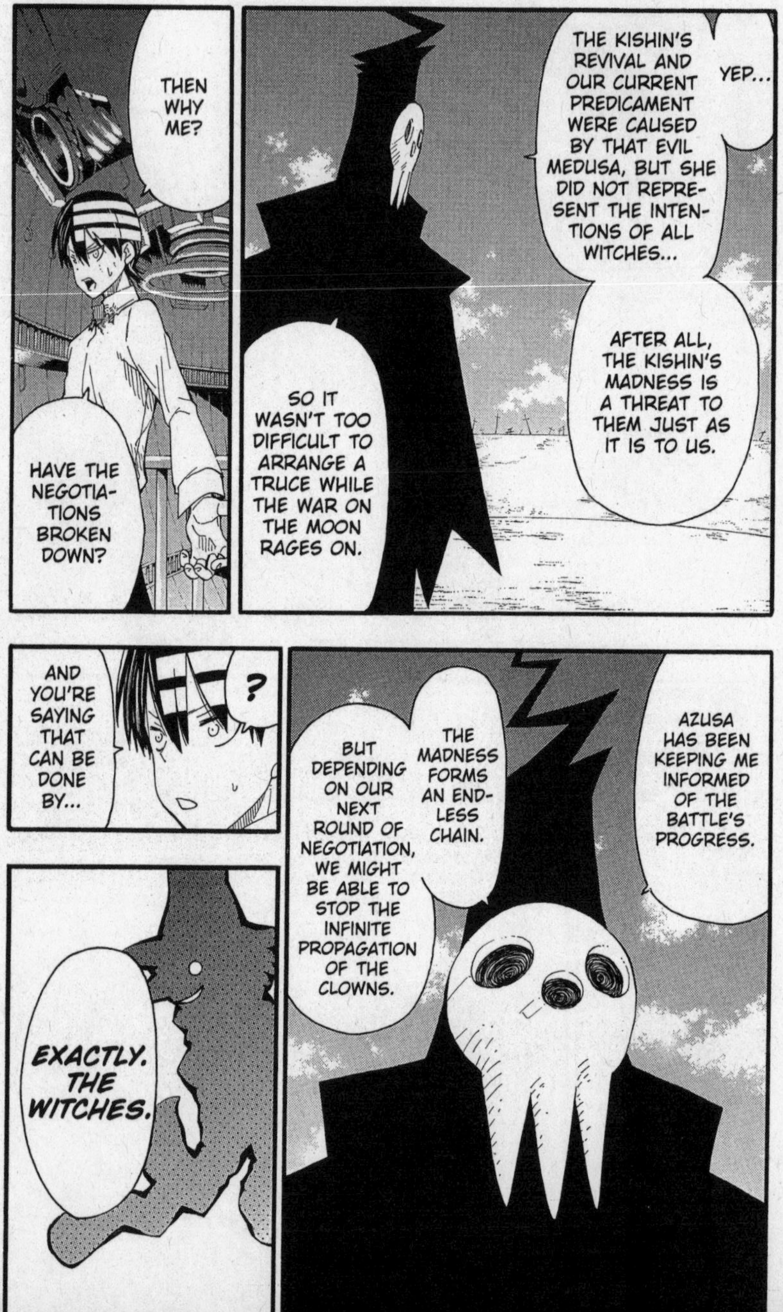
YEP...
THE KISHIN'S REVIVAL AND OUR CURRENT PREDICAMENT WERE CAUSED BY THAT EVIL MEDUSA, BUT SHE DID NOT REPRESENT THE INTENTIONS OF ALL WITCHES...
AFTER ALL, THE KISHIN'S MADNESS IS A THREAT TO THEM JUST AS IT IS TO US.
SO IT WASN'T TOO DIFFICULT TO ARRANGE A TRUCE WHILE THE WAR ON THE MOON RAGES ON.
THEN WHY ME?
HAVE THE NEGOTIATIONS BROKEN DOWN?
AZUSA HAS BEEN KEEPING ME INFORMED OF THE BATTLE'S PROGRESS.
THE MADNESS FORMS AN ENDLESS CHAIN.
BUT DEPENDING ON OUR NEXT ROUND OF NEGOTIATION, WE MIGHT BE ABLE TO STOP THE INFINITE PROPAGATION OF THE CLOWNS.
?
AND YOU'RE SAYING THAT CAN BE DONE BY...
EXACTLY. THE WITCHES.

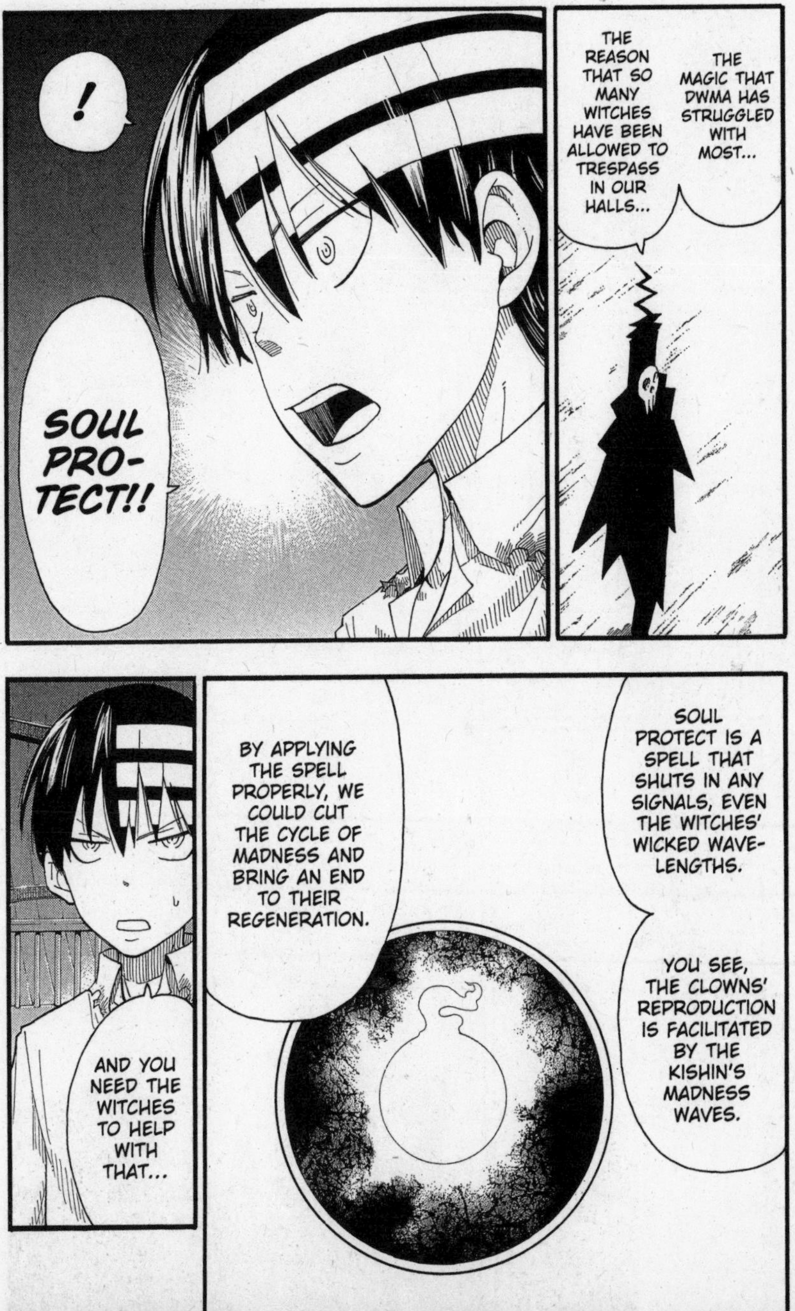
THE MAGIC THAT DWMA HAS STRUGGLED WITH MOST...
THE REASON THAT SO MANY WITCHES HAVE BEEN ALLOWED TO TRESPASS IN OUR HALLS...
!
SOUL PRO-TECT!!
SOUL PROTECT IS A SPELL THAT SHUTS IN ANY SIGNALS, EVEN THE WITCHES' WICKED WAVE-LENGTHS.
YOU SEE, THE CLOWNS' REPRODUCTION IS FACILITATED BY THE KISHIN'S MADNESS WAVES.
BY APPLYING THE SPELL PROPERLY, WE COULD CUT THE CYCLE OF MADNESS AND BRING AN END TO THEIR REGENERATION.
AND YOU NEED THE WITCHES TO HELP WITH THAT...

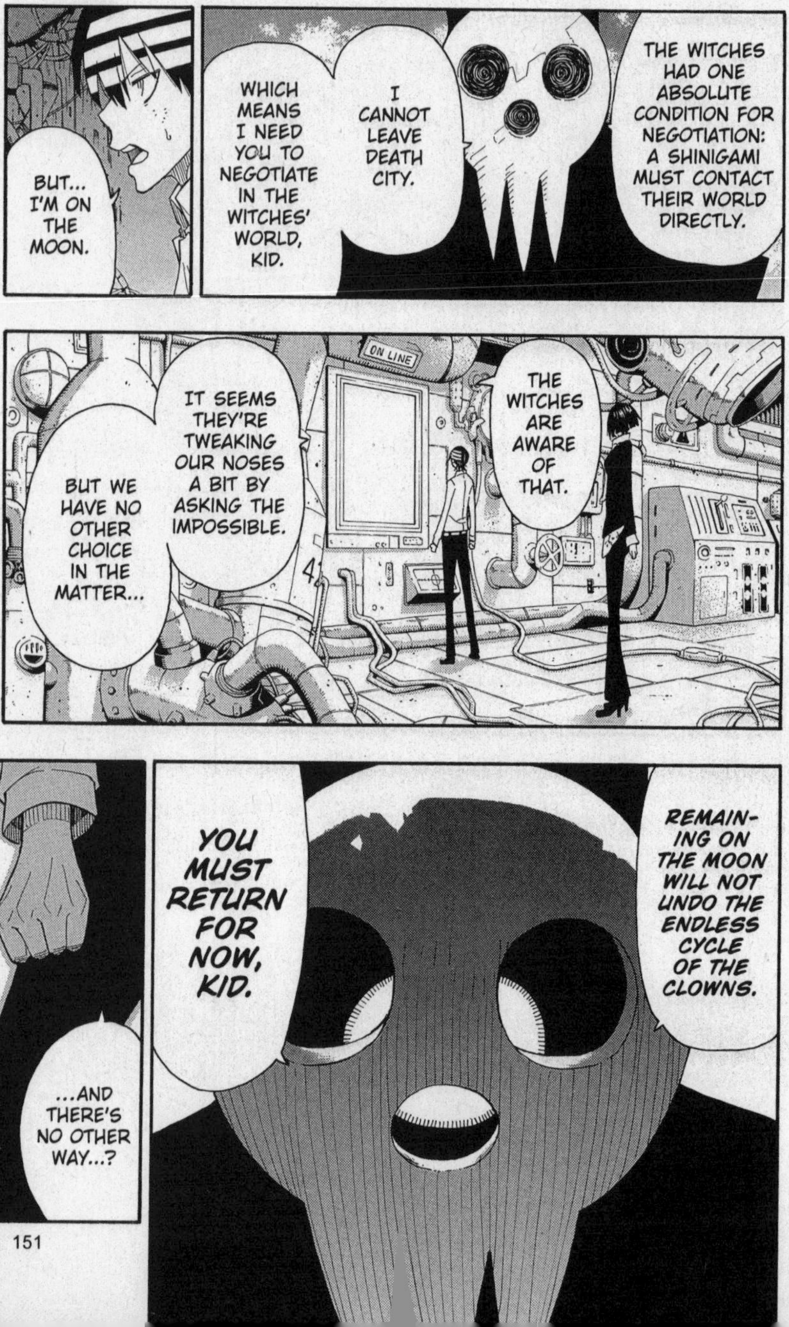
THE WITCHES HAD ONE ABSOLUTE CONDITION FOR NEGOTIATION: A SHINIGAMI MUST CONTACT THEIR WORLD DIRECTLY.
I CANNOT LEAVE DEATH CITY.
WHICH MEANS I NEED YOU TO NEGOTIATE IN THE WITCHES' WORLD, KID.
BUT... I'M ON THE MOON.
THE WITCHES ARE AWARE OF THAT.
ON LINE
IT SEEMS THEY'RE TWEAKING OUR NOSES A BIT BY ASKING THE IMPOSSIBLE.
BUT WE HAVE NO OTHER CHOICE IN THE MATTER...
REMAINING ON THE MOON WILL NOT UNDO THE ENDLESS CYCLE OF THE CLOWNS.
YOU MUST RETURN FOR NOW, KID.
...AND THERE'S NO OTHER WAY...?

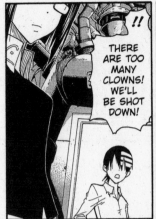

WHAT'S OUR STATUS?
ALL WOUNDED AND KILLED HAVE BEEN RE-COVERED.
READY FOR LIFTOFF!
!!
THERE ARE TOO MANY CLOWNS! WE'LL BE SHOT DOWN!
IT'S ALL RIGHT. DON'T WORRY.
!!
WAIT ...
YOU DON'T MEAN...
IT'S NOT FOR NOTHING WE'RE DEATH WEAP-ONS.

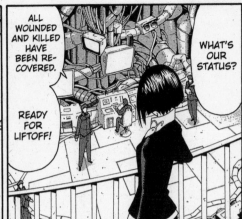

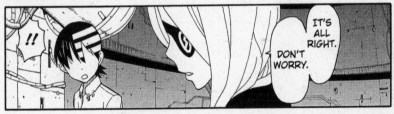

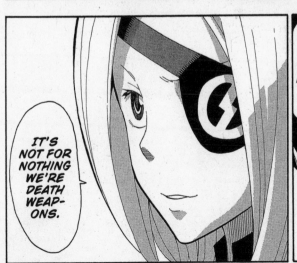

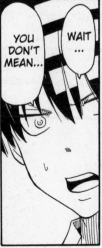

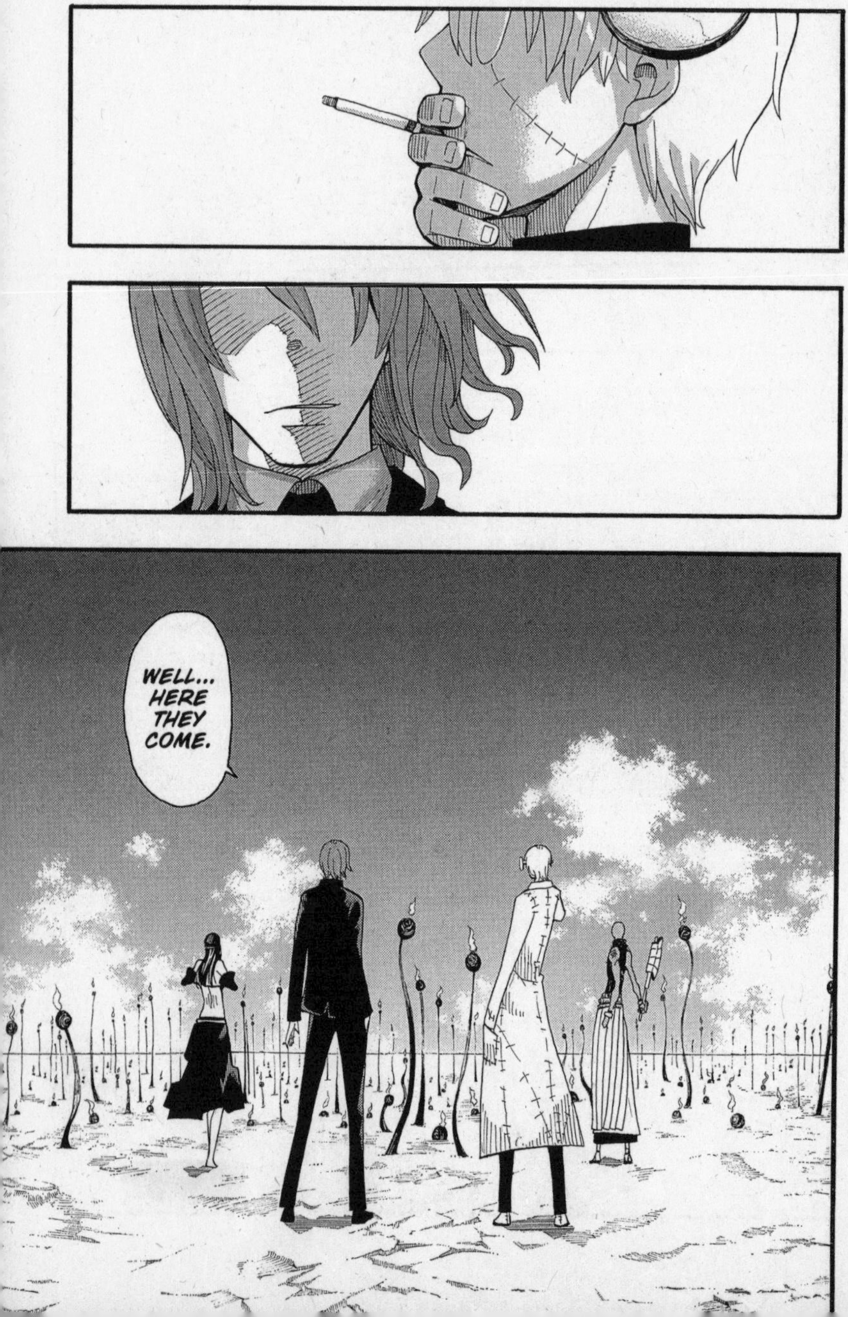
WELL... HERE THEY COME.

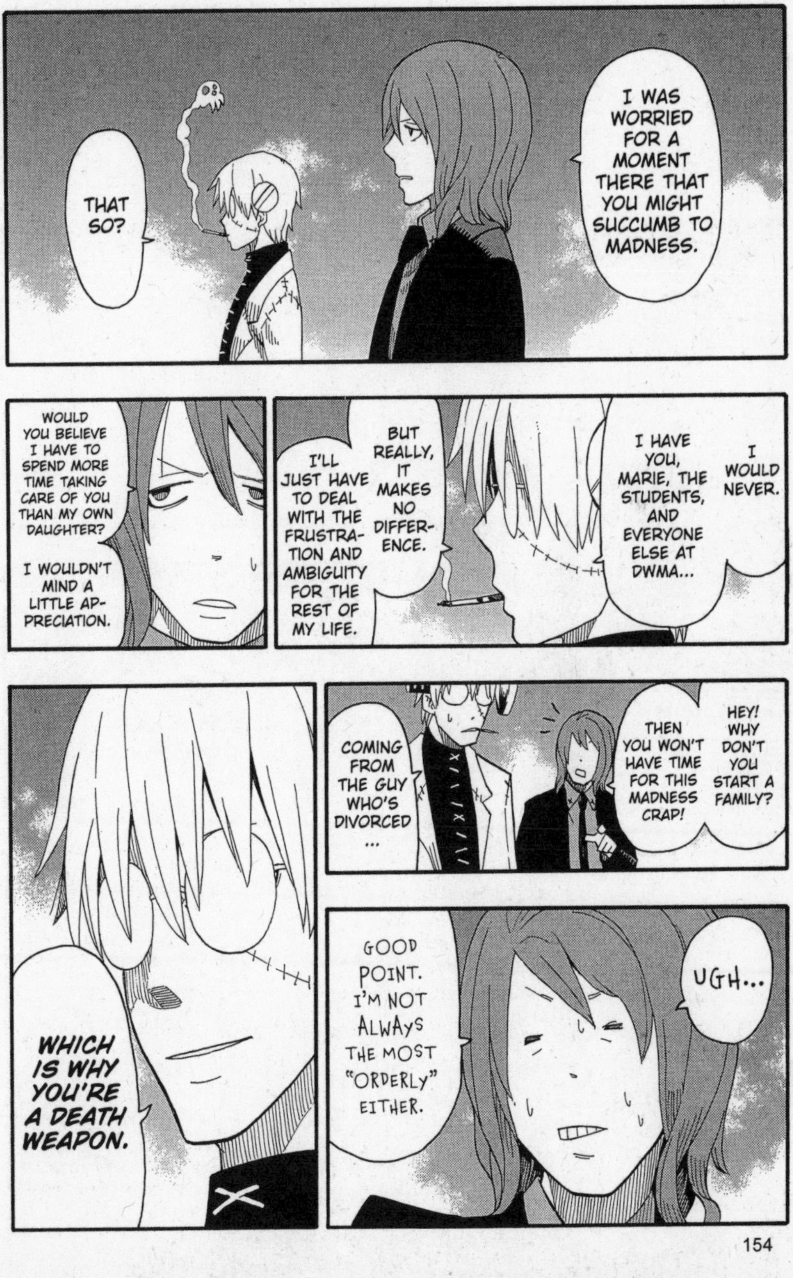
I WAS WORRIED FOR A MOMENT THERE THAT YOU MIGHT SUCCUMB TO MADNESS.
THAT SO?
I WOULD NEVER.
I HAVE YOU, MARIE, THE STUDENTS, AND EVERYONE ELSE AT DWMA...
BUT REALLY, IT MAKES NO DIFFER-ENCE.
I'LL JUST HAVE TO DEAL WITH THE FRUSTRA-TION AND AMBIGUITY FOR THE REST OF MY LIFE.
WOULD YOU BELIEVE I HAVE TO SPEND MORE TIME TAKING CARE OF YOU THAN MY OWN DAUGHTER?
I WOULDN'T MIND A LITTLE AP-PRECIATION.
HEY! WHY DON'T YOU START A FAMILY?
THEN YOU WON'T HAVE TIME FOR THIS MADNESS CRAP!
COMING FROM THE GUY WHO'S DIVORCED ...
UGH...
GOOD POINT. I'M NOT ALWAYS THE MOST "ORDERLY" EITHER.
WHICH IS WHY YOU'RE A DEATH WEAPON.

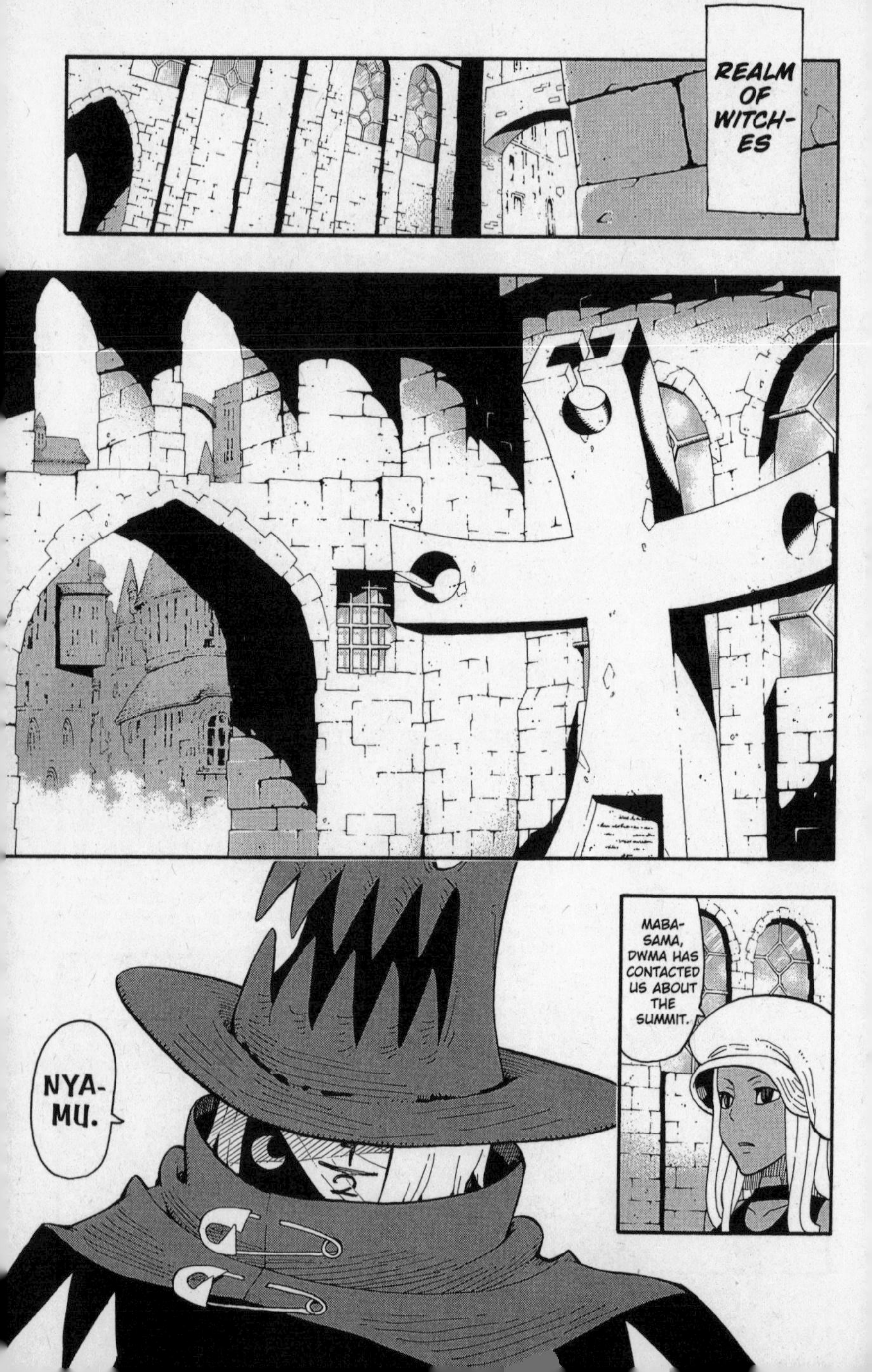
REALM OF WITCH-ES
MABA-SAMA, DWMA HAS CONTACTED US ABOUT THE SUMMIT.
NYA-MU.

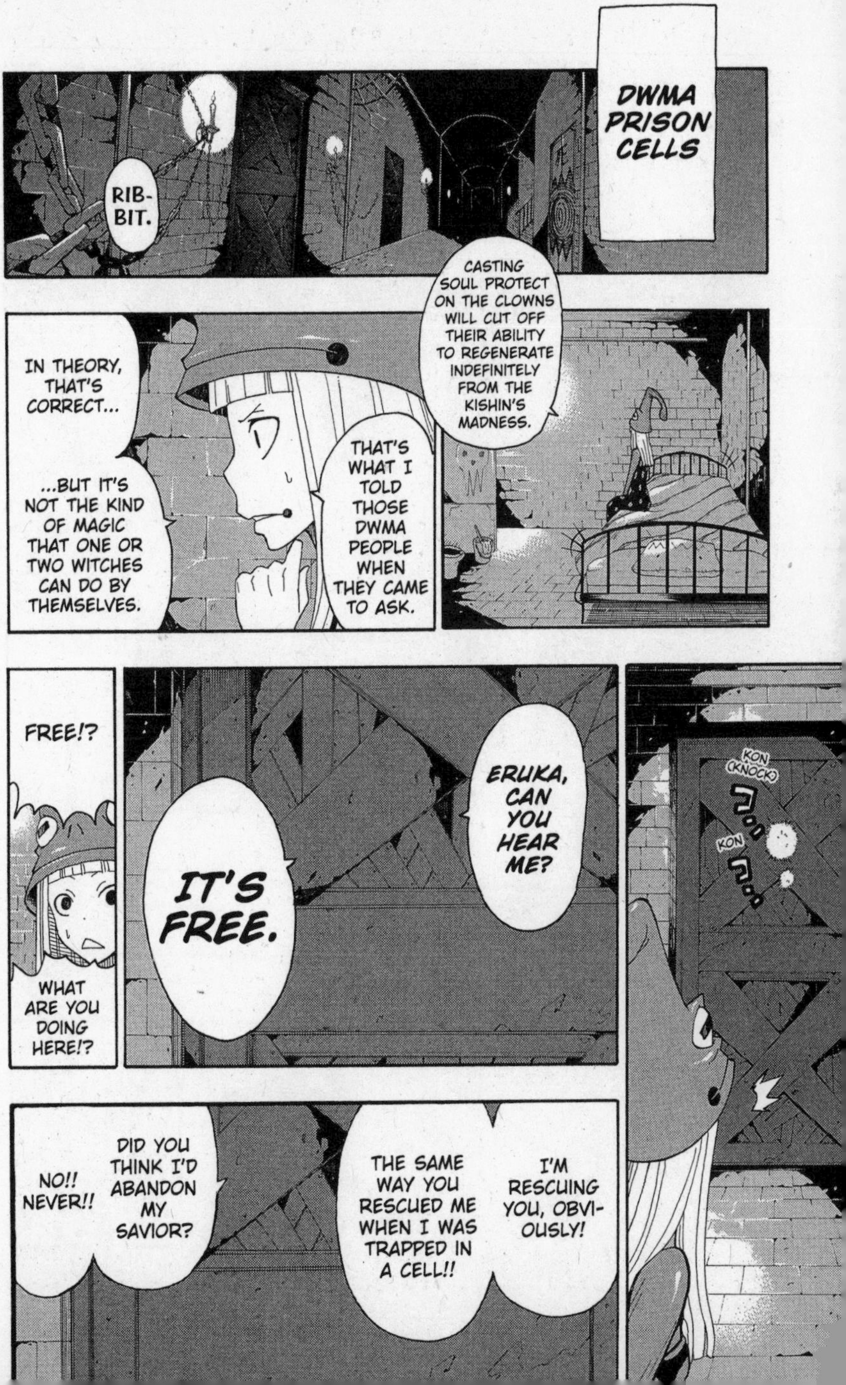
DWMA PRISON CELLS
RIB-BIT.
CASTING SOUL PROTECT ON THE CLOWNS WILL CUT OFF THEIR ABILITY TO REGENERATE INDEFINITELY FROM THE KISHIN'S MADNESS.
THAT'S WHAT I TOLD THOSE DWMA PEOPLE WHEN THEY CAME TO ASK.
IN THEORY, THAT'S CORRECT...
...BUT IT'S NOT THE KIND OF MAGIC THAT ONE OR TWO WITCHES CAN DO BY THEMSELVES.
KON (KNOCK)
KON
ERUKA, CAN YOU HEAR ME?
IT'S FREE.
FREE!?
WHAT ARE YOU DOING HERE!?
I'M RESCUING YOU, OBVI-OUSLY!
THE SAME WAY YOU RESCUED ME WHEN I WAS TRAPPED IN A CELL!!
DID YOU THINK I'D ABANDON MY SAVIOR?
NO!! NEVER!!

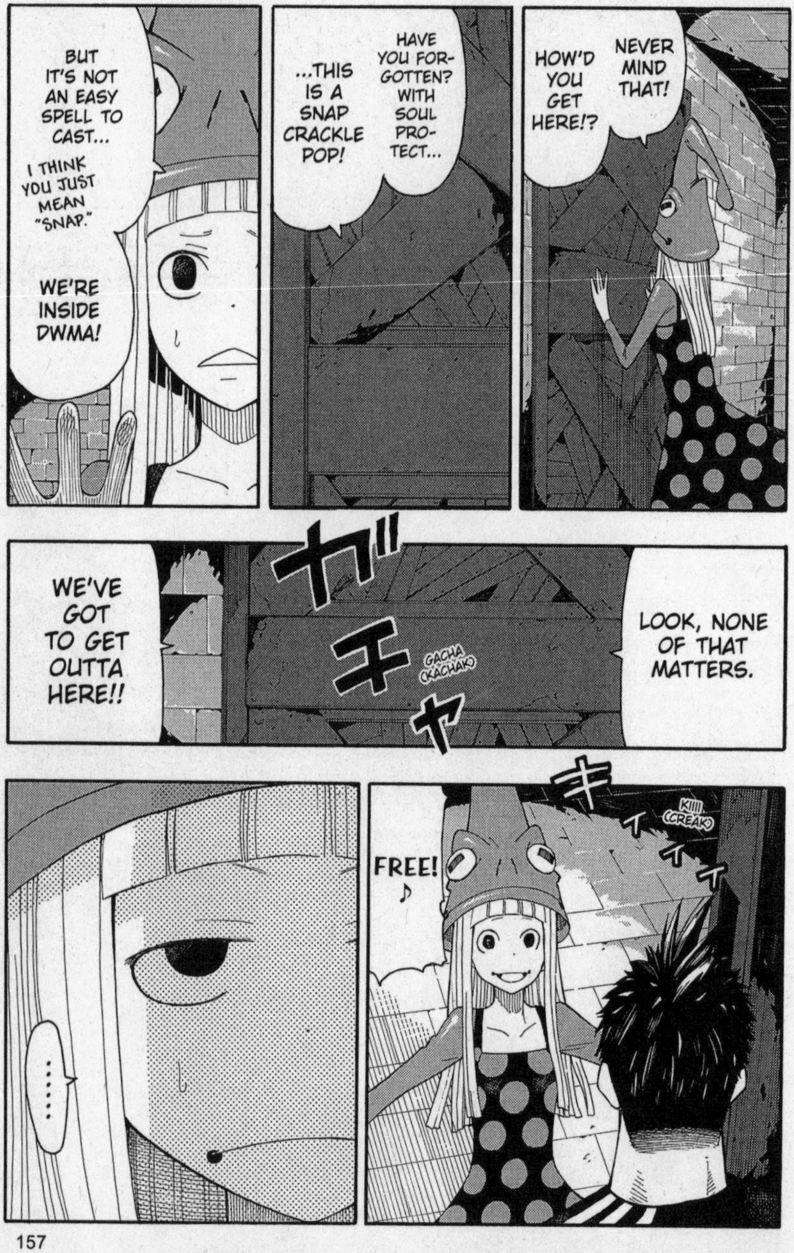
NEVER MIND THAT!
HOW'D YOU GET HERE!?
HAVE YOU FOR-GOTTEN? WITH SOUL PRO-TECT...
...THIS IS A SNAP CRACKLE POP!
BUT IT'S NOT AN EASY SPELL TO CAST...
I THINK YOU JUST MEAN "SNAP."
WE'RE INSIDE DWMA!
LOOK, NONE OF THAT MATTERS.
ガチャ
GACHA (KACHAK)
WE'VE GOT TO GET OUTTA HERE!!
キィィィ
KIIII (CREAK)
FREE! ♪
......

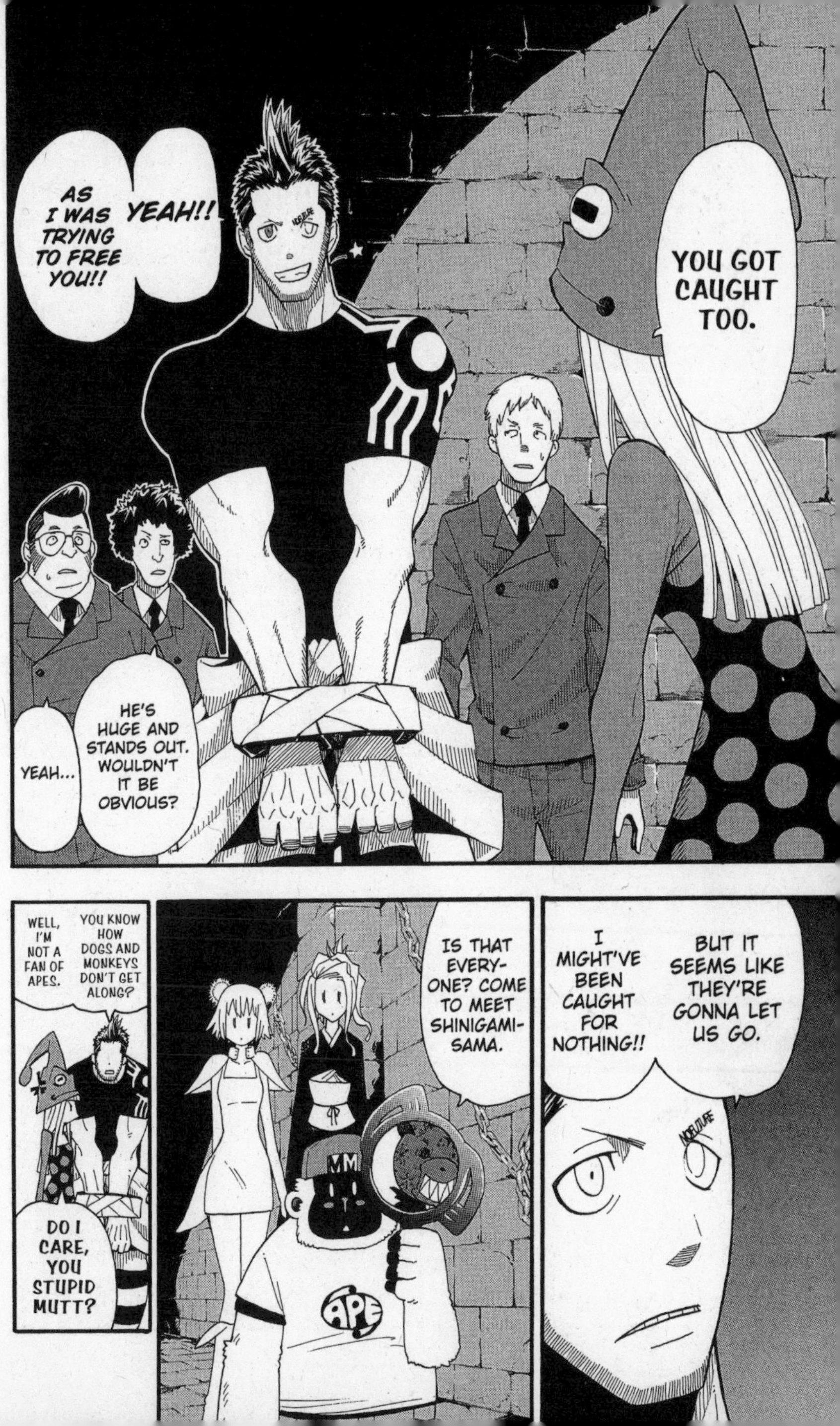
YOU GOT CAUGHT TOO.
YEAH!!
AS I WAS TRYING TO FREE YOU!!
HE'S HUGE AND STANDS OUT. WOULDN'T IT BE OBVIOUS?
YEAH...
BUT IT SEEMS LIKE THEY'RE GONNA LET US GO.
I MIGHT'VE BEEN CAUGHT FOR NOTHING!!
IS THAT EVERY-ONE? COME TO MEET SHINIGAMI-SAMA.
YOU KNOW HOW DOGS AND MONKEYS DON'T GET ALONG?
WELL, I'M NOT A FAN OF APES.
DO I CARE, YOU STUPID MUTT?
MM
APE

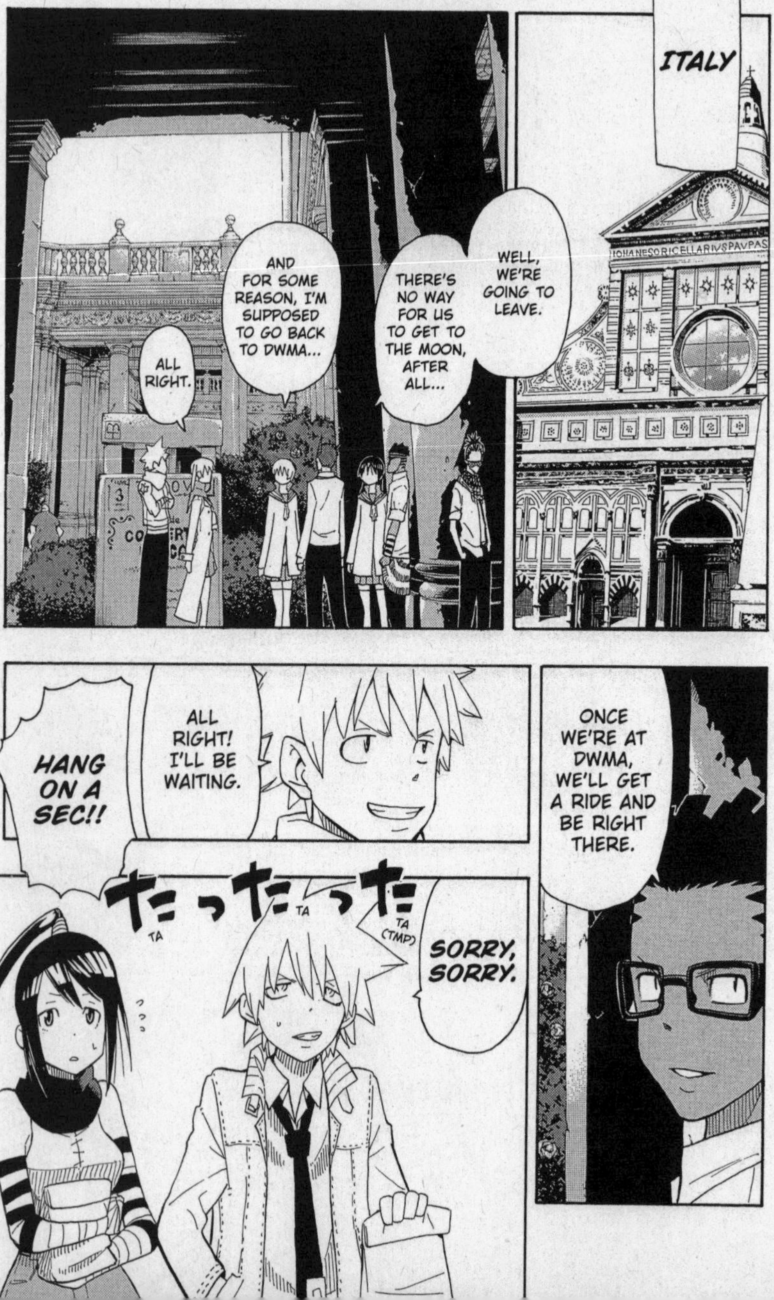
ITALY
WELL, WE'RE GOING TO LEAVE.
THERE'S NO WAY FOR US TO GET TO THE MOON, AFTER ALL...
AND FOR SOME REASON, I'M SUPPOSED TO GO BACK TO DWMA...
ALL RIGHT.
ONCE WE'RE AT DWMA, WE'LL GET A RIDE AND BE RIGHT THERE.
ALL RIGHT! I'LL BE WAITING.
HANG ON A SEC!!
たったったった
TA TA TA (TMP)
SORRY, SORRY.

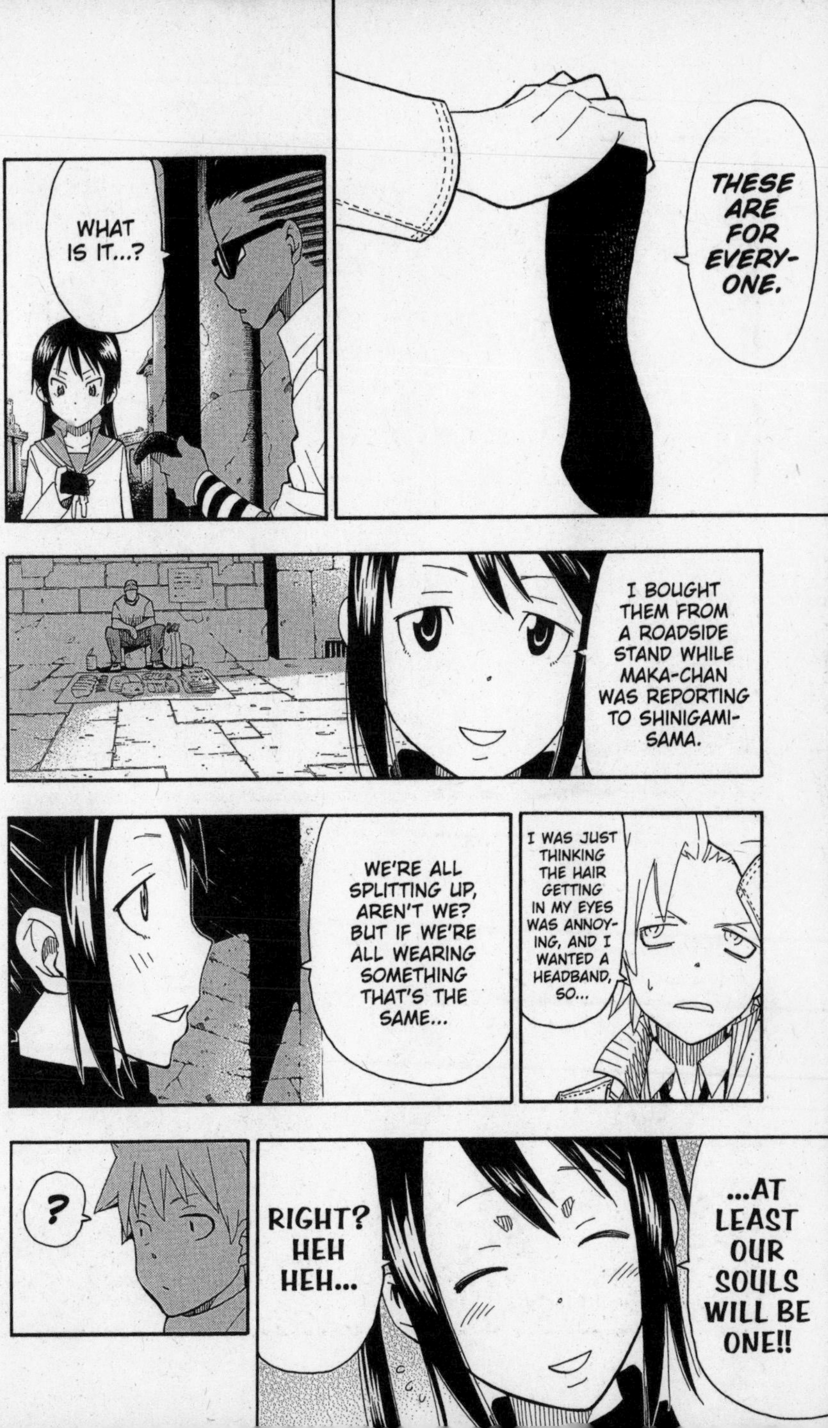
THESE ARE FOR EVERYONE.
WHAT IS IT...?
I BOUGHT THEM FROM A ROADSIDE STAND WHILE MAKA-CHAN WAS REPORTING TO SHINIGAMI-SAMA.
I WAS JUST THINKING THE HAIR GETTING IN MY EYES WAS ANNOYING, AND I WANTED A HEADBAND, SO...
WE'RE ALL SPLITTING UP, AREN'T WE? BUT IF WE'RE ALL WEARING SOMETHING THAT'S THE SAME...
...AT LEAST OUR SOULS WILL BE ONE!!
RIGHT? HEH HEH...
?

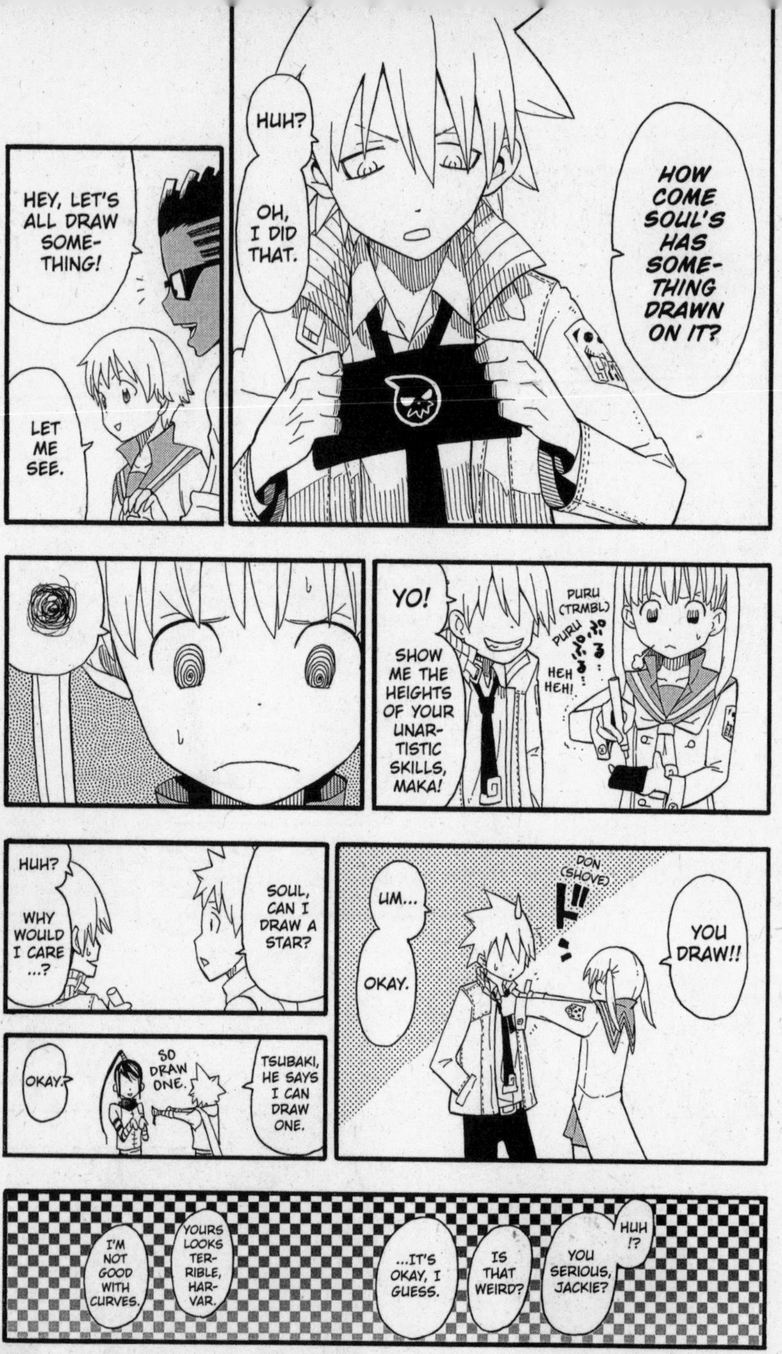
HOW COME SOUL'S HAS SOMETHING DRAWN ON IT?
HUH?
OH, I DID THAT.
HEY, LET'S ALL DRAW SOMETHING!
LET ME SEE.
YO!
SHOW ME THE HEIGHTS OF YOUR UNARTISTIC SKILLS, MAKA!
PURU (TRMBL) PURU
HEH HEH!
YOU DRAW!!
DON (SHOVE)
UM...
OKAY.
SOUL, CAN I DRAW A STAR?
HUH?
WHY WOULD I CARE ...?
TSUBAKI, HE SAYS I CAN DRAW ONE.
SO DRAW ONE.
OKAY.
HUH !?
YOU SERIOUS, JACKIE?
IS THAT WEIRD?
...IT'S OKAY, I GUESS.
YOURS LOOKS TERRIBLE, HARVAR.
I'M NOT GOOD WITH CURVES.

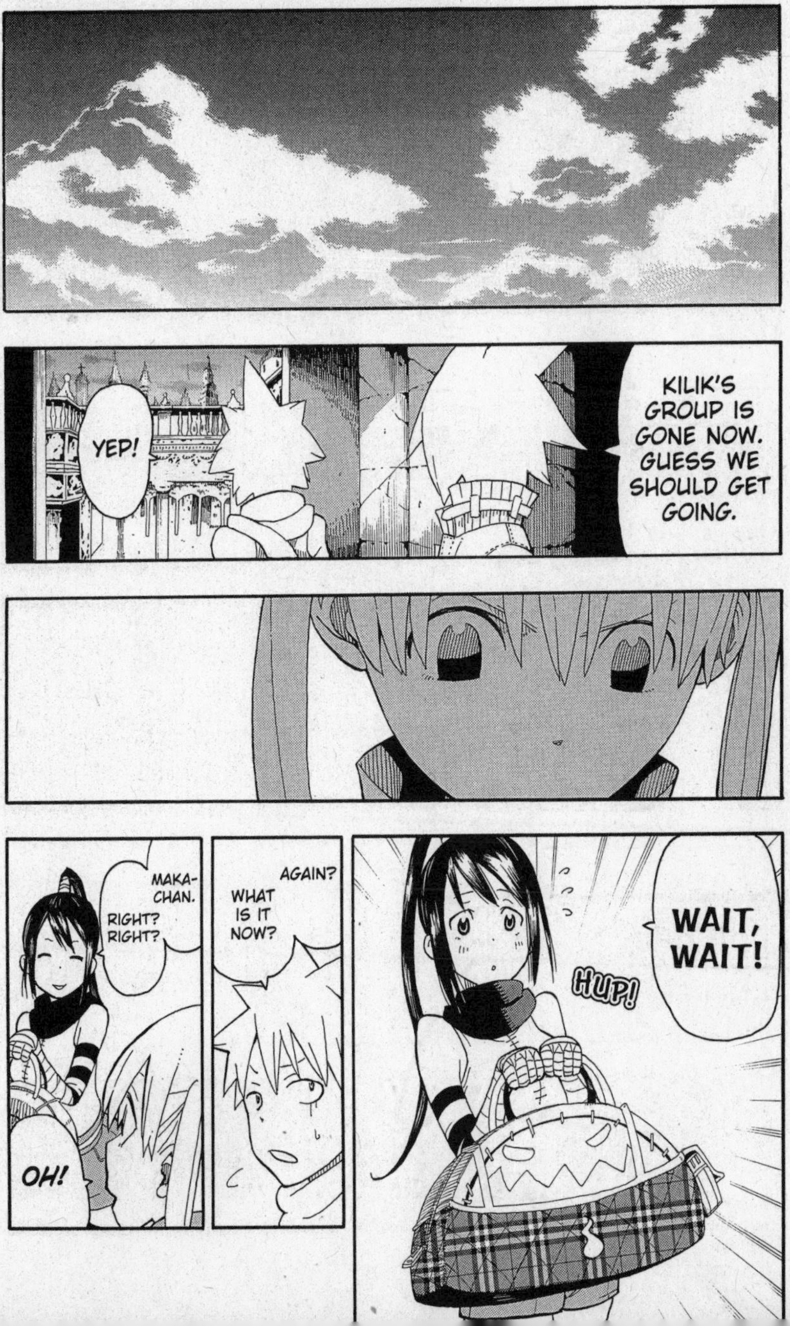
KILIK'S GROUP IS GONE NOW. GUESS WE SHOULD GET GOING.
YEP!
WAIT, WAIT!
HUP!
AGAIN?
WHAT IS IT NOW?
MAKA-CHAN.
RIGHT? RIGHT?
OH!

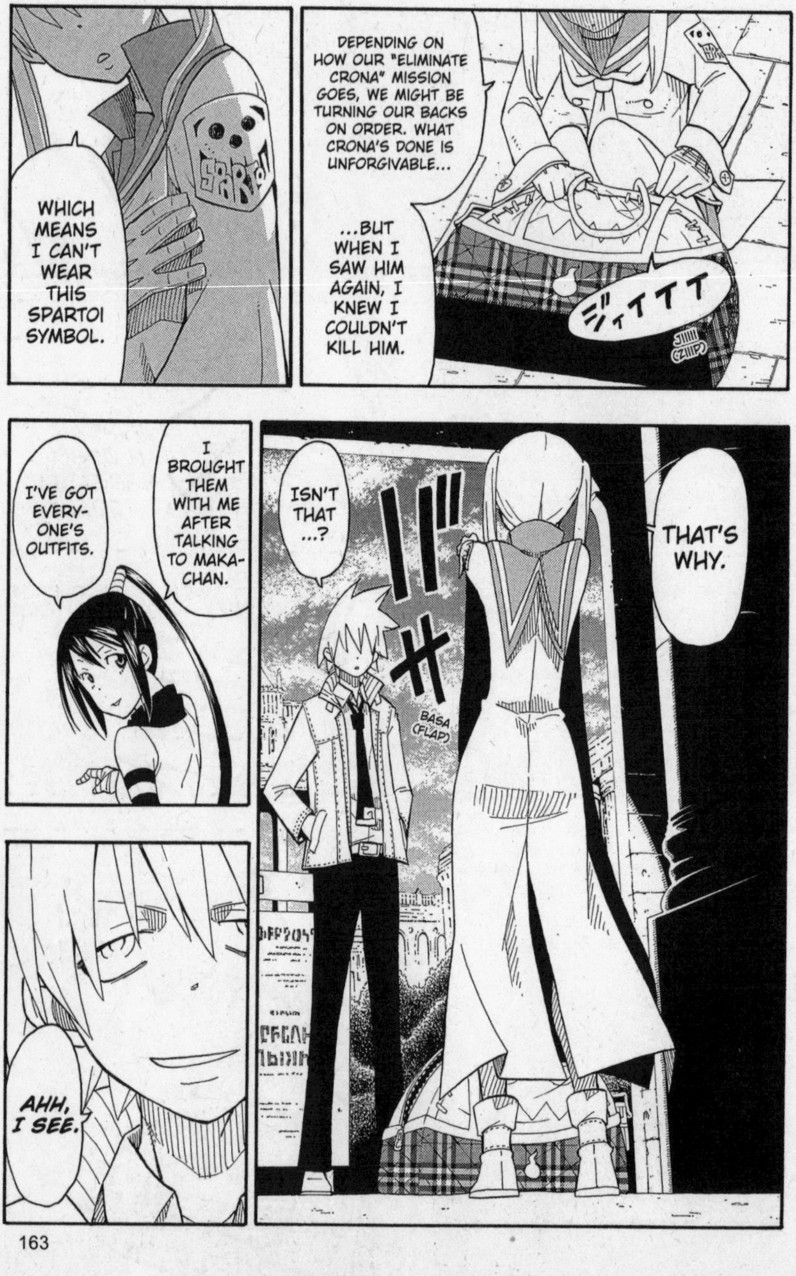
DEPENDING ON HOW OUR "ELIMINATE CRONA" MISSION GOES, WE MIGHT BE TURNING OUR BACKS ON ORDER. WHAT CRONA'S DONE IS UNFORGIVABLE...
...BUT WHEN I SAW HIM AGAIN, I KNEW I COULDN'T KILL HIM.
JIIII (ZIIIP)
WHICH MEANS I CAN'T WEAR THIS SPARTOI SYMBOL.
THAT'S WHY.
ISN'T THAT ...?
BASA (FLAP)
I BROUGHT THEM WITH ME AFTER TALKING TO MAKA-CHAN.
I'VE GOT EVERY-ONE'S OUTFITS.
AHH, I SEE.

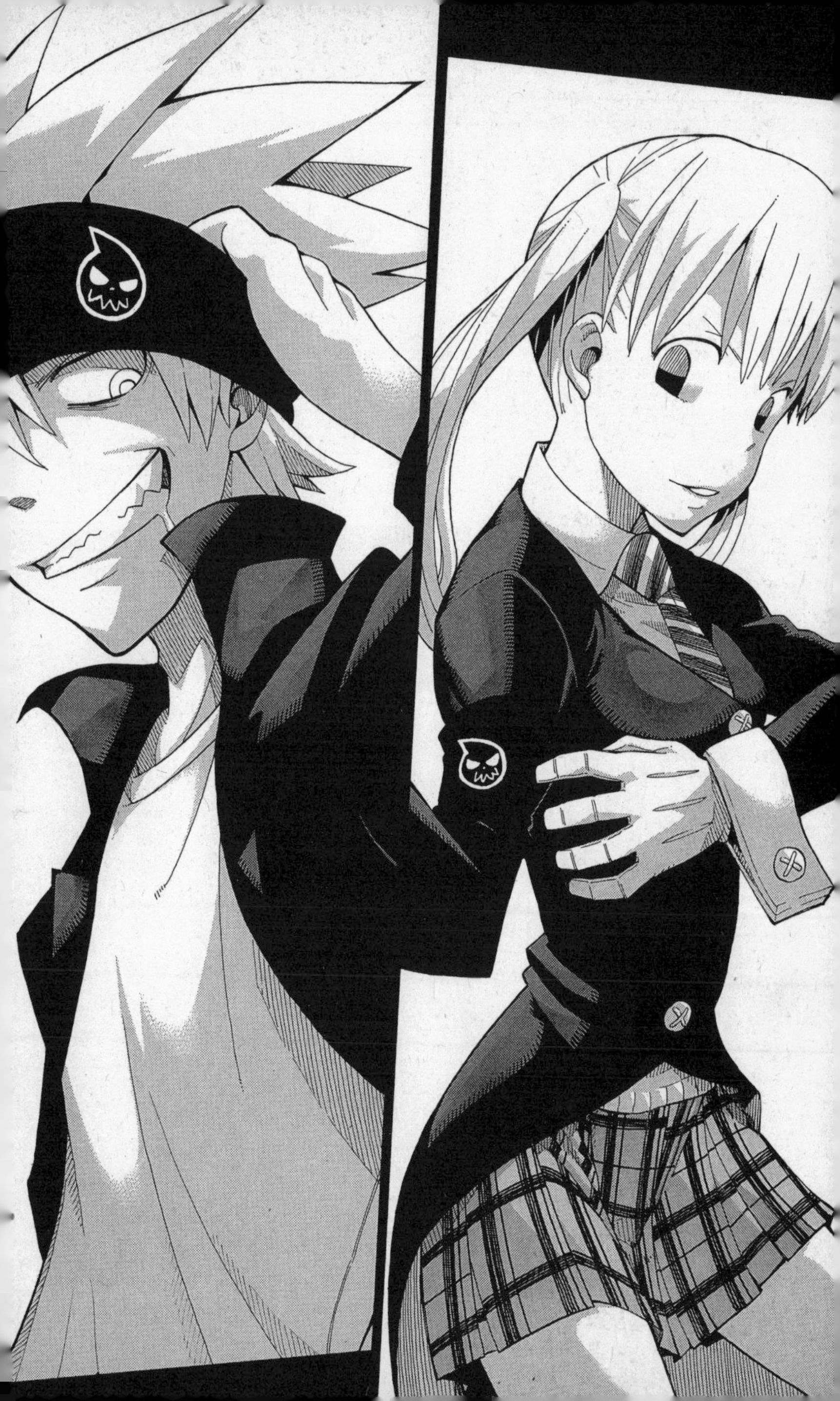

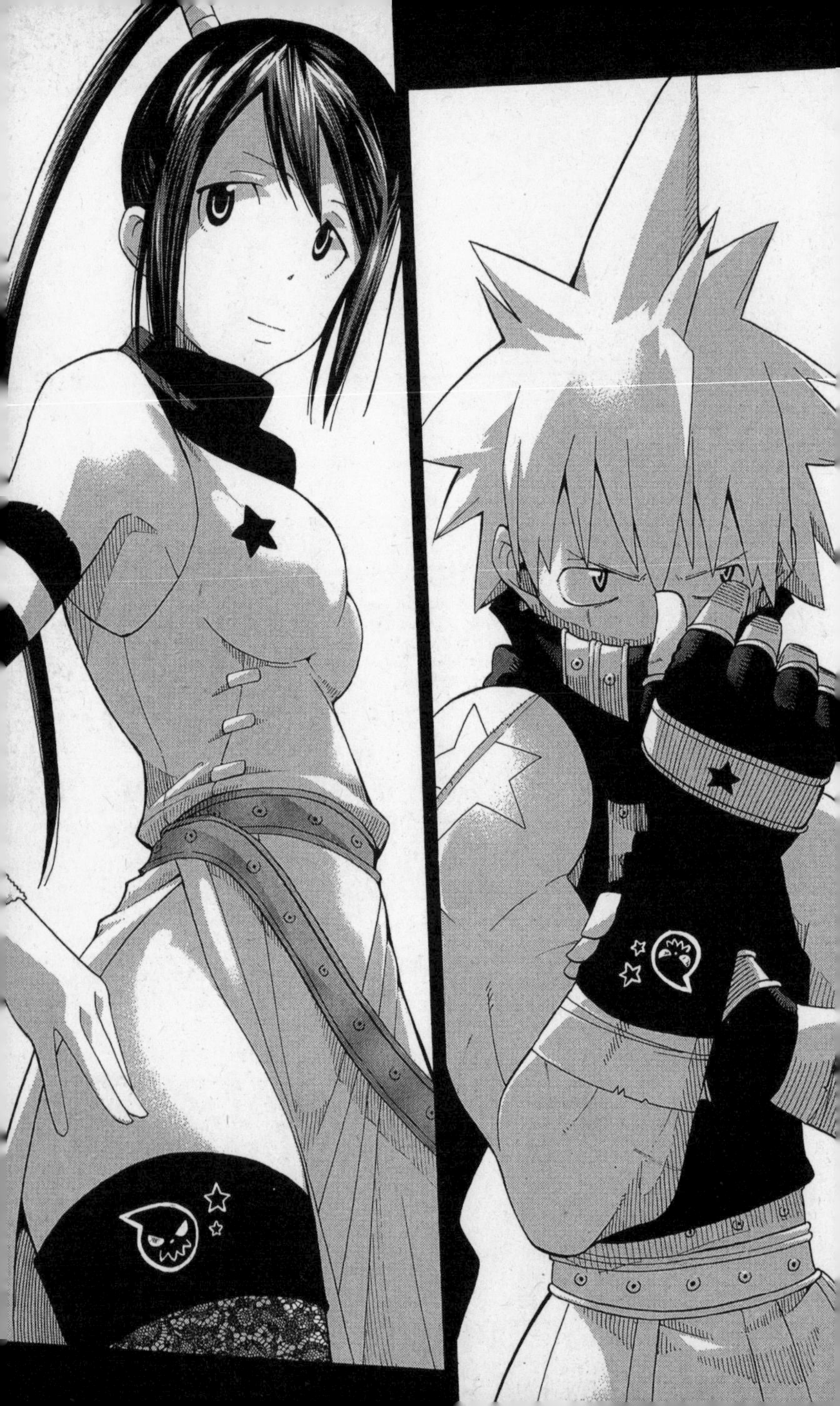

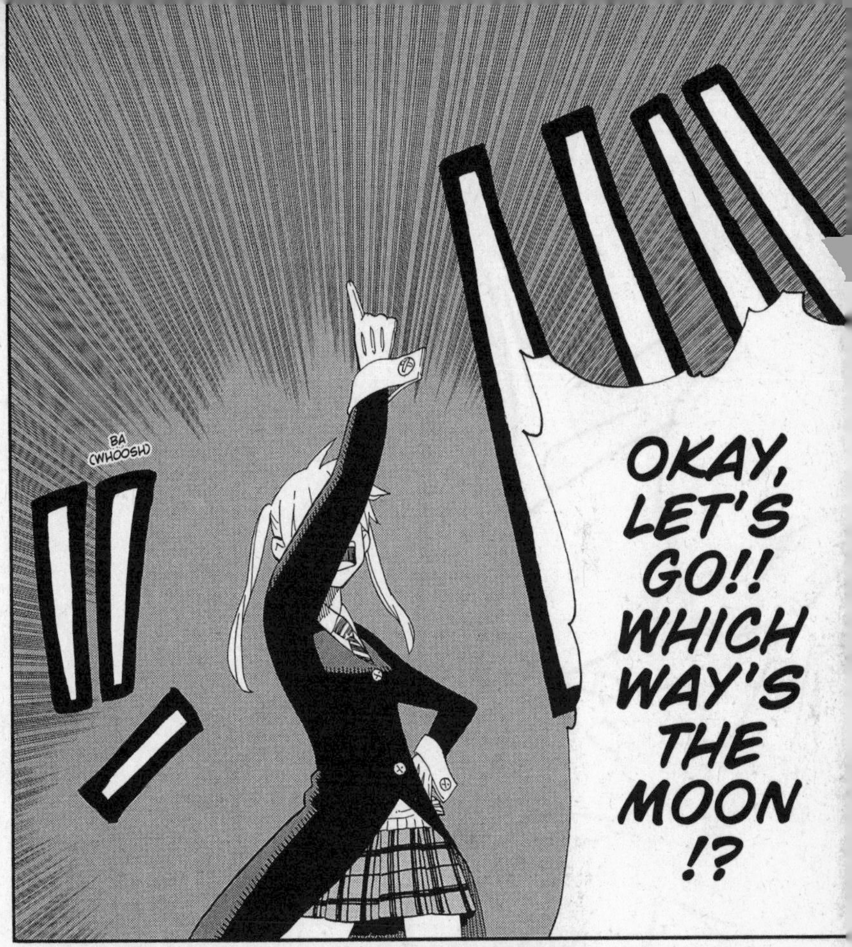
OKAY, LET'S GO!! WHICH WAY'S THE MOON!?
BA (WHOOSH)
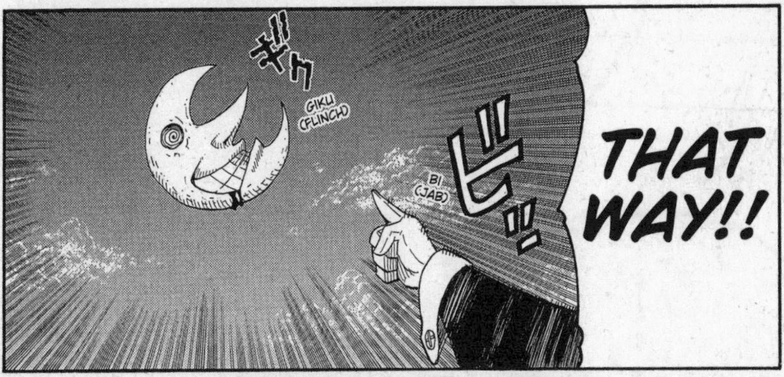
THAT WAY!!
BI (JAB)
GIKU (FLINCH)

SOUL EATER 22 END

Translation Notes

Common Honorifics

no honorific: Indicates familiarity or closeness; if used without permission or reason, addressing someone in this manner would constitute an insult.

-san: The Japanese equivalent of Mr./Mrs./Miss. If a situation calls for politeness, this is the fail-safe honorific.

-sama: Conveys great respect; may also indicate that the social status of the speaker is lower than that of the addressee.

-kun: Used most often when referring to boys, this indicates affection or familiarity. Occasionally used by older men among their peers, but it may also be used by anyone referring to a person of lower standing.

-chan: An affectionate honorific indicating familiarity used mostly in reference to girls; also used in reference to cute persons or animals of either gender.

-senpai: A suffix used to address upperclassmen or more experienced coworkers.

-sensei: A respectful term for teachers, artists, or high-level professionals.

Page 27
Pelt of the Fire Rat comes from the well-known Japanese folktale known as "The Tale of the Bamboo Cutter" or "Princess Kaguya." The sought-after Princess Kaguya tells her five princely suitors that they must each bring her a rare treasure. One of these treasures was the pelt (or robe) of the fire rat.

Page 44
Justin's **"Schmidt"** attack may be a reference to Franz Schmidt, a German executioner who held the position officially in Bamberg and Nuremberg from 1573 to 1617. During his career, Schmidt kept a journal detailing the 361 executions and 365 lesser punishments carried out over the course of his 45-year career.

Page 74
The term for **"square shoulders"** in Japanese includes the character for "rage" or "wrath," which seems to be this Noah's defining characteristic.

Page 158
The well-known Japanese phrase **"like dogs and monkeys"** refers to two people or sides being constantly at odds with one another. The Western equivalent might be "like cats and dogs."

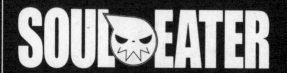

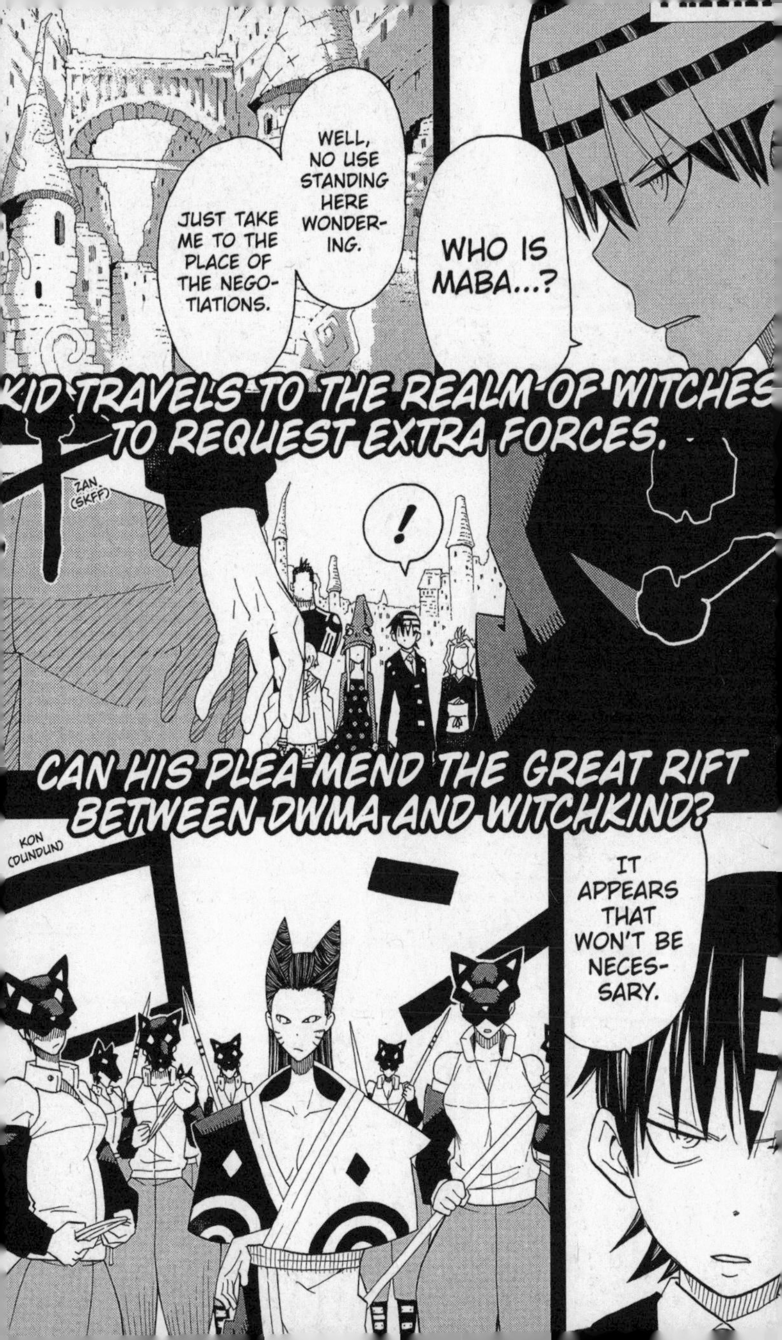
WHO IS MABA...?
WELL, NO USE STANDING HERE WONDER-ING.
JUST TAKE ME TO THE PLACE OF THE NEGO-TIATIONS.
KID TRAVELS TO THE REALM OF WITCHES TO REQUEST EXTRA FORCES.
!
ZAN (SKFF)
CAN HIS PLEA MEND THE GREAT RIFT BETWEEN DWMA AND WITCHKIND?
IT APPEARS THAT WON'T BE NECES-SARY.
KON (DUNDUN)

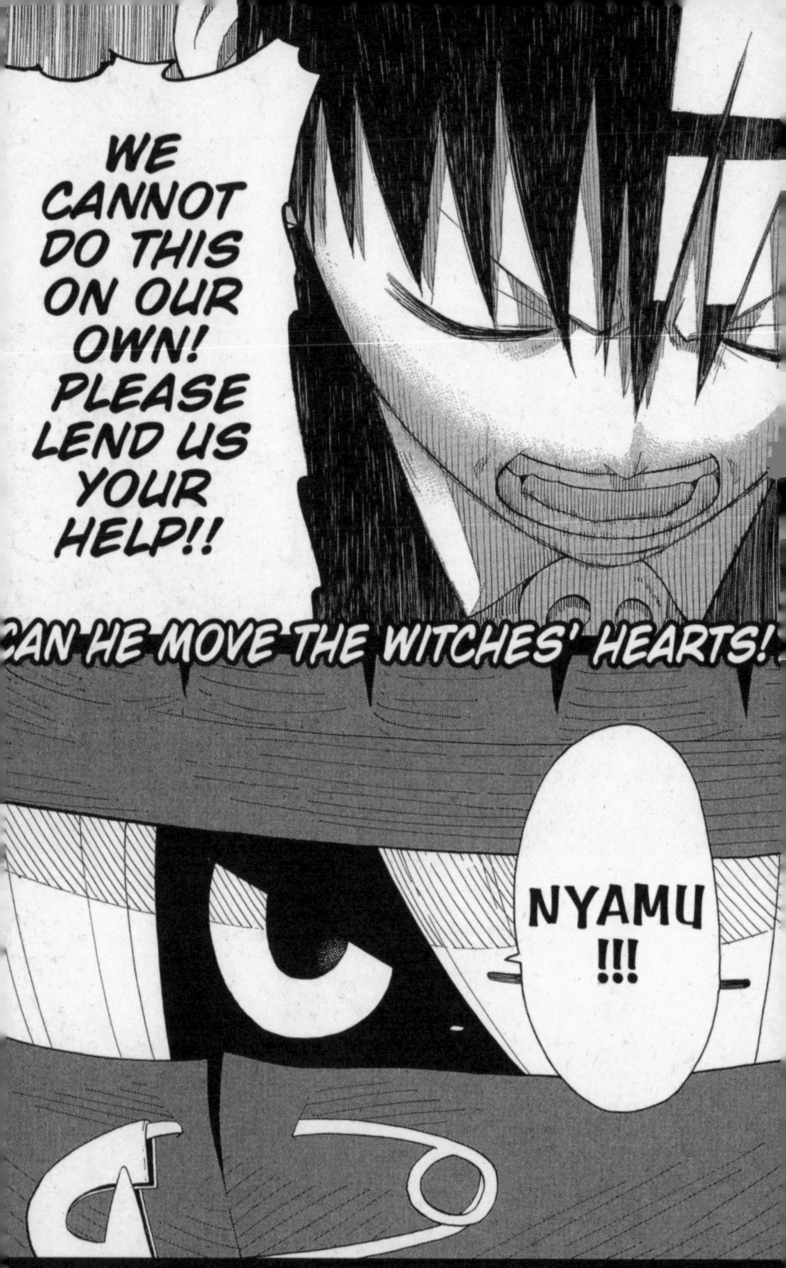
WE CANNOT DO THIS ON OUR OWN! PLEASE LEND US YOUR HELP!!
CAN HE MOVE THE WITCHES' HEARTS!
NYAMU !!!

Continued in Soul Eater Volume 23!!

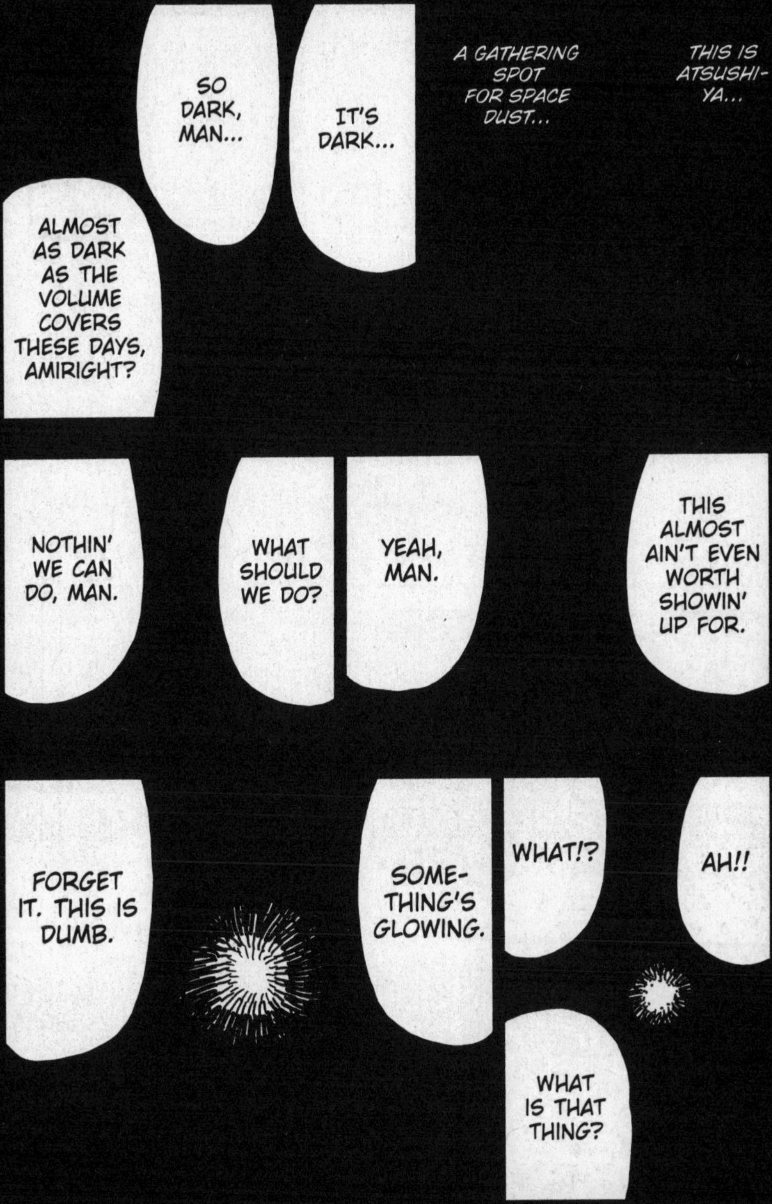
THIS IS ATSUSHI-YA...
A GATHERING SPOT FOR SPACE DUST...
IT'S DARK...
SO DARK, MAN...
ALMOST AS DARK AS THE VOLUME COVERS THESE DAYS, AMIRIGHT?
THIS ALMOST AIN'T EVEN WORTH SHOWIN' UP FOR.
YEAH, MAN.
WHAT SHOULD WE DO?
NOTHIN' WE CAN DO, MAN.
AH!!
WHAT!?
SOME-THING'S GLOWING.
FORGET IT. THIS IS DUMB.
WHAT IS THAT THING?

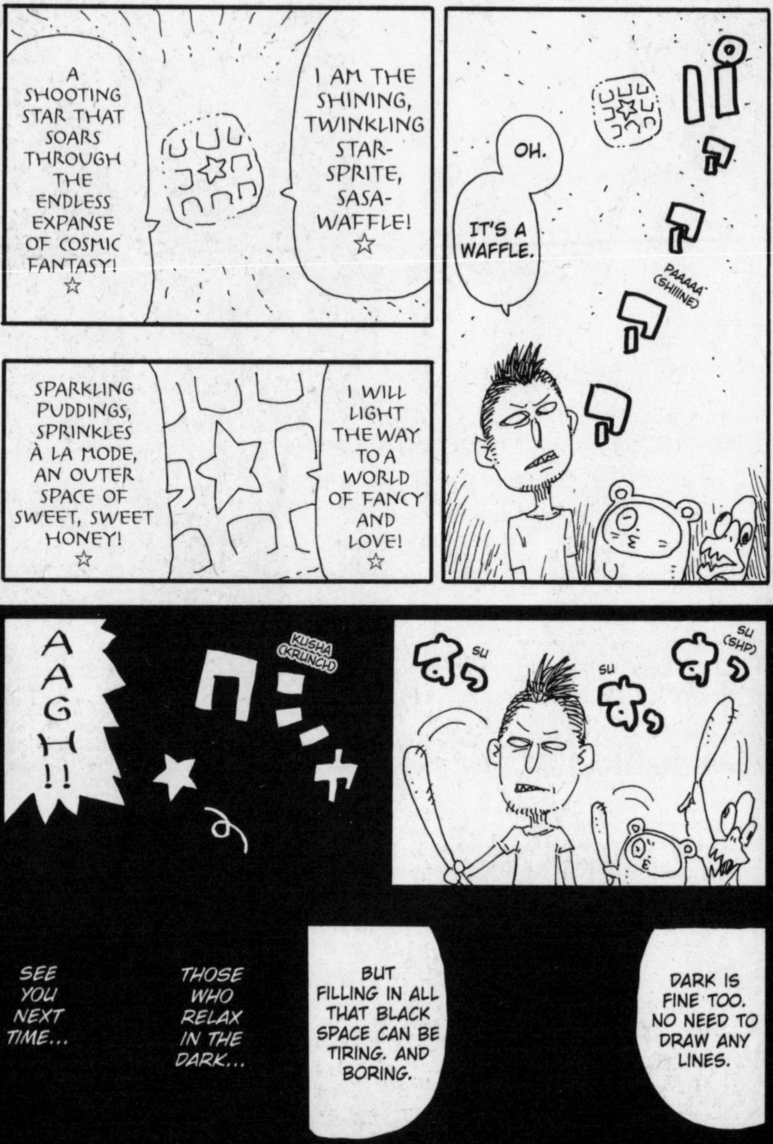
OH.
IT'S A WAFFLE.
PAAAAA (SHIIINE)
I AM THE SHINING, TWINKLING STAR-SPRITE, SASA-WAFFLE! ☆
A SHOOTING STAR THAT SOARS THROUGH THE ENDLESS EXPANSE OF COSMIC FANTASY! ☆
I WILL LIGHT THE WAY TO A WORLD OF FANCY AND LOVE! ☆
SPARKLING PUDDINGS, SPRINKLES À LA MODE, AN OUTER SPACE OF SWEET, SWEET HONEY! ☆
SU (SHP)
SU
SU
KUSHA (KRUNCH)
AAGH!!
DARK IS FINE TOO. NO NEED TO DRAW ANY LINES.
BUT FILLING IN ALL THAT BLACK SPACE CAN BE TIRING. AND BORING.
THOSE WHO RELAX IN THE DARK...
SEE YOU NEXT TIME...

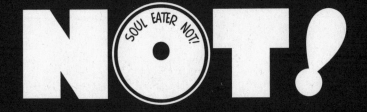

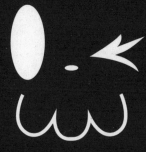

ANOTHER *SOUL EATER*?

IT'S A SAVAGE BUT
SUPER-FUN LIFE! ♪

IT'S *SOUL EATER NOT!*

If you haven't checked out our sister series yet, here's a
special preview of just a portion of Chapter 1! If you want to
read more, check out the first three volumes, on sale now!

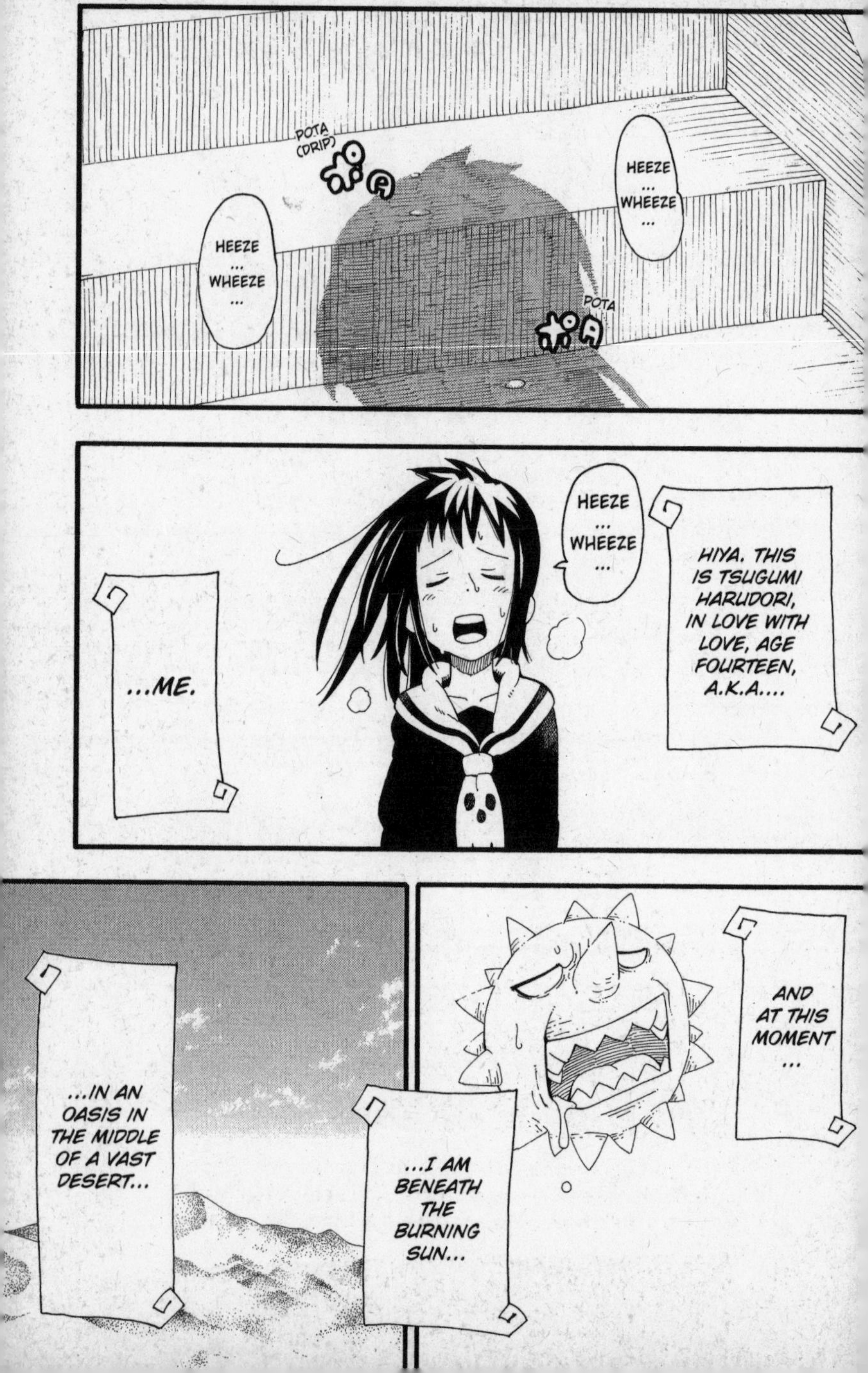
HEEZE ... WHEEZE ...
POTA (DRIP)
HEEZE ... WHEEZE ...
POTA
HIYA. THIS IS TSUGUMI HARUDORI, IN LOVE WITH LOVE, AGE FOURTEEN, A.K.A....
HEEZE ... WHEEZE ...
...ME.
AND AT THIS MOMENT ...
...I AM BENEATH THE BURNING SUN...
...IN AN OASIS IN THE MIDDLE OF A VAST DESERT...

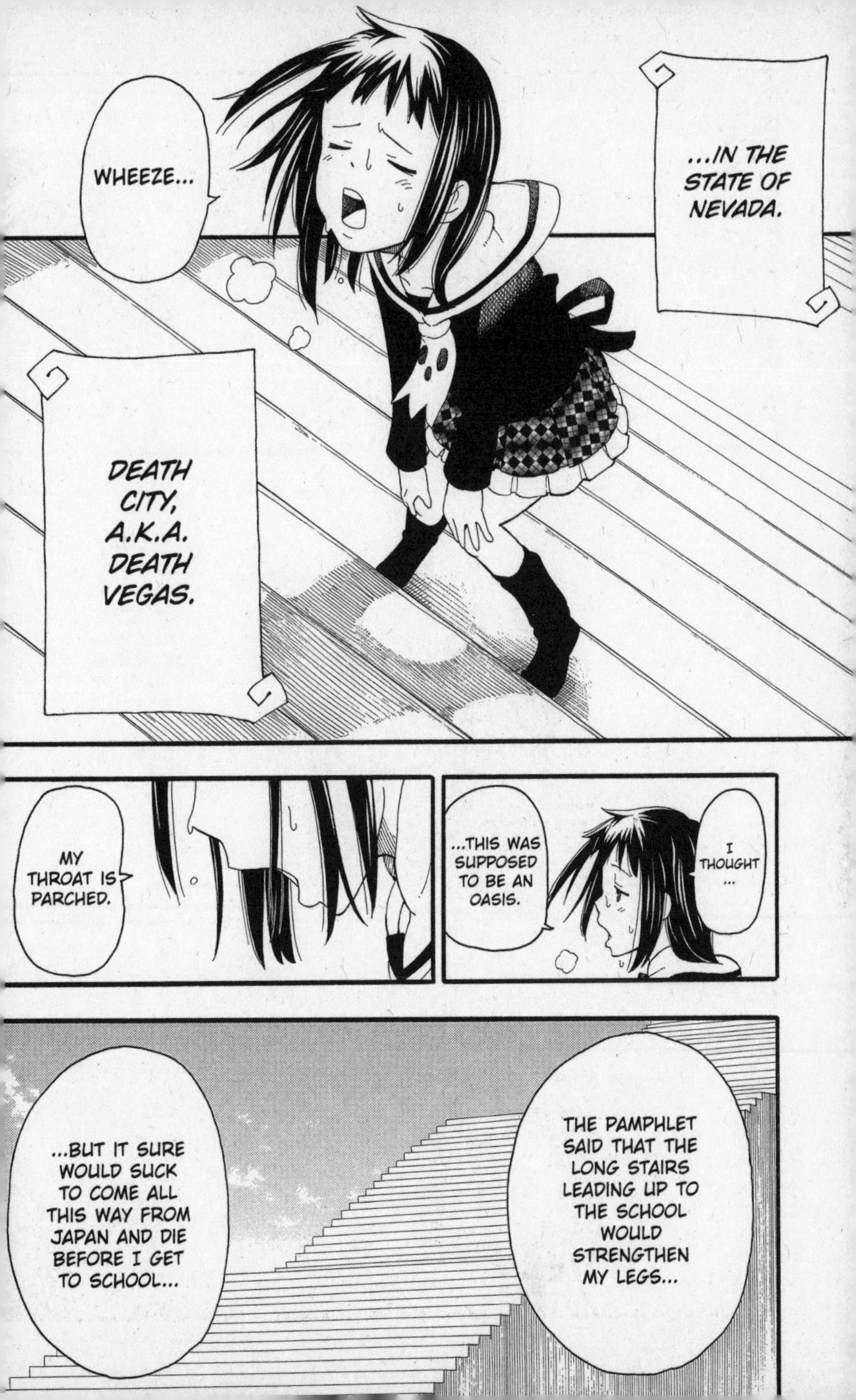
...IN THE STATE OF NEVADA.
WHEEZE...
DEATH CITY, A.K.A. DEATH VEGAS.
I THOUGHT ...
...THIS WAS SUPPOSED TO BE AN OASIS.
MY THROAT IS PARCHED.
THE PAMPHLET SAID THAT THE LONG STAIRS LEADING UP TO THE SCHOOL WOULD STRENGTHEN MY LEGS...
...BUT IT SURE WOULD SUCK TO COME ALL THIS WAY FROM JAPAN AND DIE BEFORE I GET TO SCHOOL...

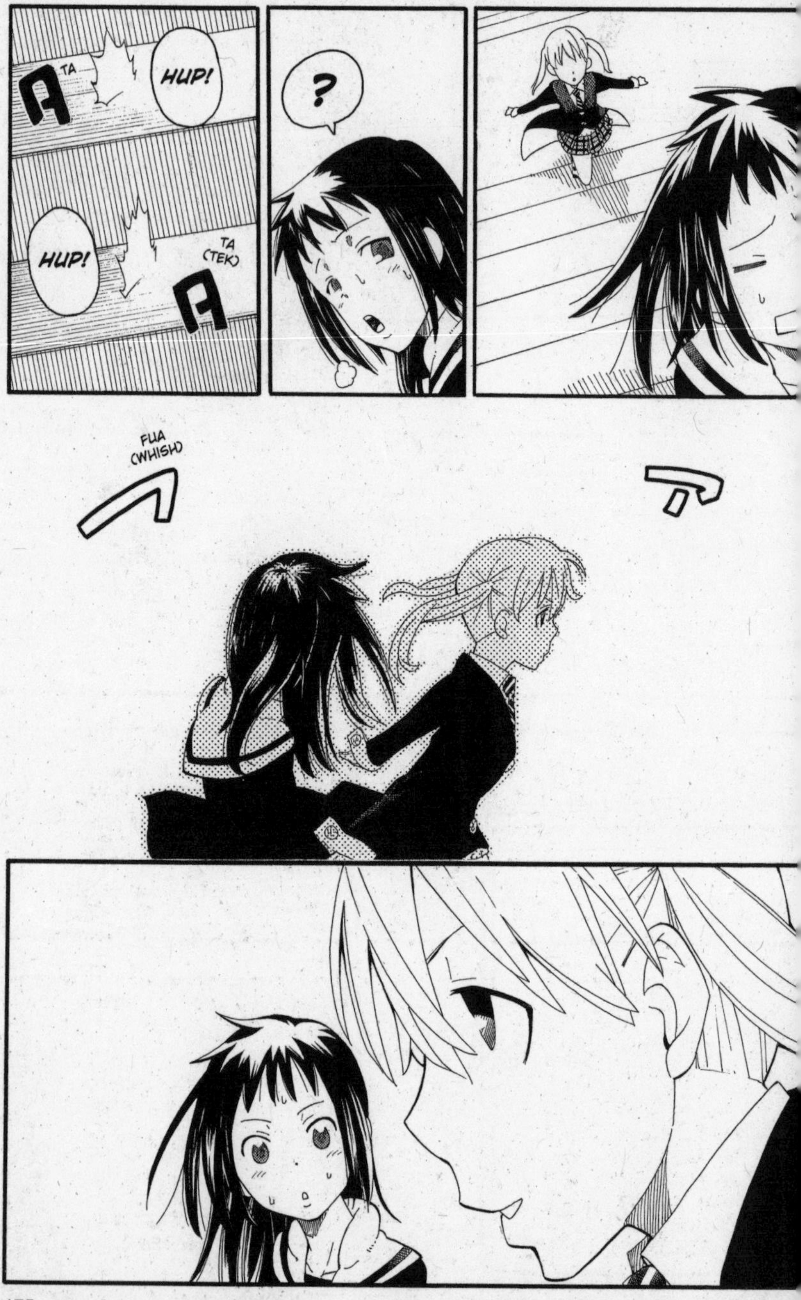
?
HUP!
TA
TA (TEK)
HUP!
FUA (WHISH)

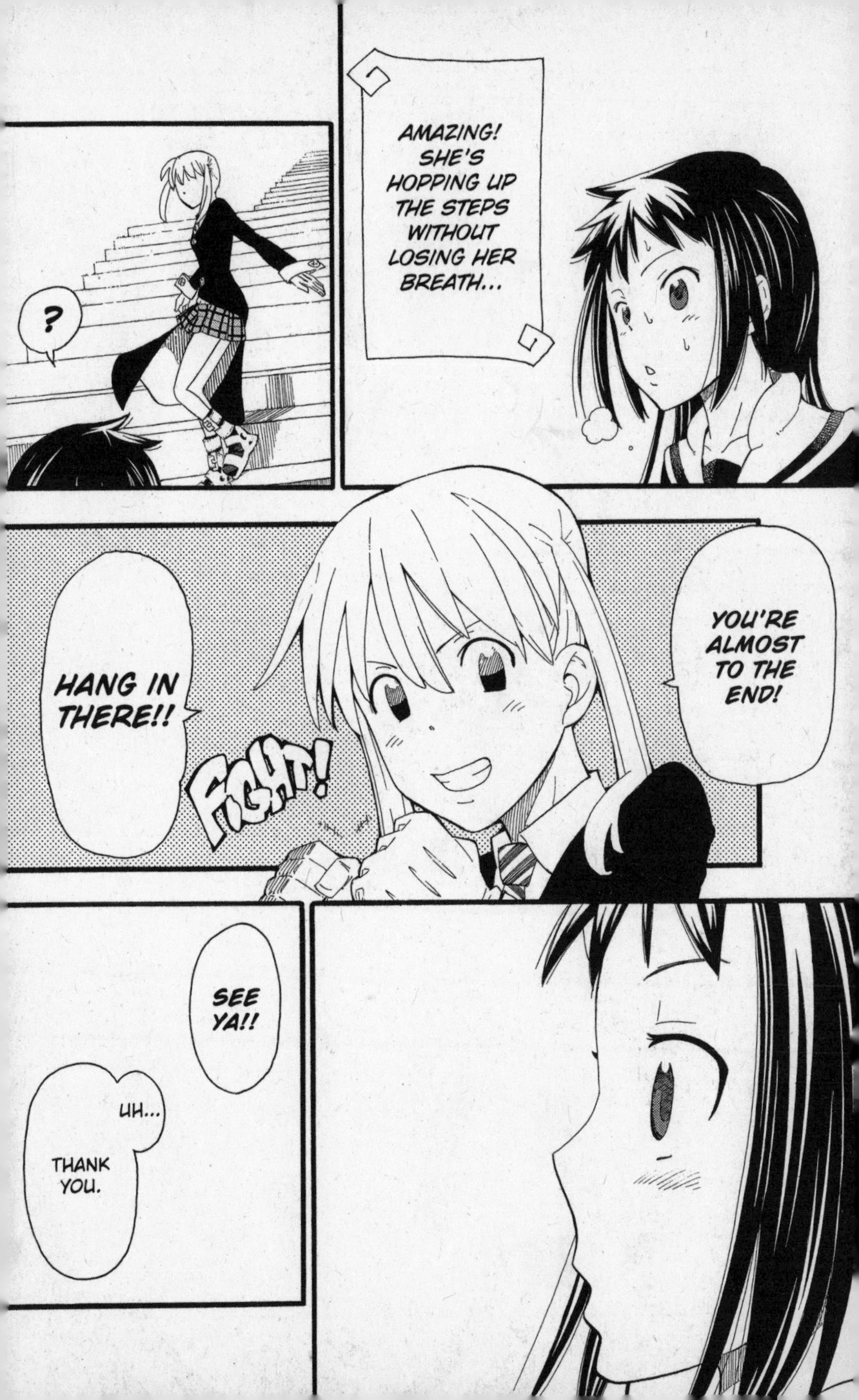
AMAZING! SHE'S HOPPING UP THE STEPS WITHOUT LOSING HER BREATH...
?
YOU'RE ALMOST TO THE END!
HANG IN THERE!!
FIGHT!
SEE YA!!
UH... THANK YOU.

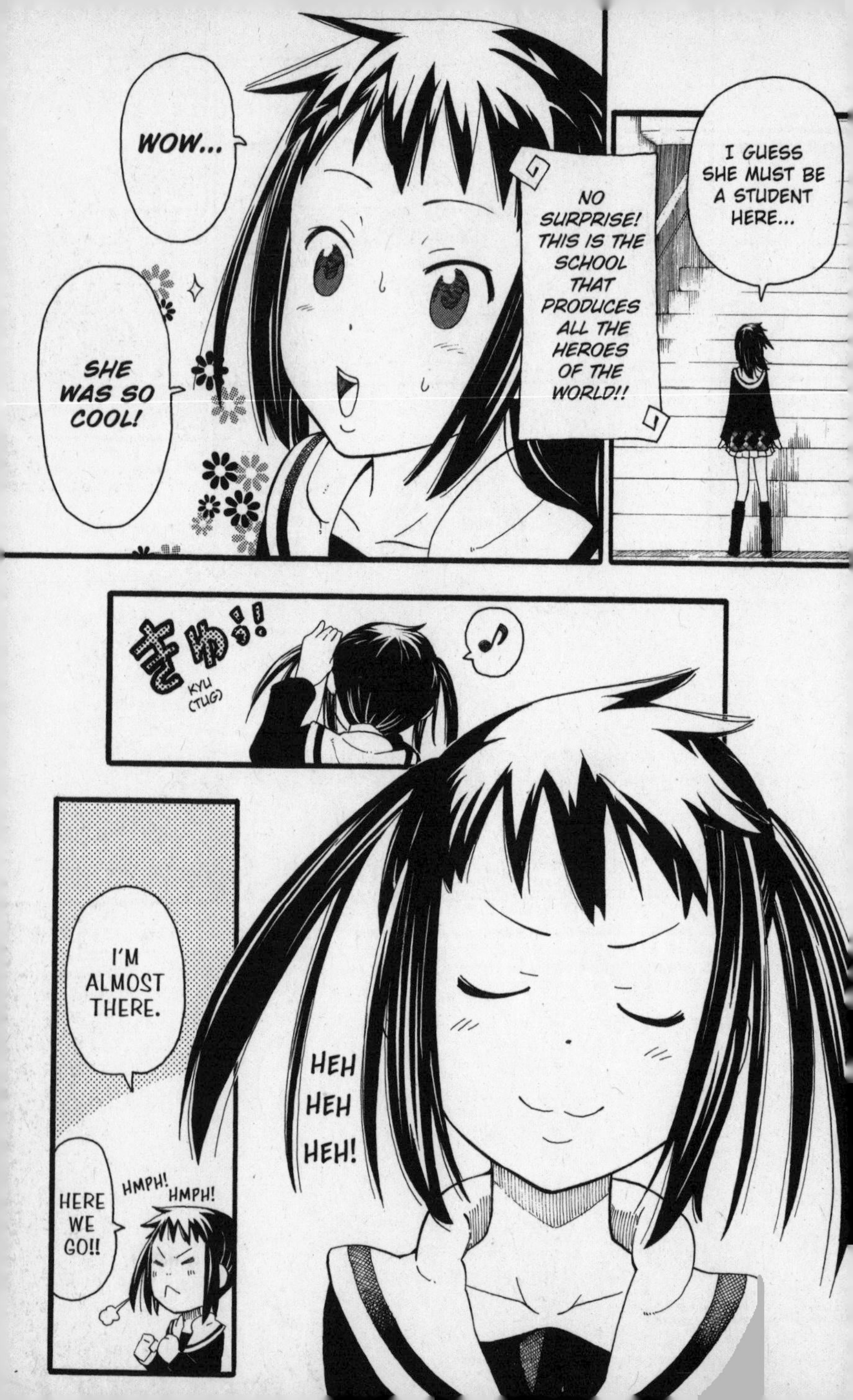
I GUESS SHE MUST BE A STUDENT HERE...
NO SURPRISE! THIS IS THE SCHOOL THAT PRODUCES ALL THE HEROES OF THE WORLD!!
WOW...
SHE WAS SO COOL!
♪
きゅっ!!
KYU (TUG)
HEH HEH HEH!
I'M ALMOST THERE.
HMPH! HMPH!
HERE WE GO!!

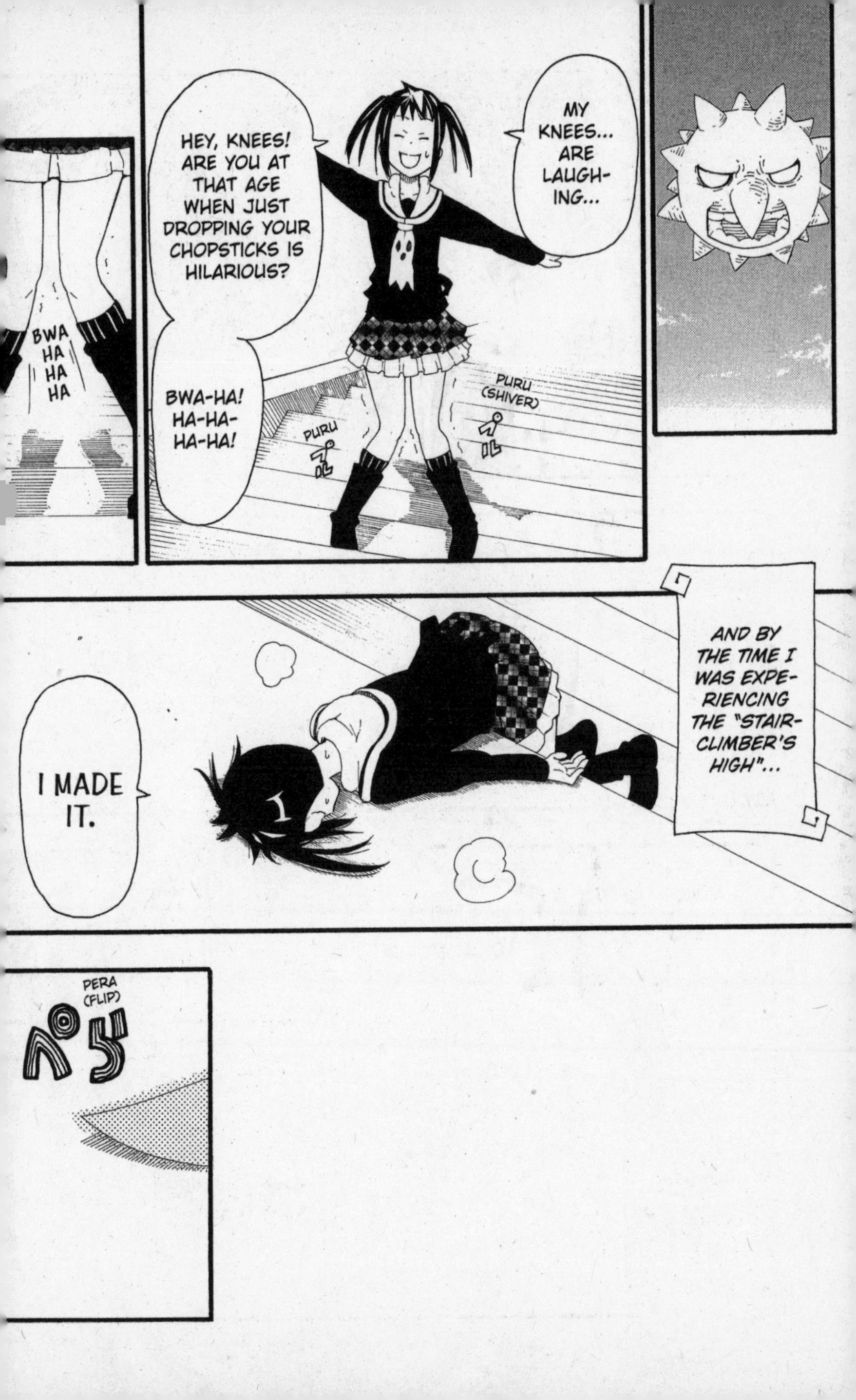
MY KNEES... ARE LAUGHING...
HEY, KNEES! ARE YOU AT THAT AGE WHEN JUST DROPPING YOUR CHOPSTICKS IS HILARIOUS?
PURU (SHIVER)
BWA-HA! HA-HA-HA-HA!
PURU
BWA HA HA HA
AND BY THE TIME I WAS EXPERIENCING THE "STAIR-CLIMBER'S HIGH"...
I MADE IT.
PERA (FLIP)

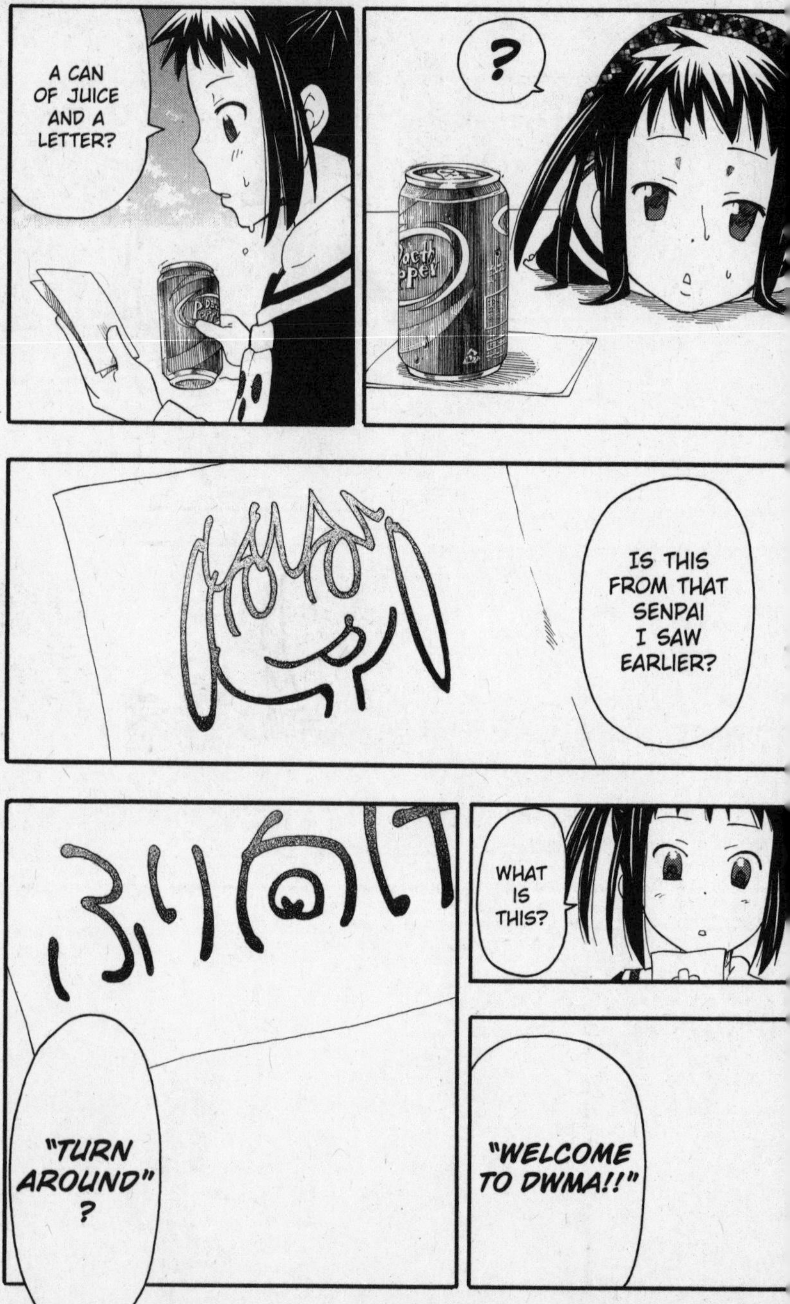
?
A CAN OF JUICE AND A LETTER?
IS THIS FROM THAT SENPAI I SAW EARLIER?
WHAT IS THIS?
"WELCOME TO DWMA!!"
ふり向いて
"TURN AROUND" ?

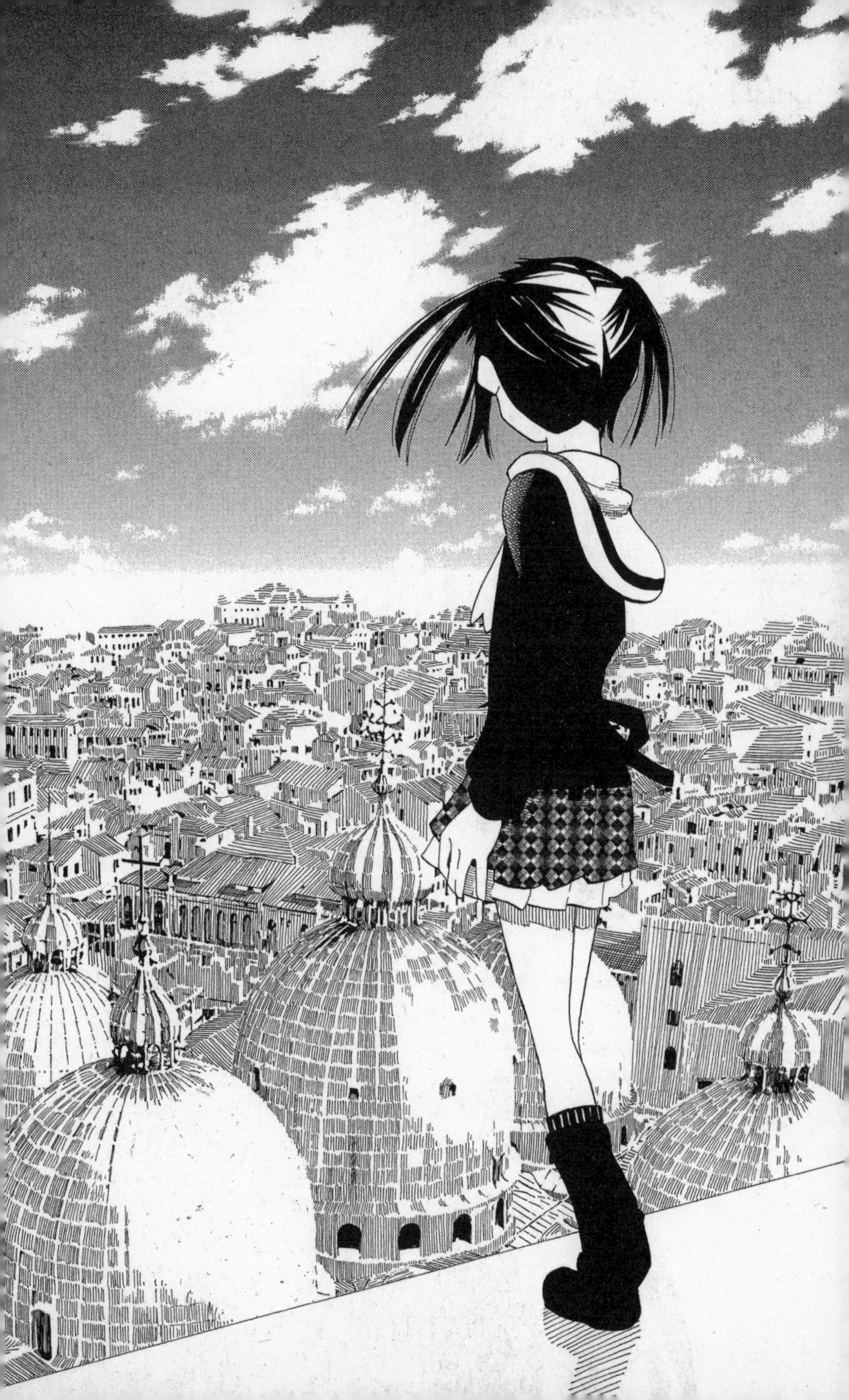

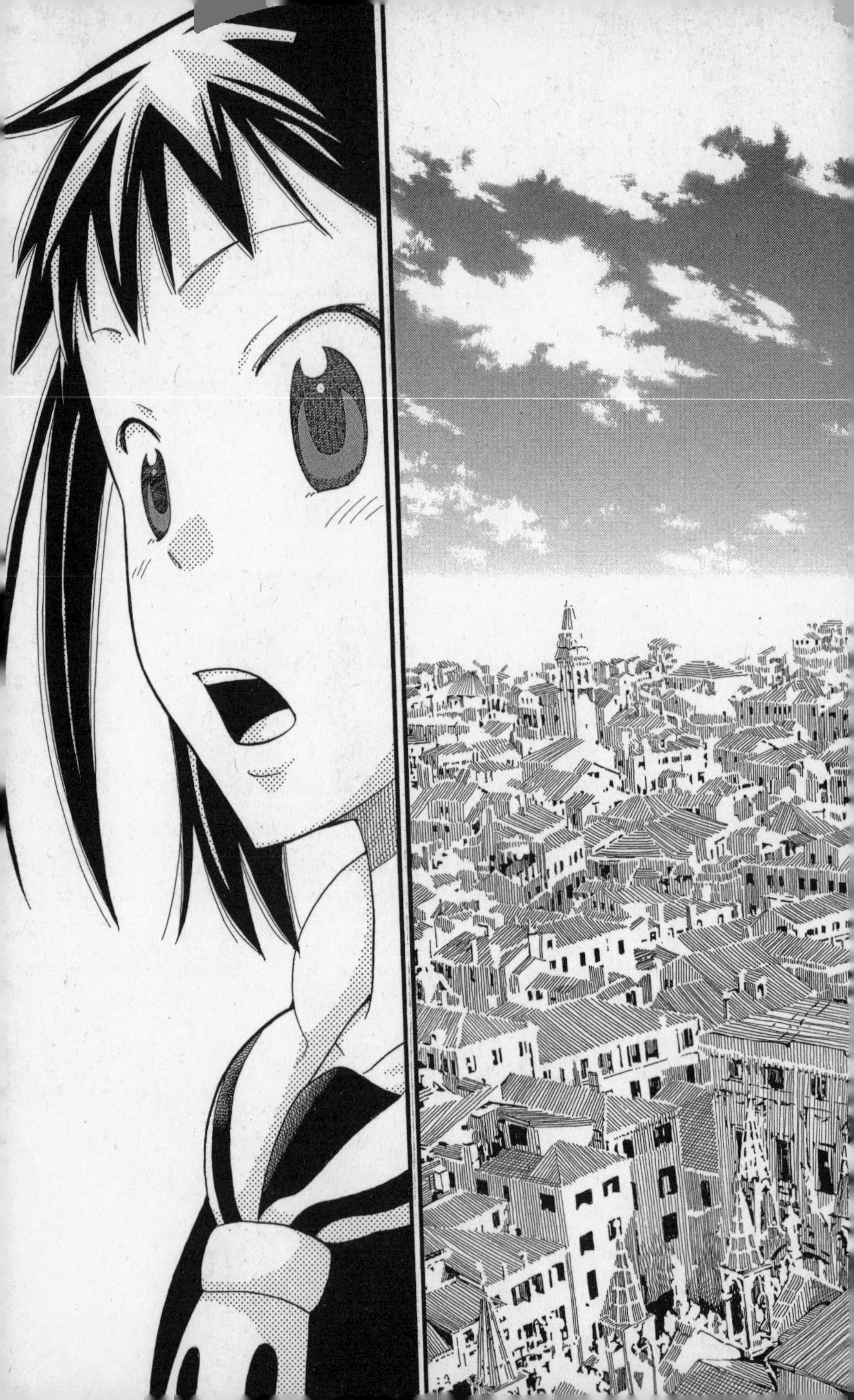

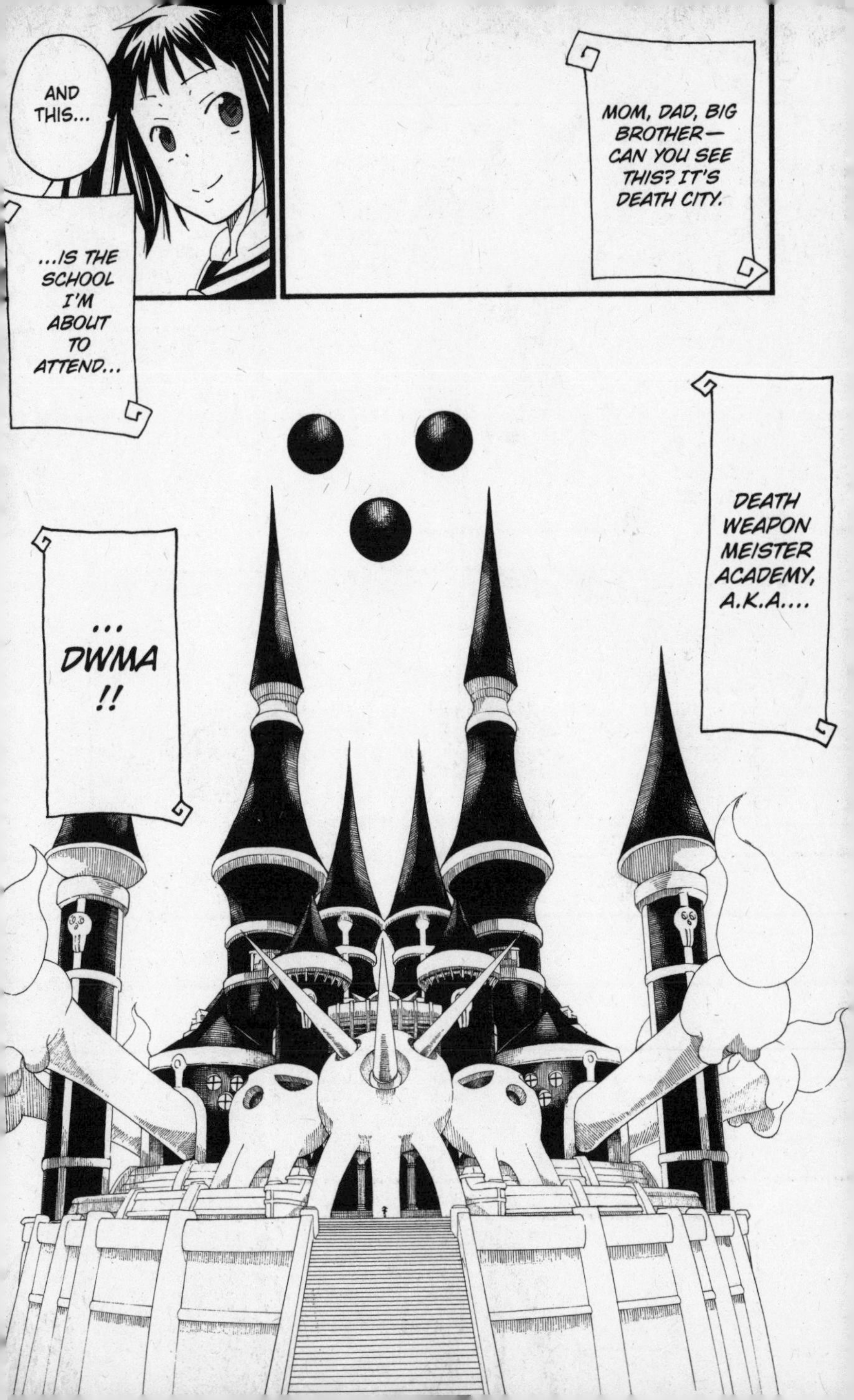
MOM, DAD, BIG BROTHER— CAN YOU SEE THIS? IT'S DEATH CITY.
AND THIS...
...IS THE SCHOOL I'M ABOUT TO ATTEND...
DEATH WEAPON MEISTER ACADEMY, A.K.A....
... DWMA !!

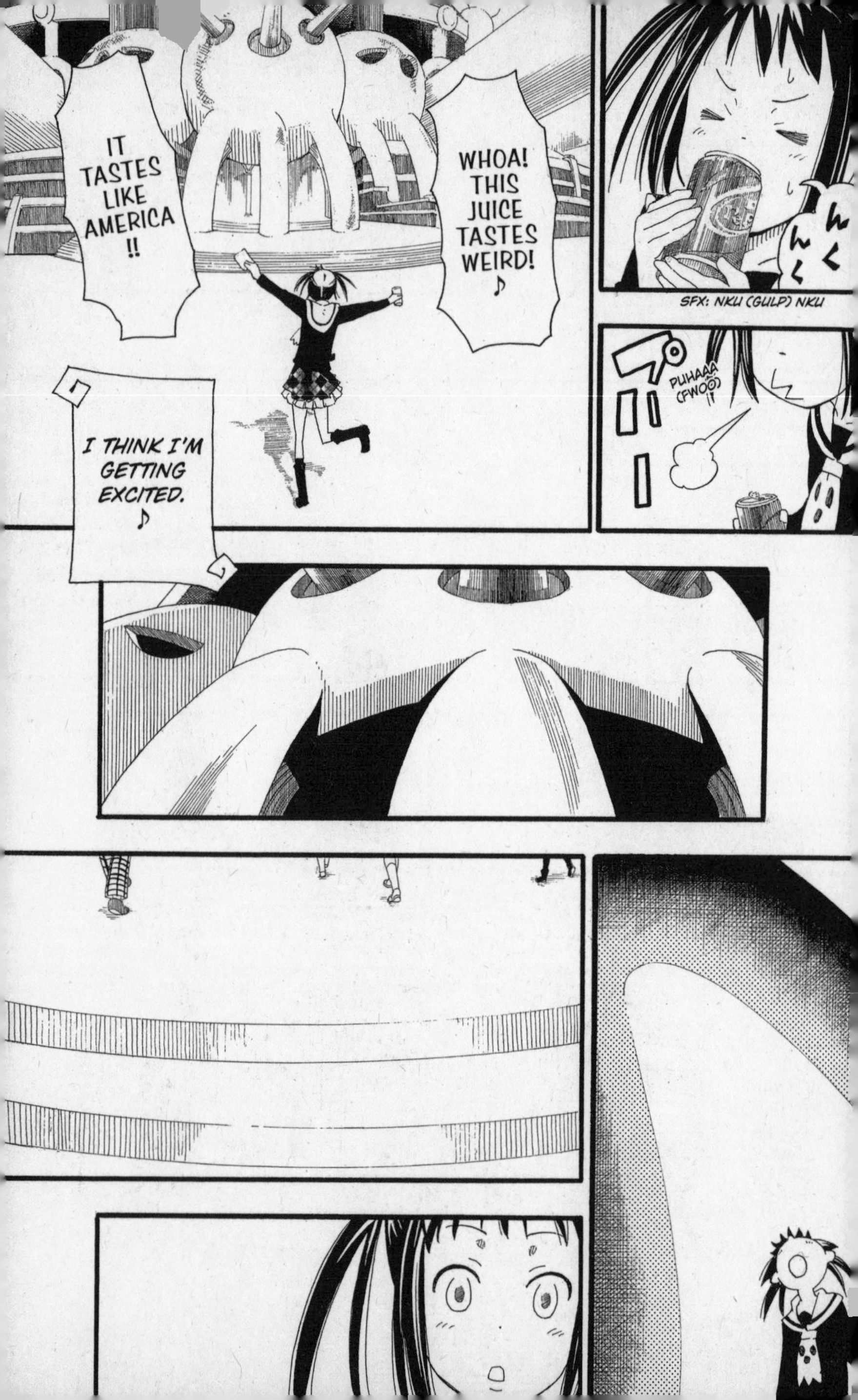
SFX: NKU (GULP) NKU
PUHAAA (FWOO)
WHOA! THIS JUICE TASTES WEIRD! ♪
IT TASTES LIKE AMERICA!!
I THINK I'M GETTING EXCITED. ♪

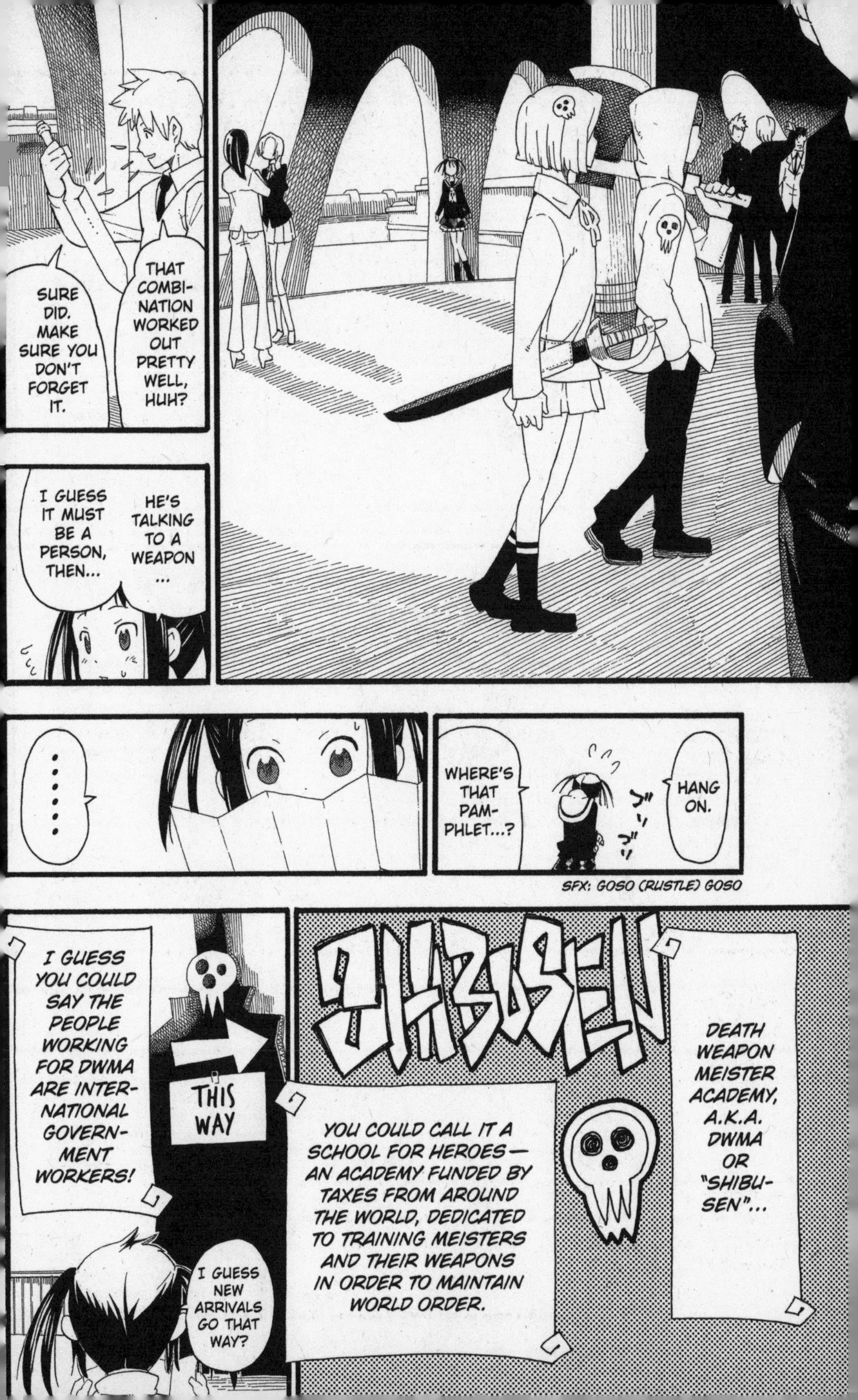
THAT COMBINATION WORKED OUT PRETTY WELL, HUH?
SURE DID. MAKE SURE YOU DON'T FORGET IT.
HE'S TALKING TO A WEAPON...
I GUESS IT MUST BE A PERSON, THEN...
HANG ON.
WHERE'S THAT PAMPHLET...?
......
SFX: GOSO (RUSTLE) GOSO
SHIBUSEN
DEATH WEAPON MEISTER ACADEMY, A.K.A. DWMA OR "SHIBUSEN"...
YOU COULD CALL IT A SCHOOL FOR HEROES—AN ACADEMY FUNDED BY TAXES FROM AROUND THE WORLD, DEDICATED TO TRAINING MEISTERS AND THEIR WEAPONS IN ORDER TO MAINTAIN WORLD ORDER.
I GUESS YOU COULD SAY THE PEOPLE WORKING FOR DWMA ARE INTERNATIONAL GOVERNMENT WORKERS!
THIS WAY
I GUESS NEW ARRIVALS GO THAT WAY?

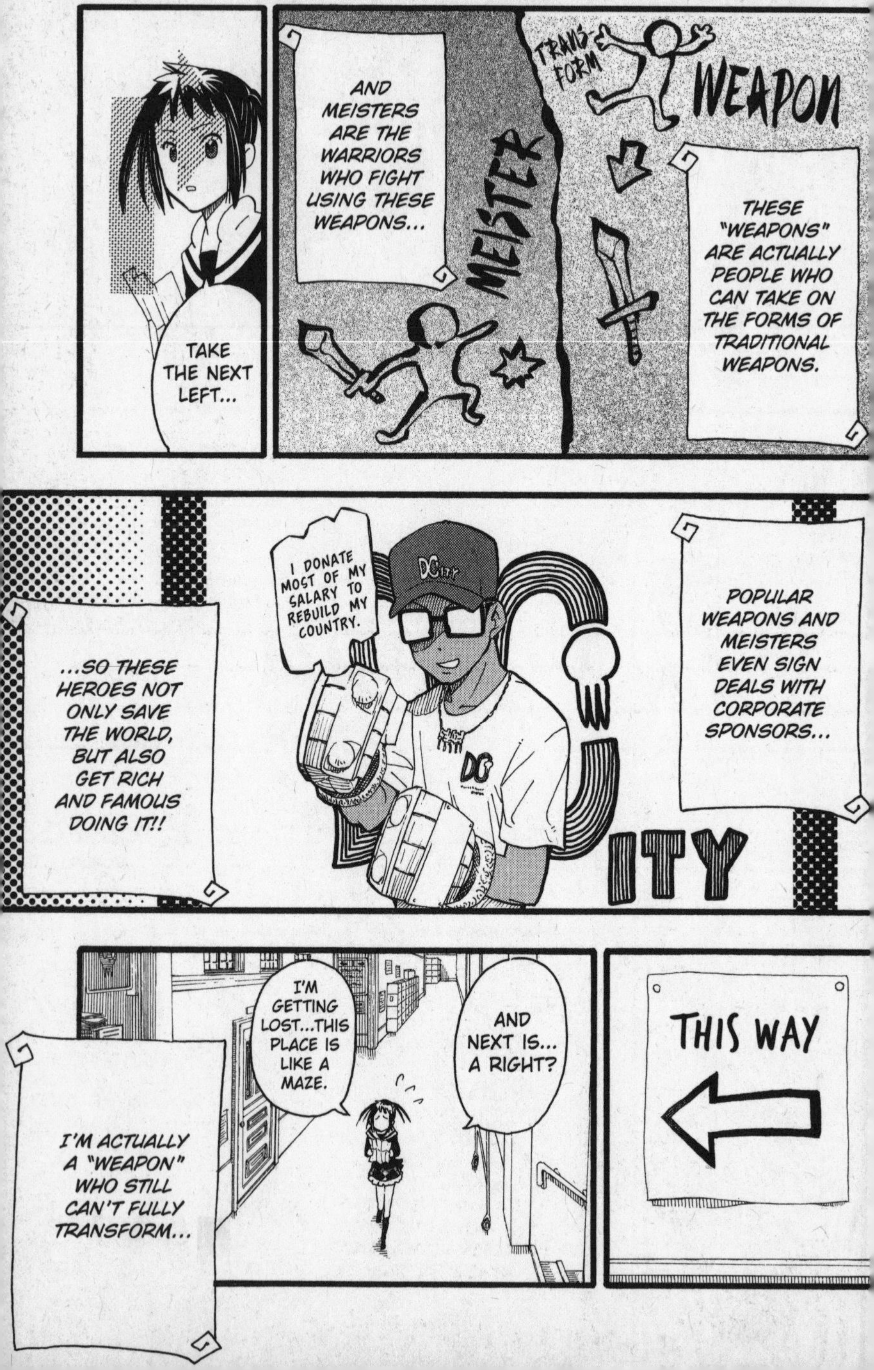
TRANS-FORM
WEAPON
THESE "WEAPONS" ARE ACTUALLY PEOPLE WHO CAN TAKE ON THE FORMS OF TRADITIONAL WEAPONS.
MEISTER
AND MEISTERS ARE THE WARRIORS WHO FIGHT USING THESE WEAPONS...
TAKE THE NEXT LEFT...
POPULAR WEAPONS AND MEISTERS EVEN SIGN DEALS WITH CORPORATE SPONSORS...
I DONATE MOST OF MY SALARY TO REBUILD MY COUNTRY.
ITY
...SO THESE HEROES NOT ONLY SAVE THE WORLD, BUT ALSO GET RICH AND FAMOUS DOING IT!!
THIS WAY
AND NEXT IS... A RIGHT?
I'M GETTING LOST...THIS PLACE IS LIKE A MAZE.
I'M ACTUALLY A "WEAPON" WHO STILL CAN'T FULLY TRANSFORM...

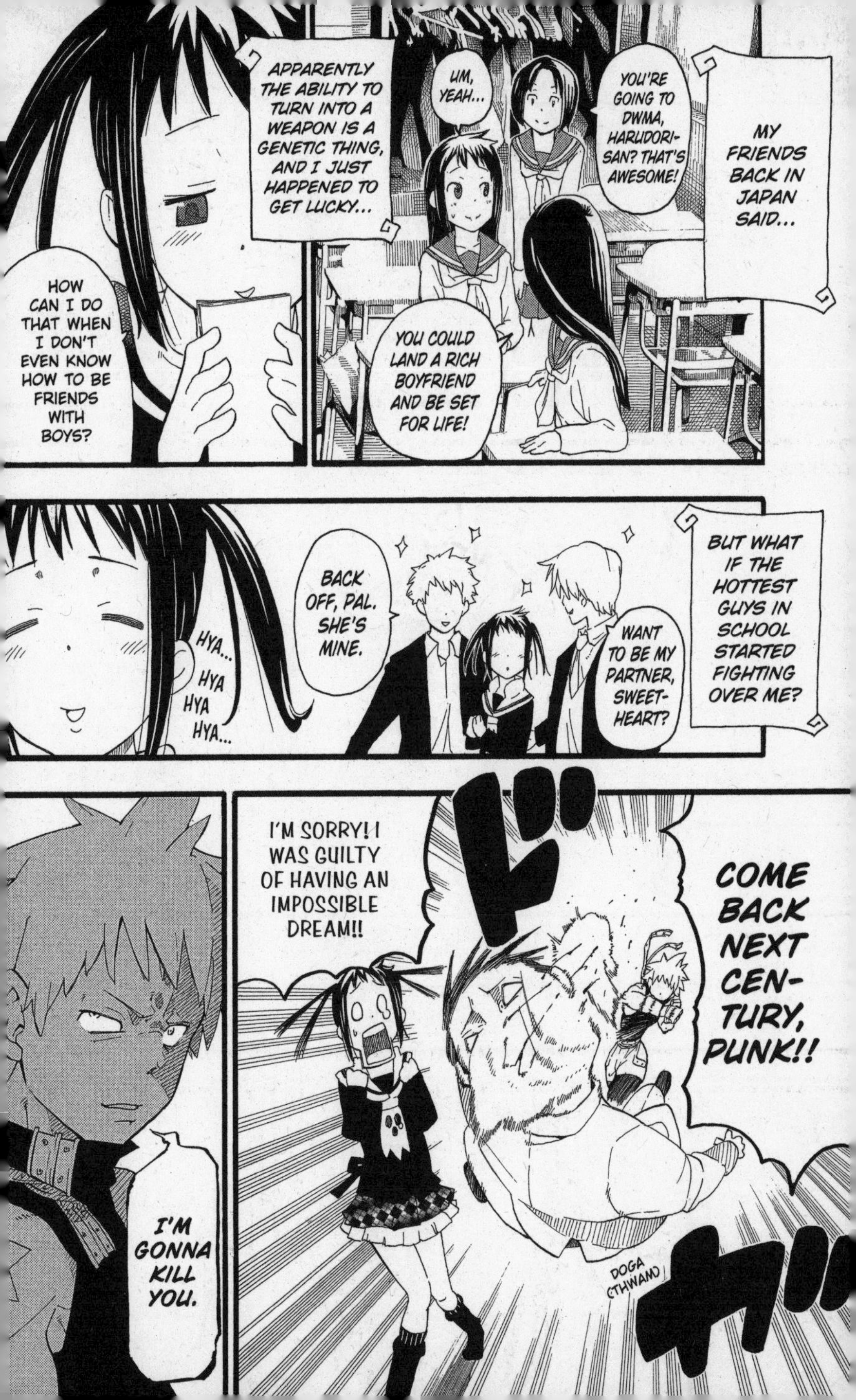
MY FRIENDS BACK IN JAPAN SAID...
YOU'RE GOING TO DWMA, HARUDORI-SAN? THAT'S AWESOME!
UM, YEAH...
YOU COULD LAND A RICH BOYFRIEND AND BE SET FOR LIFE!
APPARENTLY THE ABILITY TO TURN INTO A WEAPON IS A GENETIC THING, AND I JUST HAPPENED TO GET LUCKY...
HOW CAN I DO THAT WHEN I DON'T EVEN KNOW HOW TO BE FRIENDS WITH BOYS?
BUT WHAT IF THE HOTTEST GUYS IN SCHOOL STARTED FIGHTING OVER ME?
WANT TO BE MY PARTNER, SWEET-HEART?
BACK OFF, PAL. SHE'S MINE.
HYA... HYA HYA HYA...
COME BACK NEXT CEN-TURY, PUNK!!
I'M SORRY!! I WAS GUILTY OF HAVING AN IMPOSSIBLE DREAM!!
DOGA (THWAM)
I'M GONNA KILL YOU.

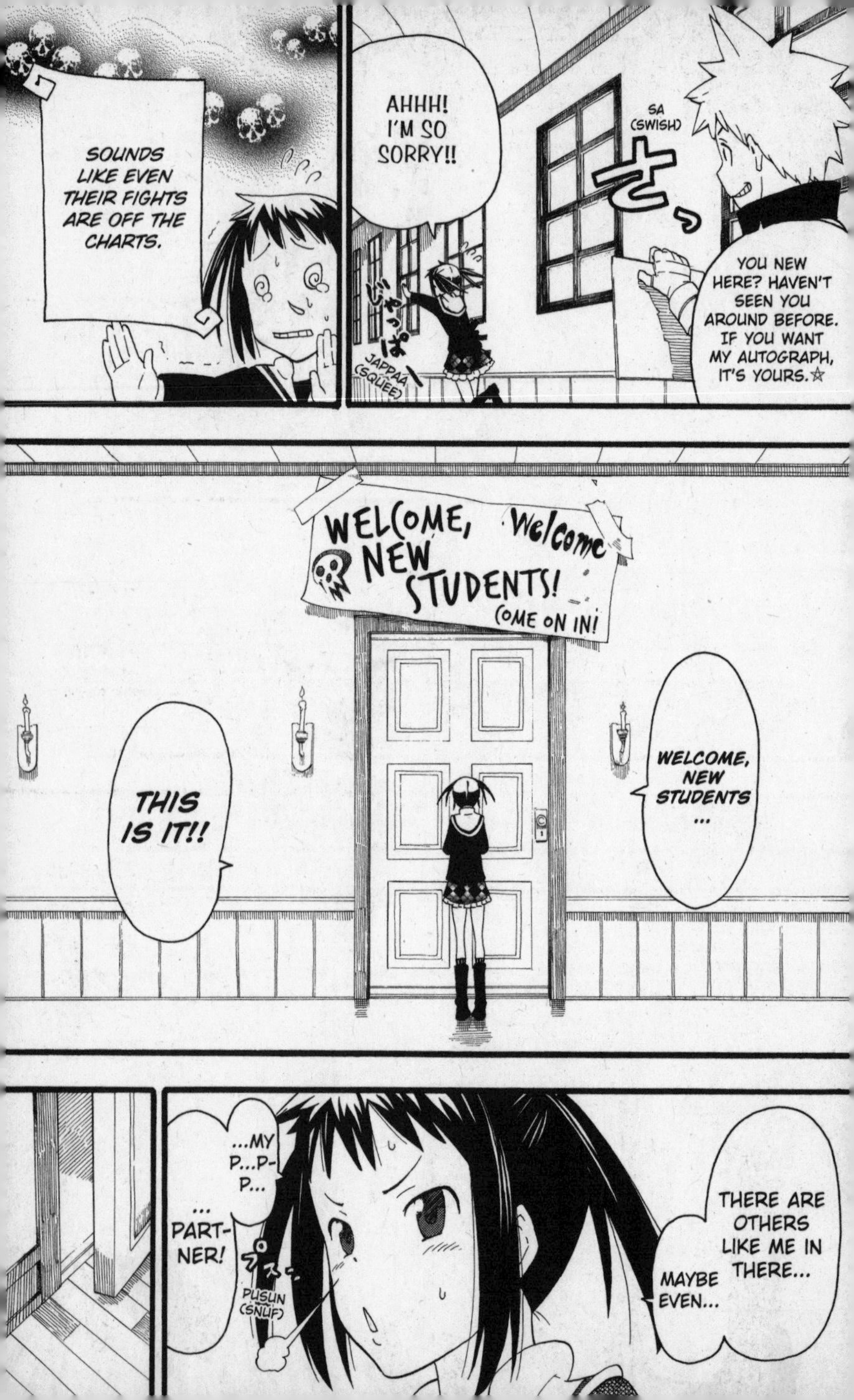
SA (SWISH)
YOU NEW HERE? HAVEN'T SEEN YOU AROUND BEFORE. IF YOU WANT MY AUTOGRAPH, IT'S YOURS.☆
AHHH! I'M SO SORRY!!
JAPPAA (SQUEE)
SOUNDS LIKE EVEN THEIR FIGHTS ARE OFF THE CHARTS.
WELCOME, NEW STUDENTS!
Welcome
COME ON IN!
WELCOME, NEW STUDENTS ...
THIS IS IT!!
THERE ARE OTHERS LIKE ME IN THERE...
MAYBE EVEN...
...MY P...P-P...
... PART-NER!
PUSUN (SNUF)

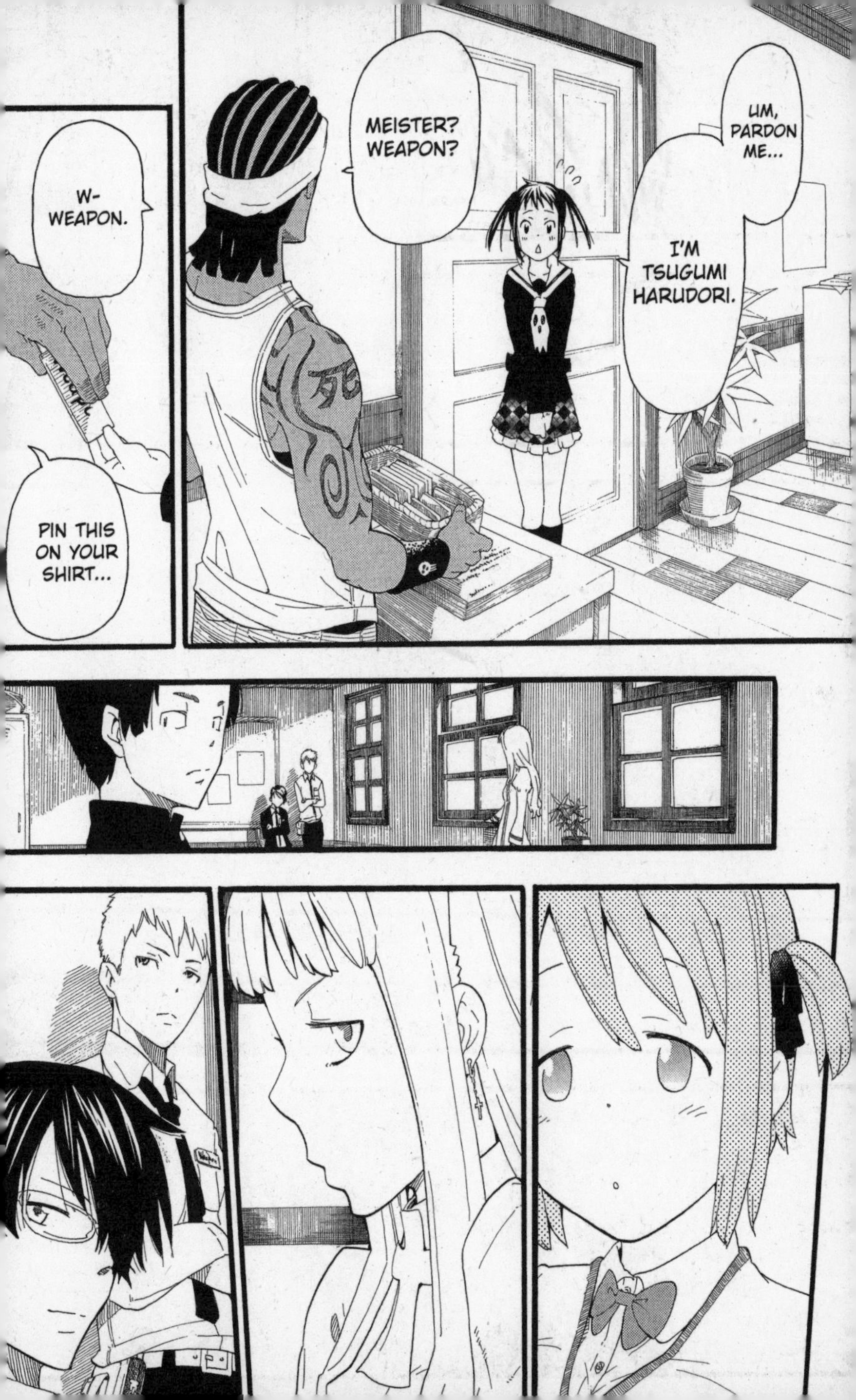

UM, PARDON ME...
I'M TSUGUMI HARUDORI.
MEISTER? WEAPON?
W-WEAPON.
PIN THIS ON YOUR SHIRT...

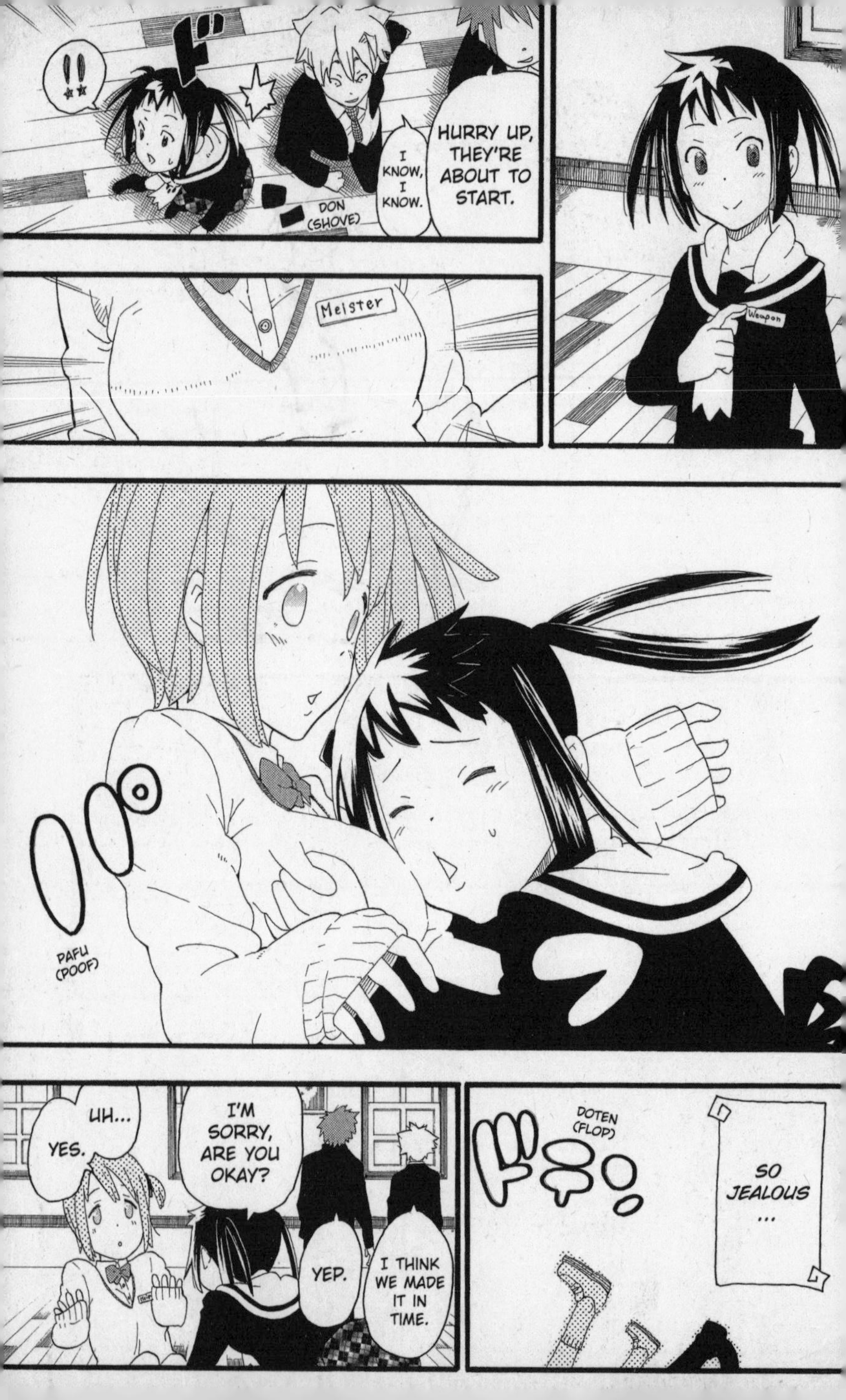
Weapon
HURRY UP, THEY'RE ABOUT TO START.
I KNOW, I KNOW.
DON (SHOVE)
!!
Meister
PAFU (POOF)
SO JEALOUS ...
DOTEN (FLOP)
I'M SORRY, ARE YOU OKAY?
UH... YES.
I THINK WE MADE IT IN TIME.
YEP.

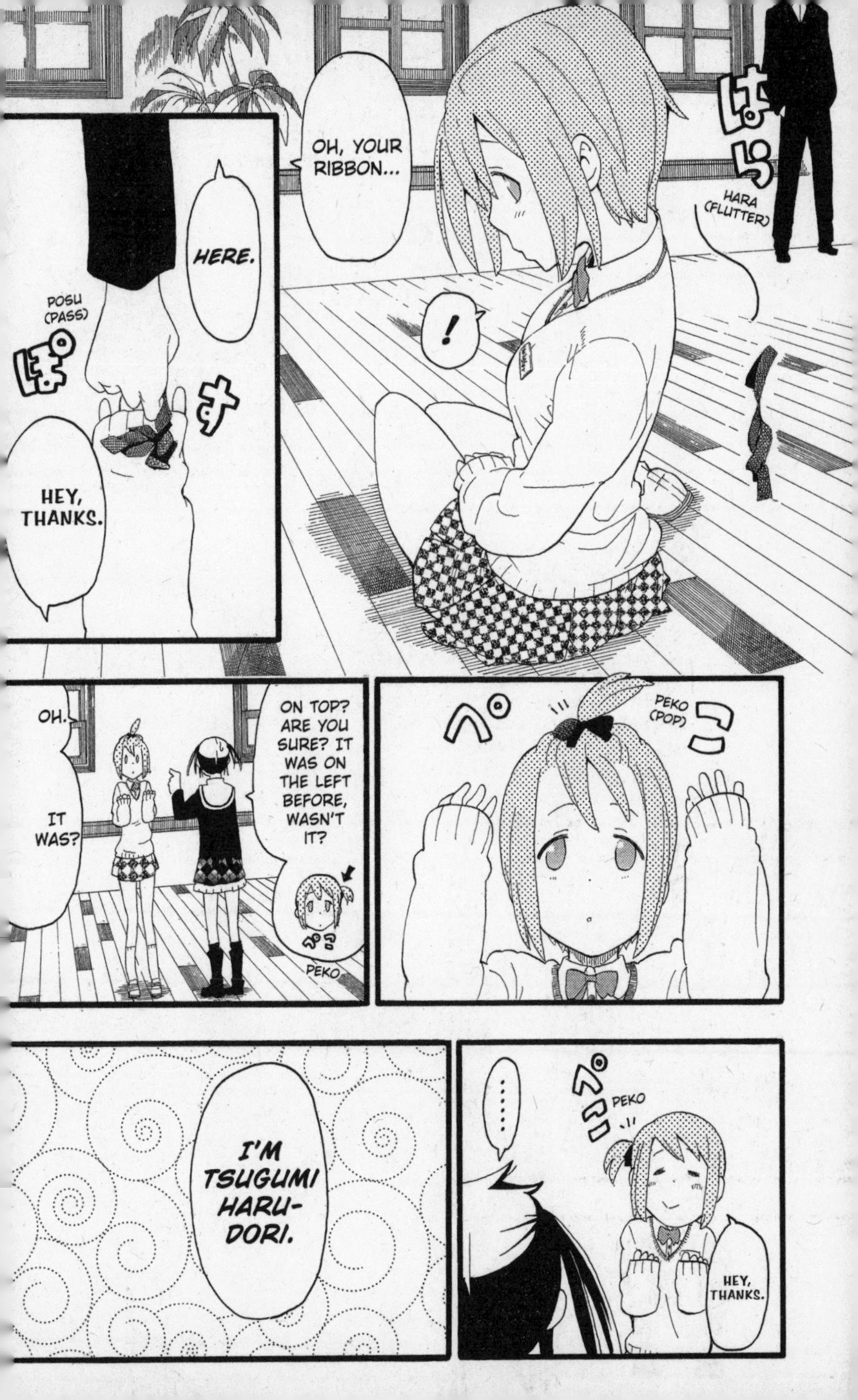
ぱら
HARA (FLUTTER)
OH, YOUR RIBBON...
!
HERE.
ぽす
POSU (PASS)
HEY, THANKS.
ぺこ
PEKO (POP)
ON TOP? ARE YOU SURE? IT WAS ON THE LEFT BEFORE, WASN'T IT?
ぺこ
PEKO
OH.
IT WAS?
......
ぺこ
PEKO
HEY, THANKS.
I'M TSUGUMI HARUDORI.

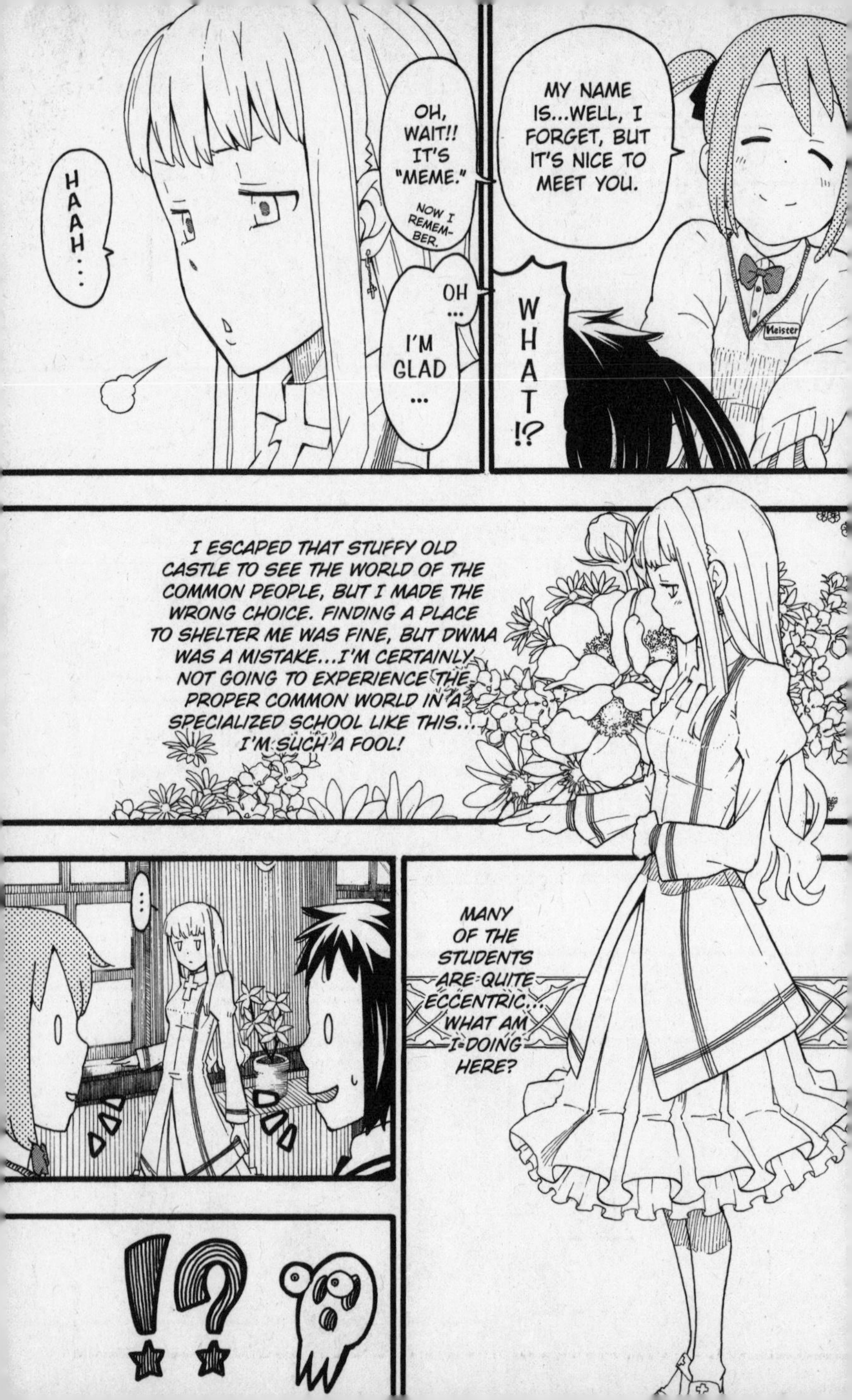

MY NAME IS...WELL, I FORGET, BUT IT'S NICE TO MEET YOU.
WHAT!?
OH, WAIT!! IT'S "MEME."
NOW I REMEMBER.
OH... I'M GLAD...
HAAH...
I ESCAPED THAT STUFFY OLD CASTLE TO SEE THE WORLD OF THE COMMON PEOPLE, BUT I MADE THE WRONG CHOICE. FINDING A PLACE TO SHELTER ME WAS FINE, BUT DWMA WAS A MISTAKE...I'M CERTAINLY NOT GOING TO EXPERIENCE THE PROPER COMMON WORLD IN A SPECIALIZED SCHOOL LIKE THIS... I'M SUCH A FOOL!
MANY OF THE STUDENTS ARE QUITE ECCENTRIC... WHAT AM I DOING HERE?
...
!?

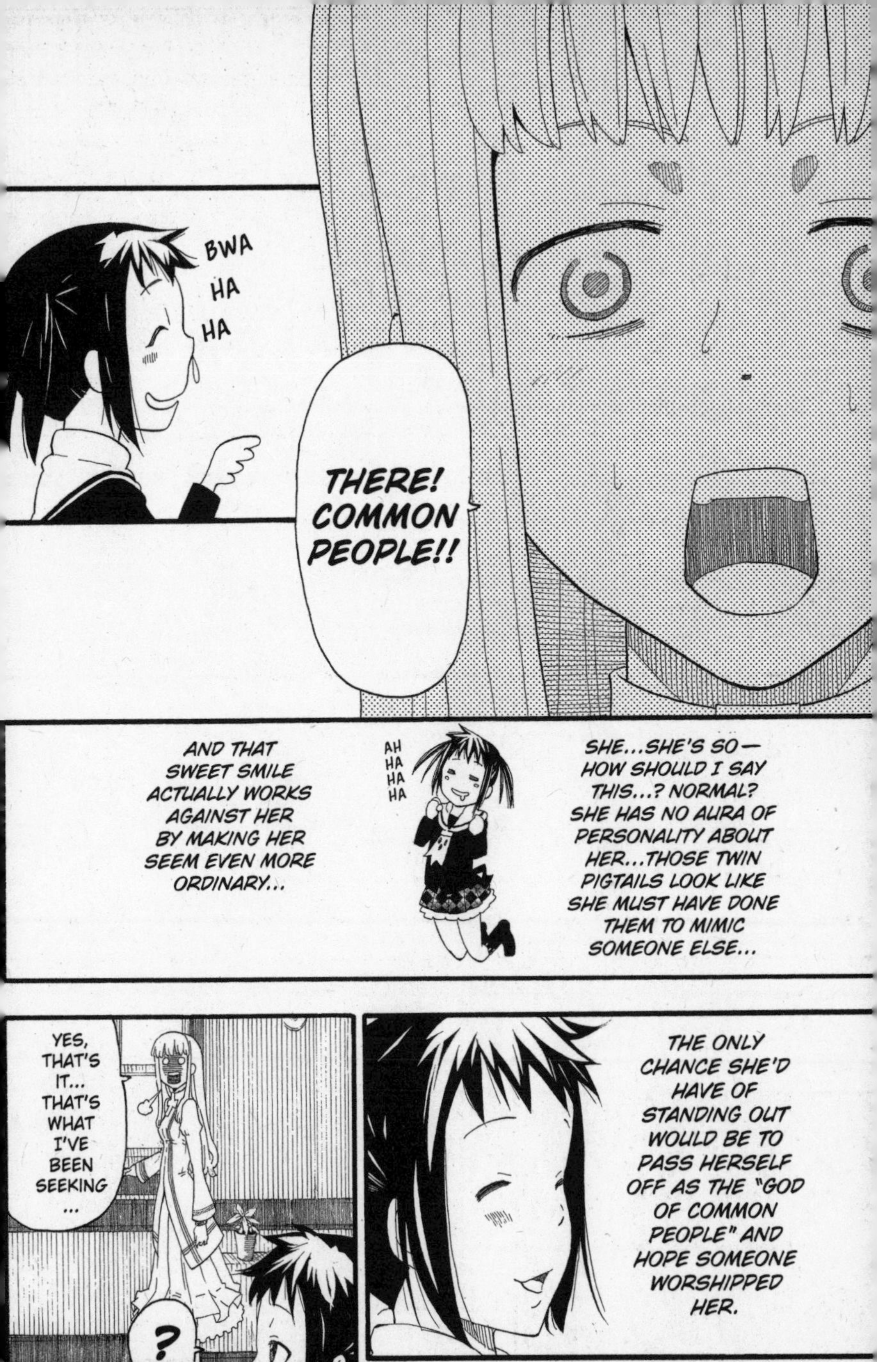
THERE! COMMON PEOPLE!!
BWA HA HA
SHE...SHE'S SO—HOW SHOULD I SAY THIS...? NORMAL? SHE HAS NO AURA OF PERSONALITY ABOUT HER...THOSE TWIN PIGTAILS LOOK LIKE SHE MUST HAVE DONE THEM TO MIMIC SOMEONE ELSE...
AH HA HA HA
AND THAT SWEET SMILE ACTUALLY WORKS AGAINST HER BY MAKING HER SEEM EVEN MORE ORDINARY...
THE ONLY CHANCE SHE'D HAVE OF STANDING OUT WOULD BE TO PASS HERSELF OFF AS THE "GOD OF COMMON PEOPLE" AND HOPE SOMEONE WORSHIPPED HER.
YES, THAT'S IT... THAT'S WHAT I'VE BEEN SEEKING...
?

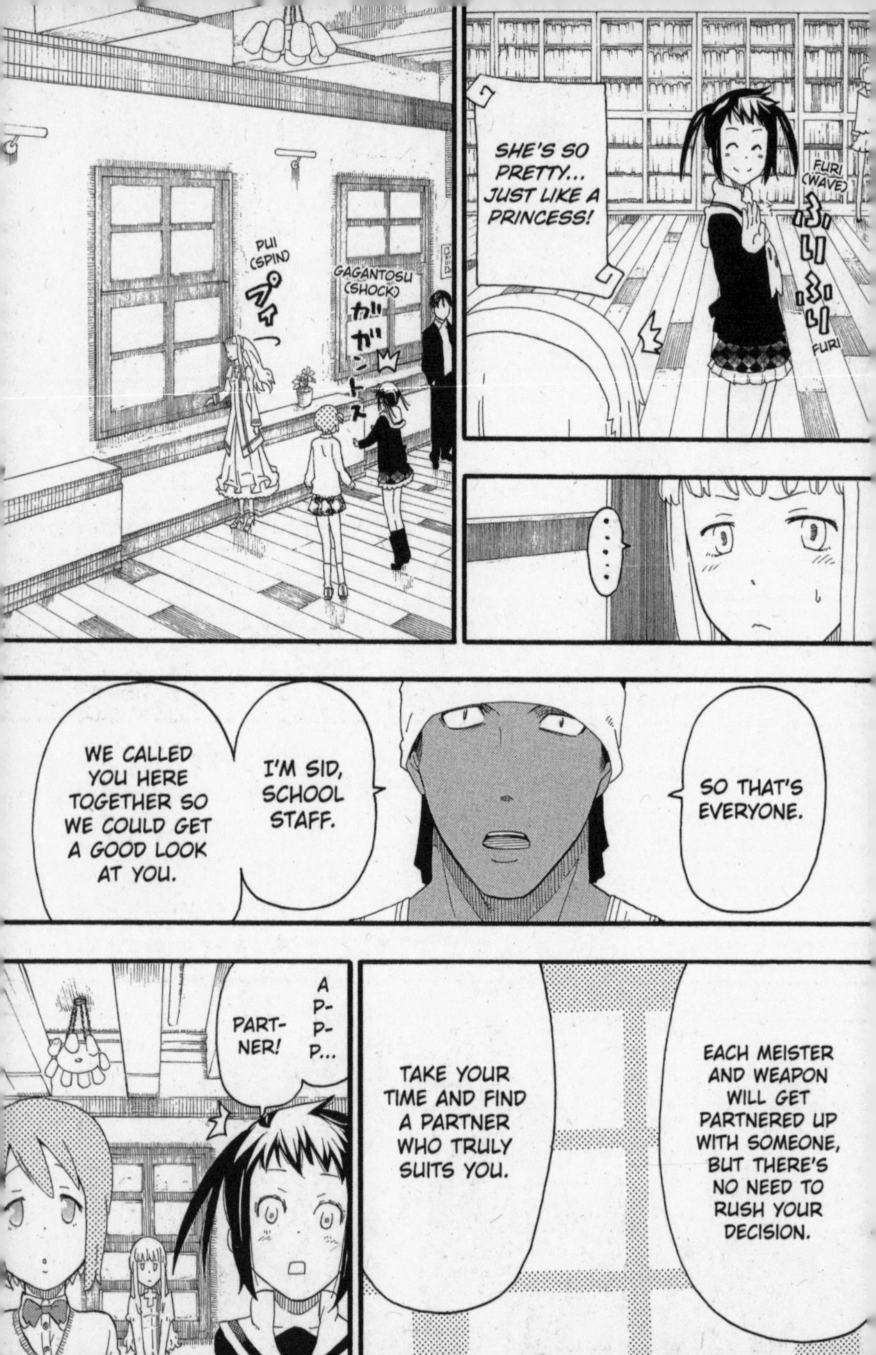
SHE'S SO PRETTY... JUST LIKE A PRINCESS!
FURI (WAVE)
FURI
.....
PUI (SPIN)
GAGANTOSU (SHOCK)
SO THAT'S EVERYONE.
I'M SID, SCHOOL STAFF.
WE CALLED YOU HERE TOGETHER SO WE COULD GET A GOOD LOOK AT YOU.
EACH MEISTER AND WEAPON WILL GET PARTNERED UP WITH SOMEONE, BUT THERE'S NO NEED TO RUSH YOUR DECISION.
TAKE YOUR TIME AND FIND A PARTNER WHO TRULY SUITS YOU.
A P-P-P...
PART-NER!

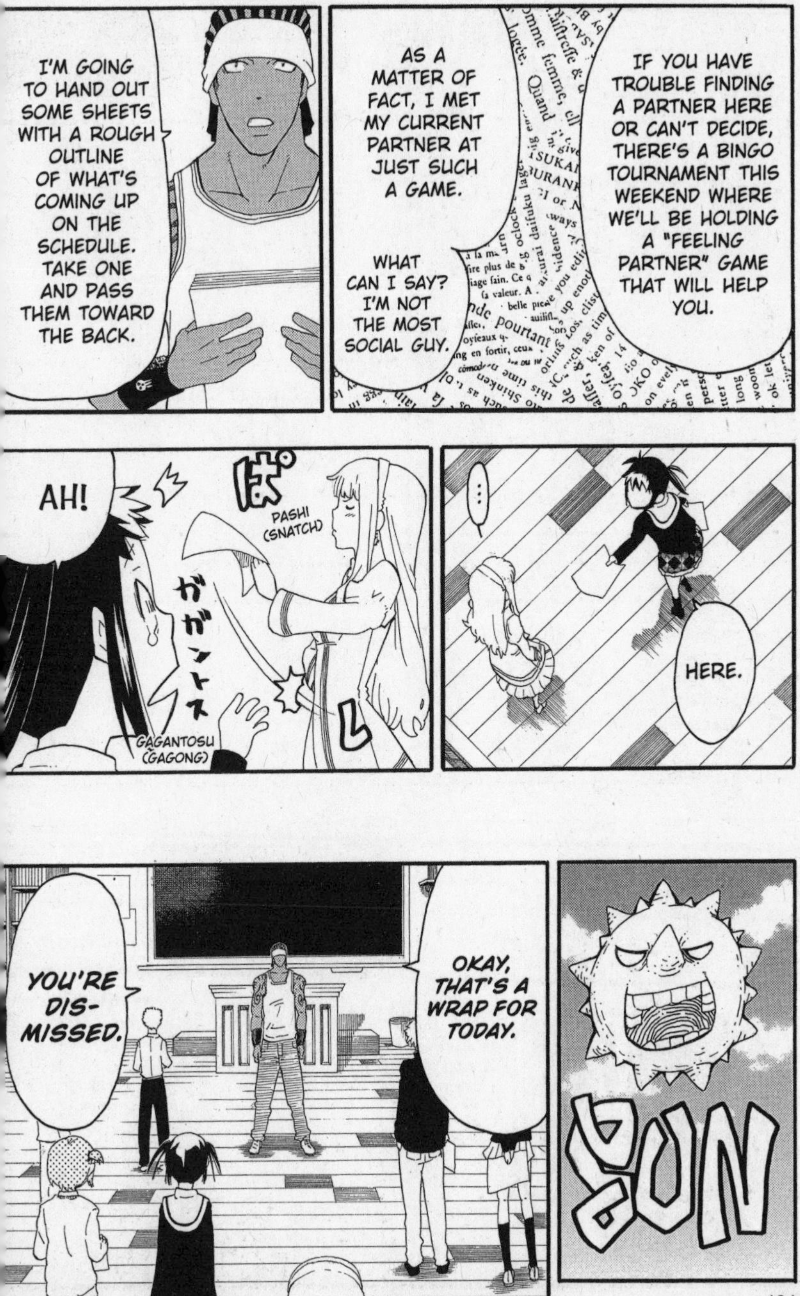
IF YOU HAVE TROUBLE FINDING A PARTNER HERE OR CAN'T DECIDE, THERE'S A BINGO TOURNAMENT THIS WEEKEND WHERE WE'LL BE HOLDING A "FEELING PARTNER" GAME THAT WILL HELP YOU.
AS A MATTER OF FACT, I MET MY CURRENT PARTNER AT JUST SUCH A GAME.
WHAT CAN I SAY? I'M NOT THE MOST SOCIAL GUY.
I'M GOING TO HAND OUT SOME SHEETS WITH A ROUGH OUTLINE OF WHAT'S COMING UP ON THE SCHEDULE. TAKE ONE AND PASS THEM TOWARD THE BACK.
...
HERE.
ぱ
PASHI (SNATCH)
AH!
ガガントス
GAGANTOSU (GAGONG)
DUN
OKAY, THAT'S A WRAP FOR TODAY.
YOU'RE DIS-MISSED.

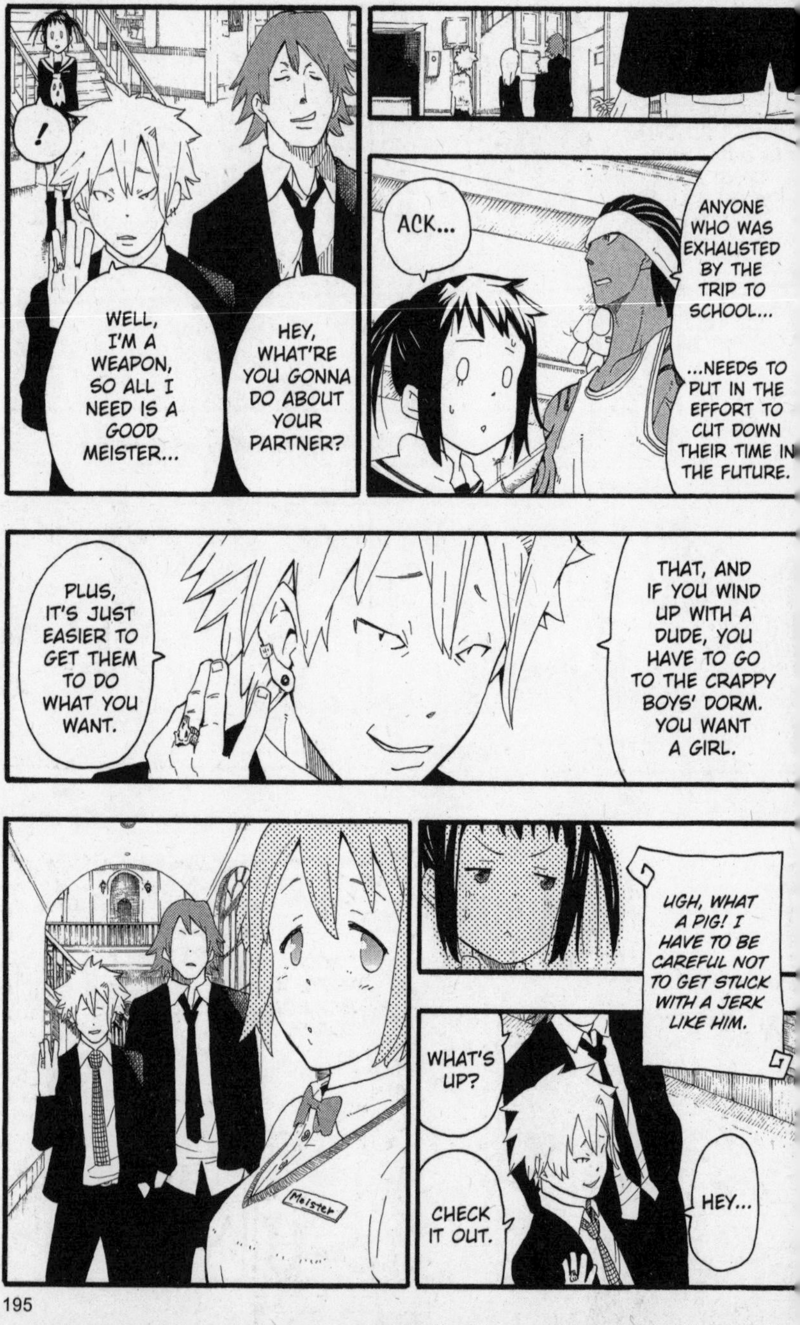
ANYONE WHO WAS EXHAUSTED BY THE TRIP TO SCHOOL...
...NEEDS TO PUT IN THE EFFORT TO CUT DOWN THEIR TIME IN THE FUTURE.
ACK...
HEY, WHAT'RE YOU GONNA DO ABOUT YOUR PARTNER?
WELL, I'M A WEAPON, SO ALL I NEED IS A GOOD MEISTER...
!
THAT, AND IF YOU WIND UP WITH A DUDE, YOU HAVE TO GO TO THE CRAPPY BOYS' DORM. YOU WANT A GIRL.
PLUS, IT'S JUST EASIER TO GET THEM TO DO WHAT YOU WANT.
UGH, WHAT A PIG! I HAVE TO BE CAREFUL NOT TO GET STUCK WITH A JERK LIKE HIM.
HEY...
WHAT'S UP?
CHECK IT OUT.
Meister

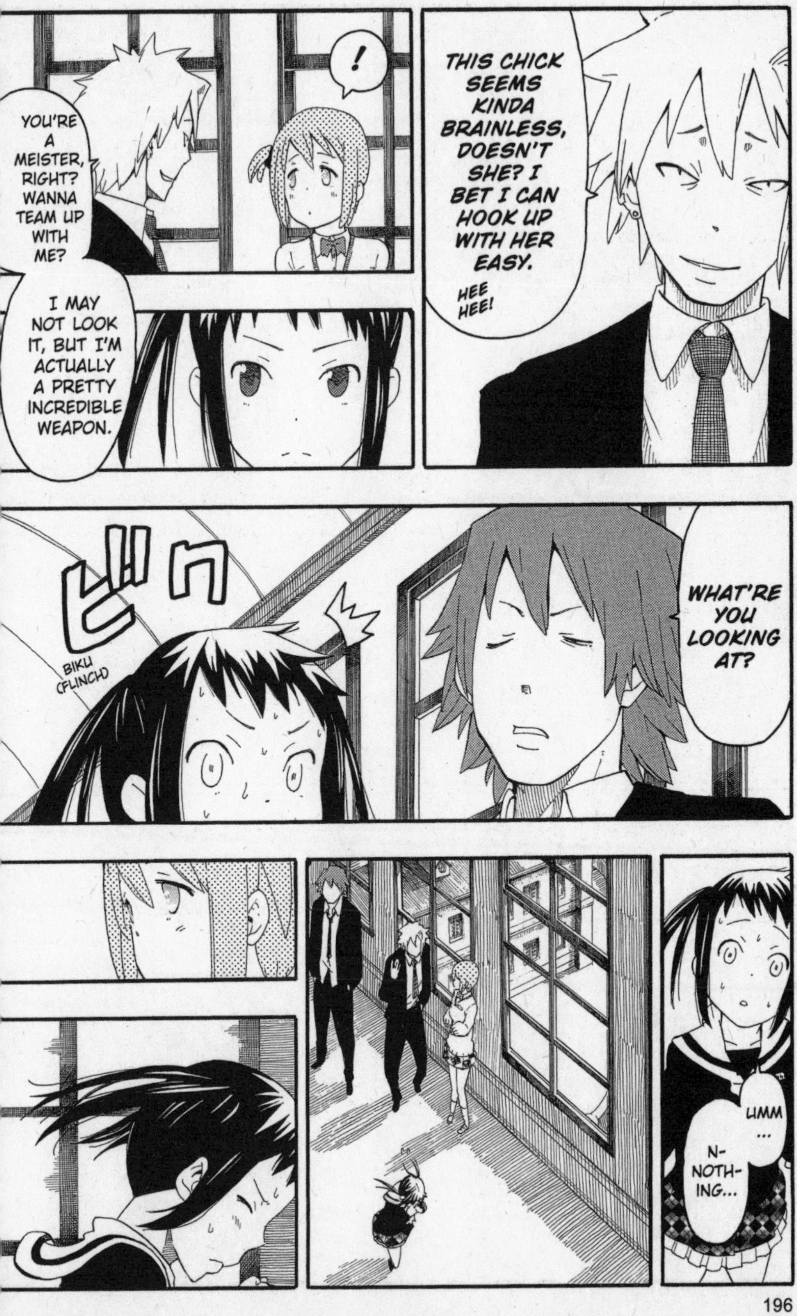
THIS CHICK SEEMS KINDA BRAINLESS, DOESN'T SHE? I BET I CAN HOOK UP WITH HER EASY.
HEE HEE!
!
YOU'RE A MEISTER, RIGHT? WANNA TEAM UP WITH ME?
I MAY NOT LOOK IT, BUT I'M ACTUALLY A PRETTY INCREDIBLE WEAPON.
WHAT'RE YOU LOOKING AT?
BIKU (FLINCH)
UMM ...
N-NOTHING...

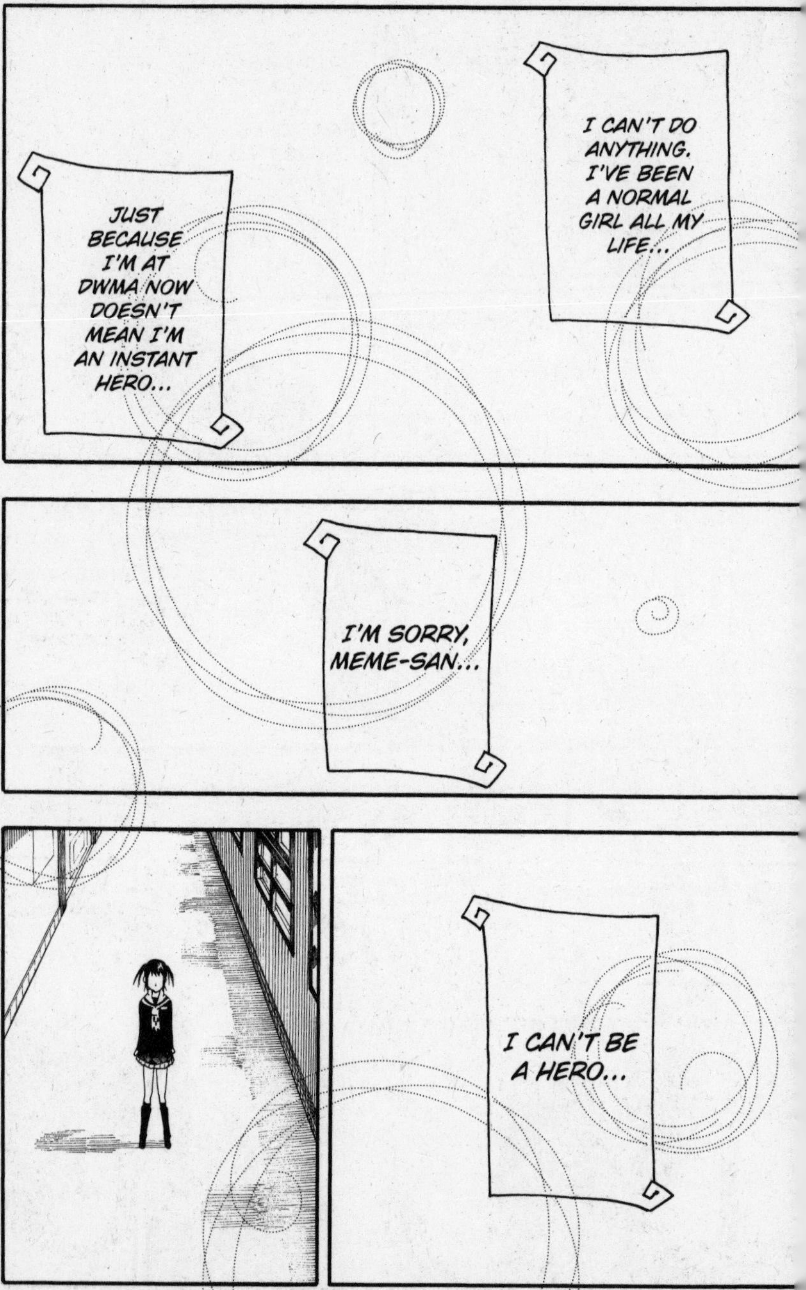
I CAN'T DO ANYTHING. I'VE BEEN A NORMAL GIRL ALL MY LIFE...
JUST BECAUSE I'M AT DWMA NOW DOESN'T MEAN I'M AN INSTANT HERO...
I'M SORRY, MEME-SAN...
I CAN'T BE A HERO...

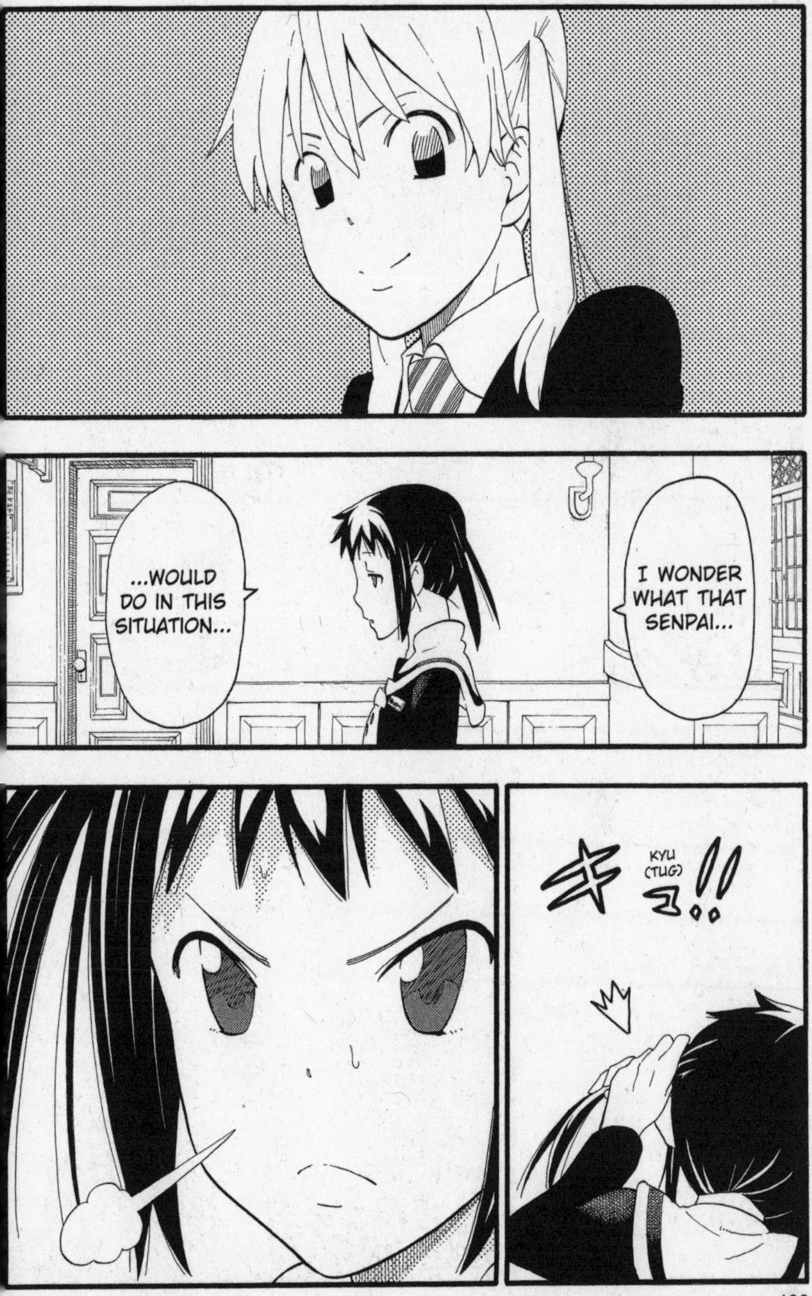
I WONDER WHAT THAT SENPAI...
...WOULD DO IN THIS SITUATION...
KYU (TUG)

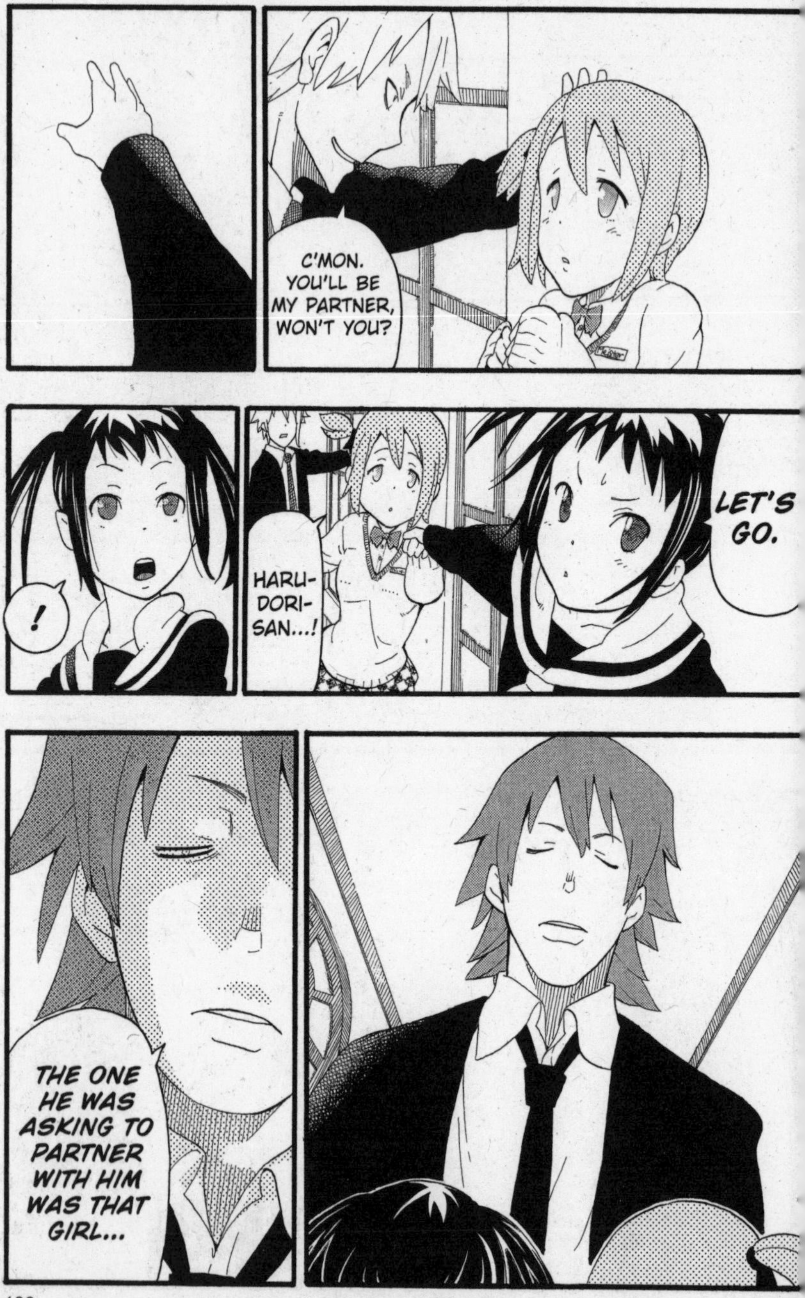
C'MON. YOU'LL BE MY PARTNER, WON'T YOU?
LET'S GO.
HARU-DORI-SAN...!
!
THE ONE HE WAS ASKING TO PARTNER WITH HIM WAS THAT GIRL...

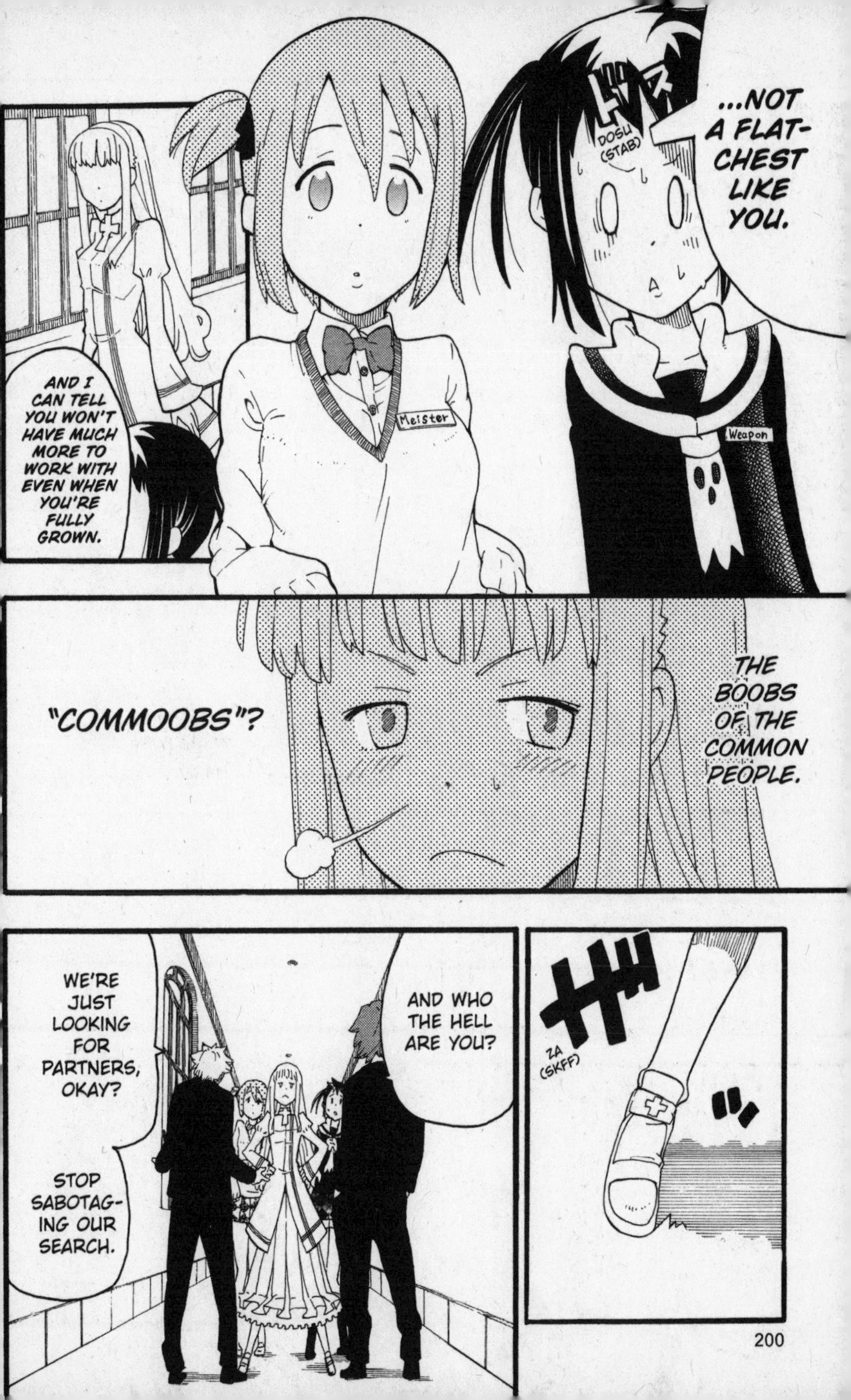
DOSU (STAB)
...NOT A FLAT-CHEST LIKE YOU.
AND I CAN TELL YOU WON'T HAVE MUCH MORE TO WORK WITH EVEN WHEN YOU'RE FULLY GROWN.
Meister
Weapon
THE BOOBS OF THE COMMON PEOPLE.
"COMMOOBS"?
ZA (SKFF)
AND WHO THE HELL ARE YOU?
WE'RE JUST LOOKING FOR PARTNERS, OKAY?
STOP SABOTAGING OUR SEARCH.

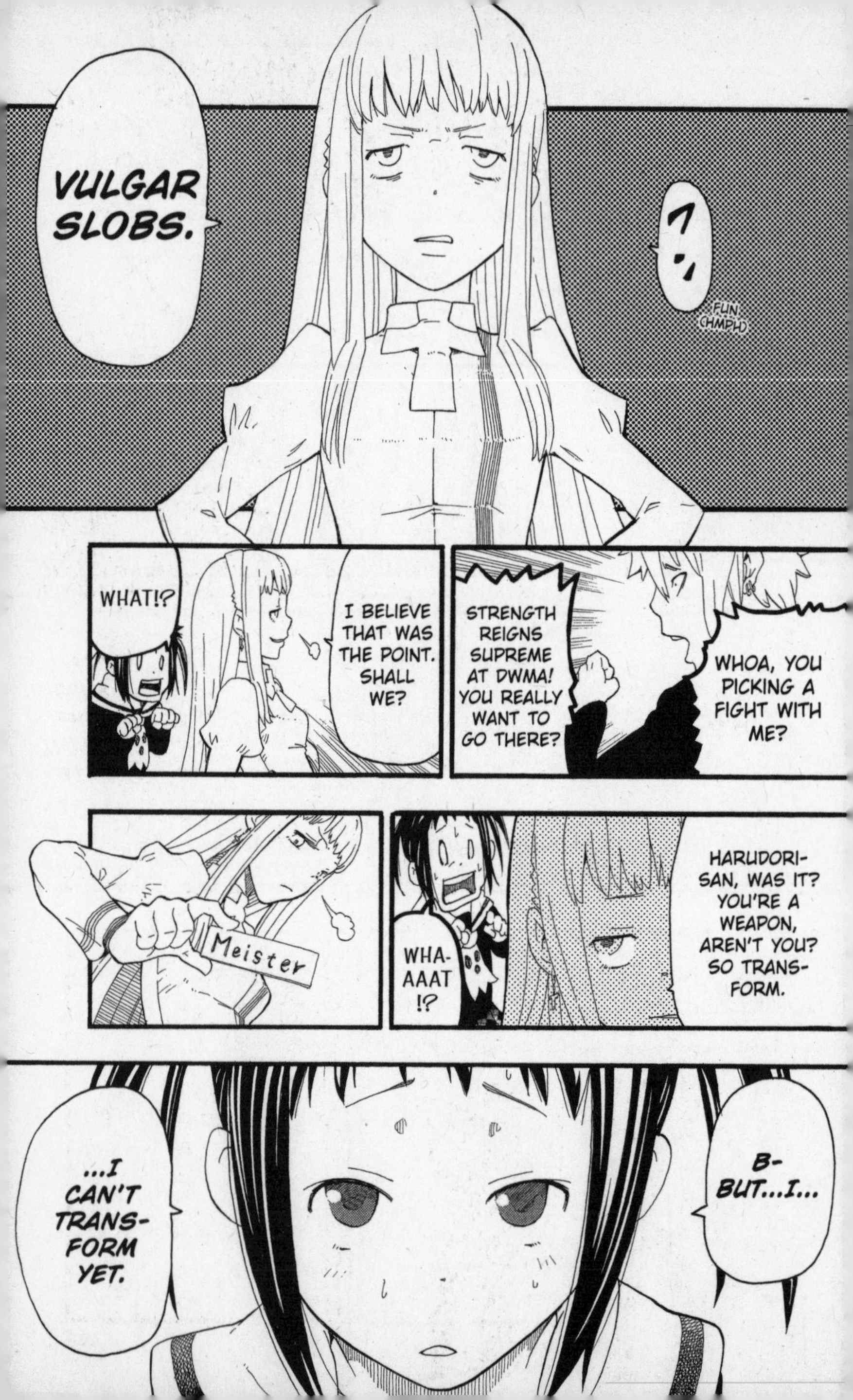
VULGAR SLOBS.
フン
FUN (HMPH)
WHOA, YOU PICKING A FIGHT WITH ME?
STRENGTH REIGNS SUPREME AT DWMA! YOU REALLY WANT TO GO THERE?
I BELIEVE THAT WAS THE POINT. SHALL WE?
WHAT!?
HARUDORI-SAN, WAS IT? YOU'RE A WEAPON, AREN'T YOU? SO TRANS-FORM.
WHA-AAAT!?
Meister
B-BUT...I...
...I CAN'T TRANS-FORM YET.

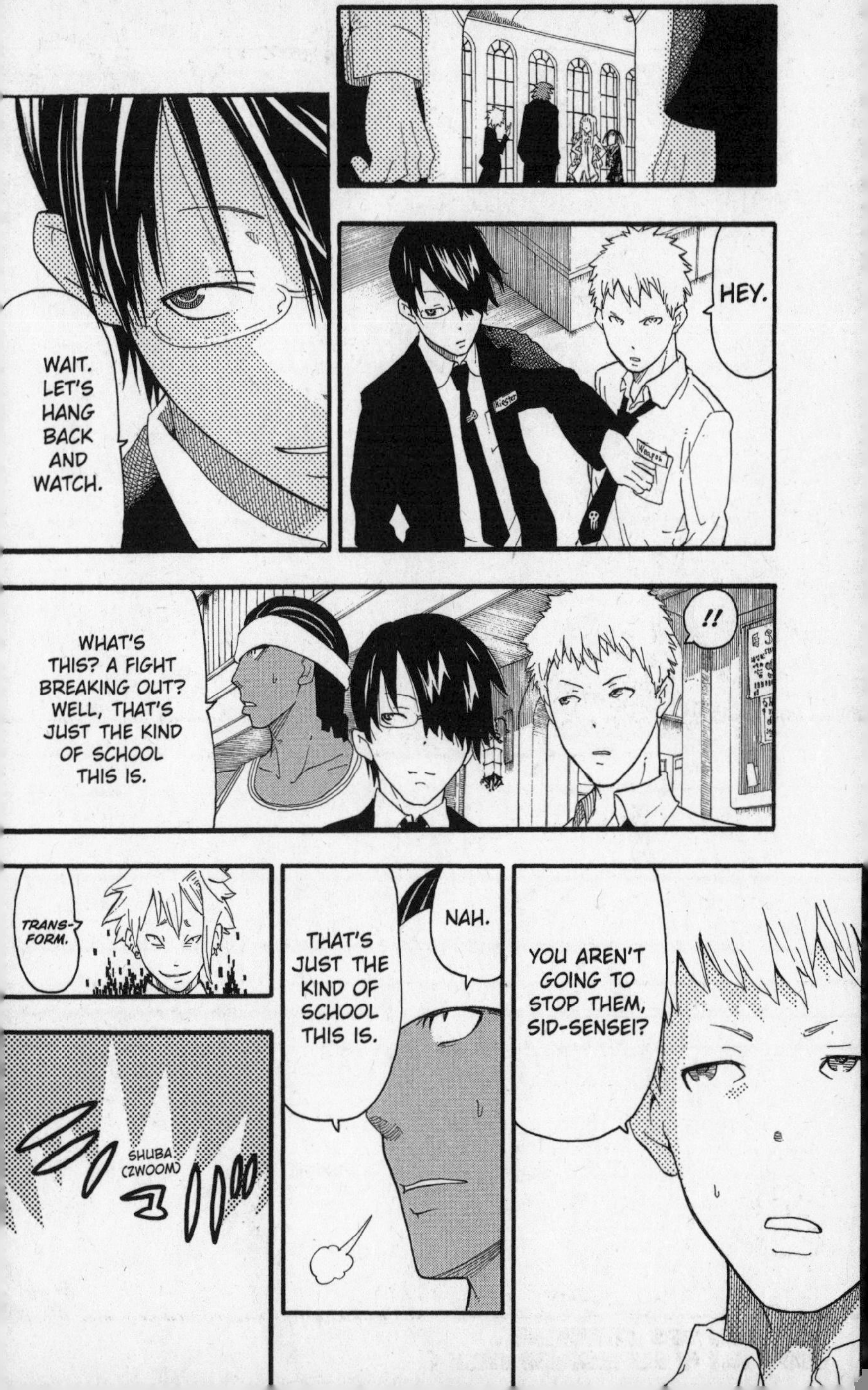
HEY.
WAIT. LET'S HANG BACK AND WATCH.
!!
WHAT'S THIS? A FIGHT BREAKING OUT? WELL, THAT'S JUST THE KIND OF SCHOOL THIS IS.
YOU AREN'T GOING TO STOP THEM, SID-SENSEI?
NAH.
THAT'S JUST THE KIND OF SCHOOL THIS IS.
TRANS-FORM.
SHUBA (ZWOOM)

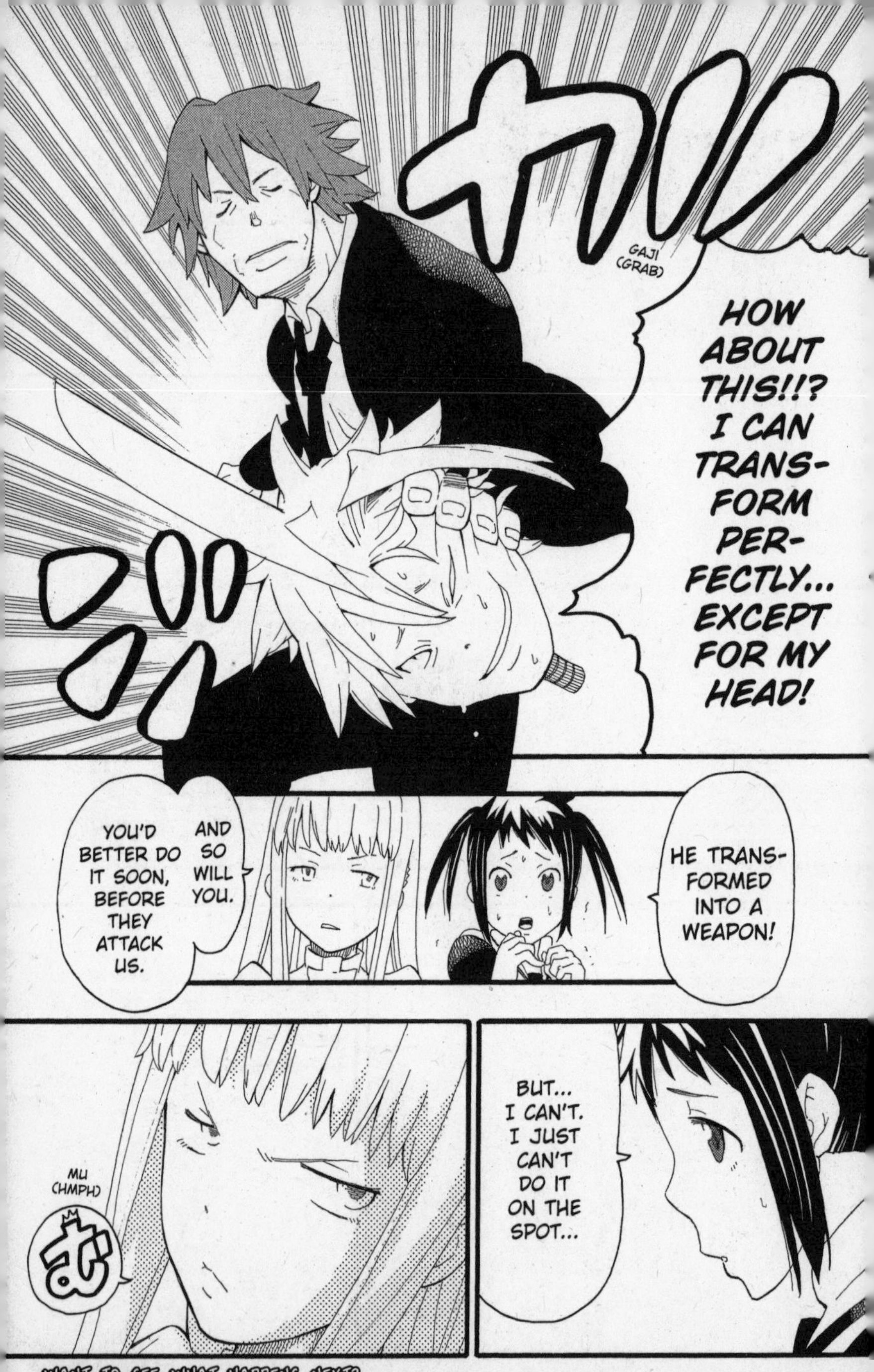
GAJI (GRAB)
HOW ABOUT THIS!!? I CAN TRANS-FORM PER-FECTLY... EXCEPT FOR MY HEAD!
HE TRANS-FORMED INTO A WEAPON!
AND SO WILL YOU.
YOU'D BETTER DO IT SOON, BEFORE THEY ATTACK US.
BUT... I CAN'T. I JUST CAN'T DO IT ON THE SPOT...
MU (HMPH)

WANT TO SEE WHAT HAPPENS NEXT?
GRAB A COPY OF SOUL EATER NOT! VOLUME 1!

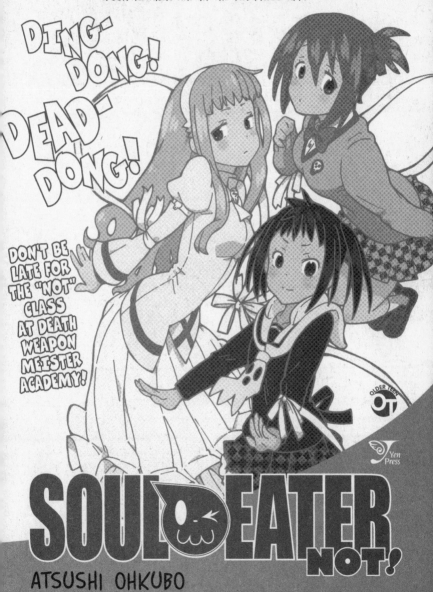

DING-DONG!

DEAD-DONG!

DON'T BE LATE FOR THE "NOT" CLASS AT DEATH WEAPON MEISTER ACADEMY!

Yen Press

SOUL EATER NOT!

ATSUSHI OHKUBO

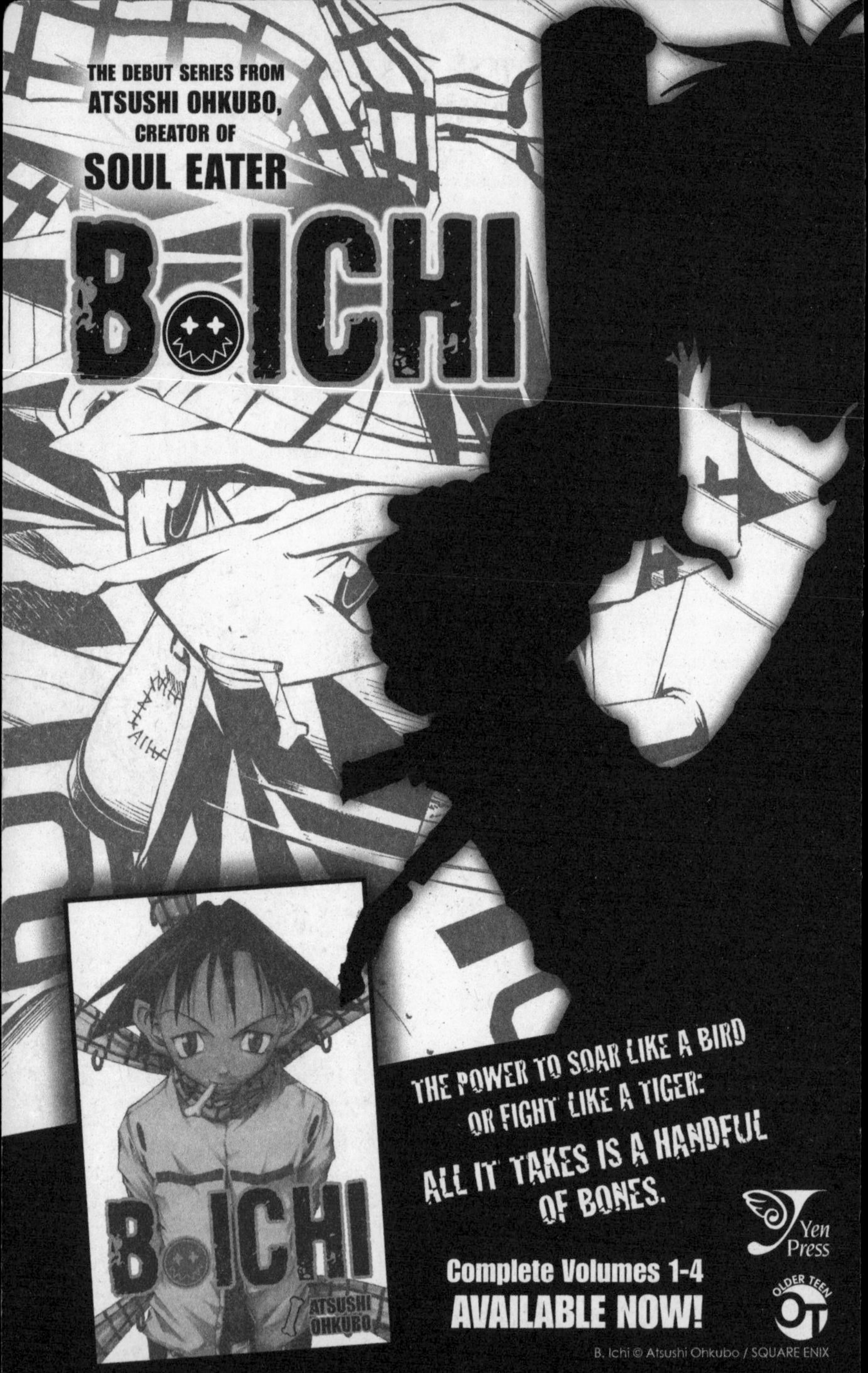

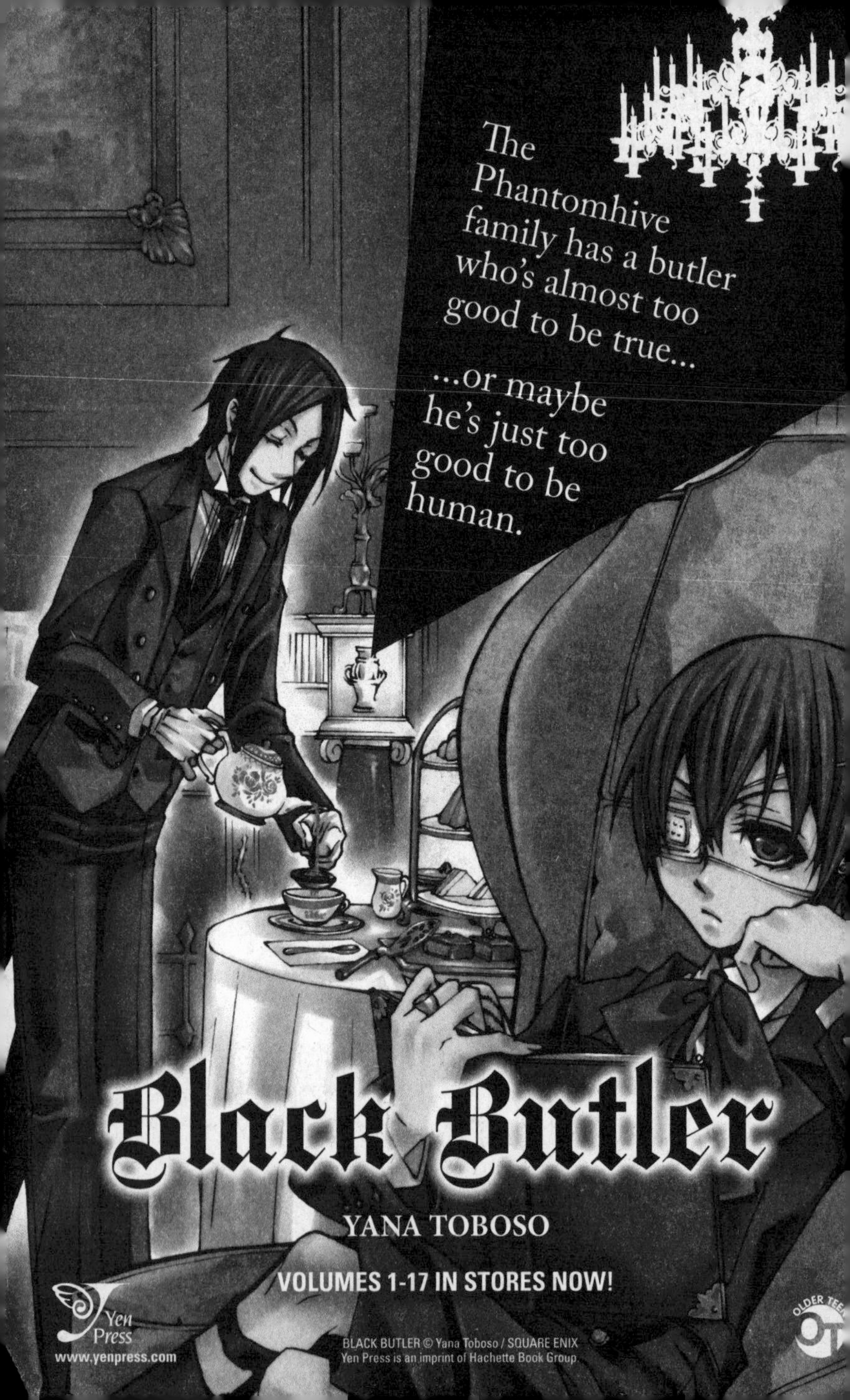

SOUL EATER ㉒

ATSUSHI OHKUBO

Translation: Stephen Paul

Lettering: Abigail Blackman

SOUL EATER Vol. 22 © 2012 Atsushi Ohkubo / SQUARE ENIX. First published in Japan in 2012 by SQUARE ENIX CO., LTD. English translation rights arranged with SQUARE ENIX CO., LTD. and Hachette Book Group through Tuttle-Mori Agency, Inc.

Translation © 2014 by SQUARE ENIX CO., LTD.

Yen Press
Hachette Book Group
237 Park Avenue, New York, NY 10017

HachetteBookGroup.com
YenPress.com

Yen Press is an imprint of Hachette Book Group, Inc. The Yen Press name and logo are trademarks of Hachette Book Group, Inc.

First Yen Press Edition: September 2014

ISBN: 978-0-316-40697-0

10 9 8 7 6 5 4 3 2 1

BVG

Printed in the United States of America